1394

Memory, Language, and Bilingualism

The relationship between memory and language, and the topic of bilingualism are important areas of research in both psychology and linguistics and are grounded in cognitive and linguistic paradigms, theories, and experimentation. This volume provides an integrated theoretical/real-world approach to second language learning, use, and processing from a cognitive perspective. A strong international and interdisciplinary team of contributors present the results of various explorations into bilingual language processing, from recent advances in studies on bilingual memory, to studies on the role of the brain in language processing and language forgetting. This is a strong yet balanced combination of theoretical/overview contributions and accounts of novel, original, empirical studies which will educate readers on the relationship between theory, cognitive experimentation, and data, and their role in understanding language learning and practice.

JEANETTE ALTARRIBA is a Professor and Chair of Psychology in the Department of Psychology, and Director of the Cognition and Language Laboratory, at the University at Albany, State University of New York (SUNY).

LUDMILA ISURIN is an Associate Professor of Second Language Acquisition in the Department of Slavic and East European Languages and Cultures at The Ohio State University.

Memory, Language, and Bilingualism
Theoretical and Applied Approaches

Edited by
Jeanette Altarriba
and
Ludmila Isurin

CAMBRIDGE UNIVERSITY PRESS

CAMBRIDGE UNIVERSITY PRESS
Cambridge, New York, Melbourne, Madrid, Cape Town,
Singapore, São Paulo, Delhi, Mexico City

Cambridge University Press
The Edinburgh Building, Cambridge CB2 8RU, UK

Published in the United States of America by Cambridge University Press,
New York

www.cambridge.org
Information on this title: www.cambridge.org/9781107008908

© Cambridge University Press 2013

This publication is in copyright. Subject to statutory exception
and to the provisions of relevant collective licensing agreements,
no reproduction of any part may take place without the written
permission of Cambridge University Press.

First published 2013

Printed and bound in the United Kingdom by the MPG Books Group

A catalogue record for this publication is available from the British Library

Library of Congress Cataloguing in Publication data
 Memory, language, and bilingualism : theoretical and applied
 approaches / edited by Jeanette Altarriba and Ludmila Isurin.
  pages cm
 ISBN 978-1-107-00890-8
 1. Bilingualism–Psychological aspects. 2. Cognition. 3. Memory.
 4. Psycholinguistics. I. Altarriba, Jeanette, 1964– II. Isurin, Ludmila.
 P115.4.M46 2012
 404′.2–dc23
 2012019856

ISBN 978-1-107-00890-8 Hardback

Cambridge University Press has no responsibility for the persistence or
accuracy of URLs for external or third-party internet websites referred to in
this publication, and does not guarantee that any content on such websites is,
or will remain, accurate or appropriate.

Contents

List of figures		*page* vii
List of tables		ix
List of contributors		x
	Introduction	1
	JEANETTE ALTARRIBA AND LUDMILA ISURIN	
1	Bilingual memory: structure, access, and processing	7
	JAMES BARTOLOTTI AND VIORICA MARIAN	
2	Lexical competition in localist and distributed connectionist models of L2 acquisition	48
	TON DIJKSTRA, FEMKE HAGA, ALEX BIJSTERVELD, AND IDA SPRINKHUIZEN-KUYPER	
3	Working memory and (second) language processing	74
	ARNAUD SZMALEC, MARC BRYSBAERT, AND WOUTER DUYCK	
4	Working memory in simultaneous interpreters	95
	TERESA M. SIGNORELLI AND LORAINE OBLER	
5	Using electrophysiological measures to track the mapping of words to concepts in the bilingual brain: a focus on translation	126
	JANET G. VAN HELL AND JUDITH F. KROLL	
6	Age effects in L2 learning: comparing child and adult learners' performance on tests of implicit and explicit memory	161
	PAVEL TROFIMOVICH, SANDRA MARTIN-CHANG, AND KYLE LEVESQUE	
7	Bilingualism, language, and aging	188
	MIRA GORAL	

8 Crossovers and codeswitching in the investigation of immigrant autobiographical memory 211
CARMIT ALTMAN, ROBERT W. SCHRAUF, AND JOEL WALTERS

9 Linguistic relativity and bilingualism 236
PANOS ATHANASOPOULOS AND FRAIBET AVELEDO

10 Testing effects for novel word learning in Chinese–English bilinguals 256
CHI-SHING TSE AND XIAOPING PU

11 The lexicon in second language attrition: what happens when the cat's got your tongue? 291
KATHLEEN BARDOVI-HARLIG AND DAVID STRINGER

12 Memory and first language forgetting 319
LUDMILA ISURIN

13 Future research directions: bilingualism, memory, and language 349
JEANETTE ALTARRIBA

Index 363

Figures

1.1	Baddeley's Working Memory Model	page 11
1.2	Kroll and Stewart's Revised Hierarchical Model	25
1.3	Van Heuven, Dijkstra, and Grainger's Bilingual Interactive Activation Model	27
1.4	Dijkstra and van Heuven's Bilingual Interactive Activation Plus Model	28
1.5	Shook and Marian's Bilingual Language Interaction Network for Comprehension of Speech	29
1.6	Green's Inhibitory Control Model	30
1.7	Li and Farkas' Self-Organizing Model of Bilingual Processing	31
2.1	The BIA+ framework of bilingual word recognition	53
2.2	The Bilingual Single Network Model	54
2.3	Processing of Dutch and English words by late learners of English	59
2.4	Processing of Dutch and English words by early Dutch–English bilinguals	59
2.5	Late learning of English words of different frequency categories in BIA+	60
2.6	The Revised Bilingual Single Network Model	63
2.7	Learning of Dutch and English words by late learners of English relative to English monolinguals	64
2.8	Learning of Dutch and English words by early Dutch–English bilinguals relative to English monolinguals	65
2.9	Late learning of English words of different frequency categories in RBSN	66
2.10	Processing by late Dutch–English bilinguals of English translation equivalents with different degrees of orthographic overlap with Dutch	67
2.11	Processing of English item types by late Dutch–English bilinguals	67

2.12	Processing of Dutch item types by late Dutch–English bilinguals	67
4.1	Verbal working memory across the literature	97
4.2	WM in interpreters vs. non-interpreters across the literature	103
4.3	WM in interpreters vs. non-interpreters: auditory stimuli across the literature	116
4.4	WM in interpreters vs. non-interpreters: print stimuli across the literature	116
5.1	The Revised Hierarchical Model	128
5.2	An illustration of the N400 component in ERP waveforms	137
6.1	Proportion of explicit recall for the combined groups of native English and French children and native English and French adults as a function of exposure condition (context vs. isolation)	177
6.2	Proportion of implicit word-stem completion for the combined groups of native English children and adults and native French children and adults as a function of exposure condition (context vs. isolation vs. control)	179
8.1	Distribution of memories in monolingual mature adults	213
8.2	Distribution of memories across the lifespan from both English and Hebrew sessions for English–Hebrew participants	221
8.3	Distribution of memories during the English and Hebrew sessions for 12 English–Hebrew adult bilinguals	222
8.4	Distribution of memories of earlier immigrants/arrival prior to age 30 and later immigrants/arrival after age 30	223
8.5	Distribution of memories in English for English–Hebrew bilinguals who immigrated before age 30 and for those who immigrated after age 30	224
8.6	Distribution of memories in Hebrew for English–Hebrew bilinguals who immigrated before age 30 and for those who immigrated after age 30	225
8.7	Mean number of same-language and crossover memories in L1 and L2 sessions/cue words among English–Hebrew bilinguals	226
10.1	Modified Revised Hierarchical Model of bilingual memory	264
10.2	Mean proportion of Swahili–English word pairs recalled in repeated study and repeated testing conditions across the 12 cycles in the acquisition phase	271
10.3	Scatterplot of testing effect and L1/L2 proficiency	276
12.1	Frequency effect	331
12.2	Contact with L1	332

Tables

4.1	Summary of the literature	*page* 99
6.1	Mean reading ability (WRAT-3) and working memory (WJ-III) scores for four participant groups	170
6.2	Mean proportion of explicit recall for the four participant groups as a function of exposure condition	176
6.3	Mean proportion of implicit word-stem completion for the four participant groups as a function of exposure condition	178
8.1	Frequency and proportion of codeswitching in same-language and crossover memories for L1 and L2 sessions	228
10.1	Mean statistics for the lexical characteristics of Swahili–English word pairs in Set A and Set B	268
10.2	Experimental stimuli	269
10.3	Mean proportions of intra-list intrusion errors, extra-list intrusion errors and omission as a function of condition in the acquisition phase and final cued-recall test	273
10.4	Pearson correlation matrix	275
12.1	Socio-linguistic background of the participants	328
12.2	Semantic interference	333
12.3	Unrecalled items	335
12.4	Recall in non-target language	335

Contributors

ALTARRIBA, JEANETTE, University at Albany, State University of New York, USA

ALTMAN, CARMIT, Bar-Ilan University, Israel

ATHANASOPOULOS, PANOS, Newcastle University, UK

AVELEDO, FRAIBET, ESRC Centre for Research on Bilingualism, UK

BARDOVI-HARLIG, KATHLEEN, Indiana University, USA

BARTOLOTTI, JAMES, Northwestern University, USA

BIJSTERVELD, ALEX, Radboud University Nijmegen, Donders Institute for Brain, Cognition and Behaviour, the Netherlands

BRYSBAERT, MARC, Ghent University, Belgium

DIJKSTRA, TON, Radboud University Nijmegen, the Netherlands

DUYCK, WOUTER, Ghent University, Belgium

GORAL, MIRA, Lehman College, City University of New York, USA

HAGA, FEMKE, Radboud University Nijmegen, Donders Institute for Brain, Cognition and Behaviour, the Netherlands

KROLL, JUDITH F., Pennsylvania State University, USA

ISURIN, LUDMILA, The Ohio State University, USA

LEVESQUE, KYLE, Dalhousie University, Canada

MARIAN, VIORICA, Northwestern University, USA

MARTIN-CHANG, SANDRA, Concordia University, Canada

OBLER, LORAINE, City University of New York, USA

List of contributors

PU, XIAOPING, The Chinese University of Hong Kong, Hong Kong

SCHRAUF, ROBERT W., Pennsylvania State University, USA

SIGNORELLI, TERESA M., Marymount Manhattan College, USA

SPRINKHUIZEN-KUYPER, IDA, Radboud University Nijmegen, Donders Institute for Brain, Cognition and Behaviour, the Netherlands

STRINGER, DAVID, Indiana University, USA

SZMALEC, ARNAUD, Ghent University, Belgium

TROFIMOVICH, PAVEL, Concordia University, Canada

TSE, CHI-SHING, The Chinese University of Hong Kong, Hong Kong

VAN HELL, JANET G., Pennsylvania State University, USA and Radboud University Nijmegen, the Netherlands

WALTERS, JOEL, Bar-Ilan University, Israel

Introduction

Jeanette Altarriba and Ludmila Isurin

Recent decades have seen a marked increase in the study of bilingualism from a scientific, empirical perspective, with the publication of various works that speak to the breadth of this subject area and the many different kinds of approaches that can be involved within this endeavor (see e.g., Altarriba & Heredia, 2008; Bhatia & Ritchie, 2005; de Groot & Kroll, 1997; Doughty & Long, 2003; Heredia & Altarriba, 2002; Randall, 2007). The purpose of the current volume is to provide a combined theoretical/applied approach to second language learning, use, and processing from a cognitive viewpoint. The chapters are meant to inform the reader regarding the relationship between memory and language, as grounded in cognitive paradigms, theories, and experimentation. The aim is not only to present results regarding various issues in bilingual language processing, but to educate the reader on the relationship between theory, cognitive experimentation, and data, and their role in understanding language learning and practice.

While psycholinguists and cognitive psychologists have extensively studied the role of memory in language processing, there remains a void in the literature as to how those studies have direct bearing on applied issues and applied areas of inquiry. That is, often times, the field of language and memory focuses either on empirical approaches or on applied approaches, but does not seek to meld or otherwise demonstrate the connections between these two perspectives. The present volume is aimed toward filling this current void.

Moreover, this volume broadens the boundaries of single disciplines and brings in cognitive, psycholinguistic, neurolinguistic, educational, and applied linguistic perspectives. From chapters on recent advances in research on bilingual memory to studies on the role of the brain in language processing, from chapters on working memory in second language acquisition (SLA) to applied investigations of SLA, from chapters on the role of memory in retaining linguistic information to those on first and second language forgetting, this volume targets a broad audience of readers and is easily accessible to anyone interested in these topics. In addition to its remarkable interdisciplinary spirit, the volume's strength is in the balanced combination of theoretical/overview contributions and accounts of novel, original, empirical studies.

The volume opens with a chapter on bilingual memory, memory structure, access, and processing (Chapter 1). Bartolotti and Marian provide an extensive overview of the research on bilingual memory. The major focus of the review is on the architecture of bilingual memory and the mechanisms involved in memory access and processing. The authors discuss the accumulated evidence related to the nature of those mechanisms, that is, whether they are language dependent or language independent. The chapter concludes with a discussion of a few models of bilingual memory, and the authors pinpoint the significance and possible shortcomings of these models.

The next chapter (Chapter 2) is a logical continuation of the discussion of bilingual memory models. Dijkstra and colleagues provide an extensive overview of research on lexical competition in localist and distributed connectionist models of second language (L2) acquisition, give an account of the extant models of L2 acquisition, and demonstrate how these models can be simulated in order to understand the way that new L2 words enter the mental lexicon and how human memory overcomes a competition between the L1 (first language) and L2 lexicon. The authors argue that each model highlights different aspects of acquisition of L2 vocabulary. The chapter concludes with a theoretical comparison of various models.

From more general models of bilingual memory to more specific memory components, the volume proceeds to a closer look at the role of working memory (WM) in bilingual language acquisition and processing. This issue is addressed by two contributions. First, the chapter by Szmalec and colleagues (Chapter 3) discusses the latest research on working memory and its role in L2 acquisition. It opens with a brief overview of the history of research on WM, major theories, and experimental paradigms. The authors discuss the role of verbal memory in the learning of new words and show how prior findings from the monolingual literature led to more recent studies on bilingual memory. Then the authors offer the most recent findings on the role of WM in lexical access and syntactic processing and discuss how bilingualism influences WM performance.

The next chapter on the role of WM in bilinguals (Chapter 4) takes the reader into the fascinating and barely researched area of simultaneous interpreters. Signorelli and Obler's contribution on WM advantages in simultaneous interpreters gives a detailed account of the extant studies in which cognitive differences between interpreters and non-interpreters are explored. The authors start their review with a discussion of the recent models of WM, especially the importance of the phonological loop and the episodic buffer as it relates to the highly demanding task of simultaneous interpretation. The review of the 13 studies pertaining to the field is broken down along a number of lines, that is, findings on WM advantages in interpreters versus those that only indicate the directionality of the effect, types of tasks and stimuli, as well as methodological variations found in the literature. The authors argue that the emergent evidence of the interpreter's cognitive advantage would have been much stronger had the inconsistencies and discrepancies in the reported studies been eliminated.

The contribution by van Hell and Kroll (Chapter 5) extends the discussion of memory paradigms into the field of electrophysiological studies on bilingual memory. The authors give a thorough overview of the findings obtained through the use of translation paradigms in the study of bilingual memory. Then they bring together the evidence from behavioral and electrophysiological studies and show how the two approaches complement and challenge each other. The chapter concludes with an outline of new directions in which the merger of the two subfields should go and what additional factors should be considered in future studies on bilingual memory.

The following two chapters look at age factors as related to second language acquisition and memory changes. The first contribution by Trofimovich and colleagues (Chapter 6) reports on a study looking into explicit and implicit memory dissociation in adults and children. The authors add a new angle to the debate of the critical period as a major adverse factor in adults' learning of a second language. Is the age factor solely responsible for children's higher achievements in L2 learning? In the experimental study probing into explicit and implicit processing among four age-matched groups of participants – native speakers of English and native speakers of French/second language learners of English – Trofimovich and colleagues pursue two goals: (1) to establish any experimental dissociations between explicit and implicit memory due to experimental processing manipulations; and (2) to test for a developmental dissociation between explicit and implicit memory.

In her contribution on aging in bilinguals (Chapter 7), Goral brings in the evidence on linguistic and cognitive changes related to age. The field of bilingualism does not have sufficient empirical evidence regarding the factors that influence the reported decline of both languages in the individual; neither do we have enough knowledge concerning the general decline of bilinguals' cognitive skills. The author gives an extensive overview of the extant findings related to the field and suggests directions for future research.

The next two contributions discuss the role of memory and cognition in two areas of research that have been growing over the past two decades. The chapter by Altman and colleagues (Chapter 8) provides insight into the autobiographical memories of bilinguals. Along the existing lines of research on autobiographical memories, the authors investigate the traditional "reminiscence bump" in English–Hebrew bilinguals' memory. However, they add a few additional angles, such as the existence of another reminiscence bump which is related to the years surrounding immigration, "crossover memories" – that is, memories retrieved in a language different from the language in which the memory was recorded – and code-switching in autobiographical memories.

The next area of research on bilingual memory and cognition relates to the renewed interest in the Linguistic Relativity Hypothesis. The question of a unique perspective of the world in bilinguals is discussed in the contribution by Athanasopoulos and Aveledo (Chapter 9). The authors give an overview of the evidence gathered over the last decade through experimental research within the framework of the Linguistic Relativity Hypothesis. They focus on a few directions of the research in the field, that is, color terms, grammatical number, and aspect realization in verbs of motion. The chapter discusses those factors that showed effects in the reported studies, such as L1 and L2 proficiency level, age of L2 acquisition, maturational constraints, amount of exposure to either of the bilingual's languages, the language of instruction in the experimental study, and the general integration in the L2 socio-cultural environment. The authors raise the question of memory involvement in the formulation of the bilingual's perceptions of the world.

The volume continues with an applied approach to the study of bilingual memory in foreign language acquisition (Chapter 10). Tse and Pu discuss the study of the acquisition of a third language vocabulary via two different routes: repeated study versus repeated testing. Through a thorough discussion of the accumulated theoretical and empirical knowledge on bilinguals' memory and acqustion of foreign language vocabulary, they build a background for testing their hypothesis. The acquisition and retention of a third language (L3) vocabulary through the L2–L3 association was shown to be stronger when the study–test procedure was used versus study alone. The study also provided evidence of the importance of L2 proficiency as a factor in the acquisition of L2 vocabulary through this paradigm.

Memory research in the field of bilingualism is inseparable from studies on language forgetting – native and foreign – in healthy individuals. The review chapter on L2 attrition by Bardovi-Harlig and Stringer (Chapter 11) expands the conceptual framework of research on L2 attrition by looking more closely at the lexicon as the most vulnerable part in language attrition. They argue that lexical storage in memory goes beyond the traditional lexical forms and incorporates certain syntactic elements as well as idioms and conventional expressions. In their comprehensive overview of research done in the field of linguistics and cognitive psychology, they attempt to bridge the two fields and conceptualize a new approach to the study of L2 attrition.

The contribution on first language attrition by Isurin (Chapter 12) reports on an empirical study of lexical access in Russian–English bilinguals who come from three distinct second language environments. Linguistic and socio-linguistic factors, such as word frequency, amount of language exposure, and length of residency in the host country, are analyzed quantitatively, whereas the effect of the second language in assigning alternative names to pictures, naming objects in the wrong language, and confusion with lexically convergent/divergent concepts is analyzed qualitatively. The author argues for the importance of combining both methods of analysis in studies of bilingual lexical access.

The volume concludes with Altarriba's overview (Chapter 13) of the main findings across the current set of chapters, with an eye toward questions and areas of research inquiry that naturally flow from these chapters. A discussion of future research directions in the field of bilingual memory focuses on such new and novel areas as the role of emotion processing within and across languages, the relationship between bilingualism and creativity, the representation of figurative language among bilingual populations, and the role of orthography or "scripts" in the encoding, maintenance, and retrieval of information from bilingual memory. These and many other areas of investigation are commented upon, reviewed, and posed for the reader in an effort to stimulate new and future research that combines aspects of bilingualism, language, and memory.

It is our hope as editors that *Memory, Language, and Bilingualism: Theoretical and Applied Approaches* will be viewed as timely, novel, and highly informative. This volume should serve as a handy, state-of-the-art compendium and reference text for researchers, scientists, and those interested in knowing more about extant findings in this area of investigation, as well as a resource for related courses at various levels of instruction. Moreover, it was compiled so as to engage an audience that is broader than that typically associated with the fields of cognitive science and cognitive psychology – an audience that should include individuals in education, other social sciences, computer science, and artificial intelligence, and several other related fields.

REFERENCES

Altarriba, J., & Heredia, R. R. (eds.) (2008). *An introduction to bilingualism: principles and processes*. New York: Lawrence Erlbaum Associates.

Bhatia, T. K., & Ritchie, W. C. (eds.) (2005). *The handbook of bilingualism*. London: Blackwell.

Doughty, C., & Long, M. H. (eds.) (2003). *The handbook of second language acquisition*. New York: Wiley-Blackwell.

de Groot, A. M. B., & Kroll, J. F. (eds.) (1997). *Tutorials in bilingualism: psycholinguistic perspectives*. Mahwah, NJ: Lawrence Erlbaum Associates.

Heredia, R. R., & Altarriba, J. (eds.) (2002). *Bilingual sentence processing*. Amsterdam: Elsevier/Academic Press.

Randall, M. (2007). *Memory, psychology, and second language learning*. Amsterdam: John Benjamins.

1 Bilingual memory: structure, access, and processing

James Bartolotti and Viorica Marian

Abstract

Language and memory are closely intertwined in the human cognitive architecture. Language acquisition depends on successful memory encoding and retrieval; at the same time, language itself is instrumental for encoding and storing knowledge. For bilinguals, the need to keep their two languages functionally distinct influences memory. In this chapter, we review the *structure* of bilingual memory, including long-term, short-term, and phonological working memory and how they are influenced by knowledge of multiple languages. We also investigate memory *access* and review research on episodic memory access in bilinguals and on semantic memory access during bilingual language comprehension and production. We then examine *processing* in the context of existing models of bilingual language and memory. Finally, we consider how the prism of novel language learning can provide insight into the interaction between memory and language. We conclude that bilingualism changes the human cognitive architecture and affects the structure, access, and processing of language and memory.

Successful acquisition and use of language requires the storage in memory of many words, their associated concepts, and grammatical rules. Access to these items in memory is accomplished with relative ease. The process by which language is stored, accessed, and processed is remarkable, yet becomes even more impressive when bilingualism is considered. A bilingual must not only store information pertaining to two languages, but also be able to access and process linguistic information according to changing linguistic contexts. The two languages have the potential to compete for memory resources and processing

Preparation of this chapter was supported in part by National Institutes of Health grant RO1 HD059858 to VM. The authors would like to thank Anthony Shook, Scott Schroeder, and Sarah Chabal for comments and feedback on earlier versions of this manuscript.

capacity. One way to avoid competitive interference would be for the bilingual architecture to include two systems that store, access, and process information in a language-specific manner. However, this characterization of the bilingual as the sum of two monolingual minds is inconsistent with a wealth of research that indicates high interactivity between the bilingual's two languages in memory and language processing (Grosjean, 1989). In the current chapter, we consider how multiple languages interact to influence memory storage, access, and processing. Whether memory is accessed selectively from one language or whether both languages are retrieved automatically has implications for long-term memory organization. Similarly, the way in which information is processed depends on what becomes activated during memory access, and how information is encoded and stored in long-term memory.

We begin by focusing on the structure of long- and short-term memory. Long-term memory is composed of substructures specific to knowledge categories, and the degree to which language-specific information is represented may differ between these categories. The manner in which information in short-term memory is processed by the working memory system is also discussed. Next, we examine how stored representations in long-term memory are accessed. Once again, we consider whether the language of retrieval affects recall success, indicating language-specific access, or whether both languages become activated automatically, indicating close integration between a bilingual's multiple languages. To address this question we examine access to episodic memory and retrieval of semantic knowledge during recognition and production of language. The chapter ends with a focus on how bilinguals process their two languages. We review the organization of several theoretical and computational models, and their capabilities in capturing aspects of bilingual language processing, after which we explore how bilingualism affects the ability to process and encode novel information, such as during novel language learning.

Structure of bilingual memory

The primary division between types of memory is made according to the timescale over which information is retained. This separation has its origins in James' (1890) *Principles of Psychology*, which differentiated between primary memory for recent experiences and secondary memory for information retained over a long period of time. The distinction received renewed attention during the 1960s with the development of the field of cognitive psychology (Neisser, 1967) and its attempts to describe the information processing capabilities of the mind. Atkinson and Shiffrin (1968) defined short-term memory as an information-maintenance system that controlled access and encoding to long-term memory. Evidence for a separation between short- and long-term memories came from patients with amnesia, who seemed to display specific impairments to one of the two memory systems (Baddeley & Warrington, 1970; Milner, 1966). The underlying architectures of long- and short-term memory are debated, but there is agreement on their functional distinction. In this section, we will consider first the storage of language in long-term memory, and then the effect of language processing and information encoding in the short-term memory system.

Long-term memory in bilinguals

Long-term memory (LTM) contains stable representations of knowledge acquired over time, including *explicit* memory for facts and events, and *implicit* memory for skills, routines, and associations. Explicit and implicit memory can be dissociated and appear to involve distinct neural components (Eichenbaum & Cohen, 2001; Mishkin, Malamut, & Bachevalier, 1984; Poldrack & Packard, 2003; Squire & Knowlton, 2000; Voss & Paller, 2008). They also differ with respect to how language is involved. Explicit memory can be consciously demonstrated by verbally recounting an event or by providing an answer to a query, while implicit memory can only be demonstrated as a non-conscious change in performance due to information gained over time. Both explicit and implicit memory play important roles in language acquisition and processing (Morgan-Short, 2007); implicit memory contributes to acquisition of grammar (Ullman, 2004), but explicit memory has been the focus of more extensive study in research on bilingual cognition (e.g., Kroll & de Groot, 1997; Pavlenko, 2000).

Explicit memory can be further divided into *semantic* memory for general facts, including word–meaning associations, and *episodic* memory for events and their linguistic environment. Memory models currently disagree on the specifics of semantic and episodic memory consolidation (the process by which information is encoded and stored in LTM). For example, *memory consolidation theory* (Paller, 1997; Scoville & Milner, 1957; Squire, Cohen, & Nadel, 1984) maintains that both semantic and episodic memories are formed by hippocampal binding of information across neocortical sites. Over time, the paired associations between neocortical sites strengthen, and the hippocampus is relied on less to reactivate memories (McClelland, McNaughton, &

O'Reilly, 1995; Norman & O'Reilly, 2003; Paller, 1997; Rempel-Clower *et al.*, 1996). Patients with hippocampal lesions are unable to consolidate new semantic and episodic memories but demonstrate preserved recall for facts and events prior to the injury, which are thought to be stored across neocortical sites. In contrast, the *multiple memory trace theory* separates the processes governing semantic and episodic memory storage (Moscovitch *et al.*, 2005; Nadel *et al.*, 2000; Rosenbaum *et al.*, 2005). Episodic memory is thought to always rely on the hippocampus for retrieval, whereas semantic memory is stored in the neocortex without hippocampal involvement (Levine *et al.*, 2002).

If semantic and episodic memories are stored independently, as the multiple memory trace theory suggests, then it is possible that they differ in whether they can mark memories for language assignment. Episodic memories are integrative and preserve a large amount of the encoding context across modalities. Language is inescapably part of this context, which may be reflected in language-specific encoding and retrieval of episodic memories. In contrast, semantic memory may forgo linking concepts to specific languages, forming targeted connections across neocortical sites. Overall, the structure of episodic and semantic memory opens the possibility for language-specific storage in the case of episodic memory and language-non-specific storage of semantic memory. Greater separation of languages in episodic memory can allow for easier access and processing in monolingual contexts and reduced interference from the non-target language. In a semantic memory system, language identity is determined during processing, after activating items in both languages. The degree to which patterns of lexical access and processing can reveal the structure of languages in LTM storage will be considered more carefully in subsequent sections.

Short-term memory in bilinguals

Information that is stored in long-term memory must be accessed and transferred to short-term memory (STM) to be processed in a meaningful way to formulate output. STM is part of the working memory (WM) system, which additionally subsumes attentional and control units involved in information processing. The structure of bilingual memory places unique demands on WM, and appears to improve the efficiency with which the system operates, improving the bilingual's ability to maintain and encode novel information.

The first issue to consider is whether STM represents a distinct neural system compared LTM or whether the two rely on the same underlying architecture. This issue has implications for defining the structure

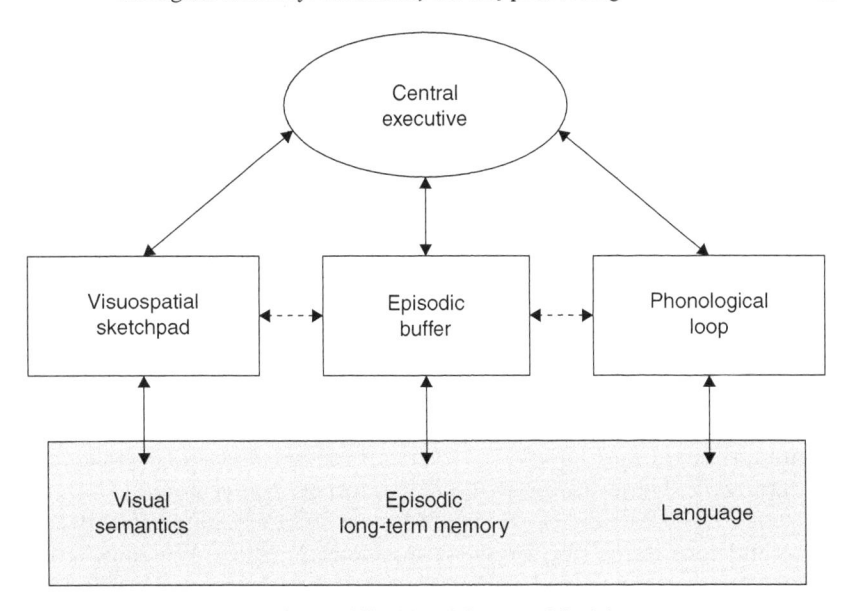

Figure 1.1 Baddeley's Working Memory Model

and functional capacity of STM. On the basis of double dissociations between LTM and STM loss in amnesic patients, multiple-store models posit distinct neural components for the two systems (Baddeley & Warrington, 1970; Shallice & Warrington, 1970; Vallar & Papagno, 2002). The working memory model of Baddeley and colleagues further subdivides WM into functional subcomponents and is shown in Figure 1.1. An independent phonological loop and visuospatial sketchpad process auditory/linguistic and mental imagery respectively, while an episodic buffer integrates across modalities and with LTM, and a central executive controls memory manipulation and attention (Baddeley, 1986, 2010; Baddeley & Hitch, 1974).

In contrast, unitary-store models propose that STM represents the reactivation of LTM representations, concluding that both systems rely on the same underlying neural architecture (Atkinson & Shiffrin, 1971; Cowan, 1988, 2000). The critical difference between multiple- and unitary-store models is in how STM capacity is represented. In multiple-store models, there is an interaction between natural item decay and the inherent limitations of the mental rehearsal mechanism – STM capacity represents the point at which information decays faster than it can be rehearsed (Baddeley, 1986, 1992). In unitary-store models, capacity is limited by the attentional network, which determines how many items from LTM can be reactivated at any given time (Cowan, 2000). While multiple- and unitary-store models describe functionally similar representations of STM, there is not yet consensus on its structure or how to represent its limits.

One of the first descriptions of STM capacity was Miller's seminal paper on a capacity limit of seven items plus or minus two (1956). The effective capacity could be augmented either by facilitating rapid encoding of items from WM to LTM, or by chunking items into larger conceptual units that could be reactivated more quickly. Examples of the latter involve the ability to remember many individual letters by combining them into seven or fewer words that can be quickly rehearsed, or by remembering a longer list of words by knowing that they all start with the same letter. The ease with which rehearsal strategies can be implemented, though, may have led to overestimations of actual capacity, by conflating WM and access to LTM resources. Experimental designs that effectively restrict access to LTM yield WM estimates of between three and four items (for a review, see Cowan, 2000). Evidence from studies using event-related potentials (ERP, e.g., Vogel & Machizawa, 2004) and functional magnetic resonance imaging (fMRI, e.g., Todd & Marois, 2004, 2005) additionally find that neurological responses related to memory encoding increase up to four items and reach an asymptote, supporting the behavioral evidence that suggests an upper limit on WM capacity of around four items. More restrictive accounts of memory capacity suggest that of these four items, only one can be the focus of attention at a time (Garavan, 1998; Oberauer, 2002).

Although there appear to be hard limits on WM capacity as a consequence of STM architecture, there is evidence to suggest that bilinguals outperform monolinguals in tasks designed to assess WM ability. A recent meta-analysis investigated the effect of bilingualism on several cognitive components, including WM (Adesope *et al.*, 2010), and found an overall advantage in WM capacity for bilinguals compared to monolinguals, with a moderate effect size. One explanation is that *functional* WM capacity may improve as a consequence of the unique demands of bilingualism, while the *architectural* WM capacity (i.e., four items with one as the focus of attention) may not be affected. As noted earlier, by employing strategies that recruit LTM, WM capacity can benefit by increasing the information density of individual items held in STM. Forming these information-chunking rules is likely to involve attentional control mechanisms to selectively activate the attributes of a set of items that allow them to be grouped as a conceptual unit, while reducing the salience of their differences (Engle 2002; Kane *et al.*, 2001). It has been shown that bilingualism can reduce age-related decline in the ability to acquire novel task-related rules that are arbitrarily defined (Bialystok *et al.*, 2004). This pattern of selective attention and executive control is closely linked to WM ability (Rosen & Engle, 1998), and has been shown to be associated with lifelong bilingualism in other domains, in terms of ability to inhibit irrelevant information (Bialystok, Craik, & Luk, 2008; Bialystok, Craik, & Ryan, 2006; Costa, Hernández, & Sebastián-Gallés, 2008) and task-switching capabilities (Bialystok, Craik, & Ruocco, 2006; Prior & MacWhinney, 2010).

Overall, the evidence suggests that the architecture of STM itself is inherently limited, but that functional capacity can be improved by recruiting LTM. By rapidly encoding novel items, STM space can be freed up, whereas by retrieving organizational schemas from LTM, multiple items can be chunked into a single unit of attention. The efficiency with which these processes operate will determine individual WM capabilities. Bilinguals demonstrate increased functional WM capacity, and their improved executive control is a likely contributor to this increased capacity by facilitating the communication between STM and LTM.

Phonological working memory in bilinguals

Phonological working memory controls the maintenance of auditory information in an articulatory loop (Baddeley, Gathercole, & Papagno, 1998). It is commonly tested by auditorily presenting a list of digits or non-words, which the participant reproduces after a brief delay. The ability to perceive and maintain novel phonological forms is a necessary step before information can be encoded and stored in LTM.

Typical implementations of phonological memory tests, however, result in cross-linguistic differences in observed WM span (Nell, 2000), where the length of individual items (i.e., digit names) can constrain WM capacity (Ellis, 1992). English digit names are shorter than Spanish and can be rehearsed faster; accordingly, English monolinguals typically show a higher digit span capacity as compared to Spanish monolinguals. However, English–Spanish bilinguals resemble neither monolingual group, and show lower English digit spans than English monolinguals and higher Spanish digit spans than Spanish monolinguals (Ardila *et al.*, 2000). In terms of storage and processing, then, the bilingual does not represent two independent monolingual language systems, but instead reflects a processing compromise. The bilingual's stored representations in each language may differ qualitatively from monolinguals, or the way in which information is processed may differ due to the demands of managing interference between languages.

One way to address problems of cross-linguistic differences while studying bilingual WM is to investigate the effect of increased bilingual experience on WM. It has been shown that early bilinguals outperform bilinguals who acquired a second language later in life on WM tasks (Ardila *et al.*, 2000), and highly proficient bilinguals show WM advantages as compared to less proficient bilinguals (Bajo, Padilla, & Padilla, 2000; Majerus *et al.*, 2008; Service *et al.*, 2002). What's clear from these studies is that there is a positive relationship between bilingualism and WM efficiency, with additional research needed to better understand the nature of this relationship.

Bilingual memory access

The manner in which linguistic information is retrieved from LTM can help to inform the structure of memory storage, in particular, the degree to which storage is language-specific or language-non-specific. Explicit knowledge is tightly connected to language, in the form of word–concept associations in semantic memory and experiences in episodic memory associated with particular language contexts. In this section, we discuss how episodic memory may be stored and accessed according to language-specific mechanisms that preserve the encoding context. We then review research on semantic memory access in bilinguals, starting with lexical access during *comprehension* and following with lexical access during *production*.

Episodic memory access

Episodic memories contain representations of previous events, places, and times; when these events are personally relevant, they become part of autobiographical memory. Episodic memories are experienced as vivid multisensory events (Mather *et al.*, 2006), and as such are subjectively distinct from the recall of semantic facts about past experiences. Episodic memories become less accessible with age, such that older adults rely more on semantic facts to describe past events (Levine *et al.*, 2002). Evidence suggests that age-related episodic memory decline can be attenuated by bilingual experience (Schroeder & Marian, 2012). As episodic memory retrieval depends in part on intact central executive functions (Baudouin *et al.*, 2009; Troyer, Graves, & Cullum, 1994), and bilingualism has been shown to protect against decline in executive control with age (Bialystok *et al.*, 2004), it is possible that the improved retrieval observed in bilinguals can be attributed to preserved executive function that facilitates episodic memory access.

Additionally, bilinguals may be able to take advantage of the linguistic context associated with an event to cue retrieval. Encoding specificity refers to the phenomenon of improved memory recall when contextual cues present at encoding are also present at recall (Tulving & Thomson, 1973), and is supported by fMRI studies that suggest reactivation of an event's brain state at encoding during retrieval (Buckner & Wheeler, 2001; Danker & Anderson, 2010). Bilinguals experience life events in one of two languages; this distinction provides an additional cue that may affect episodic memory recall. In particular, the language in which autobiographical memories are cued may influence the types of memories that become available for recall. Experimental studies and evidence from psychotherapy sessions indicate that memories that share a linguistic encoding context with the retrieval context are more numerous, more detailed, and more emotional than memories from an incongruent linguistic context of encoding (Bugelski, 1977; Larsen *et al.*, 2002; Marian & Neisser, 2000; Matsumoto & Stanny, 2006; Schrauf, 2003; Schrauf & Rubin, 1998, 2000). This pattern suggests that in contrast to language-independent access to semantic memory, episodic memories retain language-dependent information that affects retrieval.

One of the early studies investigating the effect of retrieval context on bilingual memory recall examined older Spanish–English bilingual adults who reported not speaking Spanish for the previous ten years (Bugelski, 1977). Memories were elicited with a cued-recall paradigm in which participants were asked to provide their first memory in response to a cue. Memories were elicited separately to English cues and their Spanish translation equivalents, and participants were asked to broadly designate the period of their life that the memory occurred in. Memories elicited to English words were more likely to have occurred later in life, while memories to Spanish words were more likely to have occurred in childhood. This study was one of the first to indicate that the linguistic context at retrieval influences the type of memory preferentially recalled.

As the field developed, studies on autobiographical memory in bilinguals began to take advantage of the unique situation of sequential bilingual immigrants. These are individuals who grew up monolingual, but in adulthood immigrated to a country that required them to adopt a new language. This allows one to manipulate the linguistic context in which autobiographical memories are recalled to examine whether episodes from a congruent encoding context are facilitated. There are multiple factors that contribute to a linguistic context, and they appear to have different effects on retrieval. In particular, the ambient language of the immediate environment and the language of the cue word independent of environment both influence recall (Marian & Neisser, 2000). Of these two, the language of the surrounding environment appears to exert a more powerful effect. Autobiographical memory access is effortful and typically involves a mental search through associations starting with the cue until a target memory is retrieved. The initial cue may facilitate search by biasing the language context of the first association, while the ambient language context may have a larger effect by influencing global search parameters regardless of the initial step facilitated by the word cue.

The process by which bilinguals arrive at a target memory during a mental search helps to illuminate how memory is organized. By using an autobiographical memory protocol analysis in which participants "think out loud," this mental search can be made explicit (Ericsson & Simon, 1993; Schrauf, 2003). One of the strategies bilinguals are able to use during a mental search is to spontaneously translate the cue word (Schrauf, 2003). Bilinguals' ability to use this strategy suggests that when a story could not be brought to mind, participants were aware that a word's translation equivalent might offer new mental associations. If memories are organized according to the linguistic context they were encoded in, then translating becomes a viable strategy during memory search. Another way this inner mental translation can be observed is by asking participants to report in what language a memory first came to them, before they formed a response appropriate to the retrieval context. Participants sometimes report a memory first coming to them in a language different from the language of the cue. In these cases, a language switch occurred during mental search when one language did not afford a suitable personal memory. In accordance with a language-specific encoding hypothesis, autobiographical memories that had first come to participants in their native tongue occurred at an earlier age than memories in their second language (Matsumoto & Stanny, 2006; Schrauf & Rubin, 1998, 2000).

These studies, however, necessarily confound sequential bilingualism with biculturalism. One of the ways this problem has been addressed is to examine two sets of bilingual immigrants with the same native and host countries who differ only in their age of immigration (Larsen et al., 2002). Two groups of Polish–Danish bilinguals were compared who had immigrated to Denmark at a mean age of either 24 or 34. It was found that memories that came to participants in Polish were more likely to have occurred prior to immigration, while memories in Danish were more likely to have occurred after immigration. This shift was qualitatively similar between groups, but centered around the age of immigration. Though groups differed in their cultural identities, reflected by use of inner speech in their first and second languages, in both groups, the shift in language context drove autobiographical memory retrieval.

In summary, episodic memory in bilinguals retains language-specific information that can influence the ease with which memories are accessed. Bilingualism can protect against age-related episodic memory decline, potentially by providing a cue in the linguistic context of encoding that can facilitate retrieval in a matching linguistic context. Results across multiple studies on different bilingual populations indicate that access to autobiographical memories is enhanced depending on the overlap between the linguistic context in which access is attempted and the language that was in use at the time the memory was encoded. Compared to semantic memory access, episodic memories appear to integrate language more closely and preserve the language of encoding in the memory trace.

Semantic memory access during language comprehension

The idea that bilinguals are able to shift into a monolingual language mode and restrict memory access to words in a single language is appealing (Grosjean 1985, 2001), since bilinguals are able to functionally separate their two languages and converse with monolingual speakers. However, a strict language mode hypothesis where the speaker is able to restrict access to a single language is inconsistent with evidence for activation of a non-target language that results in competitive interference, even in a monolingual context (Dijkstra & van Hell, 2003; Duyck *et al.*, 2007; Marian & Spivey, 2003a, b).

One strategy that has been used to investigate lexical access in bilinguals utilizes cross-linguistic orthographic similarity. Upon viewing a printed word, its lexical representation in LTM is accessed, but orthographic neighbors (words that differ from the target by only one letter) also become activated and can influence processing (van Heuven, Dijkstra, & Grainger, 1998). Evidence suggests that bilinguals access orthographic neighbors both in the target and in the non-target language (van Heuven *et al.*, 2008). This suggests that lexical access is language-non-specific during word recognition, as bilinguals automatically retrieve items from both languages. Research on cognates provides additional evidence suggesting that information in the non-target language is accessed. In lexical decision tasks, cognates are typically identified as words more quickly than non-cognates, since word representations in both languages are accessed and facilitate lexical decision. The magnitude of this effect is dependent upon the degree to which the orthographic representations of the cognates overlap (Dijkstra et al., 2010). Even though the task only requires participants to access words in a single language, cognate processing indicates that bilinguals activate representations in both languages.

While orthographic overlap across languages allows one to test lexical access during a monolingual task, cognates may overtly activate both languages. A strong test of language-non-specific access would restrict overt activation of the non-target language, and is possible with minimal cross-linguistic phonological overlap. In the visual world paradigm, participants view a display of several objects and are instructed to manipulate objects while their eye movements are tracked. If a participant is instructed, for example, to "pick up the candy," participants make more eye movements to objects that overlap phonologically with the target, such as a candle, compared to non-overlapping control objects. This suggests that "candle" was partially activated due to its similarity to the target word "candy" (Allopenna, 1998; Tanenhaus et al., 2000).

This paradigm has been successfully adapted to bilingual language processing to investigate whether words in a non-target language are co-activated. It was found that when Russian–English bilinguals were instructed in Russian to pick up a *marka* (the Russian word for stamp), they were significantly more likely to look at a marker than at a phonologically unrelated control (Blumenfeld & Marian, 2007; Marian & Spivey, 2003a, b; Spivey & Marian, 1999). The English names of competitor objects were never spoken, yet bilinguals accessed the lexical representations as a result of hearing words in the other language. This pattern of results provides strong support for language-non-specific lexical retrieval. It has also been shown that sentence context can reduce the magnitude of between-language competition (Chambers & Cooke, 2009).

Lexical access in these studies is thought to occur due to phonological items activating word representations in both languages non-selectively. Cross-linguistic lexical access and interference can be demonstrated in the absence of input overlap, indicating interactive processing links that facilitate lexical retrieval. In a series of studies by Thierry and Wu (2004, 2007), cross-linguistic lexical access was demonstrated in English–Chinese bilinguals. Chinese is an ideographic language that lacks orthographic form overlap with English. English–Chinese bilinguals were asked to read English word pairs and make a semantic relatedness judgment. Unbeknownst to the participants, the English words' translation equivalents in Chinese were each composed of two characters, and in half of the experimental trials, a character was repeated within a word pair. Behaviorally, there was no effect of character repetition; but when electrophysiological responses were examined, it was observed that Chinese repetition pairs elicited a larger N400 cortical response than control word pairs.[1] Despite receiving input in only one language, language-non-specific lexical access was observed, suggesting that retrieval is automatic and can cross language boundaries. Further evidence was observed in a recent study using the visual world paradigm with bimodal bilinguals (hearing users of a spoken and a signed language, such as English and American Sign Language). Although their two languages lack form overlap, covert co-activation was observed across languages, reflecting language-non-specific access (Shook & Marian, 2010, 2012).

In summary, during language comprehension, bilinguals appear to access linguistic representations in semantic memory in a language-non-specific manner. Access is not modality specific, but occurs in both orthographic and phonological contexts. The effect of non-target language activation appears to vary with task constructs, as lexical decision is facilitated by cross-linguistic activation, but target processing is interfered with as a consequence of phonological competition across languages.

Semantic memory access during language production

Language production occurs under a different set of demands compared to language recognition, and these differences are likely to influence the manner in which information is accessed. During recognition, linguistic input is initially ambiguous and is integrated as it unfolds. A system that considers lexical alternatives in either language is thus able to easily adapt to changing language contexts. During production, however, language switches are determined by the speaker, and this prior knowledge may help to constrain lexical selection and minimize interference between languages. Speech production requires two steps, an initial activation of potential lexical items to be produced and a selection process that determines the item to be articulated. During the first step of lexical access, words in both languages are thought to be accessed in parallel (Colomé, 2001; Colomé & Miozzo, 2010; Costa, Caramazza,

---

[1] The N400 is a component of the ERP signal (event-related potentials are used to assess neural responses by recording electrical activity on the scalp). The N400 occurs roughly 400 ms (milliseconds) after stimulus onset and is characterized by a negative deflection in the waveform. It is commonly thought to be a marker of semantic processing. A larger response indicates increased difficulty, in this example caused by the covert Chinese form overlap that interfered with semantic processing.

& Sebastián-Gallés, 2000; Gollan, Montoya, Fennema-Notestine, & Morris, 2005). However, bilingual production models disagree on whether the subsequent step of lexical *selection* is language-specific, precluding competition (Costa, La Heij, & Navarrete, 2006), or language-non-specific, allowing for between-language competition (Kroll, Bobb, & Wodniecka, 2006). Research from studies on cognate naming, cross-modal processing, and cross-linguistic interaction indicates that while multiple languages can interact in the bilingual mind during language production, this interaction does not result in competitive interference, as in bilingual language recognition.

As words that share cross-linguistic form and meaning overlap, cognates explicitly activate both of a bilingual's languages. If similar but non-identical cognates compete for selection, they should be difficult to produce. Instead, research suggests that bilinguals name cognates more quickly than non-cognates (Costa *et al.*, 2000). This suggests that rather than competing for selection, activation of a word in a non-target language can activate phonemes shared with the target word, facilitating production. Critically, in order for facilitation to be observed at all, initial lexical access must have been language-non-specific, allowing for the target word's translation equivalent to boost articulatory processes. Evidence from bimodal bilinguals indicates that in the absence of the biological constraints on word production in unimodal bilinguals, the language system is able to co-articulate translation equivalents, using concurrent manual signs with spoken speech (Casey & Emmorey, 2008; Emmorey *et al.*, 2008). This example demonstrates again language-non-specific lexical access during bilingual speech production.

Cross-language facilitation has also been observed during a target/distractor naming task (Colomé & Miozzo 2010). Bilingual participants viewed two superimposed red and green drawings, and were asked to name pictures of a certain color. When the name of the distractor in the non-target language overlapped phonologically with the target, target naming latency actually decreased. Even though the non-target language was never elicited and the distractor picture was clearly identified, participants appeared to spontaneously access word labels and phonological representations for the distractor in both languages, causing constructive feedback similar to that found by Costa *et al.* (2000) that facilitated target production.

By only examining instances of successful language retrieval, though, potential interference across languages may be overlooked. Words are not always accessed successfully during speech production, and these other instances of retrieval failure help to inform the interaction between lexical activation and selection. Retrieval failures commonly occur in tip-of-the-tongue (TOT) experiences, which entail an inability to retrieve a word despite a speaker's certainty that it exists in memory. The phenomenon has been well documented in monolingual speakers, particularly in cases where individuals are attempting to retrieve low-frequency words (Brown, 1991; Schwartz, 1999). During a TOT state, fragments of the target word may be accessible, including knowledge of the initial phonemes or syllables. Some TOT states are spontaneously resolved, while others can be resolved after being provided with phonological primes as cues (Abrams, White, & Eitel, 2003; James & Burke, 2000).

On the one hand, TOT states may reflect a breadth of lexical knowledge – a difficulty in accessing words may produce TOTs in individuals with large vocabularies, whereas those with lower vocabularies may simply not know the target word. On the other hand, TOTs may indicate specific failures to retrieve and a problem with lexical access. TOTs of the first sort are typically observed in older adults, and only to low-frequency words (Dahlgren, 1998; Gollan & Brown, 2006; Schwartz, 2002). Bilinguals instead show TOTs of the second sort, to words of all frequencies (Gollan & Acenas, 2004; Gollan & Brown, 2006; Gollan, Montoya, & Bonanni, 2005; Gollan & Silverberg, 2001). While superficially similar, then, TOTs in older adults are a reflection of larger vocabularies leading to more cases of attempted lexical access, whereas TOTs in bilinguals reflect a systematic disruption of lexical access.

As a result of dividing their time between two languages, bilinguals necessarily use each language less than monolingual speakers, who devote all of their communication to a single language. Frequency is an important predictor of TOTs; as seen in older adults, low-frequency words cause more TOTs than high-frequency words. Since the absolute frequency of individual words in the bilingual lexicon is lower than in monolinguals, individual items may be more difficult to retrieve. Lexical access failures in bilinguals do not appear to be driven by interference between languages, as bimodal bilinguals experience TOTs at a rate comparable to unimodal bilinguals (Pyers, Gollan, & Emmorey, 2009). The bimodal bilingual's languages cannot interfere phonologically, but it is reasonable to expect that lower absolute word frequencies drive TOTs in a manner similar to that in unimodal bilinguals.

Additional support for the word frequency account in bilinguals comes from research on TOT incidence for retrieval of proper names. An individual's proper name is consistent in different language contexts, and thus should be matched in usage frequencies across monolinguals and bilinguals. It has been shown that, in fact, bilinguals experience TOTs to proper names (either famous names or personally relevant names) at a comparable rate to monolinguals (Gollan, Montoya, & Bonanni, 2005). These results suggest that TOT incidence is sensitive to word frequency, and when the sum of a word's frequency across multiple language contexts approaches that word's frequency in a monolingual context, lexical access is comparable.

Just as proper names overlap between different language contexts and act as high-frequency words, cognates may act as high-frequency words compared to non-cognates due to form overlap that can facilitate parallel activation. Even if cognates are represented distinctly in each language, their phonological similarity may cause both items to activate in monolingual contexts. Cognates have been found to facilitate recall and reduce TOTs to the level of monolingual speakers, but only for cognates that a bilingual knew in both languages, and thus could conceivably use as often as a monolingual would (Gollan & Acenas, 2004). Even when only non-cognates were considered, words that more bilinguals were able to translate easily had reduced TOTs as compared to words without translation equivalents.

The sum of these findings suggests that translation equivalents do not impair lexical access during production. Instead of competing, words in the non-target language actually facilitate retrieval. This is consistent with models of parallel activation of lexical items in both languages during production, which can serve to increase the relative frequency of names, cognates, and translation equivalents as compared to words that a bilingual only knows in one language. The relative frequency of words within an individual bilingual lexicon determines their accessibility and may be sensitive to the strength with which those items are encoded in memory. The other finding to come from studies on TOT retrieval failures is that as a consequence of dividing their time between two languages, items in the bilingual lexicon can act as lower frequency words as compared to their equivalents in the monolingual lexicon, leading to group differences in retrieval efficiency. Thus, bilingualism results in language-non-specific access to words in both languages during production, but this parallel access does not interfere with lexical selection. Instead, difficulties in bilingual lexical access during production seem to be caused by knowing more words than monolinguals and using them less frequently.

In summary, the degree to which lexical access is language-specific versus language-non-specific depends on the type of information stored in memory. As a consequence of experiencing life in two languages, bilinguals encode information about the world in different languages according to varying linguistic contexts. These memories can be accessed in either language, resulting in situations where the language of encoding and the language of retrieval are either congruent or incongruent. The degree to which congruent language contexts affect memory access informs the specificity of LTM for individual languages. Evidence from autobiographical memory recall in bilinguals shows that congruence between encoding language and retrieval language affects retrieval, suggesting that episodic memories preserve language classification in the memory trace. Semantic memory instead shows a pattern whereby lexical items in both languages become activated and can influence language comprehension and production. During both comprehension and production, language-non-specific activation appears to be automatic, supporting the idea that information in semantic memory is accessed without regard to language classification.

Information processing in bilinguals

Although a bilingual's two languages co-activate to a certain degree during language processing, the two languages remain functionally distinct and can be used in different contexts. This separation between languages may emerge either from architectural constraints in the language system, such as separate lexicons, or it may result from an external control mechanism that manipulates global language activation. Several mechanisms for differentiating languages have been implemented in theoretical and computational models of bilingual language processing, and in this section we review the successes and limitations of a number of these models. In addition, we consider how novel language learning can be used to understand the emergence of functionally distinct languages. Whereas modeling work is vital in determining how proficient bilinguals may control access to their two languages, the process of novel language learning provides insight into how a functional separation between languages can develop. Further, by comparing novel language learning success in monolinguals and bilinguals, it is possible to determine how existing mechanisms for controlling language processing in bilinguals may extend to novel language learning success.

Modeling bilingual processing

Models of bilingual language processing have to account for the fact that although a bilingual is able to communicate effectively in a single language, both languages remain active and can potentially interfere at lower levels of lexical processing. Current models approach this problem in different ways, depending on the domain that they are specialized for. Comparing the strengths and limitations of these separate models highlights some of the primary issues that must be considered in a theory of bilingual memory and language processing, as well as potential areas of further research. In this section, we briefly review some of the more influential models of bilingual memory and language processing, and consider how these models describe language interaction during lexical processing (for a more thorough review of selected models, see Dijkstra, Haga, Bijsterveld, & Sprinkhuizen-Kuyper, this volume).

We start with the Revised Hierarchical Model (RHM; Kroll & Stewart, 1994), an early descriptive model of bilingualism that focused on associations between languages and between lexical and conceptual representations, and prompted research in the field of bilingual language organization and development. The RHM laid the groundwork for a number of specialized models, including the Bilingual Interactive Activation Model, which focuses on visual word processing and the structure of the bilingual lexicon (Dijkstra, Van Jaarsveld, & Ten Brinke, 1998; Dijkstra & van Heuven 2002; van Heuven et al., 1998), and the Bilingual Language Interaction Network for Comprehension of Speech, which focuses on auditory word processing and patterns of cross-linguistic activation (Shook & Marian, in press). Language production and control are described in the Inhibitory Control Model (Green, 2003), and the emergence of distinct languages during bilingual language acquisition has been depicted in the Self-Organizing Model of Bilingual Processing (Li & Farkas, 2002). The sample of models reviewed in this section provides a useful framework for considering the organization of language in bilingual memory, and the degree to which multiple languages interact during processing.

The Revised Hierarchical Model The Revised Hierarchical Model (RHM; Kroll & Stewart, 1994) includes separate lexicons for a bilingual's two languages, but also contains direct associative links between translation equivalents (see Figure 1.2). The RHM built on the work of Potter and colleagues (Potter et al., 1984), which separated the associative links between a bilingual's two languages and the conceptual links between words and the concepts they represent. The RHM also separates lexical and conceptual stores, with a shared conceptual store across languages that contains associations to lexical items in both languages. By varying the strength of these different connections, either between lexical items or from the individual lexicons to the conceptual store, organization of the language system can be

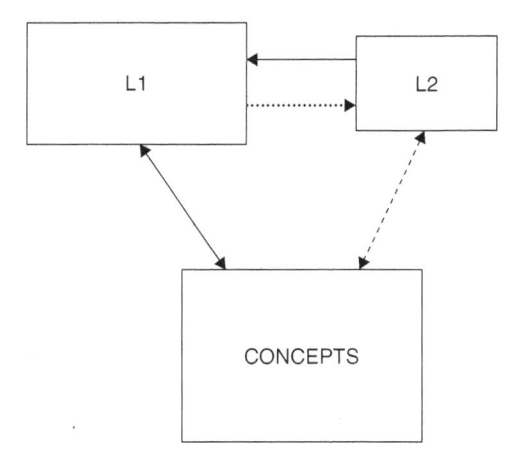

Figure 1.2 Kroll and Stewart's Revised Hierarchical Model (RHM)

modeled across development in simultaneous or sequential bilinguals. In a beginning second language learner, words in the second language (L2) are most strongly associated with their translation equivalents in the native language (L1), and contain only weak connections to the shared conceptual store. Accessing meaning for a word in the L2 is thus accomplished by activating the L1 equivalent, which then accesses semantic meaning. As L2 proficiency increases, lexical items in the L2 become more strongly associated with the conceptual store, reducing the need for L1-mediated semantic access.

The RHM plays an important role in how thinking about bilingual memory has developed, as it posited a dynamically refined system that allows for both language interaction and functional independence. However, the structure of the RHM has been challenged by some recently emerging patterns in bilingual language processing, and may be less of a good fit as compared to other language models when describing interactivity within the bilingual system (Brysbaert & Duyck, 2010). In particular, the separation of L1 and L2 into separate lexicons is inconsistent with data demonstrating effects on processing of orthographic neighbors in a non-target language (van Heuven et al., 1998), reflecting cross-linguistic word form effects that are difficult to explain using separate lexicons. Additionally, predictions of the RHM regarding asymmetric priming from the L2 to the L1 due to strong direct associative links between translation equivalents are not well supported (Schoonbaert et al., 2009). The RHM has been successful in its ability to describe changes to bilingual language storage as proficiency changes, but the basic structure of segregated language storage in the model may need further development.

The Bilingual Interactive Activation Model The Bilingual Interactive Activation (BIA) Model and its revised form, the BIA+ (Dijkstra et al., 1998; Dijkstra & van Heuven 2002; van Heuven et al., 1998), are models of bilingual visual word recognition and have been implemented computationally. The BIA and BIA+ models differ from the RHM in that they include integrated storage of the bilingual lexicon (see Figures 1.3 and 1.4). The presence of language input (orthographic only in BIA, and extending to phonological information in BIA+) non-selectively activates items that overlap with the input in either language. Non-selective language access is consistent with research showing that cognates and interlingual homographs interfere with target processing, even in a monolingual context. In the BIA+ model, to the degree that an item overlaps with the input, it will become activated regardless of its language. At higher processing levels in which a response is selected, language assignment can be enforced. The BIA+ model implements language assignment by tagging individual words in the shared lexical storage to distinct language nodes; as words in one language are activated, items with the same language tag increase in activation, while items with the opposite language tag are reactively inhibited. Task-oriented language modes can selectively activate or inhibit language tags at the response level, and in this manner, the BIA+ model relies less on the organization of language in LTM to separate languages, and instead shapes language context at the processing level. The BIA+ model has provided a useful framework for findings on bilingual semantic memory access during language comprehension. As discussed earlier in this chapter, automatic activation of both languages in response to single-language input has been supported by numerous studies, and the BIA+ model will continue to be an important resource for understanding bilingual language processing.

The Bilingual Language Interaction Network for Comprehension of Speech The Bilingual Language Interaction Network for Comprehension of Speech (BLINCS; Shook & Marian, in press) models language interaction during bilingual spoken language comprehension, in contrast to the BIA's focus on visual input. BLINCS represents a bilingual functional architecture in which the acoustic signal perceived by bilinguals travels to a feature level, then to a phonemic level, then from there to the lexical level, and further to the semantic level (see Figure 1.5). The interaction between levels is bi-directional,

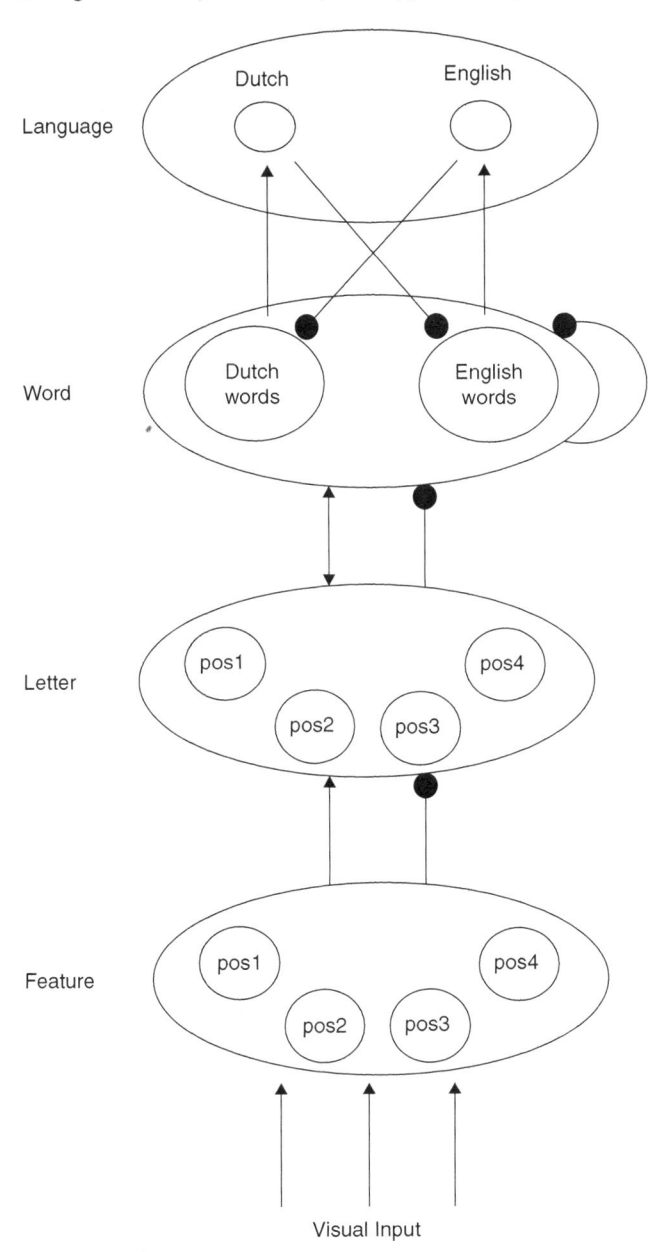

Bilingual memory: structure, access, processing 27

Figure 1.3 Van Heuven, Dijkstra, and Grainger's Bilingual Interactive Activation Model (BIA)

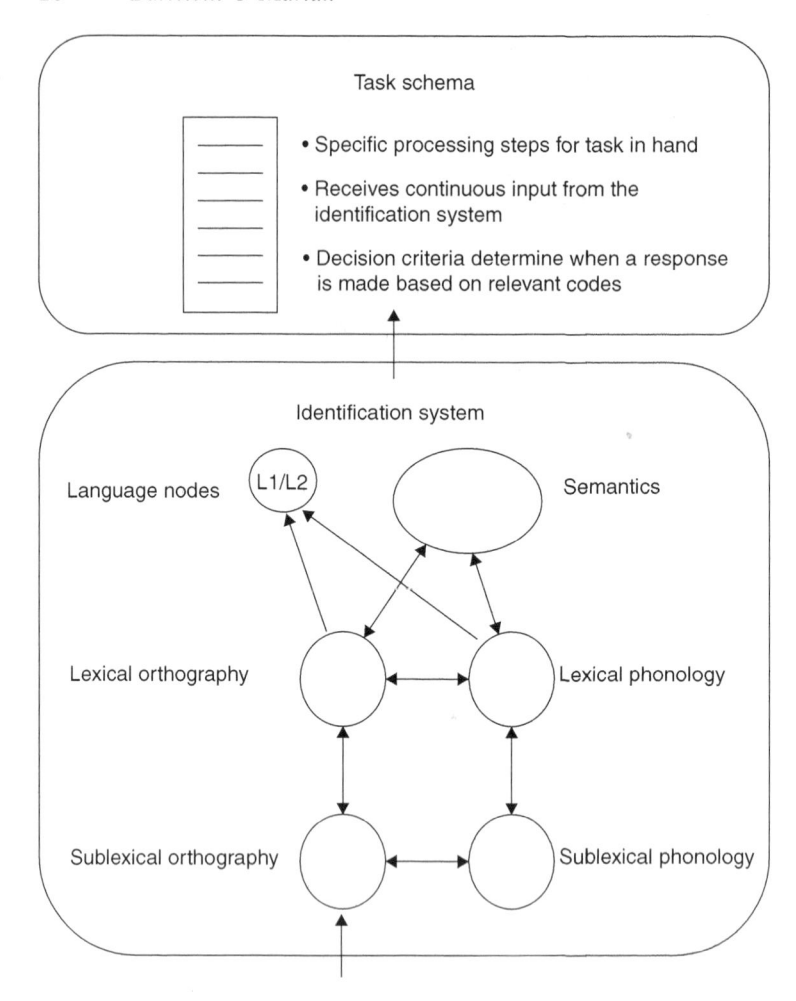

Figure 1.4 Dijkstra and van Heuven's Bilingual Interactive Activation Plus Model (BIA+)

allowing for both feed-forward and back-propagation. Within levels, language-specific and language-shared representations are included, with bi-directional connections between languages allowing for competition within and across languages. Each processing level includes a self-organizing map (see Li & Farkas, 2002 for a review) that organizes according to the amount and type of dual-language input, such that structurally similar items are grouped together. Connections between levels are bi-directional and strengthen according to the co-occurrence

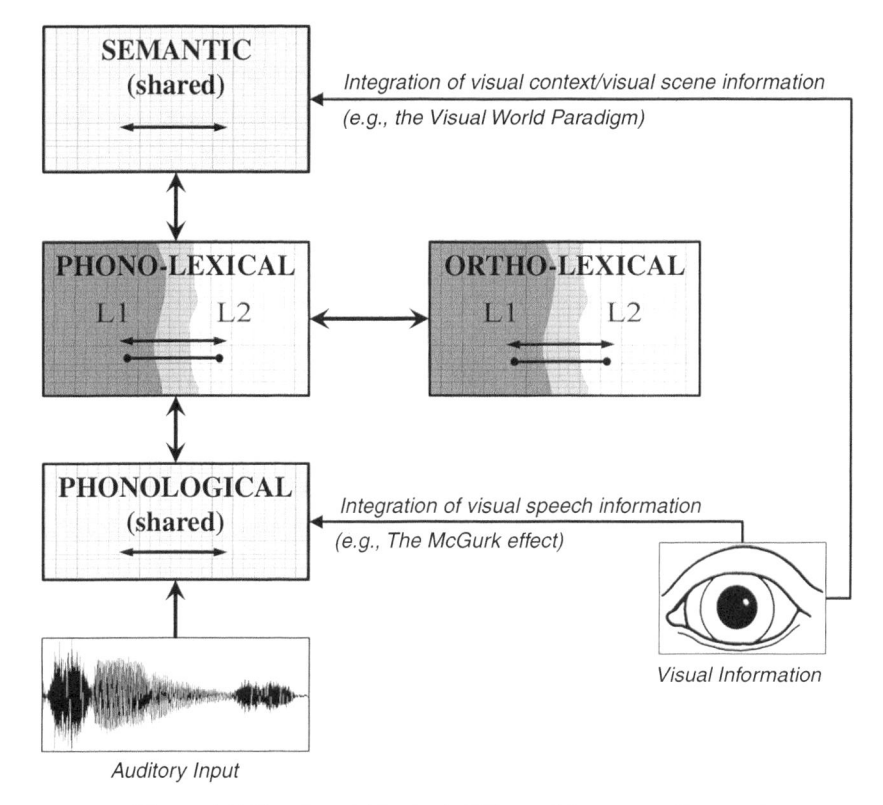

Figure 1.5 Shook and Marian's Bilingual Language Interaction Network for Comprehension of Speech (BLINCS)

of items. The model quantifies associations between items based on structural similarity regardless of language classification, as similar items occupy adjacent regions in the self-organizing maps.

The Inhibitory Control Model Although it makes few claims about the organization of multiple languages in memory, the Inhibitory Control (IC) Model (Green, 2003) plays an important role in describing the pattern through which language selection occurs when language storage and access is language-non-specific (see Figure 1.6). The IC Model includes abstract language schemas, separate from the lexical-semantic system, that compete to determine relative language activations. These language task schemas are themselves moderated by a supervisory attentional system (SAS) that regulates their activity. By inhibiting the task schema for the non-target language, communication

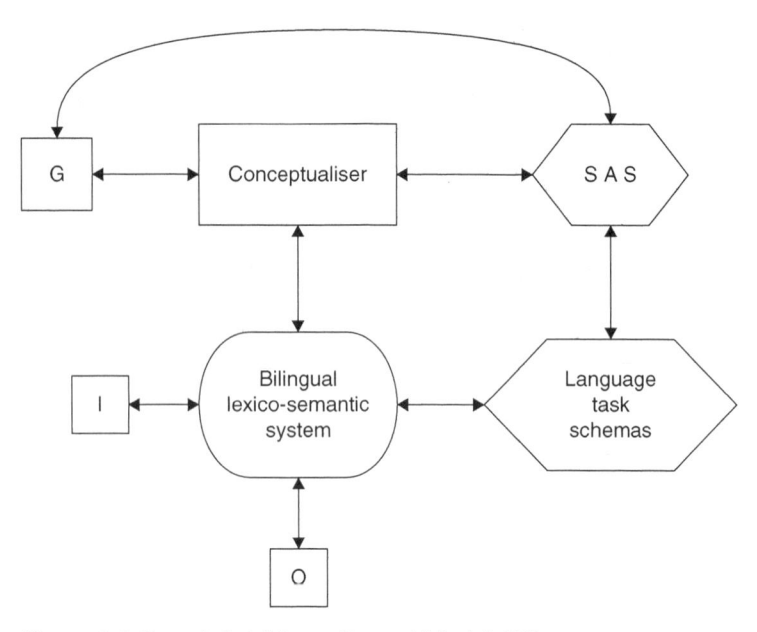

```
                    ┌──────┐     ┌──────────────┐      ┌─────────┐
                    │  G   │◄───►│ Conceptualiser│◄───►│  S A S  │
                    └──────┘     └──────────────┘      └─────────┘
                                         ▲                  ▲
                                         │                  │
                                         ▼                  ▼
                    ┌───┐      ┌──────────────┐      ┌──────────┐
                    │ I │◄───►│   Bilingual    │◄───►│ Language │
                    └───┘      │ lexico-semantic│      │   task   │
                               │    system     │      │ schemas  │
                               └──────────────┘      └──────────┘
                                         ▲
                                         │
                                       ┌───┐
                                       │ O │
                                       └───┘
```

Figure 1.6 Green's Inhibitory Control Model (IC)

in a monolingual context can occur by minimizing intrusions from the other language. In order to switch languages, then, and reactivate a previously inhibited language, latent inhibition must be overcome and will be associated with a processing cost (Meuter & Allport, 1999). As discussed earlier in this chapter, bilingual language experience appears to be associated with improved inhibitory control ability, leading to gains in attention and working memory that extend to novel language learning skill (Bajo *et al.*, 2000; Kaushanskaya & Marian, 2009b; Majerus *et al.*, 2008; Service *et al.*, 2002). However, while it seems clear that the Inhibitory Control Model accurately describes a method by which language activation can be adjusted, the efficiency with which the inhibitory demands are managed may vary between different types of bilinguals or multilinguals (Costa & Santesteban, 2004), and thus in its present form may not be broadly applicable to general bilingual processing.

The Self-Organizing Model of Bilingual Processing The Self-Organizing Model of Bilingual Processing (SOMBIP; Li & Farkas, 2002) was designed to test the ability of the language system to self-organize over time in a manner that accommodates dual-language

Figure 1.7

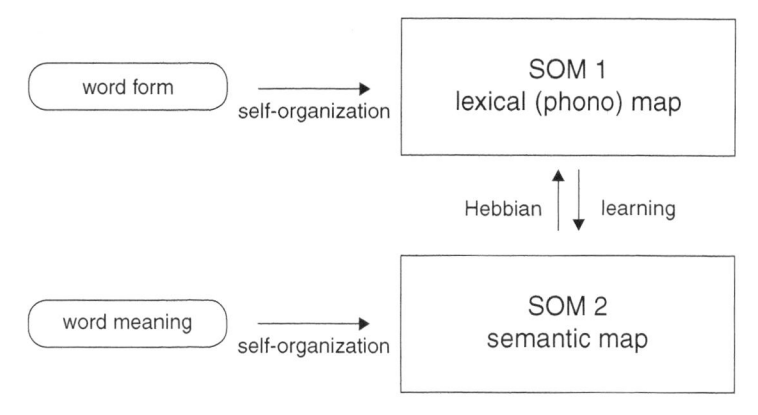

Li and Farkas' Self-Organizing Model of Bilingual Processing (SOMBIP)

- word form → (self-organization) → SOM 1: lexical (phono) map
- word meaning → (self-organization) → SOM 2: semantic map
- SOM 1 ↔ SOM 2 via Hebbian learning

input. It was developed based on connectionist models of language storage in monolinguals (Elman, 1990) and bilinguals (French, 1998) that self-organize according to statistical regularities in the input. SOMBIP has been tested on a mixed-language naturalistic input, and has been shown to successfully separate languages and store representations within a shared space. The self-organizing models in SOMBIP initially start by randomly activating patterns of nodes distributed in a two-dimensional space. Activated units and their neighbors adjust to activate more strongly to that same input in the future. The effect over time is an increased selectivity of the model's response to inputs, and the emergence of functionally distinct regions that respond to specialized types of information. SOMBIP contains two mutually interconnected self-organizing models, one that activates to phonological input and one that activates to semantic input (see Figure 1.7). The architecture of the model allows for translation equivalents to become closely associated at the phonemic level due to their similar semantic representations, and for distinct semantic concepts to become associated due to phonologically similar interlingual homographs. In contrast to other models (see de Groot & Kroll, 1997), semantic concepts in SOMBIP are not shared between languages. Instead, semantic concepts in each language are represented in a shared space within a self-organizing model for semantic information. The strength of SOMBIP is its ability to functionally separate languages within a shared storage space according to co-occurrences in the input, providing a plausible mechanism by which an integrated lexicon can form in bilingual long-term memory. SOMBIP's ability to capture aspects of bilingual language development makes it a prime candidate to incorporate the growing body of research on novel language learning success in bilinguals.

Theories of bilingual language processing necessarily make assumptions about how language and memory are organized, and how memory access occurs; even if a theory makes explicit claims only regarding one aspect of language processing, implicit assumptions are made on how the rest of the system is organized. The advantage of a model, whether it is verbally described or computationally implemented, is that it forces the researcher to confront these implicit assumptions while they construct a theory of processing. It is only when assumptions are made explicit that they can be challenged and refined, as seen in the shift away from separate lexicons in the RHM toward an integrated bilingual lexicon as seen in BIA+, BLINCS, and SOMBIP. At this stage, a challenge for models of bilingual language processing arises due to their increasing specialization. It is becoming more important that models unify the terms and frameworks in which they are based, so that competing assumptions can be recognized and compared.

Novel language learning and processing

Models of bilingual language processing have increased understanding of the unique challenges that result from organizing and processing multiple languages within a single mind. Research on novel language learning can contribute to this discussion by exploring how the language system can change to accommodate an additional language. Novel language learning entails a reorganization of the language processing system to adapt to the new language's rules of grammar and phonotactics, and to the new vocabulary. In addition to mastering the new language, the learner must be able to mitigate interference from more strongly represented proficient languages, and increasing processing demands. A bilingual's years of experience controlling access to two languages may affect these learning and memory processes in ways that improve novel language acquisition. Further, late bilinguals (those who learned a second language after acquiring their first language, instead of learning both concurrently) may be able to profitably transfer skills developed during L2 acquisition to learning a third language (L3). Novel language learning, then, can be used to compare the flexibility of monolinguals' and bilinguals' language processing abilities, and how well they are able to integrate novel vocabulary and grammatical rules. With recent advances in this area and without the confounding factors of earlier research (see Lambert, 1981), a consistent pattern has emerged where bilinguals learning an L3 outperform monolinguals learning an L2, across domains spanning vocabulary (Cenoz, 2003; Cenoz & Valencia, 1994; van Hell & Mahn, 1997; Kaushanskaya & Marian, 2009a, b; Keshavarz & Astaneh, 2004; Sanz, 2000; Thomas, 1992), grammar (Klein, 1995; Sanz, 2000; Thomas, 1992), and pragmatics (Safont Jorda, 2003). The research methods are varied, and may be primarily observational, in which performance of participants enrolled in academic language courses is investigated, or experimental, in which training occurs within a tightly controlled laboratory environment, and the target language may be either naturally occurring or artificially constructed (e.g., Cenoz & Jessner, 2000; Sanz & Lado, 2007).

Observational studies on bilingual third-language learning success in classroom environments have made important contributions by demonstrating that novel-language vocabulary learning is influenced by previous bilingual experience. In one study by Sanz (2000), English language proficiency was assessed in Catalan–Spanish bilinguals and Spanish monolinguals (mean age 16.53 years) with the CELT English Proficiency Test (Harris & Palmer, 1970). A hierarchical multiple regression analysis showed that bilingual experience contributed to third-language proficiency, and that this effect remained after controlling for the contribution of other factors including total English exposure and learning motivation. These results were in line with earlier research in a different community comprised of Spanish monolinguals and Basque–Spanish bilinguals, in which bilingual experience contributed to improved word learning, even after accounting for exposure and motivation to learn the target language (Cenoz & Valencia, 1994). Keshavarz and Astaneh (2004) compared English language knowledge of Persian monolinguals, Turkish–Persian bilinguals, and Turkish–Armenian bilinguals using a Controlled Productive Ability Test in English (Nation, 1990). All participants were enrolled in Iranian pre-university intermediate English language classes, and results indicated that both bilingual groups produced more words correctly as compared to the monolingual group, suggesting that bilingual experience improved the ability to learn and recall English vocabulary learned from classroom instruction.

The trade-off when studying language-learning performance in classroom settings is that the researcher often has minimal influence on the instructional materials and is unable to control the participants' exposure to the target language outside of the instructional setting. By training monolinguals and bilinguals on a target language within a research setting, greater control over the learner's environment is available, although the extent of language training is limited by the experimenter's time and resources. Van Hell and Mahn (1997) investigated how late bilinguals, who learned their L2 in early adolescence ("experienced foreign language learners"), compared to monolinguals ("inexperienced foreign language learners") in terms of foreign-language vocabulary learning. Participants were trained to associate Spanish words (presented visually and auditorily) with native language translations (i.e., Dutch for bilinguals or English for monolinguals). Learning performance was tested using a backward translation task in which participants viewed orthographic Spanish words and verbally provided the learned Dutch or English translations. Bilinguals were found to be more accurate and faster to respond compared to monolinguals, suggesting either that skills developed while learning an L2 may transfer to foreign-language vocabulary learning, or that years of bilingual language experience influence the organization of the language system in ways that promote further learning.

Kaushanskaya and Marian (2009b), with a conceptually similar study, showed that advantages in foreign vocabulary learning also extended to early bilinguals who had acquired two languages concurrently in childhood. The researchers taught English monolinguals, early English–Spanish bilinguals, and early Mandarin–English bilinguals words in an artificially constructed language (words in the artificial language were controlled for similarity to English, Spanish, or Mandarin). At test, participants performed a backward translation task from the novel language to English. Both immediately following training and at a one-week follow-up, the two bilingual groups achieved higher accuracy compared to monolinguals, providing additional support for a general bilingual advantage for word learning in a novel language.

Bilingualism has been shown not only to influence vocabulary learning in a third language, but also to improve acquisition of a novel language's grammar relative to monolingual speakers. Klein (1995) showed that bilinguals learning English made fewer preposition-stranding errors compared to monolinguals. Both groups made the same types of errors, but they occurred with lower frequency in the bilingual group, suggesting that bilinguals were mastering English syntactic use earlier than the monolingual learners, but were not approaching the constructions differently. The bilingual learning advantage also extends to more abstract sequence learning. In a series of studies, bilinguals and multilinguals were found to extract the underlying rules of an artificial grammar better than monolingual learners (Nation & McLaughlin, 1986; Nayak et al., 1990). Bilingual experience was also found to be associated with increased ability to segment novel words in a continuous auditory sequence using statistical probabilities that defined words (Bartolotti et al., 2011a, 2011b). Sequence learning is important for both word learning and for acquisition of syntactic rules such as word order, and may be a significant contributor to bilingual foreign language learning ability.

These bilingual advantages in novel language learning are likely the result of multiple contributing factors. For example, bilinguals may have more opportunities to transfer knowledge from known languages to the new language. Cognates, which overlap in form and meaning across languages, are typically easier to learn (MacWhinney, 2007; Murphy, 2003); bilinguals will have encountered more cognates than monolinguals, by virtue of already knowing two languages. Cenoz (1997) examined cases of language transfer from Basque and Spanish to English in children, and found that children utilized both of their known languages, but preferentially transferred word knowledge from Spanish to English, regardless of whether their native language was Basque or Spanish. English is more typologically related to Spanish than to Basque, thus the children's preference suggests that bilinguals are sensitive to which of their two known languages provides a better scaffold for L3 learning.

Other contributing factors depend not on the specific languages learned, but on the unique demands bilingualism itself places on the cognitive architecture. For example, bilingualism may increase phonological working memory ability, allowing bilinguals to sustain novel words in WM until they can be encoded in LTM (Papagno & Vallar, 1995; van Hell & Mahn, 1997). Bilingualism may also increase metalinguistic knowledge for how language operates as a system (Jessner, 1999, 2008). As a result, bilinguals rapidly acquire the understanding that the relationship between words and concepts is arbitrary; this knowledge is essential in order to associate known concepts with new words in a foreign language. Finally, bilingual experience may minimize cross-linguistic interference during novel language learning. It can be difficult to suppress aspects of a known language, such as letter-to-phoneme mappings, when they conflict with a novel language, but bilinguals are better able to minimize this conflict compared to monolinguals during novel language learning (Kaushanskaya & Marian, 2009b). In fact, it appears that advantages in resolving interference persist beyond the learning process itself and extend to novel language use. In a recent study by Bartolotti and Marian (2010, in press), monolinguals and bilinguals were taught an artificial language designed to elicit between-language competition. Specifically, words in the novel language (e.g., *shundo*, meaning acorn) overlapped phonologically with English competitor words (e.g., shovel). Activation of these native-language competitors was assessed with eye-tracking and mouse-tracking. It was found that bilinguals processed the novel language more efficiently and managed interference from the native language more successfully than monolinguals.

As bilinguals learn to use and process a novel language, it is likely that they rely on a combination of the skills discussed above, including linguistic transfer, phonological working memory, metalinguistic knowledge, and inhibitory control. Studying the role that these factors play during language learning in bilinguals can provide valuable insights into the relationship between memory and language. In particular, language learning offers a glimpse into how interaction across languages occurs and how a functional distinction between languages can develop.

Conclusions

This chapter reviews the representation of and interaction between multiple languages in bilingual memory. A central question in bilingual memory research is at what level a bilingual's two languages are differentiated, and whether information is stored, accessed, and processed in a language-specific or language-non-specific manner. This question has implications not only for bilingual research, but also for language processing in general. The bilingual's two languages provide contrasting contexts through which the links between language and memory can be investigated. It appears that episodic memory for events, especially when it is autobiographical, retains language-specific information. Episodic memories contain vivid details relating to the encoding context of the event. A bilingual's two languages contribute to this encoding context, facilitating memory recall in cases where the encoding language and the retrieval language overlap. Semantic memory for facts and word–concept associations, on the other hand, appears to be stored independently of language, as evidenced by parallel access to both languages during recognition or production. In addition, modeling work has shown that patterns of bilingual language processing can be captured in systems that integrate words across a bilingual's two languages into a single lexicon, providing a plausible account of language-non-specific storage in semantic memory. Thus, it appears that memories can be stored without being explicitly tied to individual languages, but that this link can be utilized to represent the encoding context of episodic memories.

In conclusion, a bilingual system has to accommodate the storage of multiple languages, as well as the processing demands resulting from parallel language activation. The experience of acquiring and using multiple languages improves bilinguals' ability to encode novel information relative to monolinguals, while practice managing interlingual competition improves working memory processing and inhibitory control. These cognitive benefits result from experience managing the conflict that occurs when representations in multiple languages are activated, but only one must be selected as the output. Much of the research on bilingual memory investigates what happens when this output selection mechanism fails, as these cases allow rare glimpses into the structure, access, and processing of memory. What is remarkable is that outside of the laboratory, countless bilinguals routinely perform these cognitive feats, speaking and switching languages with ease while rarely betraying the complex processes occurring unseen within the mind.

REFERENCES

Abrams, L., White, K. K., & Eitel, S. L. (2003). Isolating phonological components that increase tip-of-the-tongue resolution. *Memory & Cognition*, 31(8), 1153–1162. Retrieved from www.ncbi.nlm.nih.gov/pubmed/15058676 (last accessed July 30, 2012).

Adesope, O. O., Lavin, T., Thompson, T., & Ungerleider, C. (2010). A systematic review and meta-analysis of the cognitive correlates of bilingualism. *Review of Educational Research*, 80(2), 207–245. doi:10.3102/0034654310368803.

Allopenna, P. (1998). Tracking the time course of spoken word recognition using eye movements: evidence for continuous mapping models. *Journal of Memory & Language*, 38(4), 419–439. doi:10.1006/jmla.1997.2558.

Ardila, A., Rosselli, M., Ostrosky-Solis, F., Marcos, J., Granda, G., & Soto, M. (2000). Syntactic comprehension, verbal memory, and calculation abilities in Spanish–English bilinguals. *Applied Neuropsychology*, 7, 3–16. doi:10.1207/S15324826AN0701_2.

Atkinson, R. C., & Shiffrin, R. M. (1968). Human memory: a proposed system and its control processes. In K. W. Spence (ed.), *The psychology of learning and motivation: advances in research and theory* (Vol. 2, pp. 89–195). San Diego, CA: Academic Press.

  (1971). The control of short-term memory. *Scientific American*, 225(2), 82–90. doi:10.1038/scientificamerican0871-82.

Baddeley, A. D. (1986). *Working memory*. Oxford University Press.

  (1992). Working memory. *Science*, 255(5044), 556–559. doi:10.1126/science.1736359.

  (2010). Working memory. *Current Biology*, 20(4), R136–140. doi:10.1016/j.cub.2009.12.014.

Baddeley, A. D., & Hitch, G. J. (1974). Working memory. In G. H. Bower (ed.), *The psychology of learning and motivation* (pp. 47–90). San Diego, CA: Academic Press.

Baddeley, A. D., & Warrington, E. K. (1970). Amnesia and the distinction between long- and short-term memory. *Journal of Verbal Learning & Verbal Behavior*, 9, 176–189. doi:10.1016/S0022-5371/870/980048-2.

Baddeley, A. D., Gathercole, S., & Papagno, C. (1998). The phonological loop as a language learning device. *Psychological Review*, 105(1), 158–173. doi:10.1037/0033-295X.105.1.158.

Bajo, M. T., Padilla, F., & Padilla, P. (2000). Comprehension processes in simultaneous interpreting. In A. Chesterman, N. Gallardo San Salvador, & Y. Gambier (eds.), *Translation in context* (pp. 127–142). Amsterdam: Benjamins.

Bartolotti, J., & Marian, V. (2010). Linguistic control in monolingual and bilingual language learners. In S. Ohlsson & R. Catrambone (eds.), *Proceedings of the 32nd Annual Meeting of the Cognitive Science Society* (p. 532). Austin, TX: Cognitive Science Society.

(2012). Language learning and control in monolinguals and bilinguals. *Cognitive Science*, 36: 1129–1147. doi:10.1111/j.1551-6709.2012.01243

Bartolotti, J., Marian, V., Schroeder, S. R., & Shook, A. (2011a). Statistical learning of a Morse code language is improved by bilingualism and inhibitory ability. In L. Carlson, C. Hoelscher, & T. Shipley (eds.), *Proceedings of the 33rd Annual Conference of the Cognitive Science Society* (pp. 885–890). Austin, TX: Cognitive Science Society.

(2011b). Bilingualism and inhibitory control influence statistical learning of novel word forms. *Frontiers in Cognition*, 2(324), 1–9. doi:10.3389/fpsyg.2011.00324.

Baudouin, A., Clarys, D., Vanneste, S., & Isingrini, M. (2009). Executive functioning and processing speed in age-related differences in memory: contribution of a coding task. *Brain & Cognition*, 71(3), 240–245. doi:10.1016/j.bandc.2009.08.007.

Bialystok, E., Craik, F. I. M., Klein, R., & Viswanathan, M. (2004). Bilingualism, aging, and cognitive control: evidence from the Simon task. *Psychology & Aging*, 19(2), 290–303. doi:10.1037/0882-7974.19.2.290.

Bialystok, E., Craik, F. I. M., & Ruocco, A. C. (2006). Dual-modality monitoring in a classification task: the effects of bilingualism and ageing. *The Quarterly Journal of Experimental Psychology*, 59(11), 1968–1983. doi:10.1080/17470210500482955.

Bialystok, E., Craik, F. I. M., & Ryan, J. (2006). Executive control in a modified antisaccade task: effects of aging and bilingualism. *Journal of Experimental Psychology: Learning, Memory, & Cognition*, 32(6), 1341–1354. doi:10.1037/0278-7393.32.6.1341.

Bialystok, E., Craik, F. I. M., & Luk, G. (2008). Lexical access in bilinguals: effects of vocabulary size and executive control. *Journal of Neurolinguistics*, 21, 522–538. doi:10.1016/j.jneuroling.2007.07.001.

Blumenfeld, H. K., & Marian, V. (2007). Constraints on parallel activation in bilingual spoken language processing: examining proficiency and lexical status using eye-tracking. *Language and Cognitive Processes*, 22(5), 633–660. doi:10.1080/01690960601000746.

Brown, A. S. (1991). A review of the tip-of-the-tongue experience. *Psychological Bulletin*, 109(2), 204–223. doi:10.1037/0033-2909.109.2.204.

Brysbaert, M., & Duyck, W. (2010). Is it time to leave behind the Revised Hierarchical Model of bilingual language processing after fifteen years of service? *Bilingualism: Language & Cognition*, 13(3), 359–371. doi:10.1017/S1366728909990344.

Buckner, R. L., & Wheeler, M. E. (2001). The cognitive neuroscience of remembering. *Nature Reviews: Neuroscience*, 2(9), 624–634. doi:10.1038/35090048.

Bugelski, B. R. (1977). Imagery and verbal behavior. *Journal of Mental Imagery*, 1, 39–52.

Casey, S., & Emmorey, K. (2008). Co-speech gesture in bimodal bilinguals. *Language & Cognitive Processes*, 24(2), 290–312. doi:10.1080/01690960801916188.

Cenoz, J. (1997). The influence of bilingualism on multilingual acquisition: some data from the Basque country. In *I Simposio Internacional sobre o Bilingüismo: comunidades e individuos bilingüies* (pp. 278–287). Universidade de Vigo.

—— (2003). The additive effect of bilingualism on third language acquisition: a review. *International Journal of Bilingualism*, 7(1), 71–87. doi:10.1177/1367 0069030070010501.

Cenoz, J., & Jessner, U. (eds.). (2000). *English in Europe: the acquisition of a third language*. Clevedon, UK: Multilingual Matters.

Cenoz, J., & Valencia, J. F. (1994). Additive trilingualism: evidence from the Basque Country. *Applied Psycholinguistics*, 15(2), 195–207. doi:10.1017/S0142716400005324.

Chambers, C. G., & Cooke, H. (2009). Lexical competition during second-language listening: sentence context, but not proficiency, constrains interference from the native lexicon. *Journal of Experimental Psychology: Learning, Memory, & Cognition*, 35(4), 1029–1040. doi:10.1037/a0015901.

Colomé, A. (2001). Lexical activation in bilinguals' speech production: language-specific or language-independent? *Journal of Memory & Language*, 45(4), 721–736. doi:10.1006/jmla.2001.2793.

Colomé, A., & Miozzo, M. (2010). Which words are activated during bilingual word production? *Journal of Experimental Psychology: Learning, Memory, & Cognition*, 36(1), 96–109. doi:10.1037/a0017677.

Costa, A., & Santesteban, M. (2004). Lexical access in bilingual speech production: evidence from language switching in highly proficient bilinguals and L2 learners. *Journal of Memory & Language*, 50(4), 491–511. doi:10.1016/j.jml.2004.02.002.

Costa, A., Caramazza, A., & Sebastián-Gallés, N. (2000). The cognate facilitation effect: implications for models of lexical access. *Journal of Experimental Psychology: Learning, Memory, & Cognition*, 26(5), 1283–1296. doi:10.1037/0278-7393.26.5.1283.

Costa, A., La Heij, W., & Navarrete, E. (2006). The dynamics of bilingual lexical access. *Bilingualism: Language & Cognition*, 9(2), 137–151. doi:10.1017/S1366728906002495.

Costa, A., Hernández, M., & Sebastián-Gallés, N. (2008). Bilingualism aids conflict resolution: evidence from the ANT task. *Cognition*, 106(1), 59–86. doi:10.1016/j.cognition.2006.12.013.

Cowan, N. (1988). Evolving conceptions of memory storage, selective attention, and their mutual constraints within the human information-processing system. *Psychological Bulletin*, 104(2), 163–191. doi:10.1037/0033-2909.104.2.163.

(2000). The magical number 4 in short-term memory: a reconsideration of mental storage capacity. *Behavioral & Brain Sciences*, 24(1), 87–185. doi:10.1017/S0140525X01003922.

Dahlgren, D. J. (1998). Impact of knowledge and age on tip-of-the-tongue rates. *Experimental Aging Research*, 24, 139–153. doi:10.1080/036107398244283.

Danker, J. F., & Anderson, J. R. (2010). The ghosts of brain states past: remembering reactivates the brain regions engaged during encoding. *Psychological Bulletin*, 136(1), 87–102. doi:10.1037/a0017937.

de Groot, A. M. B., & Kroll, J. F. (eds.). (1997). *Tutorials in bilingualism: psycholinguistic perspectives*. New York: Oxford University Press.

Dijkstra, T., & van Hell, J. G. (2003). Testing the language mode hypothesis using trilinguals. *International Journal of Bilingual Education & Bilingualism*, 6(1), 2–16. doi:10.1080/13670050308667769.

Dijkstra, T., & van Heuven, W. J. B. (2002). The architecture of the bilingual word recognition system: from identification to decision. *Bilingualism: Language & Cognition*, 5(3), 175–197. doi:10.1017/S1366728902003012.

Dijkstra, T., Van Jaarsveld, H., & Ten Brinke, S. (1998). Interlingual homograph recognition: effects of task demands and language intermixing. *Bilingualism: Language & Cognition*, 1(1), 51–66. doi: 10.1017/S1366728998000121.

Dijkstra, T., Miwa, K., Brummelhuis, B., & Sappelli, M. (2010). How cross-language similarity and task demands affect cognate recognition. *Journal of Memory & Language*, 62(3), 284–301. doi:10.1016/j.jml.2009.12.003.

Duyck, W., Van Assche, E., Drieghe, D., & Hartsuiker, R. J. (2007). Visual word recognition by bilinguals in a sentence context: evidence for nonselective lexical access. *Journal of Experimental Psychology: Learning, Memory, & Cognition*, 33(4), 663–679. doi:10.1037/0278-7393.33.4.663.

Eichenbaum, H., & Cohen, N. J. (2001). *From conditioning to conscious recollection: memory systems of the brain*. New York: Oxford University Press.

Ellis, N. C. (1992). Linguistic relativity revisited: the bilingual word-length effect in working memory during counting, remembering numbers, and mental calculations. In R. J. Harris (ed.), *Cognitive processing in bilinguals* (pp. 137–155). Amsterdam: Elsevier.

Elman, J. L. (1990). Finding structure in time. *Cognitive Science*, 14(2), 179–211. doi:10.1207/s15516709cog1402_1.

Emmorey, K., Borinstein, H. B., Thompson, R., & Gollan, T. H. (2008). Bimodal bilingualism. *Bilingualism: Language & Cognition*, 11(1), 43–61. doi:10.1017/S1366728907003203.

Engle, R. W. (2002). Working memory capacity as executive attention. *Current Directions in Psychological Science*, 11(1), 19–23. doi:10.1111/1467-8721.00160.

Ericsson, K. A., & Simon, H. A. (1993). *Protocol analysis: verbal reports as data*. Cambridge, MA: MIT Press.

French, R. M. (1998). A simple recurrent network model of bilingual memory. In M. A. Gernsbacher, & S. J. Derry (eds.), *Proceedings of the 20th*

Annual Conference of the Cognitive Science Society (pp. 368–373). Mahwah, NJ: Erlbaum.
Garavan, H. (1998). Serial attention within working memory. *Memory & Cognition*, 26(2), 263–276. doi:10.3758/BF03201138.
Gollan, T. H., & Acenas, L. R. (2004). What is a TOT? Cognate and translation effects on tip-of-the-tongue states in Spanish–English and Tagalog–English bilinguals. *Journal of Experimental Psychology: Learning, Memory, & Cognition*, 30(1), 246–269. doi:10.1037/0278-7393.30.1.246.
Gollan, T. H., & Brown, A. S. (2006). From tip-of-the-tongue (TOT) data to theoretical implications in two steps: when more TOTs means better retrieval. *Journal of Experimental Psychology: General*, 135(3), 462–483. doi:10.1037/0096-3445.135.3.462.
Gollan, T. H., & Silverberg, N. B. (2001). Tip-of-the-tongue states in Hebrew–English bilinguals. *Bilingualism: Language & Cognition*, 4(1), 63–83. doi:10.1017/S136672890100013X.
Gollan, T. H., Montoya, R. I., & Bonanni, M. P. (2005). Proper names get stuck on bilingual and monolingual speakers' tip of the tongue equally often. *Neuropsychology*, 19(3), 278–287. doi:10.1037/0894-4105.19.3.278.
Gollan, T. H., Montoya, R. I., Fennema-Notestine, C., & Morris, S. K. (2005). Bilingualism affects picture naming but not picture classification. *Memory & Cognition*, 33(7), 1220–1234. doi:10.3758/BF03193224.
Green, D. W. (2003). Mental control of the bilingual lexico-semantic system. *Bilingualism: Language & Cognition*, 1(2), 67–81. doi:10.1017/S1366728998000133.
Grosjean, F. (1985). The recognition of words after their acoustic offset: evidence and implications. *Perception & Psychophysics*, 38(4), 299–310. doi:10.3758/BF03207159.
  (1989). Neurolinguists, beware! The bilingual is not two monolinguals in one person. *Brain & Language*, 36(1), 3–15. doi:10.1016/0093-934X/889/990048-5.
  (2001). The bilingual's language modes. In J. L. Nicol (ed.), *One mind two languages: bilingual language processing* (pp. 1–22). Malden, MA: Blackwell.
Harris, D. P., & Palmer, L. A. (1970). *CELT technical manual*. New York: McGraw-Hill.
James, L. E., & Burke, D. M. (2000). Phonological priming effects on word retrieval and tip-of-the-tongue experiences in young and older adults. *Journal of Experimental Psychology: Learning, Memory, & Cognition*, 26(6), 1378–1391. doi:10.1037/0278-7393.26.6.1378.
James, W. (1890). *The principles of psychology*. New York: Holt.
Jessner, U. (1999). Metalinguistic awareness in multilinguals: cognitive aspects of third language learning. *Language Awareness*, 8(3), 201–209. doi:10.1080/09658419908667129.
  (2008). A DST model of multilingualism and the role of metalinguistic awareness. *The Modern Language Journal*, 92(2), 270–283. doi:10.1111/j.1540-4781.2008.00718.x.
Kane, M., Bleckley, M. K., Conway, A. R. A., & Engle, R. W. (2001). A controlled-attention view of working-memory capacity.

Journal of Experimental Psychology: General, 130(2), 169–183. doi:10.1037/0096-3445.130.2.169.

Kaushanskaya, M., & Marian, V. (2009a). Bilingualism reduces native-language interference during novel-word learning. *Journal of Experimental Psychology: Learning, Memory, & Cognition*, 35(3), 829–835. doi:10.1037/a0015275.

(2009b). The bilingual advantage in novel word learning. *Psychonomic Bulletin & Review*, 16(4), 705–710. doi:10.3758/PBR.16.4.705.

Keshavarz, M. H., & Astaneh, H. (2004). The impact of bilinguality on the learning of English vocabulary as a foreign language (L3). *International Journal of Bilingual Education & Bilingualism*, 7(4), 295–302. doi:10.1080/13670050408667814.

Klein, E. (1995). Second versus third language acquisition: is there a difference? *Language Learning*, 45(3), 419–465. doi:10.1111/j.1467-1770.1995.tb00448.x.

Kroll, J. F., & de Groot, A. M. B. (1997). Lexical and conceptual memory in the bilingual: mapping form to meaning in two languages. In A. M. B. de Groot, & J. F. Kroll (eds.), *Tutorials in bilingualism: psycholinguistic perspectives* (pp. 169–199). Mahwah, NJ: Lawrence Erlbaum Associates.

Kroll, J. F., & Stewart, E. (1994). Category interference in translation and picture naming: evidence for asymmetric connections between bilingual memory representations. *Journal of Memory & Language*, 33, 149–174. doi:10.1006/jmla.1994.1008.

Kroll, J. F., Bobb, S. C., & Wodniecka, Z. (2006). Language selectivity is the exception, not the rule: arguments against a fixed locus of language selection in bilingual speech. *Bilingualism: Language & Cognition*, 9(2), 119–135. doi:10.1017/S1366728906002483.

Lambert, W. E. (1981). Bilingualism and language acquisition. In H. Winitz (ed.), *Native language and foreign language acquisition* (pp. 9–22). New York: The New York Academy of Sciences.

Larsen, S. F., Schrauf, R. W., Fromholt, P., & Rubin, D. C. (2002). Inner speech and bilingual autobiographical memory: a Polish-Danish cross-cultural study. *Memory*, 10(1), 45–54. doi:10.1080/09658210143000218.

Levine, B., Svoboda, E., Hay, J. F., Winocur, G., & Moscovitch, M. (2002). Aging and autobiographical memory: dissociating episodic from semantic retrieval. *Psychology & Aging*, 17(4), 677–689. doi:10.1037//0882-7974.17.4.677.

Li, P., & Farkas, I. (2002). A self-organizing connectionist model of bilingual processing. In R. Heredia, & J. Altarriba (eds.), *Bilingual sentence processing* (Vol. 134, pp. 59–85). Amsterdam: Elsevier.

MacWhinney, B. (2007). A unified model. In N. C. Ellis & P. Robinson (eds.), *Handbook of cognitive linguistics and second language acquisition* (pp. 341–371). Mahwah, NJ: Lawrence Erlbaum Associates.

Majerus, S., Poncelet, M., Van der Linden, M., & Weekes, B. S. (2008). Lexical learning in bilingual adults: the relative importance of short-term memory for serial order and phonological knowledge. *Cognition*, 107(2), 395–419. doi:10.1016/j.cognition.2007.10.003.

Marian, V., & Neisser, U. (2000). Language-dependent recall of autobiographical memories. *Journal of Experimental Psychology: General*, 129(3), 361–368. doi:10.1037//0096-3445.129.3.361.
Marian, V., & Spivey, M. J. (2003a). Bilingual and monolingual processing of competing lexical items. *Applied Psycholinguistics*, 24(2), 173–193. doi:10.1017/S0142716403000092.
(2003b). Competing activation in bilingual language processing: within- and between-language competition. *Bilingualism: Language & Cognition*, 6(2), 97–115. doi:10.1017/S1366728903001068.
Mather, M., Mitchell, K. J., Raye, C. L., Novak, D. L., Greene, E. J., & Johnson, M. K. (2006). Emotional arousal can impair feature binding in working memory. *Journal of Cognitive Neuroscience*, 18(4), 614–625. doi:10.1162/jocn.2006.18.4.614.
Matsumoto, A., & Stanny, C. J. (2006). Language-dependent access to autobiographical memory in Japanese–English bilinguals and US monolinguals. *Memory*, 14(3), 378–390. doi:10.1080/09658210500365763.
McClelland, J. L., McNaughton, B. L., & O'Reilly, R C. (1995). Why there are complementary learning systems in the hippocampus and neocortex: insights from the successes and failures of connectionist models of learning and memory. *Psychological Review*, 102(3), 419–457. doi:10.1037/0033-295X.102.3.419.
Meuter, R., & Allport, A. (1999). Bilingual language switching in naming: asymmetrical costs of language selection. *Journal of Memory & Language*, 40(1), 25–40. doi:10.1006/jmla.1998.2602.
Miller, G. A. (1956). The magical number seven, plus or minus two: some limits on our capacity for processing information. *Psychological Review*, 63(2), 81–97. doi:10.1037/0033-295X.101.2.343.
Milner, B. (1966). Amnesia following operation on the temporal lobes. In C. W. M. Whitty & O. L. Zangwill (eds.), *Amnesia* (pp. 109–133). London: Butterworth.
Mishkin, M., Malamut, B., & Bachevalier, J. (1984). Memories and habits: two neural systems. In G. Lynch, J. L. McGaugh, & N. W. Weinburger (eds.), *Neurobiology of learning and memory* (pp. 65–77). New York: Guilford Press.
Morgan-Short, K. (2007). *A neurolinguistics investigation of late-learned second language knowledge: the effects of explicit and implicit conditions*. Doctoral dissertation, retrieved from ProQuest (3282930).
Moscovitch, M., Rosenbaum, R. S., Gilboa, A., Addis, D. R., Westmacott, R., Grady, C., et al. (2005). Functional neuroanatomy of remote episodic, semantic and spatial memory: a unified account based on multiple trace theory. *Journal of Anatomy*, 207(1), 35–66. doi:10.1111/j.1469-7580.2005.00421.x.
Murphy, S. (2003). Second language transfer during third language acquisition. *Working Papers in TESOL & Applied Linguistics*, 3(1), 1–21.
Nadel, L, Samsonovich, A., Ryan, L., & Moscovitch, M. (2000). Multiple trace theory of human memory: computational, neuroimaging, and neuropsychological results. *Hippocampus*, 10(4), 352–368. doi:10.1002/1098-1063(2000)10:4<352::AID-HIPO2>3.0.CO;2-D.

Nation, I. S. P. (1990). *Teaching and learning vocabulary*. New York: Newbury House.

Nation, R., & McLaughlin, B. (1986). Novices and experts: an information processing approach to the "good language learner" problem. *Applied Psycholinguistics*, 7(1), 41–55. doi:10.1017/S0142716400007177.

Nayak, N., Hansen, N., Krueger, N., & McLaughlin, B. (1990). Language learning strategies in monolingual and multilingual adults. *Language Learning*, 40(2), 221–244. doi:10.1111/j.1467–1770.1990.tb01334.x.

Neisser, U. (1967). *Cognitive psychology*. New York: Appleton-Century-Crofts.

Nell, V. (2000). *Cross-cultural neuropsychological assessment: theory and practice*. Hillsdale, NJ: Erlbaum.

Norman, K. A., & O'Reilly, R. C. (2003). Modeling hippocampal and neocortical contributions to recognition memory: a complementary-learning-systems approach. *Psychological Review*, 110(4), 611–646. doi:10.1037/0033–295X.110.4.611.

Oberauer, K. (2002). Access to information in working memory: exploring the focus of attention. *Journal of Experimental Psychology: Learning, Memory, & Cognition*, 28(3), 411–421. doi:10.1037//0278–7393.28.3.411.

Paller, K. (1997). Consolidating dispersed neocortical memories: the missing link in amnesia. *Memory*, 5(1), 73–88. doi:10.1080/741941150.

Papagno, C., & Vallar, G. (1995). Verbal short-term memory and vocabulary learning in polyglots. *The Quarterly Journal of Experimental Psychology*, 48A(1), 98–107. doi:10.1080/14640749508401378.

Pavlenko, A. (2000). New approaches to concepts in bilingual memory. *Bilingualism: Language & Cognition*, 3(1), 1–36. doi:10.1017/S1366728999000322.

Poldrack, R. A., & Packard, M. G. (2003). Competition among multiple memory systems: converging evidence from animal and human brain studies. *Neuropsychologia*, 41(3), 245–251. doi:10.1016/S0028–3932/802/900157–4.

Potter, M. M. C., So, K. F. K., von Eckardt, B., & Feldman, L. (1984). Lexical and conceptual representation in beginning and proficient bilinguals. *Journal of Verbal Learning & Verbal Behavior*, 23(1), 23–38. doi:10.1016/S0022–5371(84)90489–4.

Prior, A., & MacWhinney, B. (2010). A bilingual advantage in task switching. *Bilingualism: Language & Cognition*, 13(2), 253–262. doi:10.1017/S1366728909990526.

Pyers, J. E., Gollan, T. H., & Emmorey, K. (2009). Bimodal bilinguals reveal the source of tip-of-the-tongue states. *Cognition*, 112(2), 323–329. doi:10.1016/j.cognition.2009.04.007.

Rempel-Clower, N. L., Zola, S. M., Squire, L. R., & Amaral, D. G. (1996). Three cases of enduring memory impairment after bilateral damage limited to the hippocampal formation. *The Journal of Neuroscience*, 16(16), 5233–5255. Retrieved from www.ncbi.nlm.nih.gov/pubmed/8756452 (last accessed July 30, 2012).

Rosen, V. M., & Engle, R. W. (1998). Working memory capacity and suppression. *Journal of Memory & Language*, 39(3), 418–436. doi:10.1006/jmla.1998.2590.

Rosenbaum, R. S., Köhler, S., Schacter, D. L., Moscovitch, M., Westmacott, R., Black, S. E., et al. (2005). The case of K. C.: contributions of a memory-impaired person to memory theory. *Neuropsychologia*, 43(7), 989–1021. doi:10.1016/j.neuropsychologia.2004.10.007.

Safont Jorda, M. P. (2003). Metapragmatic awareness and pragmatic production of third language learners of English: a focus on request acts realizations. *International Journal of Bilingualism*, 7(1), 43–68. doi:10.1177/13670 069030070010401.

Sanz, C. (2000). Bilingual education enhances third language acquisition: evidence from Catalonia. *Applied Psycholinguistics*, 21(1), 23–44. doi:10.1017/S0142716400001028.

Sanz, C., & Lado, B. (2007). Third language acquisition research methods. *Second Language Research*, 23(1), 95–114. doi:10.1177/ 0267658307071604.

Schoonbaert, S., Duyck, W., Brysbaert, M., & Hartsuiker, R. J. (2009). Semantic and translation priming from a first language to a second and back: making sense of the findings. *Memory & Cognition*, 37(5), 569–586. doi:10.3758/MC.37.5.569.

Schrauf, R. W. (2003). A protocol analysis of retrieval in bilingual autobiographical memory. *International Journal of Bilingualism*, 7(3), 235–256. doi:10.1177/13670069030070030201.

Schrauf, R. W., & Rubin, D. C. (1998). Bilingual autobiographical memory in older adult immigrants: a test of cognitive explanations of the reminiscence bump and the linguistic encoding of memories. *Journal of Memory & Language*, 39(3), 437–457. doi:10.1006/jmla.1998.2585.

(2000). Internal languages of retrieval: the bilingual encoding of memories for the personal past. *Memory & Cognition*, 28(4), 616–623. doi:10.3758/ BF03201251.

Schroeder, S., R., & Marian, V. (2012). A bilingual advantage for episodic memory in older adults. *Journal of Cognitive Psychology*. doi: 10.1080/20445911.2012.669367.

Schwartz, B. L. (1999). Sparkling at the end of the tongue: the etiology of tip-of-the-tongue phenomenology. *Psychonomic Bulletin & Review*, 6(3), 379–393. doi:10.3758/BF03210827.

(2002). *Tip-of-the-tongue states: phenomenology, mechanism, and lexical retrieval*. Mahwah, NJ: Erlbaum.

Scoville, W. B., & Milner, B. (1957). Loss of recent memory after bilateral hippocampal lesions. *Journal of Neurology, Neurosurgery, & Psychiatry*, 20(1), 11–21. doi:10.1136/jnnp.20.1.11.

Service, E., Simola, M., Metsänheimo, O., & Maury, S. (2002). Bilingual working memory span is affected by language skill. *European Journal of Cognitive Psychology*, 14(3), 383–408. doi:10.1080/09541440143000140.

Shallice, T., & Warrington, E. K. (1970). Independent functioning of verbal memory stores: a neuropsychological study. *The Quarterly Journal of Experimental Psychology*, 22(2), 261–273. doi:10.1080/00335557043000203.

Shook, A., & Marian, V. (2010). Interactivity during spoken word recognition: evidence from bimodal bilinguals. In S. Ohlsson & R. Catrambone (eds.), *Proceedings of the 32nd annual meeting of the Cognitive Science Society* (pp. 790–795). Austin, TX: Cognitive Science Society.

(in press). The Bilingual Language Interaction Network for Comprehension of Speech. *Bilingualism: Language and Cognition.*

(2012). Bimodal bilinguals coactivate both languages during spoken comprehension. *Cognition,* 124, 314–324. doi: 10.1016/j.cognition.2012.05.014.

Spivey, M. J., & Marian, V. (1999). Cross talk between native and second languages: partial activation of an irrelevant lexicon. *Psychological Science,* 10(3), 281–284. doi:10.1111/1467-9280.00151.

Squire, L. R., & Knowlton, B. J. (2000). The medial temporal lobe, the hippocampus, and the memory systems of the brain. In M. S. Gazzaniga (ed.), *The new cognitive neurosciences* (pp. 765–780). Cambridge, MA: MIT Press.

Squire, L. R., Cohen, N. J., & Nadel, L. (1984). The medial temporal region and memory consolidation: a new hypothesis. In H. Weingartner & E. Parker (eds.), *Memory consolidation* (pp. 185–210). Hillsdale, NJ: Lawrence Erlbaum Associates.

Tanenhaus, M. K., Magnuson, J. S., Dahan, D., & Chambers, C. G. (2000). Eye movements and lexical access in spoken-language comprehension: evaluating a linking hypothesis between fixations and linguistic processing. *Journal of Psycholinguistic Research,* 29(6), 557–580. Retrieved from www.ncbi.nlm.nih.gov/pubmed/11196063 (last accessed July 30, 2012).

Thierry, G., & Wu, Y. J. (2004). Electrophysiological evidence for language interference in late bilinguals. *Neuroreport,* 15(10), 1555–1558. doi:10.1097/01.wnr.0000134214.57469.c2.

(2007). Brain potentials reveal unconscious translation during foreign-language comprehension. *Proceedings of the National Academy of Sciences,* 104(30), 12530–12535. doi:10.1073/pnas.0609927104.

Thomas, J. (1992). Cognitive processing in bilinguals. *Advances in Psychology,* 83, 531–545. doi:10.1016/S0166-4115(08)61515-0.

Todd, J. J., & Marois, R. (2004). Capacity limit of visual short-term memory in human posterior parietal cortex. *Nature,* 428, 751–754. doi:10.1038/nature02466.

(2005). Posterior parietal cortex activity predicts individual differences in visual short-term memory capacity. *Cognitive, Affective, & Behavioral Neuroscience,* 5(2), 144–155. doi:10.3758/CABN.5.2.144.

Troyer, A., Graves, R., & Cullum, C. (1994). Executive functioning as a mediator of the relationship between age and episodic memory in healthy aging. *Aging Neuropsychology,* 1(1), 45–53. doi:10.1080/09289919408251449.

Tulving, E., & Thomson, D. M. (1973). Encoding specificity and retrieval processes in episodic memory. *Psychological Review,* 80(5), 352–373. doi:10.1037/h0020071.

Ullman, M. T. (2004). Contributions of memory circuits to language: the declarative/procedural model. *Cognition,* 92(1–2), 231–270. doi:10.1016/j.cognition.2003.10.008.

Vallar, G., & Papagno, C. (2002). Neuropsychological impairments of verbal short-term memory. In A. Baddeley, M. Koppeley, & B. Wilson (eds.), *The handbook of memory disorders* (2nd edn, pp. 249–270). Chichester: Wiley.

van Hell, J. G., & Mahn, A. C. (1997). Keyword mnemonics versus rote rehearsal: learning concrete and abstract foreign words by experienced and inexperienced learners. *Language Learning*, 47(3), 507–546. doi:10.1111/0023-8333.00018.

van Heuven, W. J. B., Dijkstra, T., & Grainger, J. (1998). Orthographic neighborhood effects in bilingual word recognition. *Journal of Memory & Language*, 39(3), 458–483. doi:10.1006/jmla.1998.2584.

van Heuven, W. J. B., Schriefers, H., Dijkstra, T., & Hagoort, P. (2008). Language conflict in the bilingual brain. *Cerebral Cortex*, 18(11), 2706–2716. doi:10.1093/cercor/bhn030.

Vogel, E. K., & Machizawa, M. G. (2004). Neural activity predicts individual differences in visual working memory capacity. *Nature*, 428, 748–751. doi:10.1038/nature02447.

Voss, J. L., & Paller, K. A. (2008). Brain substrates of implicit and explicit memory: the importance of concurrently acquired neural signals of both memory types. *Neuropsychologia*, 46(13), 3021–3029. doi:10.1016/j.neuropsychologia.2008.07.010.

2 Lexical competition in localist and distributed connectionist models of L2 acquisition

Ton Dijkstra, Femke Haga, Alex Bijsterveld, and Ida Sprinkhuizen-Kuyper

Abstract

Learning a second language (L2) implies the incorporation of its words into a lexicon that already contains words of the native language (L1). This chapter considers whether special mechanisms must protect L2 learning in its early stages, how learning the L2 early or late affects the organization of and access to bilingual memory, and how "special" words, like cognates and false friends, are acquired and processed. In addition, it examines the role of competition (inhibition) mechanisms in L2 word learning and L2 word identification according to localist and distributed connectionist models. Simulations with a localist model show that it can account for orthographic aspects of L2 acquisition without assuming any special mechanisms beyond lateral inhibition. The model differentiates the development of the L2 lexicon into stages of sequential or simultaneous L1/L2 learning for various types of words. Simulations with a distributed model show that cognate facilitation and false friend interference effects can be understood not only in terms of an on-line identification perspective but also from a learning perspective. A theoretical comparison of model types concludes the chapter.

Language learning is life-long learning. When we grow up, we continuously enrich the lexicon of our native language with less frequent and more sophisticated new words. We do not stop after learning concrete words like "elephant" and "ice cream," but also master more abstract words like "redemption" and "regression." When we choose a job as an insurance agent or biologist, we further acquire specialized words like "inflation" or "Crustacea." Learning new words and, unfortunately,

---

We thank Erik Lormans for his courtesy in making available the basic programs underlying the RBSN model.

forgetting them sometimes is a dynamic process of knowledge representation, waxing and waning across the seasons of our life.

The authors of this chapter believe that learning words from a second language (L2) is in many respects comparable to learning new words in a first language (L1). For instance, just as for L1 words, an L2 learner must learn the orthographic and semantic representations of L2 words. Thus, they may ask: "What is the word form for 'horse' in the foreign language I am mastering? And what word form in my native language has the same meaning as 'blight'?"

However, one important difference between first and second language learning is that an L2 learner already possesses tens of thousands of L1 words to convey meaning to other language users. This implies that for many of the new L2 word forms, there will be existing L1 word forms with largely overlapping meanings (their translation equivalents). Such L1 words might compete with L2 words during L2 learning and during reading, listening, or speaking. Therefore, an important issue is whether the just-acquired and still fragile L2 words need to be protected against their strong, well-established L1 competitors.

In the following sections, we discuss these issues of learning L2 words against a background of competing L1 words. First, we consider available models for L2 acquisition that take different theoretical approaches; next, we develop new computational models in the localist-connectionist and distributed-connectionist tradition, to examine in detail how the recognition of a new word is affected by lexical competitors from the same or a different language. We conclude the chapter with a comparison of this process according to the different types of models.

Models of bilingual processing and L2 learning

At present, three types of model have been proposed to account for bilingual processing in adults and in L2 learners (see French & Jacquet, 2004, and Thomas & van Heuven, 2005, for more extensive reviews): verbal models, like the Revised Hierarchical Model (RHM; Kroll & Stewart, 1994); localist connectionist models, like the Bilingual Interactive Activation Plus model (BIA+; Dijkstra & van Heuven, 2002); and distributed connectionist models, like the Self-Organizing Model of Bilingual Processing (SOMBIP; Li & Farkas, 2002) and the Bilingual Single Network model (BSN; Thomas, 1997, 1998). In this section, we will briefly describe these models (also see Bartolotti & Marian, this volume).

A "classic" example of a *verbal model* for L2 acquisition and word translation in late bilinguals is the Revised Hierarchical Model (RHM; e.g., Kroll & Stewart, 1994; Kroll & Tokowicz, 2001; Kroll et al., 2010). The RHM assumes that L1 and L2 word forms are stored in lexicons of different sizes (large for L1, smaller for L2), while there is an integrated store with meaning representations for both. There are links between word forms and meaning representations, and between word forms of different languages. In early phases of learning, the retrieval of the meaning (M) of an L2 word proceeds via its translation equivalent's orthographic representation in L1. For instance, a beginning English learner of Dutch maps the English word form "horse" onto its Dutch equivalent *paard* and then retrieves the meaning of *paard* via the Dutch word form (L2 → L1 → M). With increasing proficiency in the L2, the mapping of the L2 word form on its meaning representation is assumed to be strengthened and a more direct retrieval of meaning becomes prominent (L2 → M), although the word association route remains active in the background.

As recent reviews attest, the RHM has been a source of inspiration for hundreds of studies (Brysbaert & Duijck, 2010; Kroll et al., 2010). Nevertheless, a number of the model's theoretical assumptions are under debate given the results of more recent empirical research (Bartolotti & Marian, this volume). For instance, in contrast to the RHM's predictions, several studies have observed conceptual mediation effects even in beginning L2 learners (e.g., Altarriba & Mathis, 1997; Brenders, van Hell, & Dijkstra, under revision; Comesaña et al., 2009; de Groot & Poot, 1997). Furthermore, the RHM does not specify the lexical activation and selection processes that underlie word recognition and word translation (Dijkstra & Rekké, 2010).

There are inherent limitations to the explanations and predictions that RHM or any other verbal model can provide (see Dijkstra & De Smedt, 1996, for a discussion). For instance, verbal model explanations and predictions are usually qualitative in nature (does condition A differ from condition B?) and are hard to put in quantitative terms (how much does condition A differ from condition B?). In addition, the coherence, consistency, and completeness of verbal model assumptions can often be questioned.

In these respects, implemented models are quite different from verbal models, because they force the modeler to make detailed assumptions about the structures and processes of the domain under scrutiny. Such model implementation is difficult but rewarding, because it makes a model empirically testable at a quantitative level and leads to a better understanding of complex interactions between multiple factors (such interactions are notoriously hard to understand without an algorithmic or mathematical formulation).

It will therefore be a step forward to implement the RHM or other accounts of L2 learning in terms of a computational (computer) model (Dijkstra & Rekké, 2010). The best-known models of this type belong to the class of connectionist models (Dijkstra, 2005). Connectionist models of word recognition appeared in the 1980s, when personal computers became more generally available. Because the software and algorithms underlying these models were soon widely distributed, researchers quickly became familiar with them. Inspired by ideas of how the human brain works, computation in connectionist models takes the form of cooperative and competitive interactions among large numbers of simple, neuron-like processing units (see Rumelhart & McClelland, 1986, for an introduction).

In *localist connectionist models* or *interactive activation (IA) models*, words and other functional notions to be modeled are represented by single network nodes, and the weights on connections between these nodes are preprogrammed by the network designer. Each network node receives excitatory and inhibitory input from other connected nodes, and previous and current input establish the node's activation state, which can be transformed into an output value. Word recognition takes place if the target word node's activation meets an absolute (e.g., threshold) or relative activation criterion (e.g., Luce choice rule). IA models are characterized by *lateral inhibition* (between nodes at the same level) and *top-down feedback* (from nodes at a higher level downward).

In contrast, in *distributed connectionist models* (also called *parallel distributed processing or PDP models)*, theoretical concepts are associated with activation patterns over several nodes in the network, simultaneously. Thus, representations are *subsymbolic*. The network learns to categorize and generalize input signals by adjusting the weights on connections between units depending on the statistical structure of the environment over space and time. Usually, a limited a priori structural organization (e.g., different subsystems for different modalities) is assumed, but the further network structure in terms of weights on connections is established during a learning phase. Various learning rules (e.g., Hebbian, delta, backpropagation) have been proposed, which differ in their psychological and neurophysiological plausibility. During testing, the network generates either the correct word candidate or another similar one. Many distributed models, though learning by backpropagation, have feed forward connections only. This may seem paradoxical, because interactivity was once seen as typical of connectionist models.

Localist connectionist models in bilingualism

So far, localist connectionist models have predominantly addressed bilingual processing in adults. One well-known localist connectionist framework for bilingual word recognition in proficient late bilinguals is that of the Bilingual Interactive Activation Plus or BIA+ Model (Dijkstra & van Heuven, 1998, 2002; van Heuven, Dijkstra, & Grainger, 1998). This model was developed on the basis of an existing model for word recognition within a language, commonly referred to as the Interactive Activation Model (McClelland & Rumelhart, 1981, 1988). The model, presented in Figure 2.1, assumes that words are recognized in a series of steps. Suppose one reads the word WORK. The curved and straight lines on paper first activate matching letter representations for each letter position in memory. These letters then activate possible words, like CORK, FORK, WORN, and WORK. Such similar words that differ in only one letter position from the presented word are called "neighbors." Importantly, all activated word candidates suppress each other. This process of lexical competition is called *lateral inhibition*. Through a gradual process of elimination, the neighbors are excluded as potential targets and in the end, only the presented word, WORK, remains active. Complex facilitatory and inhibitory interactions between letters and words make the activation process difficult to predict without actual simulation. In addition, the task that must be performed (e.g., name the word, decide whether a letter string is a word or not, or categorize the word's meaning) is important in determining the ultimate response time.

Recently, it has been argued that localist connectionist models can in principle be applied to L2 learning. Grainger, Midgley, and Holcomb (2010) argued that an implemented localist connectionist model such as BIA would be able to account for the development of L2 word retrieval from L2 → L1 → M toward L2 → M if this latter link were strengthened over time by a Hebbian learning process. In a Hebbian learning process, the connection strength between two representations is increased if they are active together, and decreased if they are not (Hebb, 1949). An actual implementation of this idea would achieve two goals at the same time: the development of a localist connectionist model of L2 acquisition (dubbed BIA-d by Grainger et al., 2010) and a direct test of the RHM's proposed stages in L2 development.

Below, we will choose an alternative way of simulating L2 learning, by slicing L2 development into discrete stages and considering for each stage the corresponding L1–L2 distributions in the bilingual's lexicon. The theoretical framework of BIA+ will serve as the basis for this simulation exercise.

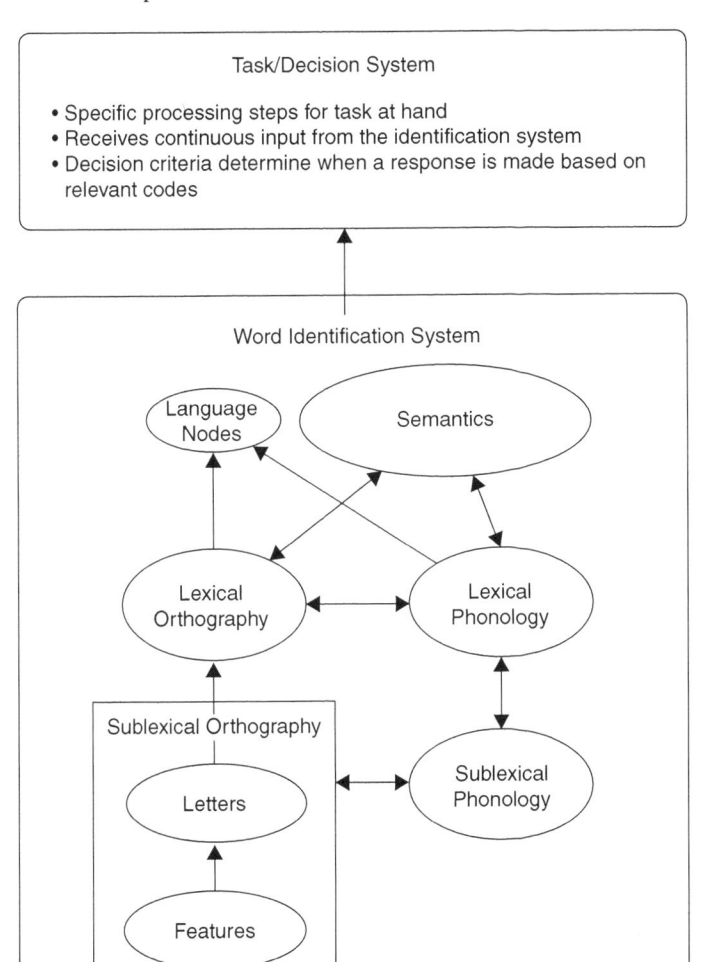

Lexical competition in connectionist models 53

```
┌─────────────────────────────────────────────┐
│           Task/Decision System              │
│                                             │
│  • Specific processing steps for task at hand│
│  • Receives continuous input from the        │
│    identification system                     │
│  • Decision criteria determine when a        │
│    response is made based on relevant codes  │
└─────────────────────────────────────────────┘
                      ▲
┌─────────────────────────────────────────────┐
│          Word Identification System          │
│                                             │
│      Language          Semantics            │
│       Nodes                                 │
│                                             │
│      Lexical          Lexical               │
│    Orthography       Phonology              │
│                                             │
│   ┌─Sublexical Orthography─┐                │
│   │      Letters    │      Sublexical       │
│   │                 │      Phonology        │
│   │     Features    │                       │
│   └─────────────────┘                       │
└─────────────────────────────────────────────┘
```

Figure 2.1 The BIA+ framework of bilingual word recognition

Distributed connectionist models in bilingualism

Because learning mechanisms are at the core of distributed connectionist models, such models have focused on the issues of language acquisition and language loss. Extensive research by Seidenberg, McClelland, Plaut, Shallice, and others has clarified how orthographic

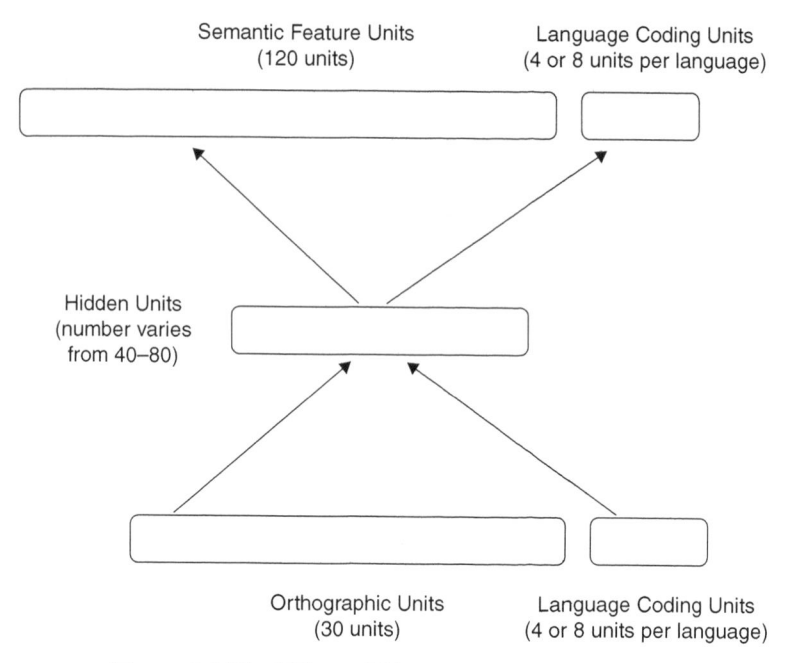

```
          Semantic Feature Units        Language Coding Units
               (120 units)              (4 or 8 units per language)
```

Hidden Units
(number varies
from 40–80)

```
          Orthographic Units            Language Coding Units
               (30 units)               (4 or 8 units per language)
```

Figure 2.2 The Bilingual Single Network (BSN) Model

representations of L1 may develop and how they map onto semantic and phonological representations (Plaut, 1997; Plaut et al., 1996; Plaut & Shallice, 1993; Seidenberg & McClelland, 1989). Two distributed connectionist models that have addressed L2 acquisition are the BSN model by Thomas (1997, 1998; Thomas & van Heuven, 2005) and the Developmental Lexicon (DevLex) model called SOMBIP (Self-Organizing Map model for Bilingual Processing) by Li and colleagues (Li & Farkas, 2002; Li, Zhao, & MacWhinney, 2007).

The *Bilingual Single Network (BSN) model* for bilingual word recognition learned to map orthographic word forms of two languages onto semantic representations (see Figure 2.2). Artificial languages were used as input for the model. To scale down the size of the training set, the lexicon of each language consisted of 96 words composed of 5 consonants and 5 vowels of a ten-letter alphabet. The resulting orthographic representations were similar to those in the BIA model in that they involved a position-specific encoding of letters in monosyllabic words (see Dijkstra, 2005, for an evaluation of this type of representation). Of the words, 40 were orthographically legal in both languages, 40 so-called "singles" were legal in only one language, 8 were "cognate homographs" and 8 were "noncognate homographs." Cognate homographs were assigned the same form and meaning across languages, whereas for noncognate homographs shared word forms had a different meaning in the two languages. An example of a cognate homograph in daily life is the word FILM that shares its meaning and orthography across many European language combinations, like English and Dutch. An example of an English–Dutch noncognate homograph is a word like ROOM that means "cream" in Dutch. A binary vector of 120 semantic feature units was used to generate a meaning representation for each word. Each feature had a 10 percent probability of being active in a given meaning (cf. de Groot, 1992). In addition, the frequency of word forms presented to the model during learning was varied. Translation equivalents were created by randomly pairing singles of the same frequency and then assigning the same meaning to them.

Because all words were stored in a single network, information specifying language membership was associated with each item (as a binary vector) to allow language differentiation. Language coding was added to both input and output vectors. The reasons for adding language coding to the output vectors were to emphasize the salience of language representation and to allow classification of ambiguous inputs. The three-layer feedforward network of Figure 2.2 was used to learn the mappings between orthographic and semantic codes.

During word recognition, the relevant units for the letters of the word are turned on. Connections with varying weights (strengths) then carry this activation to the internal ("hidden") processing units. Next, the linked semantic features of the target words are activated. Thus, in two steps, the model transforms an orthographic input activation pattern into a meaning representation. The activation patterns of the "hidden units" can be considered as the representations that the model has developed to recognize the words in two languages.

The model has led to a series of interesting results, some of which were the following. Due to the inclusion of language membership information in input and output, frequency-dependent distinct representations were developed for words of different languages. Moreover, noncognate homographs were sensitive to within-language frequency effects and, relative to cognate homographs, showed a between-language disadvantage in learning. In contrast, cognate homographs in L2 showed a facilitatory effect. As a potential problem, Thomas and van Heuven (2005) indicated there was a possibility of "catastrophic forgetting" when the model acquired the L2 sequentially, in particular if the salience of language membership was not high enough.

As we will see below, we extended and revised the BSN from the original artificial and restricted lexicons to more realistic lexicons containing hundreds of English and Dutch words. In addition, we implemented a more recently proposed learning algorithm, called LEABRA (discussed below). The simulations by the Revised BSN were then compared to those by a localist connectionist model for L2 learning (a version of BIA+).

The *Self-Organizing Connectionist Model of Bilingual Processing (SOMBIP)* was developed in an extensive series of publications by Li and colleagues (e.g., Li & Farkas, 2002; Li, Zhao, & MacWhinney, 2007; Li, 2009). SOMBIP is a distributed, developmental computational model that incorporates a refined representation of English and Chinese phonology and uses a training set derived from a bilingual child language corpus. The model applies "self-organizing maps" and neurally inspired learning algorithms and constraints (see Bartolotti & Marian, this volume). When exposed to a set of training patterns, self-organizing maps develop a two-dimensional similarity structure of the domain in question (e.g., orthographic representations of similar words will be stored closely together in space). SOMBIP learned two self-organizing maps, one representing the sounds of words in English and Chinese, and one representing the meanings of words; associative links were then learned between the two maps. Although the resulting orthographic and semantic representations for English and Chinese were quite separated in the topographic maps, unpublished work by Leoné (2009) in collaboration with Dijkstra has shown that language nonselective maps may develop for mixed L1–L2 learning conditions.

Developing localist and distributed connectionist models of L2 learning

A comparison of localist and distributed connectionist models of L2 learning is interesting, because they differ in their underlying processing mechanisms. Localist models consider lateral inhibition (i.e., mutual interference) between activated words as an important and inherent mechanism to word identification. Distributed models do not assume this type of competition, but they allow indirect competition during the process of learning words in terms of establishing increasingly strong connections. The two types of model therefore differ considerably in their assumptions about interactions between words, and a comparison of them will allow an assessment of the role of lexical competition during L2 learning and L2 word identification.

To ensure a proper theoretical comparison, we implemented new versions of the two model types that were applied to learning similar Dutch–English lexicons and also considered the contribution of comparable factors. First, the two model types were compared with respect to *L2 acquisition in early and late bilinguals*. This comparison allowed us to assess the effect of learning L2 at the same time as L1 or after L1 is already strongly established but still in use. One issue here is whether L2 learning should be protected by an increased inhibition of L1 words in late learners, to compensate for the large interference exerted by the strong L1. Second, we considered how the gradual increase in *L2 word frequency* over learning time affects the recognition and learning of words in the two types of model. Third, we considered how the two types of model handle the recognition and learning of *"special" words*, such as cognates, noncognate homographs, translation equivalents, and language-specific words (i.e., with a concept in only one language). Cognates are defined here as translation equivalents with orthographic form overlap. They may be identical across languages, like the Dutch–English cognate homograph FILM, or similar, like the English word TOMATO, which is TOMAAT in Dutch. As defined earlier, an example of a noncognate Dutch–English homograph is the word ROOM, which means "cream" in Dutch; an example of translation equivalent is the word pair BIKE–FIETS (where FIETS is Dutch for BIKE).

Using BIA+ as a localist connectionist model of L2 learning

In 2002, several researchers noted that BIA+ did not provide any account of L2 acquisition (Jacquet & French, 2002; Thomas, 2002; van Hell, 2002). It is indeed an important question how L2 acquisition can be implemented in a localist connectionist framework. As mentioned above, Grainger et al. (2010) suggested that a special Hebbian learning process could be included on top of the localist connectionist architecture to describe how L2 words, once learned, can be mapped onto their meaning. Here we will present an alternative approach, based on the following line of argumentation. Consider a monolingual Dutch speaker who starts to learn English as a second language at a later age (since 1993, all Dutch primary-school children learn English from about the age of 10 onwards, and nowadays, they begin to acquire English even earlier). With a considerable degree of simplification, it can be argued that in the months following their first lessons in English, the L2 learners' native Dutch mental lexicon will contain a variety of words that are used more or less frequently, whereas even the highest-frequency English words (according to native speakers of English) in fact have only a low subjective frequency for them. After a year of learning English, however, the first-learned words have acquired a somewhat higher subjective frequency of use, and other new words have been added to the lexicon, which are as yet of a lower subjective frequency. Across the lifespan of the adolescent and adult Dutch–English bilingual, English (L2) learning proceeds, while Dutch (L1) is still used daily, so, after many years, the subjective frequency distributions of English and Dutch may reach a more stable state, possibly approaching distributions similar to those of native English or Dutch monolinguals (but perhaps based on a lower total frequency for each, following Gollan *et al.*, 2008).

The general consequence of this reasoning is that different stages of L2 acquisition can be simulated in the BIA+ model by assuming that at each point in time, the L2 consists of words of varying frequency that are some factor lower than those of an L2 native speaker (because they have been used only a fraction of the time relative to their usage by monolinguals). The L1 lexicon, however, remains distributionally the same in all stages (it always consists of the complete lexicon of the native language). In all simulations to be reported, we considered word learning and word processing by Dutch–English bilinguals or by Dutch monolinguals learning English late as their L2. Thus, in all simulations, L1 refers to Dutch and L2 to English.

(a) How late bilinguals process L1 and L2 words Figure 2.3 shows a simulation of L1 and L2 word processing by late bilinguals differing in their L2 proficiency. It represents how long it takes late Dutch–English bilinguals to process L1 (Dutch) and L2 (English) words at different L2 (English) proficiency stages with L1 already in place. The remarkable finding is that, overall, neither the processing in L2 nor that in L1 suffers much from the introduction of new words. There are probably several reasons for this (see Dijkstra, 2003, for a more extensive discussion). A first reason is that words from English have an orthographic make-up that is somewhat different from the Dutch words, which decreases the degree of competition they mutually exert. A second reason is that the competitive effect of the new English words on Dutch words is decreased because they also compete with other English words. A third reason for a relatively low effect of English on Dutch is that initially, the English words' frequency is low relative to that of the well-established Dutch words.

(b) How early bilinguals learn L1 and L2 words Following the same reasoning, it is possible to simulate the L1 and L2 word learning processes of early bilinguals. In this case, the number and frequency of words from both L1 and L2 are increased in stages. Figure 2.4 also depicts this learning process for L2 (English) words in Dutch–English

Lexical competition in connectionist models

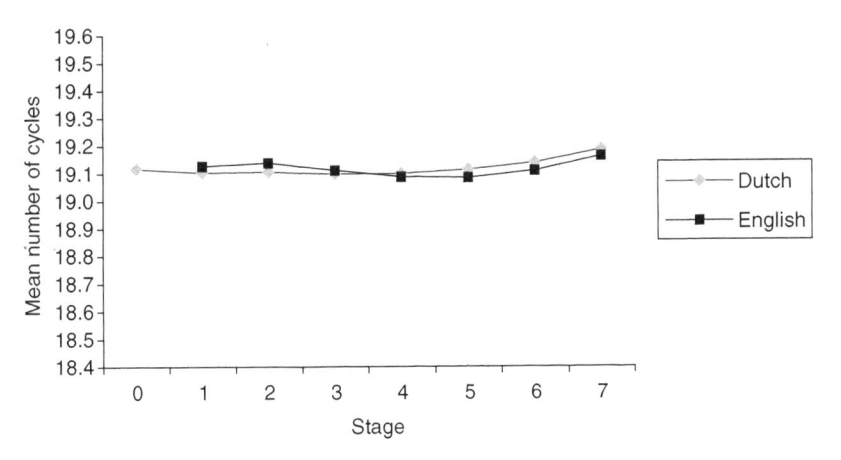

Figure 2.3 Processing of Dutch and English words by late learners of English

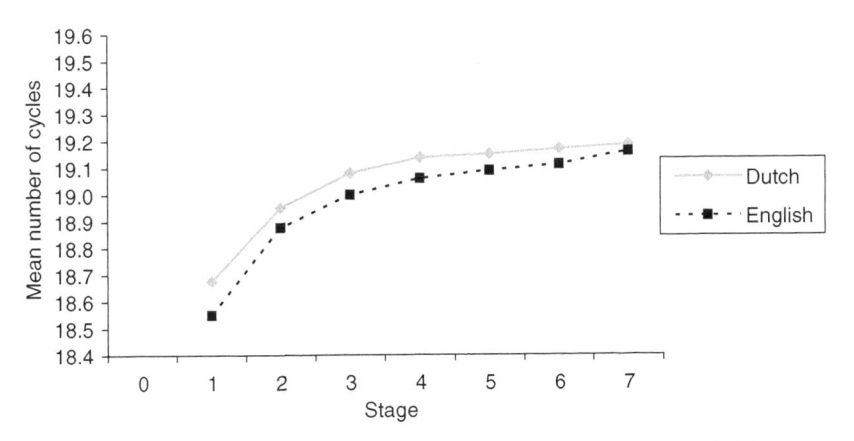

Figure 2.4 Processing of Dutch and English words by early Dutch–English bilinguals

bilinguals. As can be seen, the time in cycles to recognize both Dutch and English words slowly increases when more and more words of both languages are learned. The differences between Dutch and English word learning curves must be a consequence of the different compositions of the lexicons of the two languages. When the words of both languages are fully learned (at stage 7), the required processing times of course converge to those in Figure 2.3 for learning L2 after L1.

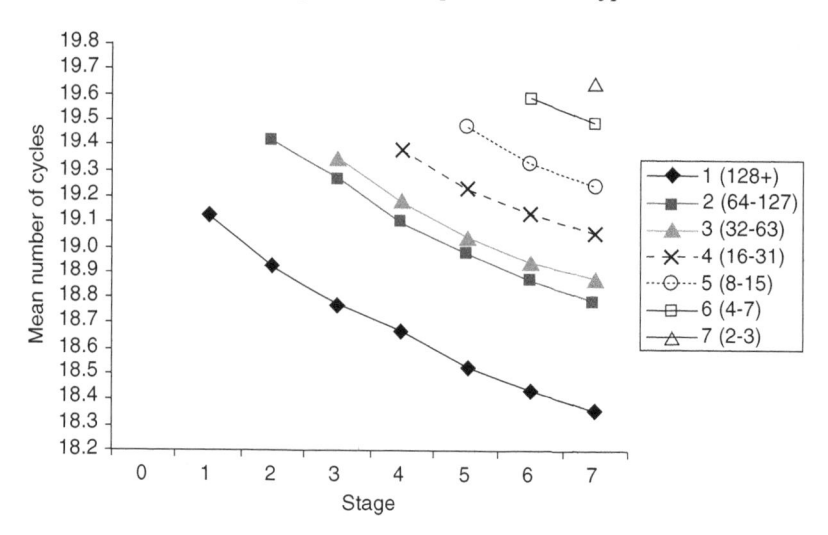

60 Dijkstra, Haga, Bijsterveld, & Sprinkhuizen-Kuyper

Figure 2.5 Late learning of English words of different frequency categories in BIA+

(c) How late bilinguals process L2 words of different frequencies Simulations also allow us to consider the processing of L2 words of different frequencies by late bilinguals at each moment in the learning process. Figure 2.5 again displays the different stages of learning an L2 (English) when the L1 (Dutch) is already established, but now words of different frequency categories are differentiated. In each progressive stage of learning (going from 1 to 7), additional words are learned that have a lower frequency in native speakers. The L1 frequency range of the added words is indicated (e.g., 64–127 occurrences per million in learning stage 2). The figure shows that, while each frequency category of words becomes processed more quickly across learning stages, later learned words (initially all of a low frequency for the learner) are slowed down by the presence of earlier words from the same language through lexical competition (lateral inhibition) in the model. Except for the second stage, the time cycles needed for new words (as indicated by the top nodes) increase (the exception may be due to coincidental characteristics of the new words introduced in stage 2). However, the increase is limited (just over half a time cycle, which would correspond to 10–15 milliseconds). This is in line with findings by Ransdell and Fischler (1987), who suggested that bilinguals might be at a disadvantage relative to monolinguals in speeded tasks.

Because the simulations with the developmental BIA+ presented here only include orthographic representations, they cannot directly show us how L2 words with orthographic or semantic overlap with L1 words are learned. Thus, the model does not account for the learning of cognate and noncognate homographs. However, empirical studies on word recognition in more proficient bilinguals often show L2 facilitation effects for cognates and L2 inhibition effects for noncognate homographs, so it is important to consider how such item types are learned. Dijkstra (2005, 2009; also see Dijkstra *et al.*, 2010) has proposed that cognates and noncognate homographs are characterized by overlapping form representations and largely shared semantic representations. In this account, cognate facilitation effects can be ascribed to two sources: (1) the increased semantic activation that arises from the co-activation of two translation equivalents (e.g., both TOMAAT and TOMATO activate the same meaning); and (2) the resonance between the overlapping form representations in the two languages via their shared semantics. Using a new localist connectionist model called Multilink, Dijkstra and Rekké (2010) demonstrated that cognate facilitation effects can indeed be simulated upon the basis of a representation like that proposed by Dijkstra (2005).

For noncognate homographs (also called "false friends"), empirical studies have observed null effects or inhibition effects in terms of their latencies relative to single-language control words (cf. Dijkstra, Van Jaarsveld, & Ten Brinke, 1998). To account for the observed effects, Dijkstra (2005) proposed that noncognate homographs had overlapping form representations but non-overlapping semantic representations. How this item type is processed would also depend considerably on the task at hand (e.g., Smits *et al.*, 2006).

If we assume that L2 word form representations are gradually strengthened with learning experience, as proposed above, the following predictions about the L2 acquisition of cognates and noncognate homographs can be made. In the initial stages of L2 acquisition by unbalanced late bilinguals, there will be a large effect of L1 on L2, due to differences in L1 and L2 subjective word frequency for these items. There will be hardly any effect of L2 words on L1. Gradually, the effects of L1 on L2 will become less strong, while those in the other direction will become stronger. In balanced late bilinguals, L1 and L2 should have similar effects on each other. The effects are expected to be more facilitatory for cognates due to semantic overlap, and more inhibitory for noncognate homographs due to lateral inhibition at the word form level.

To conclude, the results of simulations and Gedanken (thought) experiments with a localist connectionist framework show that it can be applied not only to adult bilingual processing but to L2 acquisition as well. The predictions presented above can be tested in future experimental studies (see Brenders, van Hell, & Dijkstra, 2011, for a developmental study on cognate and noncognate homographs). In other words, they provide an answer to those researchers who asked how the BIA+ framework can handle L2 acquisition.

Importantly, the presented simulations indicate that it is not necessary to protect L2 words in any special way during the first phases of L2 acquisition. Lateral inhibition in the interactive activation framework ascertains that the presented word, even when it is of low frequency, is recognized in an acceptable time. Note that the precise parameter settings in the model are crucial here, because they ensure that a very low frequency word (with a frequency of 1) is always recognized, even in the context of neighbors with an extremely high frequency. It remains to be seen if this statement can be maintained for even earlier stages of learning (when words have been encountered with a frequency of far less than 1 per million). In this context, it may be noted that, like bilinguals, monolinguals also keep learning new words when they become older, for instance, because they develop a specialized vocabulary in particular areas of expertise (in electronics, botany, or sailing, for example).

A distributed connectionist model of L2 learning: the Revised BSN

As shown by Thomas (1997, 1998) and Thomas and van Heuven (2005), L2 vocabulary acquisition can also be simulated in distributed connectionist models. We extended Thomas's Bilingual Single Network (BSN) model to accept a "realistic" Dutch–English lexicon. Because the new model also included a different type of learning rule, we will refer to it as the Revised Bilingual Single Network (RBSN) Model (see Figure 2.6). The model was revised as follows. First, the Dutch and English lexicons were extended to include 40 cognates and 40 noncognate homographs, 80 translation equivalents (four groups of 20 words with 0–3 letter overlap) and (depending on the simulations done, maximally) 160 control words. Translation equivalents were words with completely different orthographic representations in Dutch and English, but a shared semantic representation. In contrast, control words were completely different in orthography and meaning in the two languages (like the items called singles in Thomas, 1997). The Dutch–English lexicon was a selection of 50 percent of the Dutch words and 50 percent of the English words. All items were existing four-letter words, instead of the three-letter units of the BSN model and potentially consisted of all

```
                Semantic Feature Units      Langugage Coding Units
                     (120 units)              (1 unit per language)
              ┌──────────────────────────┐   ┌──┐
              │                          │   │  │
              └──────────────────────────┘   └──┘
                         ▲                    ▲
                          \                  /
                           \                /
   Hidden Units             \              /
   (400 units)        ┌──────────────────┐
                      │                  │
                      └──────────────────┘
                           ▲        ▲
                          /          \
                         /            \
              ┌──────────────────────────┐   ┌──┐
              │                          │   │  │
              └──────────────────────────┘   └──┘
                  Orthographic Units        Language Coding Units
                     (104 units)              (1 unit per language)
```

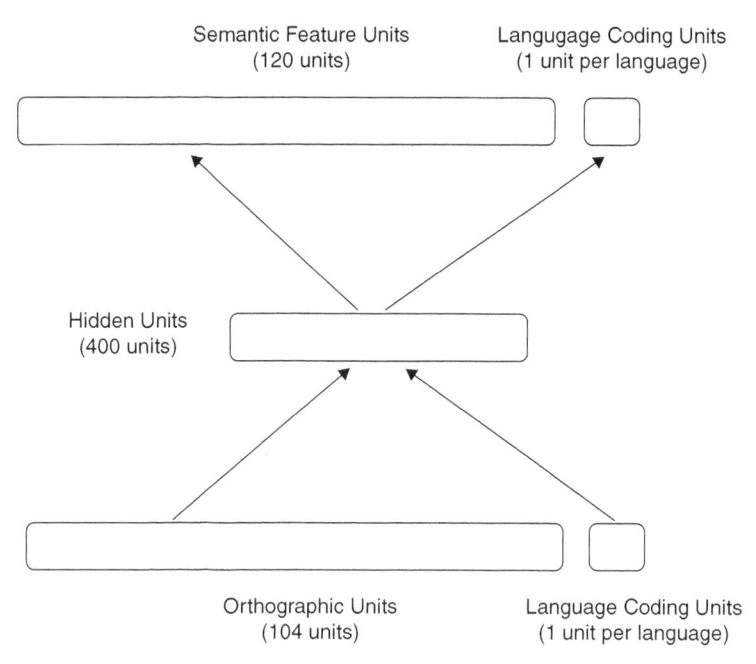

Figure 2.6 The Revised Bilingual Single Network (RBSN) Model

letters of the alphabet. To make this possible, the model's Orthographic Input Unit was extended to 104 units, 26 units for each of the four letter positions in a word (BSN: 30). The Language Coding Unit (LCU) consisted of only one unit per language (BSN: 4 or 8 units) that could have a value of 0 (indicating that a word is Dutch) or 1 (indicating that it is English). The RBSN had 400 units in the hidden layer (BSN: 60). The output layer consisted of 120 Semantic Feature Units with the same structure as in the BSN. It also had its own Language Coding Units. The RBSN model was developed in an open-source C++ software environment called Emergent (see http://grey.colorado.edu/emergent/index.php/Main_Page, last accessed 3 August, 2012). This environment supports multiple different learning and processing algorithms for neural networks, from backpropagation to more biologically based algorithms. The learning algorithm used was LEABRA, which stands for Local, Error-driven and Associative, Biologically Realistic Algorithm. This algorithm implements a balance between Hebbian and error-driven learning on top of a biologically based point neuron activation function with inhibitory competition dynamics.

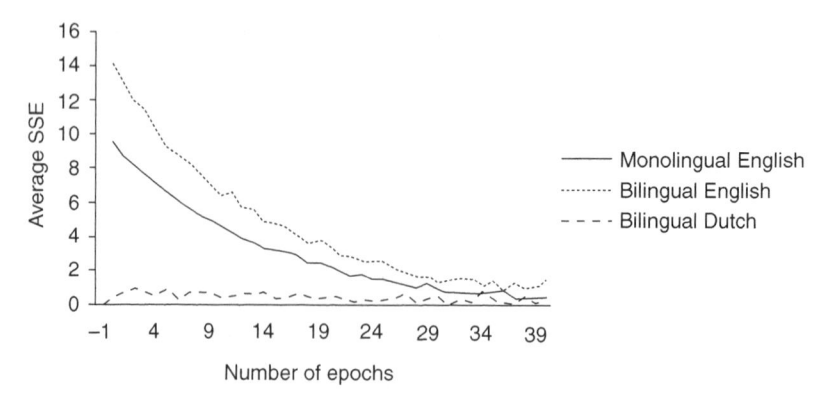

Figure 2.7 Learning of Dutch and English words by late learners of English relative to English monolinguals

(a) How late bilinguals process L1 and L2 words In a first series of simulations with RBSN, we again considered L1 and L2 word processing by late bilinguals differing in their L2 proficiency. Figure 2.7 shows the learning of an L2 (English) vocabulary as the only language (monolingual English) or after L1 (Dutch) has already been acquired (bilingual English). First, 69 control words of the L1 (Dutch) were learned during each epoch until the squared summed error rate (SSE) was zero (an epoch is a series of learning trials involving one presentation of all training items). At that point in time, the input changed from mere L1 words to a mix of L1 and L2 words to avoid catastrophic forgetting. Now, during each epoch, 69 Dutch control words and 69 English control words were presented for learning. As can be seen in Figure 2.7, learning English as an L2 when Dutch as the L1 is already established proceeds more slowly than when English is the only language to be learned. The figure also shows that the L1 does not suffer much from the transition to bilingual input: the average SSE remains close to zero. Thus, in a network that has a sufficient capacity to serve both L1 and L2, L1 can be maintained when L2 is introduced.

(b) How early bilinguals learn L1 and L2 words Next, we simulated the L1 and L2 word learning processes of early bilinguals, using the same set of words as before. Like Figure 2.7, Figure 2.8 shows the learning of an L2 (English) vocabulary as the only language (monolingual English), but now compares it to the learning of both L2 (English) and L1 (Dutch) words by an early Dutch–English bilingual (i.e., when words of both languages are learned simultaneously). As can be seen,

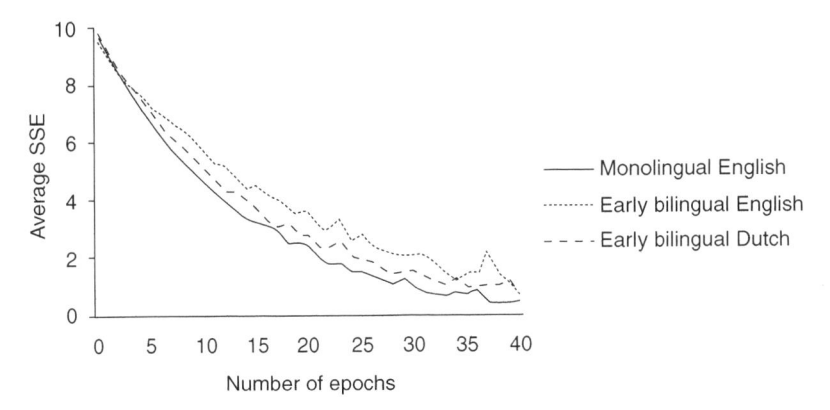

Lexical competition in connectionist models 65

Figure 2.8 Learning of Dutch and English words by early Dutch–English bilinguals relative to English monolinguals

there is a cost to learning both languages at the same time, especially in the intermediate stages of L2 learning. However, in the long run the advantage is, of course, that two languages rather than one can be mastered at a high level of proficiency (i.e., with a small error rate).

(c) How late bilinguals process L2 words of different frequencies We further considered the processing of words of different frequencies during L2 word learning. Figure 2.9 shows how the frequency of English words affected their learning by Dutch language users. First, the log frequency of the English control words in the model lexicon (according to the CELEX database) was taken. Next, the words were allocated to three approximately equally large frequency groups: words with low frequency (with log frequencies smaller than 2), middle frequency (with log frequencies from 2 to up to 4), or high frequency (with log frequencies above 4). In the simulations, low-frequency words were presented only once for each epoch, middle-frequency words twice, and high-frequency words 4 times. As will be clear from Figure 2.9, frequency of occurrence did indeed affect the learning process in these late bilinguals and resulted in faster learning for higher frequency words.

(d) How late bilinguals learn "special" types of L2 words Finally, the distributed connectionist approach allows us to simulate how "special" types of L2 words are learned, such as cognates, noncognate homographs, and non-overlapping translation equivalents, by varying the mapping of orthographic input representations onto semantic output representations. Figures 2.10–12 show the results of simulations

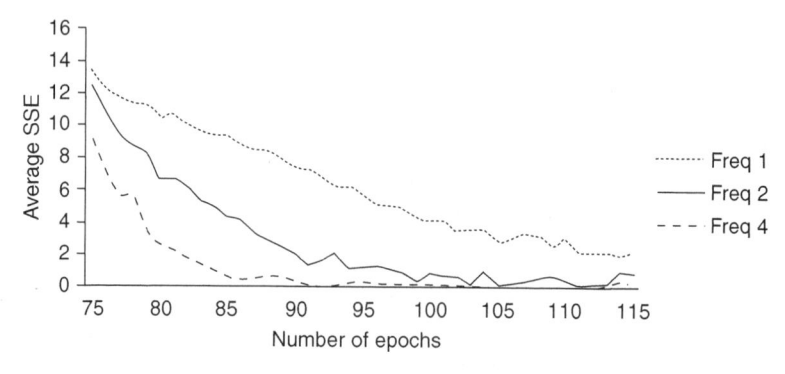

66   *Dijkstra, Haga, Bijsterveld, & Sprinkhuizen-Kuyper*

Figure 2.9 Late learning of English words of different frequency categories in RBSN

with these types of item. Figure 2.10 shows that translation equivalents are learned faster when the cross-linguistic overlap increases from 0 (no overlap) to maximal overlap (cognates, with overlap 4). Figure 2.11 shows that newly learned L2 (English) words are especially sensitive to their orthographic and semantic relationship with L1 (Dutch) words. Relative to control words, cognates and translation equivalents benefit from their cross-linguistic links, while noncognate homographs (false friends) are slightly disadvantaged. Figure 2.12 shows that the already-known L1 (Dutch) words are hardly affected by the acquisition of L2 (English) words. Only noncognate homographs experience some difficulty, which surely must have something to do with mapping one and the same orthographic representation onto a new meaning.

General discussion

In this chapter, we have presented simulations of the L2 acquisition process by localist and distributed connectionist models. These paradigms differ in several respects, one of which is how they implement competition between lexical candidates during word identification. This competition is directly visible in localist models (lateral inhibition), but functions only indirectly in distributed models (presenting a word affects the setting of connection parameters). Because there is a "hot" debate about whether inhibition between word candidates during identification is to be preferred to varying decision settings, it is important to compare the two types of model.

A comparison of the results for localist and distributed models requires us to make particular assumptions. For instance, we can follow

Lexical competition in connectionist models

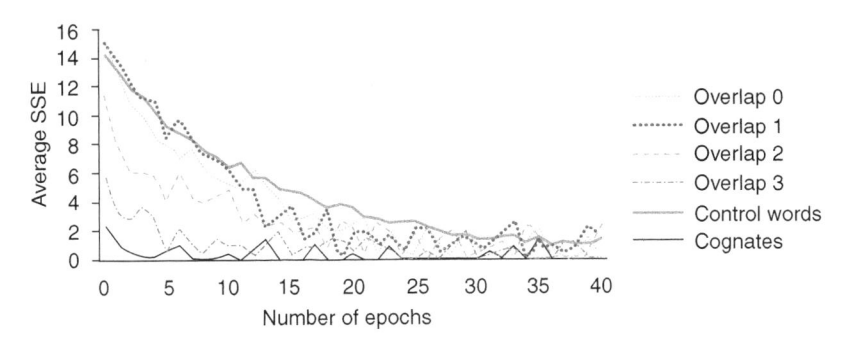

Figure 2.10 Processing by late Dutch–English bilinguals of English translation equivalents with different degrees of orthographic overlap with Dutch

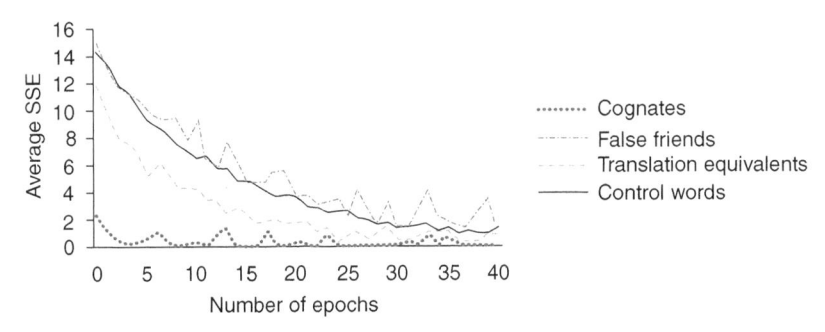

Figure 2.11 Processing of English item types by late Dutch–English bilinguals

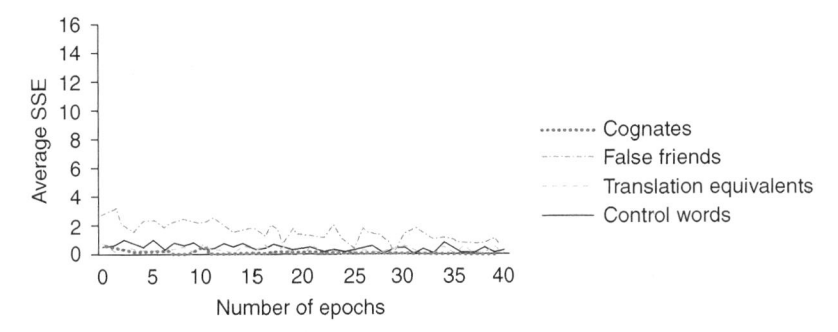

Figure 2.12 Processing of Dutch item types by late Dutch–English bilinguals

Seidenberg and McClelland (1989) in making the assumption that error rates and response times are two sides of the same coin. In empirical studies, they usually go the same way, unless there is a speed–accuracy trade-off. In this type of reasoning, the orthographic error score can be seen to reflect the average speed of word retrieval. However, it may be safer to examine the similarities between the simulations of the two model types in terms of similarities between learning and word identification. Indeed, many similarities were found on learning and on-line processing in terms of the moment of learning the L2 (early/late) and the type of words acquired. This happened even though in the present simulations with the BIA+ model, we simulated only how L2 orthographic representations develop, whereas our RBSN simulations dealt with learning the L2 mapping of orthography on semantics (the orthographic–semantic interface in localist connectionist models is further discussed in Dijkstra & Rekké, 2010). The similarities between the two types of simulation can be summarized as follows.

First, both localist and distributed connectionist simulations suggest that learning L2 after L1 has already been established is somewhat more difficult than learning L2 on its own as a first language. In the first situation, processing times were just over half a cycle slower in the localist simulations (Figures 2.3 and 2.4) and it took somewhat longer to learn the L2 words without error in the distributed simulations (Figures 2.7 and 2.8). Nevertheless, the effect was surprisingly small (for instance, under the assumption that a time cycle in the localist model represents about 25 ms). In addition, L2 learning led to only slightly worse performance relative to L1 in terms of processing time and error rates.

Second, L2 word frequency was shown to affect both learning and identification time: a higher frequency facilitates both (Figures 2.5 and 2.9). The facilitatory effect of frequency in learning was a consequence of a finer-tuned setting of the links between form and meaning connections for high-frequency words (cf. Seidenberg & McClelland, 1989), while that in identification was due to a higher resting activation level and an associated higher degree of competitive force (cf. McClelland & Rumelhart, 1981).

Third, according to the discussed models, special words like cognates and noncognate homographs have similar effects on learning and identification (Figures 2.10 and 2.11). Late bilinguals learn and identify L2 cognates faster than other L2 words, while noncognate homographs are learned and identified more slowly. L1 items hardly suffer from the L2 learning process, with the exception of noncognate homographs (Figure 2.12). In addition, cross-linguistic overlap in terms of orthography facilitates the learning of translation equivalents and cognates

(Figure 2.10). A similar effect is obtained for on-line processing in more proficient bilinguals, as shown in reaction time studies such as Dijkstra *et al.* (2010).

The similarities in results for the two types of model indicate that the advantage for cognates in both learning and identification is a consequence of their nature. Joint semantics and overlapping orthography led to faster learning as well as to faster identification. Thus, according to the present simulations, the well-known cognate effect is both a learning effect and an identification effect. There is also a similarity between the model types with respect to learning and identification for noncognate homographs. Their two identical word forms can compete in localist models and their mapping onto different semantic representations leads to slower learning in distributed connectionist models.

We noticed one interesting difference between the two types of simulation. Whereas learning an L2 in the distributed model invoked a relatively temporary and limited effect on the error rates of L1 words, L2 development in the localist model resulted in consistent inhibitory effects on L1 word identification time. This is the one case in which a direct effect of lateral inhibition was found in our simulations. It will be interesting to see if on-line studies display differences in identification times in the presence of about equal error rates.

Conclusion

In this chapter, we performed actual simulations with localist and distributed connectionist models for bilingual word recognition. The models in question were straightforward examples of localist and distributed models, using the standard paradigms in each case. The simulations demonstrated that learning and identification processes were nearly always in line. Because of space limitations, we were not able to discuss simulations for L1 targets as processed by early and late bilinguals, but these conclusions also hold under those circumstances.

Because localist models assume explicit inhibitory links between word units but distributed models do not, one might perhaps have expected different performance characteristics. However, although inhibition between word units is not explicitly operative in distributed connectionist models, at the moment the error score for a target word is computed, different words all put their mark on the word recognition network by affecting the settings of its parameters in the learning phase, depending on their frequencies of usage (presentation) and the similarities between the target word and other words.

In all, the simulations show that one must be cautious in drawing conclusions about inhibition mechanisms in word learning and processing. Different types of inhibition may play a role in word processing: during learning, during identification, and also when a response must be chosen from among a series of strong or active lexical candidates.

In spite of this warning, it is, of course, of the utmost importance for the development of L2 learning models that assumptions about lexical competition and inhibition are made explicit. By specifying the processing details of the models and preferably implementing them as computer programs, precise quantitative predictions can be made. We believe that the comparison of bilingual processing models (such as BIA, RHM, and Green's, 1998, Inhibitory Control model) will benefit from an implementation of the various assumptions about inhibition mechanisms and task dependence. Computational models of L2 learning will be most informative if their consequences are assessed in simulations with stimulus materials approximating those in daily life and in experimental studies.

REFERENCES

Altarriba, J., & Mathis, K. M. (1997). Conceptual and lexical development in second language acquisition. *Journal of Memory and Language*, 36, 550–568.

Brenders, P., van Hell, J. G., & Dijkstra, T. (2011). Word recognition in child second language learners: evidence from cognates and false friends. *Journal of Experimental Child Psychology*, 109(4), 383–396.

(under revision). *The development of lexical and conceptual processing in L2 learners: electrophysiological and behavioral studies.*

Brysbaert, M., & Duijck, W. (2010). Is it time to leave behind the Revised Hierarchical Model of bilingual language processing after fifteen years of service? *Bilingualism: Language and Cognition*, 13, 359–371.

Comesaña, M., Perea, M., Piñeiro, A., & Fraga, I. (2009). Vocabulary teaching strategies and conceptual representations of words in L2 in children: evidence with novice learners. *Journal of Experimental Child Psychology*. doi: 10.1016/j.jecp.2008.10.004.

de Groot, A. M. B. (1992). Determinants of word translation. *Journal of Experimental Psychology: Learning, Memory, and Cognition*, 18(5), 1001–1018.

de Groot, A. M. B., & Poot, R. (1997). Word translation at three levels of proficiency in a second language: the ubiquitous involvement of conceptual memory. *Language Learning*, 47, 215–264.

Dijkstra, T. (2003). Lexical processing in bilinguals and multilinguals: the word selection problem. In J. Cenoz, B. Hufeisen, & U. Jessner (eds.), *The multilingual lexicon* (pp. 11–26). Dordrecht: Kluwer Academic.

(2005). Word recognition and lexical access II: connectionist approaches. In D. A. Cruse, F. Hundsnurscher, M. Job, & P. R. Lutzeier (eds.), *Lexikologie vol. II* [*Lexicology vol. II*] (pp. 1722–1730). Berlin: Walter de Gruyter.
(2009). The multilingual lexicon. In D. Sandra, J.-O. Östman, & J. Verschueren (eds.), *Cognition and pragmatics* (*Handbook of pragmatics highlights*). Amsterdam: John Benjamins.
Dijkstra, T., & De Smedt, K. (1996). Computer models in psycholinguistics: an introduction. In A. Dijkstra & K. De Smedt (eds.), *Computational Psycholinguistics: AI and connectionist models of human language processing* (pp. 3–23). London: Taylor & Francis.
Dijkstra, T., & van Heuven, W. J. B. (1998). The BIA-model and bilingual word recognition. In J. Grainger & A. Jacobs (eds.), *Localist connectionist approaches to human cognition* (pp. 189–225). Hillsdale, NJ: Lawrence Erlbaum Associates.
(2002). The architecture of the bilingual word recognition system: from identification to decision. *Bilingualism: Language and Cognition*, 5, 175–197.
Dijkstra, T., & Rekké, S. (2010). Towards a localist-connectionist model of word translation. *The Mental Lexicon*, 5, 403–422.
Dijkstra, T., Van Jaarsveld, H., & Ten Brinke, S. (1998). Interlingual homograph recognition: effects of task demands and language intermixing. *Bilingualism: Language and Cognition*, 1, 51–66.
Dijkstra, T., Miwa, K., Brummelhuis, B., Sappelli, M., & Baayen, H. (2010). How cross-language similarity affects cognate recognition. *Journal of Memory and Language*, 62, 284–301.
French, R. M., & Jacquet, M. (2004). Understanding bilingual memory: models and data. *Trends in Cognitive Science*, 8, 87–93.
Gollan, T. H., Montoya, R. I., Cera, C. M., & Sandoval, T. C. (2008). More use almost always means a smaller frequency effect: aging, bilingualism, and the weaker links hypothesis. *Journal of Memory and Language*, 58, 787–814.
Grainger, J., Midgley, K., & Holcomb, P. J. (2010). Re-thinking the bilingual interactive-activation model from a developmental perspective (BIA-d). In M. Kail & M. Hickmann (eds.), *Language acquisition across linguistic and cognitive systems* (pp. 267–284). Amsterdam: John Benjamins.
Green, D. W. (1998). Mental control of the bilingual lexico-semantic system. *Bilingualism: Language and Cognition*, 1, 67–81.
Hebb, D. O. (1949). *The organization of behavior*. New York: Wiley & Sons.
Jacquet, M., & French, R. M. (2002). The BIA++: extending the BIA+ to a dynamical distributed connectionist framework. *Bilingualism: Language and Cognition*, 5, 202–205.
Kroll, J. F., & Stewart, E. (1994). Category interference in translation and picture naming: evidence for asymmetric connections between bilingual memory representations. *Journal of Memory and Language*, 33, 149–174.
Kroll, J. F., & Tokowicz, N. (2001). The development of conceptual representation for words in a second language. In J. Nicol (ed.), *One mind, two languages: bilingual language processing* (pp. 49–71). Malden, MA: Blackwell.

Kroll, J. F., van Hell, J. G., Tokowicz, N., & Green, D. W. (2010). The Revised Hierarchical Model: a critical review and assessment. *Bilingualism: Language and Cognition*, 13, 373–381.

Leoné (2009). *A self-organizing model of sequential and simultaneous late language learning.* Unpublished Master's Thesis Artificial Intelligence, Radboud University Nijmegen.

Li, P. (2009). Lexical organization and competition in first and second languages: computational and neural mechanisms. *Cognitive Science*, 33, 629–664.

Li, P., & Farkas, I. (2002). A self-organizing connectionist model of bilingual processing. In R. Heredia & J. Altarriba (eds.), *Bilingual sentence processing* (pp. 59–85). North Holland: Elsevier Science.

Li, P., Zhao, X., & MacWhinney, B. (2007). Dynamic self-organization and early lexical development in children. *Cognitive Science: a Multidisciplinary Journal*, 31, 581–612.

McClelland, J. L., & Rumelhart, D. E. (1981). An interactive activation model of context effects in letter perception, Part 1: an account of basic findings. *Psychological Review*, 88, 375–405.

(1988). *Parallel distributed processing: explorations in the microstructure of cognition: a handbook of models, programs, and exercises.* Cambridge, MA: Bradford Books.

Plaut, D. C. (1997). Structure and function in the lexical system: insights from distributed models of word reading and lexical decision. *Language and Cognitive Processes*, 12, 765–805.

Plaut, D. C., & Shallice, T. (1993). Deep dyslexia: a case study of connectionist neuropsychology. *Cognitive Neuropsychology*, 10, 377–500.

Plaut, D. C., McClelland, J., Seidenberg, M. S., & Patterson, K. (1996). Understanding normal and impaired word reading: computational principles in quasi-regular domains. *Psychological Review*, 103, 56–115.

Ransdell, S. E., & Fischler, I. (1987). Memory in a monolingual mode: when are bilinguals at a disadvantage? *Journal of Memory and Language*, 26, 392–405.

Rumelhart, D. E., & McClelland, J. L. (1986). *Parallel distributed processing: explorations in the microstructure of cognition.* Volume I. Cambridge, MA: MIT Press.

Seidenberg, M. S., & McClelland, J. L. (1989). A distributed, developmental model of word recognition and naming. *Psychological Review*, 96, 523–568.

Smits, E., Martensen, H., Dijkstra, A., & Sandra, D. (2006). Naming interlingual homographs: variable competition and the role of the decision system. *Bilingualism: Language and Cognition*, 9, 281–297.

Thomas, M. S. C. (1997). *Connectionist networks and knowledge representation: the case of bilingual lexical processing.* Unpublished D.Phil. thesis, Oxford University.

(1998). Bilingualism and the single route/dual route debate. *Proceedings of the 20th Annual Conference of the Cognitive Science Society* (pp. 1061–1066). Mahwah, NJ: Lawrence Erlbaum Associates.

(2002). Theories that develop. *Bilingualism: Language and Cognition*, 5, 216–217.

Thomas, M. S. C., & van Heuven, W. J. B. (2005). Computational models of bilingual comprehension. In J. F. Kroll, & A. M. B. de Groot (eds.), *Handbook of bilingualism: psycholinguistic approaches* (pp. 202–225). Oxford University Press.

van Hell, J. G. (2002). Bilingual word recognition beyond orthography: on meaning, linguistic context and individual differences. *Bilingualism: Language and Cognition*, 9, 209–212.

van Heuven, W. J. B., Dijkstra, T., & Grainger, J. (1998). Orthographic neighborhood effects in bilingual word recognition. *Journal of Memory and Language*, 39, 458–483.

3 Working memory and (second) language processing

Arnaud Szmalec, Marc Brysbaert, and Wouter Duyck

Abstract

> This chapter discusses the interactions between two of the most important human cognitive functions: memory and language. First, the concept of working memory is introduced, along with a brief summary of the evolutions that working memory theory has undergone in the last decades. The second part of the chapter focuses on the role of (verbal) working memory in language acquisition and processing. It is argued that working memory, and especially the ability to temporarily represent serial-order information, is crucially involved in both native and foreign word learning, and perhaps also in sentence and text comprehension. The third and final part of the chapter explores the other direction of the interaction, by questioning whether language processing can influence working memory functioning. This question is addressed with recent behavioral and neurological evidence for a general executive control advantage in bilinguals, which makes a strong case for the trainability of some aspects of working memory.

From intelligence testing to working memory

In 1887, Jacobs published a series of studies in which he reported that older children could repeat longer strings of digits read out to them than younger children. Jacobs (1887) also reported that intelligent children (as assessed by the teacher) could repeat more digits than less intelligent children. This idea was picked up by Binet and Simon in the early twentieth century when they developed the first valid intelligence test. They found that 3-year-old children could repeat only sequences of two digits, whereas children of 4 years could repeat sequences of three digits, and most healthy children of 7 years could repeat sequences of five digits. Therefore, Binet and Simon included digit repetition in their intelligence test (Binet & Simon, 1905). Ever since, the digit-span task (as it became called) has been part of intelligence tests, because it correlates reasonably well with the scores of other subtests of intelligence (such as arithmetic, general information, and the discovery of similarities). The task received further impetus when Miller (1956) argued it was a good measure of a person's short-term memory capacity.

In the early 1970s several authors felt uneasy with the digit span as a measure of memory capacity. It seemed to consider short-term memory too much as a passive storage buffer rather than an active part of human information processing. As a result, the concept of working memory, representing both storage and executively controlled manipulation of information, was put forward. An important publication in this respect was the working memory model of Baddeley and Hitch (1974). This model consisted of three parts: (i) a modality-free central executive related to attention, (ii) a phonological loop holding information in a speech-based form, and (iii) a visuospatial sketchpad for the coding of visual and spatial information. A further milestone was the publication of an article by Daneman and Carpenter (1980) in which they presented the reading-span task as a measure of working-memory capacity. This task (also known as the complex span task) was developed to tax the storage and processing functions of working memory simultaneously. Participants had to read sentences (the processing component) while maintaining and retrieving the final words of the sentences (the storage component). An example of a test item with two sentences was:

- When at last his eyes opened, there was no gleam of triumph, no shade of anger.
- The taxi turned up Michigan Avenue where they had a clear view of the lake.

After reading aloud these two sentences the participant had to retrieve the two last words (anger, lake). The number of sentences was increased until the participants made errors.

Daneman and Carpenter observed that reading span typically varied from two to five words. They further discovered that this span correlated much better with reading comprehension and performance on the Scholastic Aptitude Test (SAT; a standardized test for college admission in the USA) than the traditional, passive word span (measured by presenting lists of words of varying length to participants and asking them to repeat the lists). Subsequent reviews confirmed the high correlations between working memory capacity and language comprehension (Daneman & Merikle, 1996), and between working memory capacity and fluid intelligence (Ackerman, Beier, & Boyle, 2005; Engle et al., 1999).

A wide variety of immediate serial recall tasks and complex span measures are in use today to increase our understanding of the structure and the functioning of working memory. At the same time, the conceptualization of working memory has gone through some substantial changes. Whereas Daneman and Carpenter (1980) considered working memory as a unitary system with a single capacity, later research provided evidence for several subcomponents with their own capacities. For instance, Jarrold and Towse (2006), in line with Baddeley and Hitch's (1974) model, argued that working memory capacity depended on (i) processing efficiency, (ii) storage capacities for the maintenance of verbal/numerical information and spatial information, and (iii) controlled attention needed for the coordination and integration of storage and processing, and for the inhibition of irrelevant information.

Still other working memory theorists started to question the idea of working memory as a separate module. Partly inspired by the work of Cowan (1988), which was further elaborated by Oberauer (2009), they have questioned the multiple-component view of memory and argued that short-term memory, long-term memory, and working memory are not separate structures but differ from each other in terms of activation levels of representations in memory and the amount of attentional control dedicated to those representations. Working memory, then, is seen as an activated subset of long-term memory, with information in a directly accessible state and shielded against interference from other memory contents through attentional control (e.g., Szmalec, Verbruggen, Vandierendonck, & Kemps, 2011). In this view, the same memory processes (recall, recognition, recollection, stimulus familiarity, etc.) operate in the entire memory system (e.g., Goethe & Oberauer, 2008; Oztekin & McElree, 2007) and the structural differentiation between memory subsystems is largely abandoned. This assumption is based on a wide variety of behavioral and neurophysiological evidence showing that long-term and working memory are in much closer interaction than initially thought (which also led to the introduction of the episodic buffer in the traditional working memory model; Baddeley, 2000). Probably one of the best examples of the close collaboration between working memory and long-term memory is language acquisition.

How working memory supports language acquisition

Why a working memory for verbal information?

A longstanding tradition in memory research draws a distinction between verbal and visuospatial information, on which different memory processes operate. This division was explicitly present in the working memory model of Baddeley and Hitch (1974) and it remains present in many recent models. The need for a visuospatial (working) memory is easy to assert on the basis of evolutionary grounds. A visuospatial working memory provides a survival advantage because it allows for the retention of visual and spatial information when the information is no longer accessible from the sensory registers (see Vandierendonck and Szmalec, 2011, for a collection of recent papers on spatial working memory theory). Such a memory system allows an organism, for example, to keep track of its nest and to remember where prey is hiding or where predators are likely to be waiting.

Scientists have sought similar evolutionary factors behind the verbal part of (working) memory: why did humans evolve the capacity to (briefly) retain speech-based information? What is the evolutionary purpose of working memory for speech-based materials? It seems unlikely that verbal working memory developed to perform well in cognitive psychology experiments, where participants are asked to recall lists of digits, syllables, telephone numbers, words or other artificial stimuli cognitive psychologists are interested in. What could be the etiology of verbal working memory?

An important breakthrough was published in a seminal paper by Baddeley, Gathercole, and Papagno (1998). On the basis of a literature review, they proposed that verbal working memory primarily represents "the processes and mechanisms by which the sound patterns of the words of the native language are learned by the child" (p. 159). Similar perspectives on verbal working memory had been introduced before, as in the work of Martin and Saffran (1992), who suggested that short-term memory for verbal information was merely an emergent property of the temporary activation of linguistic information. However, the conceptualization of Baddeley *et al.* (1998) was more dynamic and open to individual differences, as typically investigated in working memory research. As a result, Baddeley *et al.* (1998) have been highly influential and stimulated a lot of new research, which is summarized below.

Verbal working memory and the learning of new words

Baddeley *et al.* (1998) reviewed a large amount of evidence from adults, children, and patients in support of the idea that verbal working memory primarily is a language learning device. For example, positive correlations were reported between measures of verbal working memory capacity (e.g., nonword repetition) and native vocabulary knowledge in children of various ages (Bowey, 2001; Gathercole & Adams, 1993,

1994). Further experimental evidence was found by Gathercole and Baddeley (1990) when they taught 5- to 6-year-old children to learn unfamiliar names (e.g., Pimas) for new toy animals. This was considered an operationalization of naturalistic *word* learning, namely the mapping of a new word form to a referent in the real world. As expected, performance was worse for children with low nonword repetition scores than for children with high scores. Further experiments tried to make sure that the correlation between memory performance and learning new words was really due to constraints imposed by working memory capacity on language learning, and not due to a third, confounded variable, or to the fact that the working memory capacity of an individual depends on the language learning skills of the individual (see also Gathercole, 2006). A first line of research (Duyck *et al.*, 2003; Papagno, Valentine, & Baddeley, 1991) used the dual-task methodology to demonstrate that loading verbal working memory resulted in poorer learning of word–nonword pairs, such as finger–*vilsan* (in which participants had to name the nonword upon hearing the word, or vice versa), but not in learning word–word pairs (e.g., frog–nail), in both adults and 11- to 13-year-old children.

Other research examined patients with verbal short-term memory deficits, to see whether these patients found it hard to learn new vocabulary while at the same time retaining the language capacities they had before the lesion. For instance, Baddeley (1993) reported a case study of such a patient, SR, who indeed performed very poorly on a word–new word association task (pairing English with Finnish words), unless he could associate both words by forming very elaborate semantic associations. There is also good evidence that children with specific language impairment have a reduced verbal working memory capacity and that the latter is causally linked to language acquisition difficulties (Baddeley *et al.*, 1998).

The importance of serial-order memory for novel word learning

More recent research has focused on the question of *what* must be learned in a word–new word association task (different from a word–word association task) and how working memory is related to this. Is verbal working memory especially important for learning the new word form itself, for associating the old with the new word form, or for mapping the semantic representation of the old word form to the new word form? Or could it be that the effect of verbal working memory on word–new word association is simply due to the fact that a new, conflicting, name must be given to existing information, which already has a name?

In the latter case, working memory would play a role in the learning of a new language (where existing objects get new names) but not in the learning of new names of new objects.

An important model to describe the acquisition of new names for new objects (as happens in children acquiring language) was proposed by Page and Norris (1998). The rationale behind their Primacy Model of immediate serial recall can be summarized as follows. Learning a novel word form consists of learning both a sequence of sounds (letters) and the correct order of the sounds. Learning the new word *artecey*, for example, involves learning both the identity and the order of the phonemes: *ar*, *te*, *cey*. According to Page and Norris (2009), learning such a word is similar to learning the sequence of letters in a letter span task (i.e., repeating the letters R T C in an immediate serial recall task). In other words, the model of Page and Norris bridges the gap between verbal working memory and language acquisition by hypothesizing that the working memory mechanisms involved in immediate serial recall of letters are the same as those involved in the acquisition of novel word forms. In this view, naturalistic word-form learning consists of extracting regularities from the auditory information in the environment. If a baby repeatedly hears the sequence *ar*, *te*, *cey* in this specific order, it will develop a lexical representation for *artecey*, which may then be linked to a real-world referent that is always present when the baby hears this particular sequence of sounds.

Page and Norris (2009) argued that the above naturalistic word-learning process can be mimicked in a laboratory setting using the Hebb repetition effect (Hebb, 1961). The Hebb repetition effect is observed in an immediate verbal serial recall task when a particular sequence of digits/syllables is repeated across trials. In such a situation, recall of the repeated sequence improves over time relative to that of unrepeated sequences. In essence, Page and Norris (2009) argued that the Hebb repetition effect showed how information related to a sequence of items (like letters or syllables) in working memory gradually develops into a stable long-term memory trace that has the same characteristics as a newly acquired word form. The first empirical evidence supporting Page and Norris's computational exercise was reported by Mosse and Jarrold (2008). They found a positive correlation between the steepness of the Hebb learning curve and performance in a paired-associate learning task with nonwords, in a sample of 5- to 6-year-olds. More recently, Szmalec *et al.* (2009) presented the first experimental demonstration of the idea that the verbal Hebb effect can be used as a laboratory analogue of novel word-form learning. They presented adult participants with sequences of syllables in a standard Hebb learning paradigm (e.g., *zi-lo-ka-ho-fi-se-be-ru-mo*). Then, the same participants took part in a lexical decision experiment including nonwords that were constructed with syllables from the Hebb experiment (*ziloka, hofise, berumo*). Szmalec and colleagues observed that participants were slower to reject the Hebb-based nonwords compared to matched control nonwords. This suggests that the immediate serial recall of repeated Hebb sequences leads to representations in lexical memory similar to those of existing words, just as would happen when people acquire novel words.

The idea that the Hebb repetition effect operationalizes the memory mechanisms that support language learning raises the question whether the Hebb effect can also be used to shed some light on language impairment. In this context, Szmalec, Loncke, Page, and Duyck (2011) demonstrated that adults with dyslexia show impaired Hebb learning across verbal and visuospatial stimulus modalities. On the basis of these findings, they put forward a new, memory-based account of dyslexia, in which the various difficulties experienced by people with dyslexia are assumed to originate from an impairment affecting the learning of serial-order information in memory, of which Hebb repetition learning is an example. Assuming that a newly learned word form is simply an ordered sequence of sublexical items, the Hebb learning account of dyslexia proposes that the lexical representation's constituent elements are not optimally consolidated as a single entry in long-term memory. Hence, lexical access for that entry during reading will be impaired and normal procedures for mapping grapheme sequences to phoneme sequences are disrupted (Whitney & Cornelissen, 2005).

Similar ideas have been proposed by Gupta (2009), who also sees a new word (or a nonword) as a novel sequence of sounds, similar to a sequence of digits or letters to be learned in an immediate serial recall task (or span task). Based on this assumption, Gupta hypothesized that effects typically observed in immediate serial recall tasks should be present in the learning of new words or nonwords as well. In a series of elegant studies, he indeed observed that the phonemes of syllables within a newly learned word form are subject to primacy and recency effects (Gupta, 2005; Gupta *et al.*, 2005). The primacy effect refers to the finding that the items presented first in a series are better recalled than items presented later, independent of whether the test follows immediately after the presentation of the series or after a distraction task that depletes short-term memory. The recency effect refers to the finding that the items presented last are better recalled when the test immediately follows the series presentation but not when a distraction task intervenes.

The fact that the same effects are observed in new word learning and serial recall further strengthens the claim that naturalistic word-form learning and immediate serial recall rely on the same working memory mechanisms. Based on these findings, Gupta (2009; Gupta & Tisdale, 2009) developed a computational model that could simulate the various effects by making a distinction between a lexical (word) level and a sublexical (sound) level of item representations and a serial-order mechanism that encoded the order of the lexical and sublexical elements.

A third model stressing the analogy between serial-order learning in short-term memory tasks and language learning was developed by Burgess and Hitch (1999, 2006). An interesting feature of this model is that it is a connectionist model consisting of nothing but layers of nodes connected to each other. This allowed the authors to provide a common explanatory mechanism for effects like serial position, lexicality and Hebb repetition. Of further importance is that the model made an explicit distinction between serial-order information for unknown stimuli (new words) and item information for known stimuli (old words), which were based on different processes.

Finally, the distinction between memory for item information and memory for order information has been documented in neuroscientific and neuropsychological research as well (Majerus et al., 2001; Majerus, Poncelet, Elsen, & Van der Linden, 2006; Majerus, Poncelet, Greffe, & Van der Linden, 2006; Majerus et al., 2004). Using a correlational approach, Majerus, Poncelet, Elsen, & Van der Linden (2006) explored the contribution of three different short-term memory skills to novel word-form learning in patients. These were short-term memory for serial-order information, item recall, and item recognition. The results showed that only memory for serial order played a role in acquiring novel phonological word forms and, therefore, supported the hypothesis that the representation of item and order information are distinct factors in word learning. Majerus, Poncelet, Elsen, & Van der Linden (2006) further explored the item versus order distinction with functional magnetic resonance imaging (fMRI). They observed that memory for order and items activated different brain regions. Order relied on the right intraparietal sulcus, the right cerebellum, and the bilateral premotor cortex, whereas item memory activated two regions associated with language processing, namely the superior temporal gyrus and the left fusiform gyrus.

Overall, the above findings provide compelling evidence for a causal relation between short-term serial recall and naturalistic word-form learning. Therefore, they reinforce the assumption that the primary purpose of human verbal working is to support the acquisition of language.

Verbal working memory and second language word learning

Evidently, the findings described in the previous sections have implications for second language (L2) learning. One of the key requirements of L2 learning is the acquisition of new word forms, which initially are nothing but sequences of sounds and letters.

Service (1992) was one of the first to specifically examine the relationship between nonword repetition and learning new words in L2. She ran a longitudinal study of Finnish-speaking primary-school children learning English. At the beginning of the study, a nonword repetition task was administered and the scores on this test were correlated with English performance levels nearly three years later. Service observed that the nonword spans were a significant, independent predictor of L2 proficiency. Cheung (1996) ran another early study. He correlated nonword span with the number of trials 7th grade participants from Hong Kong needed to acquire new English L2 words. Cheung found the expected inverse relationship (participants with higher nonword spans learned the words faster), at least for the participants with vocabulary sizes lower than average, in line with the idea that verbal working memory is particularly important for acquiring new words and less so for the processing of familiar words.

The studies of Service (1992) and Cheung (1996) have since been replicated and extended in several studies with convergent results, a good review of which is given by Hummel and French (2010). So, there is little doubt that verbal working memory is involved in the acquisition of L2 words as much as it is in the acquisition of new native language (L1) words. It also seems reasonable to assume that the working memory processes involved in L2 and L1 word learning are the same, although there is not much empirical evidence on this aspect yet, except for a study by Majerus, Poncelet, Van der Linden, and Weekes (2008). At the same time, there is fMRI evidence that for low-proficiency bilinguals order encoding may be less efficient in L2 than in L1 (Majerus *et al.*, 2008), suggesting that in early stages L2 word learning may be more difficult than L1 word learning.

Working memory involvement in other aspects of language processing

So far, we have reviewed evidence showing that verbal working memory (more precisely memory for serial order and item information) supports the acquisition of novel lexical forms, both in native and foreign languages. It is important to realize, however, that hypotheses about the involvement of working memory in the human language system have not been restricted to word learning. In the final section of this part, we briefly review some more ideas that have been proposed about how working memory may be involved in the integration of individual words into coherent sentences and discourse representations. Indeed the correlation between working-memory-span measures and reading comprehension, originally discovered by Daneman and Carpenter (1980), strongly points to the importance of working memory for text understanding. However, it has been very difficult thus far to design paradigms that are as convincing as those for novel word acquisition.

One of the first questions addressed by working memory proponents was whether working memory is involved in sentence parsing (Just & Carpenter, 1992; Waters & Caplan, 1996). Sentence parsing refers to the processes needed to organize the words of a sentence into a proposition (or set of propositions) summarizing who did what to whom. Indeed, it seems obvious that verbal working memory (or the phonological loop in Baddeley and Hitch's model) is needed to retain the surface structure of a sentence until the proper syntactic interpretation has been made. Sentences can be syntactically complex with large distances between related parts (e.g., between the subject and the verb, as in "when the girl with the red hood, who was dancing in the wood, saw..."). In addition, many sentences are locally ambiguous and may require some kind of reanalysis. This is shown most clearly in so-called garden-path sentences, such as "the horse chased past the barn fell." For these sentences, participants are likely to experience parsing difficulties because the structure of the sentence does not agree with the initially preferred interpretation (i.e., "the horse that was chased" vs. "the horse that was chasing"). Given the need to retain word-order information until the correct syntactic interpretation has been found, it seems reasonable to assume that people with high working memory capacity will perform better on sentence parsing than people with low capacity (e.g., Swets et al., 2007; Vallar & Baddeley, 1984).

A problem with this intuitively appealing hypothesis, however, is that syntactic comprehension seems to be affected little by neurological conditions resulting in reduced working memory capacity. Only for very complex sentences can an effect be shown. This finding led Caplan and Waters (1999) to argue that sentences are interpreted by a system independent of working memory (the so-called separate sentence interpretation resource), giving rise to a lively discussion about whether or not verbal working memory as traditionally measured is needed for sentence parsing (e.g., Lauro et al., 2010, for a recent installment). O'Brien et al. (2006), for instance, claimed that verbal working memory capacity (as measured with nonword repetition) predicts the development of narrative and grammatical competences in L2, in English-speaking adults learning Spanish. Still, it cannot be denied that the consequences of reduced memory span are much more severe for novel word learning than for sentence parsing, suggesting that the involvement of verbal working memory will be less for the understanding of sentences than for the learning of new words.

In a review article on the relationship between working memory and language, Baddeley (2003) mentioned two other possible contributions of working memory to language understanding. He thought it likely that visuospatial working memory would be involved in maintaining a representation of the page and its layout during reading. Readers are amazingly accurate at locating previously read words. This can be seen, for instance, when they make regressions upon encountering a comprehension problem in text reading. These regressive eye movements are usually remarkably accurate (Kennedy et al., 2003) and seem to require access to a spatial map of the text. Baddeley (2003) further hypothesized that visuospatial working memory may also be involved in the understanding of spatial information (e.g., grammatical structures involving spatial terms such as above, below, shorter, and so on). Both ideas, however, still need to be tested.

How language processing supports working memory

Thus far, we have summarized findings showing that working memory is crucially involved in language acquisition. Of equal interest is the reverse question, namely whether working memory's processing (executive control) and storage (span/capacity) functions are also influenced by language processing, or whether they remain unchanged. One research area that has proven particularly fruitful in this respect concerns the consequences of bilingualism for executive control functions.

Executive control advantages in bilingualism

Recent studies point toward important cognitive benefits of being bilingual. Bialystok, Craik, and Freedman (2007), for example, found that the age of onset of dementia is on average four years later in bilinguals than in monolinguals. Cognitive advantages of bilingualism are assumed to originate from the requirement to continuously control the activation of lexical representations from the non-target language so that they do not interfere with the ongoing language processing (Green, 1998).

There is now a good consensus that both languages of a bilingual are always to some extent active in lexical memory and interact with each other (Brysbaert & Duyck, 2010). For instance, it has been observed that bilinguals read L1 words faster if the L2 translations are similar in form (i.e., when they are so-called cognates, such as apple and *appel* in English and Dutch). This is even true when the participants are reading complete sentences in L1 (Van Assche *et al.*, 2009), which indicates that lexical access in bilinguals is not language selective. Similarly, there is evidence for unremitting competition between word forms from different languages in speech production. Ivanova and Costa (2008), for example, reported that L1 speech production is slower in Spanish–Catalan bilinguals than in monolinguals. Gollan and Acenas (2004) observed that bilinguals experience more tip-of-the-tongue states than monolinguals (these are situations in which one cannot retrieve the correct lexical entry for a concept).

Despite the fact that the languages of a bilingual are constantly in competition with each other, there is little evidence for control *failures*, as can be concluded from the few switching errors made. These are rare in comparison with other types of errors and hesitations in speech. Hence, bilinguals seem to have an efficient cognitive control mechanism dealing with the language competition in a highly interactive bilingual language processing system. This raises questions about the nature and the functioning of such a cognitive control system and the extent to which it is specialized for language or generalizes to other cognitive domains.

Interest in the language control of bilinguals took off after the publication of papers by Meuter and Allport (1999) and Costa and Santesteban (2004). In the former study, bilinguals were required to name pictures in the language indicated by an external cue. The experiment contained trials in which the language was the same as in the previous trial, and trials in which the language switched. Meuter and Allport observed that bilinguals were slower in the switch trials than in the non-switch trials, and that the switching costs were larger when the language changed from L2 to L1 than vice versa. They interpreted the latter finding as being due to the fact that more inhibition of L1 is required when participants speak in L2 than the other way around.

Costa and Santesteban (2004) adopted the same paradigm, and additionally manipulated second language proficiency in a group of Spanish–Catalan bilinguals. For unbalanced bilinguals, they replicated the findings of Meuter and Allport (1999): a cost when switching languages, and a larger switching cost when switching to the dominant language. However, for balanced Spanish–Catalan bilinguals (who used both languages interchangeably and equally often), the language-switching cost was symmetrical, equally large in both directions. Surprisingly, the switching cost remained symmetrical when in a later experiment switching between L1 and a much weaker third language (L3) was studied. On the basis of this finding, Costa and Santesteban argued that balanced bilinguals develop a qualitatively different mechanism of lexical selection, which can also be used for a weaker language (L3). Similarly, Costa, Santesteban and Ivanova (2006) found no asymmetrical switching cost in balanced Spanish–Catalan bilinguals who were switching between L2 and L3. These participants did show an asymmetry, however, when they were asked to switch between L3 and fourth language (L4), leading Costa and colleagues to argue that there are limits to the extent to which the specific control mechanism can be applied.

All in all, it looks as though the continuous language control and the repeated practice of language switching provide bilinguals with efficient control mechanisms, which generalize to some extent beyond the specific language pair for which they are needed (see the symmetrical language switching cost for L3 in Costa & Santesteban, 2004). This has led researchers to investigate whether bilinguals also perform differently, more efficiently, in tasks that do not require verbal processing.

Within this framework, Bialystok and colleagues compared bilinguals with monolinguals on a wide variety of tasks tapping into executive control, such as the Simon task. In this task, participants are required to make a spatial response (e.g., press the left or right key) to a non-spatial characteristic (e.g., the green or red color) of a stimulus, which has a particular spatial position (e.g., left or right of the fixation location). A robust finding in this paradigm is that the irrelevant position of the stimulus interferes with the response, such that participants are faster to respond to congruent trials (pressing the left key to a stimulus presented left of fixation) than to incongruent trials (pressing the right key to a stimulus presented left of fixation). This is the so-called Simon effect. Interestingly, Bialystok *et al.* (2004) found a smaller Simon effect in English–Tamil bilinguals than in monolinguals. Similarly, Bialystok, Craik, and Ryan (2006) observed that bilinguals had fewer problems moving their eyes in the direction opposite to the one where the stimulus appeared (e.g., moving the eyes to the right when a light flash appears to the left; this is the so-called antisaccade task). Emmorey *et al.* (2008) found a comparable bilingual executive control advantage using a flanker task, in which irrelevant flanking stimuli had to be ignored for good task performance. The findings that bilinguals show better performance than monolinguals on a variety of executive control tasks suggest that the cognitive benefits of bilingualism are not restricted to language control. They generalize to other situations in which a dominant response must be suppressed for good performance.

The cognitive mechanisms underlying the bilingual executive control advantage were further explored by Prior and Gollan (2011), who manipulated the degree of language switching in their participants. They compared a group of balanced Spanish–English bilinguals who regularly switched between languages, to a group of balanced Mandarin–English bilinguals who switched between languages less often. Only the Spanish–English bilinguals showed a reduced task-switching cost. On the basis of this finding, Prior and Gollan concluded that only bilinguals who often switch between languages train their executive control capacities, resulting in improved task-switching performance.

Also, at the neural level there is evidence that language control makes use of the same brain structures as other, non-verbal control mechanisms. Pioneering work was done by Hernandez and colleagues (Hernandez, Martinez, & Kohnert, 2000; Hernandez *et al.*, 2001), who used a picture-naming task. They observed stronger activation in the dorsolateral prefrontal cortex when bilinguals had to switch response languages. Using event-related fMRI, Wang *et al.* (2007) reported stronger activation in the frontal cortices bilaterally and in the left anterior cingulate cortex when Chinese–English bilinguals switched picture naming from L1 to L2, but not from L2 to L1. The dorsolateral prefrontal cortex also showed stronger activation on switch trials, but this pattern of activation did not interact with switching direction. Similarly, a positron emission tomography study by Crinion *et al.*, (2006) identified involvement of the basal ganglia (caudate) in language control in German–English and Japanese–English bilinguals. Finally, Abutalebi and Costa (2008) reported that naming in the first language in a bilingual context (compared with monolingual contexts) increased activation in the left caudate and anterior cingulate cortex. The brain areas that have been found to be involved in such language-switching tasks highly overlap with the neural circuits identified in domain-general executive control research (Brass and von Cramon, 2002, 2004; Ridderinkhof *et al.*, 2004). Recent models of the anterior cingulate cortex assume that it is involved in conflict processing (Botvinick *et al.*, 2001). Also, the basal ganglia are known to be crucial for cognitive flexibility (Aron *et al.*, 2003).

Working memory capacity and bilingualism

Another question that has been raised is whether bilingualism can boost total working memory capacity. Is it the case that bilinguals have a higher working memory capacity than monolinguals?

Some of the early research indicated that multilingual adults indeed have greater short-term memory and working memory spans (as measured with digit and nonword repetition) than IQ-matched monolingual participants. Papagno and Vallar (1995) compared Italian polyglots and controls on a series of tasks related to: fluid intelligence (Raven Progressive Matrices), L1 vocabulary (the Wechsler Adult Intelligence Scale subtest), auditory digit span, nonword repetition, visuospatial span (Corsi blocks), visuospatial learning (the number of sequences participants needed to learn a supra-span sequence on the Corsi blocks), paired-associate learning of words, and paired-associate learning of words and nonwords. Multilinguals had similar or inferior performance to the controls for fluid intelligence, L1 vocabulary, visuospatial span, visuospatial learning, and paired-associate word–word learning. In contrast, they had better performance on digit and nonword repetition and on paired-associate word–nonword learning. Furthermore, a principal component analysis indicated that the latter three tasks were part of the same component (i.e., the participants' scores on these tests correlated substantially).

Not all findings have been positive, however. French and O'Brien (2008) tested Arabic and English nonword repetition before and after French-speaking children took part in an intensive English-as-a-second-language program. Whereas performance on the English nonwords improved (as expected from the finding that the memory span is larger for meaningful words than for nonwords), no difference was observed for Arabic nonword repetition. Similarly, Vejnović, Milin, and Zdravković (2010) compared reading spans of Serbian–English bilinguals in L1 and L2 as a function of L2 proficiency. Whereas the L2 span was significantly longer for high-proficiency bilinguals than for low-proficiency bilinguals, there was only a nonsignificant trend for the L1 span. More powerful designs will have to be used to find out whether this trend is a genuine effect, as suggested by Papagno and Vallar (1995), or a difference too small to be of practical value.

The issue whether the working memory capacity of bilinguals is larger than that of monolinguals has implications for the literature about the extent to which this capacity can be increased by training or is stable within an individual (Shipstead, Redick, & Engle, 2010). The question whether or not working memory can be trained is currently highly contested (Jaeggi *et al.*, 2011; Shipstead *et al.*, 2010). Some findings suggest that training one cognitive ability may extend to other cognitive abilities and, hence, be beneficial in general. Jaeggi *et al.* (2008), for example, reported higher fluid intelligence in participants who were trained on an *n*-back task, a working memory task which relies heavily on executive control resources. Other researchers, however, have identified several methodological concerns with these artificial training studies and claim that to this day no study has convincingly demonstrated that cognitive abilities can be trained, over and above (strategic) improvements in specific task demands (Shipstead *et al.*, 2010).

Further interesting findings of Vejnović *et al.* (2010) were that even for the highly proficient L2 speakers the reading spans were substantially shorter in L2 than in L1, and that there was quite a high correlation between the L1 and L2 reading spans. The latter finding is in line with the assumption that reading spans measure stable individual differences in working memory capacity. The former finding agrees with the observation that L2 processing is more demanding than L1 processing. As Hummel and French (2010) argued, the shorter working memory span in L2 than L1 is likely to have implications for learning in L2, because it may put bilinguals at the same disadvantage as monolinguals with a reduced memory span. Hummel and French suggested that one way to counter this problem might be to provide L2 learners with additional written support when spoken instruction is used extensively (as in communicative classroom contexts or immersion projects), so that L2 learners can try to decrease the working memory load.

Conclusions

The aim of this chapter was to demonstrate that although the relation between memory and language has remained poorly specified for many years, the last decade has witnessed an important step forward in understanding how these key features of the human cognitive system interact. On the one hand, native and foreign language acquisition appear to be achieved through the ability to represent serial-order information in working memory, while language perception and production rely on attentional control functions. The latter functions are not specific to language processing and their continuous use seems to provide the bilingual brain with a greater mental flexibility, although it may not increase working memory capacity as measured by (reading) span tasks.

REFERENCES

Abutalebi, J., & Costa, A. (2008). Acquisition, processing and loss of L2: functional, cognitive and neural perspectives. *Journal of Neurolinguistics*, 21, 473–476.

Ackerman, P. L., Beier, M. E., & Boyle, M. O. (2005). Working memory and intelligence: the same or different constructs? *Psychological Bulletin*, 131, 30–60.

Aron, A. R., Watkins, L., Sahakian, B. J., Monsell, S., Barker, R. A., & Robbins, T. W. (2003). Task-set switching deficits in early-stage Huntington's disease: implications for basal ganglia function. *Journal of Cognitive Neuroscience*, 15, 629–642.

Baddeley, A. D. (1993). Short-term phonological memory and long-term learning: a single-case study. *European Journal of Cognitive Psychology*, 5, 129–148.

(2000). The episodic buffer: a new component of working memory? *Trends in Cognitive Sciences*, 4, 417–423.

(2003). Working memory: looking back and looking forward. *Nature Reviews: Neuroscience*, 4, 829–839.

Baddeley, A. D., & Hitch, G. J. (1974). Working memory. In G. H. Bower (ed.), *The psychology of learning and motivation* Vol. 8 (pp. 47–89). New York: Academic Press.

Baddeley, A. D., Gathercole, S. E., & Papagno, C. (1998). The phonological loop as a language learning device. *Psychological Review*, 105, 158–173.

Bialystok, E., Craik, F. I. M., Klein, R., & Viswanathan, M. (2004). Bilingualism, aging, and cognitive control: evidence from the Simon task. *Psychology and Aging*, 19, 290–303.

Bialystok, E., Craik, F. I. M., & Ryan, J. (2006). Executive control in a modified anti-saccade task: effects of aging and bilingualism. *Journal of Experimental Psychology: Learning, Memory, and Cognition*, 32, 1341–1354.

Bialystok, E., Craik, F. I. M., & Freedman, M. (2007). Bilingualism as a protection against the onset of symptoms of dementia. *Neuropsychologia*, 45, 459–464.

Binet, A., & Simon, T. (1905). Application des méthodes nouvelles au diagnostic du niveau intellectual chez les enfants normaux et anormaux d'hospice et d'école primaire. *L'Année Psychologique*, 11, 245–336.

Botvinick, M. M., Braver, T. S., Barch, D. M., Carter, C. S., & Cohen, J. D. (2001). Conflict monitoring and cognitive control. *Psychological Review*, 108, 624–652.

Bowey, J. A. (2001). Nonword repetition and young children's receptive vocabulary: a longitudinal study. *Applied Psycholinguistics*, 22, 441–469.

Brass, M., & von Cramon, D. Y. (2002). The role of the frontal cortex in task preparation. *Cerebral Cortex*, 12, 908–914.

(2004). Selection for cognitive control: an fMRI study on the selection of task relevant information. *The Journal of Neuroscience*, 24, 8847–8852.

Brysbaert, M., & Duyck, W. (2010). Is it time to leave behind the revised hierarchical model of bilingual language processing after 15 years of service? *Bilingualism: Language and Cognition*, 13, 359–371.

Burgess, N., & Hitch, G. J. (1999). Memory for serial order: a network model of the phonological loop and its timing. *Psychological Review*, 106, 551–581.

(2006). A revised model of short-term memory and long-term learning of verbal sequences. *Journal of Memory and Language*, 55, 627–652.

Caplan, D., & Waters, G. S. (1999). Verbal working memory and sentence comprehension. *Behavioral and Brain Sciences*, 22, 77–94.

Cheung, H. (1996). Nonword span as a unique predictor of second-language vocabulary learning. *Developmental Psychology*, 32, 867–873.

Costa, A., & Santesteban, M. (2004). Lexical access in bilingual speech production: evidence from language switching in highly proficient bilinguals and L2 learners. *Journal of Memory and Language*, 50, 491–511.

Costa, A., Santesteban, M., & Ivanova, I. (2006). How do highly proficient bilinguals control their lexicalization process? Inhibitory and language-specific selection mechanisms are both functional. *Journal of Experimental Psychology: Learning, Memory and Cognition*, 32, 1057–1074.

Cowan, N. (1988). Evolving conceptions of memory storage, selective attention, and their mutual constraints within the human information-processing system. *Psychological Bulletin*, 104, 163–191.

Crinion, J., Turner, R., Grogan, A., Hanakawa, T., Noppeney, U., Devlin, J. T., *et al.* (2006). Language control in the bilingual brain. *Science*, 312, 1537–1540.

Daneman, M., & Carpenter, P. A. (1980). Individual differences in working memory and reading. *Journal of Verbal Learning and Verbal Behavior*, 19, 450–466.

Daneman, M., & Merikle, P. M. (1996). Working memory and language comprehension: a meta-analysis. *Psychonomic Bulletin & Review*, 3, 422–433.

Duyck, W., Szmalec, A., Kemps, E., & Vandierendonck, A. (2003). Verbal working memory is involved in associative word learning unless visual codes are available. *Journal of Memory & Language*, 48, 527–541.

Emmorey, K., Luk, G., Pyers, J. E., & Bialystok, E. (2008). The source of enhanced cognitive control in bilinguals. *Psychological Science*, 19, 1201–1206.

Engle, R. W., Tuholski, S. W., Laughlin, J. E., & Conway, A. R. A. (1999). Working memory, short-term memory, and general fluid intelligence: a latent-variable approach. *Journal of Experimental Psychology: General*, 128, 309–331.

French, L., & O'Brien (2008). Phonological memory and children's second language grammar learning. *Applied Psycholinguistics*, 29, 463–487.

Gathercole, S. E. (2006). Complexities and constraints in nonword repetition and word learning. *Applied Psycholinguistics*, 27, 599–613.

Gathercole, S. E., & Adams, A. M. (1993). Phonological working memory in very young children. *Developmental Psychology*, 29, 770–778.

  (1994). Children's phonological working memory: contributions of long-term knowledge and rehearsal. *Journal of Memory and Language*, 33, 672–688.

Gathercole, S. E., & Baddeley, A. D. (1990). The role of phonological memory in vocabulary acquisition: a study of young children learning new names. *British Journal of Psychology*, 81, 439–454.

Goethe, K., & Oberauer, K. (2008). The integration of familiarity and recollection information in short-term recognition: modeling speed–accuracy trade-off functions. *Psychological Research*, 72, 289–303.

Gollan, T. H., & Acenas, L. A. R. (2004). What is a TOT? Cognate and translation effects on tip-of-the-tongue states in Spanish–English and Tagalog–English bilinguals. *Journal of Experimental Psychology: Learning, Memory, and Cognition*, 30, 246–269.

Green, D. W. (1998). Mental control of the bilingual lexico-semantic system. *Bilingualism: Language and Cognition*, 1, 67–81.

Gupta, P. (2005). Primacy and recency in nonword repetition. *Memory*, 13, 318-324.

(2009). A computational model of nonword repetition, immediate serial recall, and nonword learning. In A. Thorn and M. Page (eds.), *Interactions between short-term and long-term memory in the verbal domain* (pp. 108-135). Hove: Psychology Press.

Gupta, P., & Tisdale, J. (2009). Does phonological short-term memory causally determine vocabulary learning? Toward a computational resolution of the debate. *Journal of Memory and Language*, 61, 481-502.

Gupta, P., Lipinski, J., Abbs, B., & Lin, P.-H. (2005). Serial position effects in nonword repetition. *Journal of Memory and Language*, 53, 141-162.

Hebb, D. O. (1961). Distinctive features of learning in the higher animal. In J. F. Delafresnaye (ed.), *Brain mechanisms and learning* (pp. 37-46). Oxford: Blackwell.

Hernandez, A. E., Martinez, A., & Kohnert, K. (2000). In search of the language switch: an fMRI study of picture naming in Spanish-English bilinguals. *Brain and Language*, 73, 421-431.

Hernandez, A. E., Dapretto, M., Mazziotta, J., & Bookheimer, S. (2001). Language switching and language representation in Spanish-English bilinguals: an fMRI study. *NeuroImage*, 14, 510-520.

Hummel, K., & French, L. (2010). Phonological memory and implications for the second language classroom. *Canadian Modern Language Review*, 66, 371-391.

Ivanova, I., & Costa, A. (2008). Does bilingualism hamper lexical access in speech production? *Acta Psychologica*, 127, 277-288.

Jacobs, J. (1887). Experiments on "prehension." *Mind*, 12, 75-79.

Jaeggi, S. M., Buschkuehl, M., Jonides, J., & Perrig, W. J. (2008). Improving fluid intelligence with training on working memory. *Proceedings of the National Academy of Sciences of the United States of America*, 105, 6829-6833.

Jaeggi, S. M., Buschkuehl, M., Jonides, J., & Shah, P. (2011). Short and long-term benefits of cognitive training. *Proceedings of the National Academy of Sciences of the United States of America*, 108, 10081-10086.

Jarrold, C., & Towse, J. N. (2006). Individual differences in working memory. *Neuroscience*, 139, 39-50.

Just, M. A., & Carpenter, P. A. (1992). A capacity theory of comprehension: individual differences in working memory. *Psychological Review*, 98, 122-149.

Kennedy, A., Brooks, R., Flynn, L.-A., & Prophet, C. (2003). The reader's spatial code. In J. Hyönä, R. Radach, & H. Deubel (eds.), *The mind's eye: cognitive and applied aspects of eye movement research* (pp. 193-212). Amsterdam: North-Holland.

Lauro, L. J., Reis, J., Cohen, L. G., Cecchetto, C., & Papagno, C. (2010). A case for the involvement of phonological loop in sentence comprehension. *Neuropsychologia*, 48, 4003-4011.

Majerus, S., Lekeu, F., Van der Linden, M., & Salmon, E. (2001). Deep dysphasia: further evidence on the relationship between phonological short-term memory and language processing impairments. *Cognitive Neuropsychology*, 18, 385-410.

Majerus, S., Van der Linden, M., Mulder, G., Meulemans, T., & Peters, F. (2004). Verbal short-term memory reflects the sublexical organization of the phonological language network: evidence from an incidental phonotactic learning paradigm. *Journal of Memory and Language*, 51, 297–306.

Majerus, S., Poncelet, M., Elsen, B., & Van der Linden, M. (2006). Exploring the relationship between new word learning and short-term memory for serial order recall, item recall, and item recognition. *European Journal of Cognitive Psychology*, 18, 848–873.

Majerus, S., Poncelet, M., Greffe, C., & Van der Linden, M. (2006). Relations between vocabulary development and verbal short-term memory: the relative importance of short-term memory for serial order and item information. *Journal of Experimental Child Psychology*, 93, 95–119.

Majerus, S., Poncelet, M., Van der Linden, M., & Weekes, B. (2008). Lexical learning in bilingual adults: the relative importance of short-term memory for serial order and phonological knowledge. *Cognition*, 107, 395–419.

Martin, N., & Saffran, E. M. (1992). A computational account of deep dysphasia: evidence from a single case study. *Brain and Language*, 43, 240–274.

Meuter, R. F. I., & Allport, A. (1999). Bilingual language switching in naming: asymmetrical costs of language selection. *Journal of Memory and Language*, 40, 25–40.

Miller, G. A. (1956). The magical number seven, plus or minus two: some limits on our capacity for processing information. *Psychological Review*, 63, 81–97.

Mosse, E. K., & Jarrold, C. (2008). Hebb learning, verbal short-term memory, and the acquisition of phonological forms in children. *The Quarterly Journal of Experimental Psychology*, 61, 505–514.

O'Brien, I., Segalowitz, N., Collentine, J., & Freed, B. (2006). Phonological memory and lexical, narrative, and grammatical skills in second-language oral production by adult learners. *Applied Psycholinguistics*, 27, 377–402.

Oberauer, K. (2009). Design for a working memory. *Psychology of Learning and Motivation*, 51, 45–100.

Oztekin, I., & McElree, B. (2007). Proactive interference slows recognition by eliminating fast assessments of familiarity. *Journal of Memory and Language*, 57, 126–149.

Page, M. P. A., & Norris, D. (1998). The primacy model: a new model of immediate serial recall. *Psychological Review*, 105, 761–781.

(2009). A model linking immediate serial recall, the Hebb repetition effect and the learning of phonological word-forms. *Philosophical Transactions of the Royal Society B*, 364, 3737–3753.

Papagno, C., & Vallar, G. (1995). Short-term memory and vocabulary learning in polyglots. *Quarterly Journal of Experimental Psychology*, 48A, 98–107.

Papagno, C., Valentine, T., & Baddeley, A. D. (1991). Phonological short-term memory and foreign-language learning. *Journal of Memory and Language*, 30, 331–347.

Prior, A., & Gollan, T. H. (2011). Good language-switchers are good task switchers: evidence from Spanish–English and Mandarin–English bilinguals. *Journal of the International Neuropsychological Society*, 682–691.

Ridderinkhof, K. R., Ullsperger, M., Crone, E. A., & Nieuwenhuis, S. (2004). The role of medial frontal cortex in cognitive control. *Science*, 306, 443-447.

Service, E. (1992). Phonology, working memory, and foreign- language learning. *Quarterly Journal of Experimental Psychology*, 45A, 21-50.

Shipstead, Z., Redick, T. S., & Engle, R. W. (2010). Does working memory training generalize? *Psychologica Belgica*, 50, 245-276.

Swets, B., Desmet, T., Hambrick, D. Z., & Ferreira, F. (2007). The role of working memory in syntactic ambiguity resolution: a psychometric approach. *Journal of Experimental Psychology: General*, 136, 64-81.

Szmalec, A., Duyck, W., Vandierendonck, A., Barberá Mata, A., & Page, M. P. A. (2009). The Hebb repetition effect as a laboratory analogue of novel word learning. *Quarterly Journal of Experimental Psychology*, 62, 435-443.

Szmalec, A., Loncke, M., Page, M., & Duyck, W. (2011). Order or disorder? Impaired Hebb learning in dyslexia. *Journal of Experimental Psychology: Learning, Memory, and Cognition*, 37, 1270-1279.

Szmalec, A., Verbruggen, F., Vandierendonck, A., & Kemps, E. (2011). Control of interference during working memory updating. *Journal of Experimental Psychology: Human Perception and Performance*, 37, 137-151.

Vallar, G., & Baddeley, A. D. (1984). Fractionation of working memory: neuropsychological evidence for a phonological short-term store. *Journal of Verbal Learning and Verbal Behaviour*, 23, 151-161.

Van Assche, E., Duyck, W., Hartsuiker, R. J., & Diependaele, K. (2009). Does bilingualism change native-language reading? Cognate effects in sentence context. *Psychological Science*, 20, 923-927.

Vandierendonck, A., & Szmalec, A. (eds.) (2011). *Spatial Working Memory*. Hove: Psychology Press.

Vejnović, D., Milin, P., & Zdravković, S. (2010). Effects of proficiency and age of language acquisition on working memory performance in bilinguals. *Psihologija*, 43, 219-232.

Wang, Y., Xue, G., Chen, C., Xue, F., & Dong, Q. (2007). Neural basis of asymmetric language switching in second-language learners: an ER-fMRI study. *NeuroImage*, 35, 862-870.

Waters, G. S., & Caplan, D. (1996). The capacity theory of sentence comprehension: critique of Just and Carpenter (1992). *Psychological Review*, 103, 761-772.

Whitney, C., & Cornelissen, P. (2005). Letter-position encoding and dyslexia. *Journal of Research in Reading*, 28, 274-301.

4 Working memory in simultaneous interpreters

Teresa M. Signorelli and Loraine Obler

Abstract

Simultaneous interpretation – the continuous, immediate, oral translation from one language to another – permits researchers to consider bilingual processing in real-life professional situations. The task is physically and cognitively demanding, taking years to master. Most professional interpreters receive considerable graduate-level training following a rigorous selection process which requires expertise in three or more languages and skills in a range of other cognitive abilities. Working memory – the ability to store and process incoming information verbatim for a brief period – has been posited as a cognitive skill heavily called upon throughout the simultaneous interpretation process. Since the brain's structure and function are influenced by experience, and working memory is considered crucial to interpretation, it has been postulated that simultaneous interpreters may have better working memory skills than non-interpreters. The evidence in the literature has been contradictory, however. A number of studies indicate superior working memory for interpreters relative to non-interpreters, while others do not. This chapter weighs the data in support of working memory advantages for interpreters against that suggesting no difference between the two groups, concluding that the strength of the arguments favors greater working memory skills in interpreters.

Simultaneous interpretation provides a platform to study bilingual processing under high-stress situations. Only relatively high-proficiency bilinguals (generally, multilinguals) can serve as simultaneous interpreters, and the task itself requires that both languages be available at all times. While it is not a task that any bilingual can naturally do at a professional level, those who are expert in it provide us with a window

We thank the following individuals for their input at various stages on this and related projects: Henk Haarmann, Barbara Köpke, Kilian Seeber, Barbara Moser-Mercer, Miriam Shlesinger and Elise Wagner.

into the cognitive underpinnings of bilingual language comprehension and production. Most prominent among the cognitive processes that have been studied in interpreters is working memory (WM), which is the focus of the current chapter.

In simultaneous interpreting, an auditory message in a source language is orally translated into a target language as the message continues. Since word-by-word translation would reduce meaning substantially, the focus instead is on providing the meaning of the message. The simultaneous interpreting process taxes WM in that the interpreter must concurrently keep input in mind until a sufficient amount permits the interpreter to comprehend it, translate it, and produce a response quickly. Some researchers maintain that interpreters have better WM as a result of their extensive training and practice in the task of simultaneous interpreting (e.g., Darò, 1994). There is inconsistent evidence in the literature, however, as to whether or not interpreters actually have better WM skills than non-interpreter multilinguals (non-interpreters). In this chapter, we will review the literature on WM and propose reasons for the discrepancies in the literature. Our goal is to consider what the study of WM in simultaneous interpreters tells us about memory in bilingual and multilingual speakers.

Working memory

WM is the cognitive system that stores and processes information over brief periods of time. It contrasts with long-term memory, which can be thought of as permanent knowledge. Baddeley (2000) describes three main components of WM (see Figure 4.1). This model includes an attention-allocating system, known as the central executive, and two subordinate systems. The central executive is a regulatory mechanism that controls information flow in WM, information retrieval from other memory systems, and information storage and processing in WM. Some scholars think of it as part of the executive-function systems that have been reported to be particularly strong in older bilinguals and multilinguals (see Hilchey & Klein, 2011, for a review of the complexities of this literature, however). One subsystem of WM, the visuospatial sketchpad, processes visual and spatial information, so we do not address it here. The other subsystem that we do address is the phonological loop, which manages verbal information. The phonological loop consists of a phonological store where information is held for about two seconds before it begins to decay. The second component of the phonological

```
┌─────────────────────────────────────────────────────────┐
│              Central Executive                          │
│       (Controls information flow & retrieval)           │
│                                                         │
│   ┌──────────────────────┐   ┌──────────────────────┐   │
│   │  Phonological Loop   │   │   Episodic Buffer    │   │
│   │                      │   │                      │   │
│   │ A storage │   An     │   │ A limited-capacity   │   │
│   │ process   │articulation  │ semantic storage &   │   │
│   │ maintains │ process  │   │ processing system    │   │
│   │ information│refreshes│   │                      │   │
│   │ for about 2│information  │                      │   │
│   │ seconds   │via subvocal  │                      │   │
│   │ before    │articulation  │                      │   │
│   │ decaying  │         │   │                      │   │
│   └──────────────────────┘   └──────────────────────┘   │
│ Adapted from Baddeley (2000)                            │
└─────────────────────────────────────────────────────────┘
```

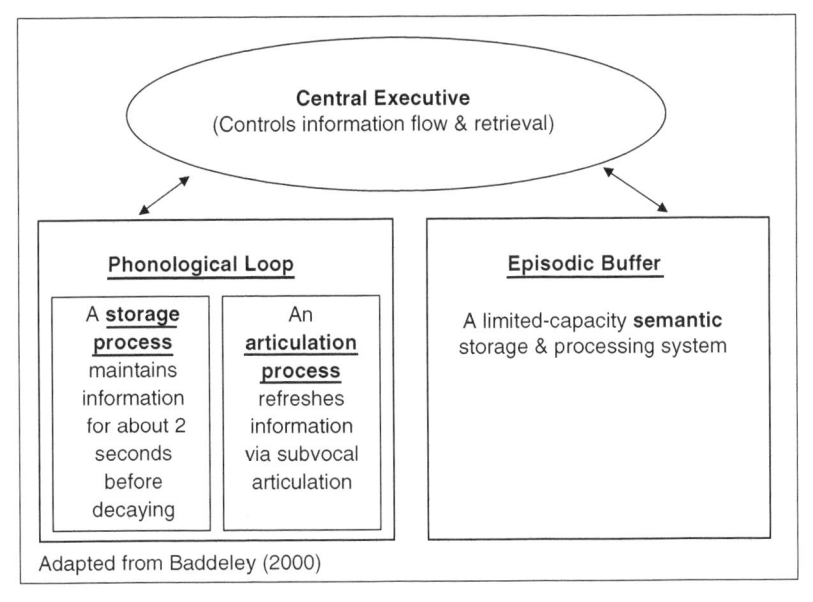

Figure 4.1 Verbal working memory across the literature

loop is a rehearsal process that refreshes information in the store via subvocal articulation.

A relatively new component to the Baddeley (2000) model is the episodic buffer. The buffer is a limited-capacity storage system that integrates various types of information, such as visual and phonological information, to provide recall for the gist of a message. This is important since many verbal WM tasks involve visual stimuli (e.g., participants may read lists of sentences or words). Similar to the components of the phonological loop, the episodic buffer is controlled by the central executive. The central executive accesses the episodic buffer consciously and influences its contents by attending to an information source (e.g., long-term memory or the phonological loop). The episodic buffer was added to the model to account for the recall and processing of prose (i.e., verbal information beyond the capacity limitations of the phonological loop).

The dissociation of the components of WM is seen in their independent breakdown in brain damage and in different regions of activation in brain-imaging studies (see Martin, Shelton, & Yaffee, 1994, regarding brain damage and Crosson et al., 1999, regarding brain regions). It is also seen in behavioral studies on healthy individuals.

Haarmann and colleagues, for example, demonstrated the dissociation of semantic WM from other forms of working and long-term memory with their Conceptual Span Test (Haarmann, Davelaar, & Usher, 2003; Haarmann & Usher, 2001), and semantic-category cued recall (Haarmann & Usher, 2001). They found that word-length effects (i.e., better recall for shorter relative to longer words) that are associated with phonological-loop function were absent in cued recall for semantic information. This suggests that semantic-category cued recall invokes phonological rehearsal strategies to a lesser degree than do overt phonological tasks (e.g., serial-order cued recall).

Baddeley (2000) proposes specific components of WM that account for a variety of behavioral phenomena noted in WM tasks, such as the recency (better recall of list-final items), primacy (better recall of list-initial items), and word-length effects. The Baddeley model, in particular, explains WM effects for lists of information, which has been the focus in the simultaneous interpreting literature to date and will be the primary focus of this review.

In summary, there is ample evidence of the modularity of phonological and semantic information in WM from a range of literature. There is also a distinction between phonological and semantic information in the simultaneous interpreting process. Phonological information must be retained until semantic processing of the clause in question is assured. We find the Baddeley model (2000) useful to help us understand how WM differences are seen in some studies and not in others.

WM in interpreters: evidence from the literature

Many of the studies that have looked at WM in interpreters have used measures of memory span that reflect WM capacity. These studies are summarized in Table 4.1.

There are two basic types of span measure, those that use words and those that use sentences. In word-span tasks, WM capacity is established as the maximum number of items an individual is able to repeat back immediately following presentation of a list of words. Sentence-span tasks are also referred to as phrase- or reading-span tasks. These tasks determine capacity in terms of the number of sentence-final words an individual can recall from presented sets of sentences. Word-span measures are typically considered to be representative of phonological-loop function and typically reveal primacy, recency, and word-length effects. Recall that the phonological-loop functions to store and refresh

Table 4.1 Summary of the literature

Key for word-stimulus papers
1 = Relative to what is reported in the general span literature
2 = Pattern of superior interpreter performance
3 = Scores not reported, so pattern direction judgment cannot be made
4 = Student interpreters significantly better. Professionals had a pattern in the direction of better performance relative to controls.
5 = For second-, not first-year interpreting students
PSI = Professional simultaneous interpreter
NIM = Non-interpreter multilingual

Article	Participants	Language of testing	Context	Auditory stimuli	Print stimuli	On par performance	Superior interpreter performance
Word-span Tasks							
Darò & Fabbro (1994)	Student interpreters	L1/L2	Normal	Digits			✓[1]
Chincotta & Underwood (1998)	Student interpreters, NIMs	L1/L2	Normal / Articulation suppression		Digits	✓[2] ✓[2]	
Padilla et al. (1995)	PSIs, student interpreters, NIMs	NA	Normal	Digits			✓
Christoffels et al. (2006)	Interpreters, bilingual students, English teachers	L1/L2	Normal		Words		✓

Table 4.1 (cont.)

Article	Participants	Language of testing	Context	Auditory stimuli	Print stimuli	On par performance	Superior interpreter performance
Köpke & Nespoulous (2006)	PSIs, student interpreters, multilinguals, monolinguals	L1	Normal	Words		✓[2]	
Tzou et al. (2011)	Student interpreters, NIMs	L1/L2	Normal	Digits			✓[5]

Word-list Recall

Free Recall

Article	Participants	Language of testing	Context	Auditory stimuli	Print stimuli	On par performance	Superior interpreter performance
Padilla et al. (1995)	PSIs, student interpreters, NIMs	NA	Normal Articulation suppression		Words	✓[2]	✓
Köpke & Nespoulous (2006)	PSIs, student interpreters, multilinguals, monolinguals	L1	Normal Articulation suppression	Words		✓[3]	✓[4]

Final Recall					
Padilla et al. (1995)	PSIs, student interpreters, NIMs	NA	Normal Articulation suppression	Words	✓
Cued Recall					
Köpke & Nespoulous (2006)	PSIs, student interpreters, multilinguals, monolinguals	L1	Normal (Non-articulation suppression)	Words Phonological cues	✓[3]
				Words Semantic cues	✓[2]
Signorelli et al. (2011)	PSIs, NIMs	L2		Words Phonological cues	✓[2]
				Words Semantic cues	✓[2]

Related Word-Stimulus Tasks

Non-word Repetition

Signorelli et al. (2011)	PSIs, NIMs	L2	Normal	Words	✓

Table 4.1 (*Cont.*)

Key for phrase-stimulus papers
1 = New students had just begun interpretation study
2 = Pattern for better performance with more interpreting experience
3 = Only student interpreters had significantly better performance than controls. Students and professionals did not differ.
PSI = Professional simultaneous interpreter
NIM = Non-interpreter multilingual

Phrase Span
(This is a collective term. Different studies also used labels such as reading and listening span)

Article	Participants	Language of testing	Auditory stimuli	Print stimuli	On par performance	Superior interpreter performance
Padilla et al. (1995)	PSIs, student interpreters, NIMs,	NA		✓		✓
Liu et al. (2004)	PSIs, advanced student interpreters, new students[1]	L2	✓		✓[2]	
Christoffels et al. (2006)	Interpreters, bilingual students, English teachers	L1/L2		✓		✓
Köpke & Nespoulous (2006)	PSIs, student interpreters, multilinguals, monolinguals	L1	✓		✓[3]	✓[3]
Signorelli et al. (2011)	PSIs, NIMs	L2		✓		✓
Tzou et al. (2011)	Student interpreters and NIMs	L1/L2		✓		✓

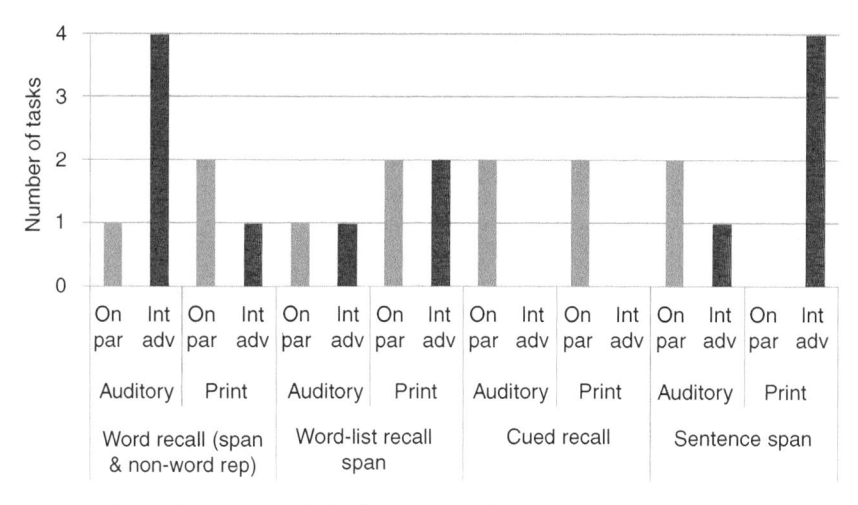

Figure 4.2 WM in interpreters vs. non-interpreters across the literature

Note: Int adv stands for Interpreter Advantage.

verbatim speech-sound information in WM. Sentence-span tasks generally reflect complex storage-and-processing in WM.

In what follows, we consider the data by grouping the studies into those that support WM superiority in interpreters over non-interpreters, in the first section, followed by those that provide evidence for equal WM skills across these two groups. The literature on WM in interpreters is small. Many of the studies contain multiple experiments with mixed results within an article. As a result, the reader will find a number of the same articles mentioned in both the section supporting superiority for interpreters and in the section supporting parity of WM between interpreters and non-interpreters. Within each of these sections we secondarily organize the studies by stimulus type (i.e., word-based stimuli and sentence-based stimuli) as performance for these different stimulus types turns out to help explain the somewhat conflicting results (see Figure 4.2 for an overview of the findings in the literature).

Evidence of superior interpreter performance over non-interpreters

Word-list stimuli There is evidence in the WM literature employing word-list stimuli that suggests that interpreters have better phonological-loop function than non-interpreters. The first three studies we include use numbers as the stimuli to measure WM in a task called "digit span." They report higher than average digit spans for interpreters relative to non-interpreters. Darò and Fabbro (1994) studied a group of 24 student interpreters as they participated in a series of digit-span tasks. The student interpreters ranged in age between 22 and 27 (average age 24.5) and had been in simultaneous interpreting training between 12 and 60 months (average 29 months) for 10 to 40 hours a week. They were described as highly proficient in their native Italian as well as two other languages among a set of four: German, English, Spanish, and French. The authors divided the participants into two groups according to the languages in which they worked. Group A performed the task in Italian and Group B performed the task in English. No details were reported regarding how group placement was determined.

The authors presented strings composed of digits from 1–9 binaurally over headsets. The series began with two sets of three digits, then two sets of four digits, up to, two sets of nine digits. Participants immediately recalled the numbers in the order they had been presented after the end of each set. The task yielded a span of 8.38 for Group A and a span of 8.90 for Group B. The combined average span was 8.65. These figures are higher than the reported average of seven digits in non-interpreters (Darò, 1994) and support the proposal that interpreters have better phonological-loop function than non-interpreters.

A second digit-span experiment showing superior interpreter WM performance is that of Padilla *et al.* (1995). They studied four groups of bilingual participants with varied experience in simultaneous interpreting. One group of ten participants included practicing interpreters, five were recent graduates of the School of Translators and Interpreters, and five had been practicing in the field for about five years. These individuals had a mean age of 30 years. A second group of ten participants were third-year interpreting students described only as having some simultaneous interpreting training. A third group of ten participants were students in the second year of their program, who had had training in translation (of written materials), but not simultaneous interpreting. The fourth group of ten participants consisted of bilinguals with no formal translation or interpreting experience. Age information was not reported for the student groups. In this study, too, no other information regarding background history of the participants was provided.

As in Darò and Fabbro's (1994) study, the participants in Padilla *et al.* (1995) listened to sets of digits and were asked to recall the digits in order of presentation. The task commenced with three sequences of four digits. Each set of sequences increased by one digit so that the second set had three sequences of five digits. Sets were presented in these increasing sizes until a participant was unable to recall the digits in order. The result was that the interpreter group had significantly longer digit spans than the other groups. Although the group digit-span means were not directly reported, graphed data indicated that the interpreter group had spans of just over seven digits on average, whereas the other groups had spans of just over six digits. The authors suggested that the interpreter advantage was due to interpretation training, since the second-year students with training only in translation performed comparably to the non-interpreter groups. The authors, however, do not comment on their third-year interpreting students, who are described only as having received some simultaneous interpretation training. It is possible that the amount of training for this group may not have been sufficient to yield the differences in memory skills that other studies find.

Indeed, the digit-span experiment of Tzou, Eslami, Chen, and Vaid (2011) is just such a study, showing better performance for second-year interpreter students relative to first-year students and non-interpreters. These authors compared 20 student interpreters (11 first-year and 9 second-year students) to 16 non-interpreter graduate students matched for education and language history. The participants ranged in age from 20 to 32 years, were native speakers of Mandarin, spoke English as a second language, and had been living in the United States for about three years. The researchers presented single-digit numbers recorded in both Mandarin and English. Stimulus sets began with three sets of four and increased incrementally as the digits from all three sets were recalled correctly through three sets of ten digits. It is unclear why Tzou *et al.* found an advantage for interpreters in the second year of study, while Padilla *et al.* did not. We know that training in interpretation only started in the second year for the participants in Padilla *et al.*; perhaps it started in the first year, or was more intensive, for the students in the population of Tzou *et al.*

Consistent with the digit-span single-word stimuli mentioned above, studies using non-digit word stimuli also found interpreter superiority. Christoffels, de Groot, and Kroll (2006) looked at interpreters and highly proficient bilinguals. The first of two control groups consisted of 39 Dutch–English bilingual university students who spoke Dutch as a first language. All had at least six years of formal education in English as a second language and used English textbooks for their university coursework. The second control group consisted of 15 Dutch teachers of English. The teachers had an average of 19 years' experience teaching English in the Netherlands at the higher levels of secondary education. The experimental group of interpreters also included native Dutch speakers who used English as one of their languages of interpretation. The interpreters, teachers, and students had mean ages of 48.5, 43.5, and 21.1, respectively.

The Christoffels *et al.* (2006) participants saw words one at a time on a computer screen in sets of three to ten words. They were then asked to recall each set in order after the presentation of the final word in its list. The task was executed in both Dutch and English. The results revealed statistically superior performance by the interpreters over both groups of non-interpreters. The interpreter group achieved word spans of 5.00 and 5.92 in Dutch and English, respectively. The students achieved word spans of 3.59 and 3.05 in Dutch and English, respectively. The English teachers achieved word spans of 3.80 and 2.40 in Dutch and English, respectively. The significant differences lay between the interpreters and the other two groups.

Superior interpreter performance in WM relative to non-interpreters is also reported in a task involving word-list recall. Word-list recall is a task that is somewhat similar to span measures like those mentioned above. A list of words is presented and items from the list must be recalled. Such tasks especially call upon the phonological loop that stores and refreshes speech-sound information in WM. Superior phonological-loop function in interpreters was supported by the Padilla *et al.* (1995) study mentioned earlier in another set of experiments that employed list recall with articulation suppression, a method commonly employed to assess storage in the phonological loop. This method assesses the storage component of the phonological loop because subvocal rehearsal of the items to be remembered is prevented by participants being required to repeat a nonsense syllable so that information in WM cannot be refreshed.

Padilla *et al.* (1995) ran their experimental groups mentioned earlier in a series of word-list recall tasks with articulation suppression. In these tasks, participants silently read three lists of 16 printed words, presented at the rate of one word every three seconds. They articulated the nonsense syllable "*bla*" repeatedly during list presentation. In a free-recall condition of this articulation-suppression task, participants recalled each word list at the conclusion of list presentation in any order they chose. In a final-recall condition, participants recalled as many words as possible after all three lists had been presented.

In these articulation-suppression recall tasks, the interpreter group recalled significantly more words than the non-interpreter and novice groups in both free and final recall. The means were not reported, but the figures indicated that the interpreter group recalled approximately 55 words compared to the other groups, whose performances approached only 40 words. This suggests that interpreters have better WM skills than non-interpreters, at least when the rehearsal process of the phonological loop is effectively removed from WM function.

(Note that Padilla *et al.*, 1995, ran this task without articulation suppression, as well. The results of this second condition are discussed in the following section on performance parity between interpreters and non-interpreters.)

Another word-based study involving lists of words with articulation suppression is that of Köpke and Nespoulous (2006). These authors found a result similar to Padilla *et al.* (1995) when comparing professional simultaneous interpreters, student interpreters, bilingual speakers, and monolingual speakers. However, they used auditory stimuli, in contrast to Padilla *et al.*'s (1995) print stimuli mentioned just above. Köpke and Nespoulous' professional interpreter group consisted of 21 individuals who ranged in age from 29 to 61 years (mean age 44.4 years) and had between 4 and 35 years of interpreting experience. The student interpreter group consisted of 18 individuals, aged 23 to 38 years (mean age 26.2), who were in their second year of studies and had just begun their training in simultaneous interpreting. There was one control group that consisted of 20 bi- and multilingual speakers who ranged in age from 27 to 63 years (mean age 44.7 years) and a second control group of 20 monolingual speakers who ranged in age from 18 to 26 (mean age 21.5). All testing was done in French, the dominant language of all the participants. All the multilingual participants were highly proficient in at least English and sometimes other languages as well. No other specifics were given as to what the languages were, how they were used, or how they were acquired.

In the Köpke and Nespoulous (2006) free-recall task, the participants heard word lists of 12 items while repeating the syllable "*bla.*" At the end of a list, they recalled the words in any order. Significant group differences were reported. Contrary to the patterns in other studies, the student interpreters had the best performance (mean of 5.24), followed by the professional interpreters (mean of 4.79), the monolingual non-interpreters (mean of 4.41), and then the multilingual non-interpreters (mean of 4.37). Thus, these authors reported that the novice interpreter group outperformed the experts and that the experts outperformed the two non-interpreter control groups. (Köpke and Nespoulous also ran their free-recall task without articulation suppression in addition to a number of other tasks. These findings will be discussed in the section on performance parity.)

Another type of task we include in our review of word stimuli that yielded superior interpreter performance in WM is non-word repetition. Non-words, having no meaning, permit the study of processing of speech-sound information independent of semantic information.

This allows for a more accurate picture of speech-sound processing. Signorelli, Haarmann, and Obler (2011) found superior performance for interpreters over non-interpreters in a non-word repetition task. The interpreter group consisted of 22 individuals ranging in age from 35 to 57 years and interpreting experience of eight months to 42 years, with a mean of 13 years' experience. The non-interpreter group consisted of 17 individuals, aged 32 to 64 years, with no interpreting experience. All testing was performed in English, which was no participant's first language but which was, for each, a language in which they were highly proficient. The participants all began learning English at comparable ages and had similar language experience with English. The participants performed the non-word repetition subtest of the Comprehensive Test of Phonological Processing (CTOPP) (Wagner, Torgesen, & Rashotte, 1999). They repeated 18 non-words, one at a time, that increased in length from one to seven syllables. The results showed significantly stronger non-word repetition performance for interpreters, who performed with 54 percent accuracy relative to the non-interpreters who performed with 43 percent accuracy, again indicating that interpreters have better phonological WM than non-interpreters.

In summary, a series of WM experiments using word-based stimuli reported that interpreters outperformed non-interpreters. The simple memory-storage advantages for interpreters seen in the regular span tasks are further substantiated by the tasks employing articulation suppression that prohibit phonological rehearsal to refresh information stored in WM. Advantages for interpreters relative to non-interpreters were seen for stimuli that were both auditory and print in nature. While these findings support those who argue that interpreters have better WM skills than non-interpreters, there is another set of word-based studies that suggest there is no difference on such tasks and, thus, in WM. These will be addressed in the parity section later in the present chapter. First, we turn to the data for superior WM in interpreters from experimental tasks that have used sentence-based stimuli.

Sentence stimuli As mentioned above, sentences are also used in span tasks to assess the complex storage-and-processing component of WM. Padilla *et al.* (1995) ran their four groups of participants in a reading-span task. The task was a Spanish adaptation of Daneman and Carpenter's (1980) reading-span task. Reading span is a complex storage-and-processing task in contrast to the simple storage-span task of word recall. Participants read sets of sentences presented one at a time, then recall as many final words from as many sentences as possible from a set. The number of sentences per set increases as the task progresses. The maximum number of final words recalled indicates participants' phrase span. Padilla *et al.*'s (1995) interpreter group had significantly longer reading spans than the other groups. Figure data for reading span indicated spans of five items for the interpreter group and spans of just under four items for the other groups. Again, as with their digit-span task, the second-year translation students (without simultaneous interpreting training) performed comparably to the non-interpreter group. Thus, in this sentence-span task, professional interpreters outperformed both groups of interpreting students and multilingual controls. This suggests that better complex storage-and-processing skills within WM in interpreters relative to non-interpreters manifests only after a certain amount of interpreting experience.

The Christoffels *et al.* (2006) study mentioned earlier in the word-span section also found superior interpreter performance in a reading-span task. Their participants read aloud 42 English sentences in sets of two, three, four, and five, recalling the final word of each sentence aloud at the end of each set. Significant group differences manifested, with the interpreters outperforming the non-interpreters. The interpreter group achieved reading-span scores of 35.39 and 34.54 (out of a possible 42) in Dutch and English, respectively. The teacher and student groups achieved reading-span scores of 32.06 and 30.73 in Dutch and 34.00 and 31.13 in English. Thus, these data also support superior WM in terms of complex storage-and-processing in interpreters over non-interpreters.

The results of Christoffels *et al.* (2006) were substantiated in a close replication by Signorelli *et al.* (2011), the study discussed with respect to its non-word span results above. Using the Christoffels' *et al.* English stimulus list and methodology, Signorelli and colleagues tested 19 interpreters and 19 non-interpreters in their highly proficient, non-L1 English. On this task, like the non-word recall task, interpreters had significantly better performance (86%) than non-interpreters (81%). Superiority for interpreters with sentence-based stimuli was also supported in the Tzou *et al.* (2011) study. They found superior performance in the combined performance of their first- and second-year interpreting students relative to non-interpreter graduate students in a reading-span task. After reading each set of sentences, which increased from two to five sentences, participants wrote down the final word from each sentence. The group mean scores were 29.19, 34.73, and 34.11 for non-interpreters, first-year, and second-year interpreting students, respectively, in Chinese. The group means were 25.31, 28.18, and 31.78 for the groups, respectively, in English. Thus, evidence even with interpreting students, relative to professional interpreters, shows a WM advantage for interpreters over non-interpreters.

Another sentence-based task that shows an arguable interpreter advantage was found in a listening-span task in the Köpke and Nespoulous (2006) study discussed above. Their professional interpreters, student interpreters, multilinguals, and monolinguals listened to spoken sets of sentences. This auditory sentence task contrasts with the sentence-stimulus tasks mentioned above, which used written stimuli. The Köpke and Nespoulous participants repeated each sentence and were asked to remember the last word. After a set was presented, the participants were asked to recall the last word from each sentence in the order of presentation. The results indicated that the student interpreters had the highest mean score (4.54) followed by the professional interpreters (3.91), then bilingual (3.51), and monolingual controls (3.45). No difference emerged between the two interpreter groups; curiously, statistical significance was found only between the student-interpreter and the non-interpreter groups.

In summary, as with word-based tasks, tasks that involve sentence-based stimuli in memory-span tasks have shown an advantage for interpreters relative to non-interpreters. Thus, it is not only simple storage tasks with words that interpreters (or, in some cases, interpreting students) excel in, complex storage-and-processing tasks using sentences also show an interpreter advantage in WM. The studies above do not tell the whole story, however. The next set of data we review show that word-based (simple storage) and sentence-based (complex storage and processing) stimuli show parity of performance for interpreters and non-interpreters in WM skills.

Evidence of parity of WM skill in interpreters and non-interpreters

Among the studies that suggest there may be no WM differences between the groups, the reader will find the articles mentioned above. In these studies more than one experiment was included, and mixed results were seen across their several experiments, some showing superior performance by interpreters, others not (i.e., Christoffels *et al.*, 2006; Köpke & Nespoulous, 2006; Padilla *et al.*, 1995; Signorelli *et al.*, 2011; Tzou *et al.*, 2011). In this section, then, we discuss those articles again, along with articles by Chincotta and Underwood (1998) and Liu, Schallert, and Carroll (2004), which found no significant differences between interpreters and non-interpreters using similar tasks to those used in the studies that did find group differences. After reviewing this set of articles, in our final section of the current chapter, we consider why such apparently conflicting findings may have arisen.

Word-list stimuli supporting parity   As mentioned in the previous section on interpreter superiority in WM, Padilla *et al.* (1995) ran their four participant groups on free- and final-recall word-list tasks. In the articulation-suppression condition, when forced to repeat *"bla"* during stimulus presentation, interpreters outperformed non-interpreters in their ability to recall the words presented. However, when participants simply listened to the lists and then recalled them, either immediately (free recall) or after a delay (final recall), as described above, no group differences manifested in the number of words recalled. The interpreter superiority disappeared. This finding – along with the fact that virtually all studies that employed articulation suppression reported interpreter advantages – suggests that only when the system is stressed, interpreter superiority in WM is evident.

Results of some digit-span tasks also appear to demonstrate parity of performance. Contrary to Padilla *et al.*'s (1995) and Tzou *et al.*'s (2011) digit-span results of significant group differences using auditory stimuli, Chincotta and Underwood's (1998) findings indicate no significant differences in memory span for printed digits between student interpreters and non-interpreters. Chincotta and Underwood compared 12 student interpreters from the University of Turku, with a minimum of 100 hours of experience interpreting between Finnish and English, to a group of 12 Finnish English majors. The participants were all described as Finnish dominant, Finnish–English bilinguals. No other information on language history or age was reported.

The participants saw four sets of digits presented one at a time, sequentially on a monitor. Each set began with two series of two digits and then two series of three digits, increasing by one digit every series up to two series of 13 digits. Following a prompt tone at the end of each series, the participants orally recalled as many numbers as possible in both Finnish and English conditions. The stimuli were also presented in normal and suppressed conditions. In the suppressed condition, participants articulated the nonsense syllable *"la-la"* continually, beginning four seconds prior to the initial stimulus presentation and ending four seconds after presentation of the last digit stimulus. The results indicated no significant differences between groups in mean digit span in either language. Thus, this is the one articulation-suppression study that finds no difference in WM skills between interpreters and non-interpreters with printed digit stimuli.

Other evidence of word-list stimuli demonstrating equal WM performance between interpreters and non-interpreters was found in a different task from the one discussed above, in the Köpke and Nespoulous (2006) study. The authors, as mentioned earlier, compared professional simultaneous interpreters, student interpreters, multilingual speakers, and monolingual speakers. Participants performed auditory word-span tasks with real words, non-words, semantically similar words, and phonologically related words. In the span tasks, participants listened to word lists four to 12 words in length and repeated them back in order as best they could. Results of these span tasks revealed no significant differences across the groups. Also, as mentioned, participants performed a free-recall task without articulation suppression. Recall that in the articulation-suppression condition, group differences were found. Without articulation suppression, however, Köpke and Nespoulous, like Padilla *et al.* (1995) and Chincotta and Underwood (1998), did not find significant group differences.

Cued recall is another type of word-based task distinct from the others reviewed so far, in that it is used in these studies to dissociate phonological from semantic WM. In Köpke and Nespoulous' (2006) phonological cued-recall condition, after listening to the word list, the participants were given a probe word and had to report if the probe word rhymed with one of the words in the list by responding "yes" or "no." In the category condition, participants had to report if the probe word belonged to the same semantic category as one of the words in the list. No group differences were noted in the phonological condition. The category condition revealed group differences by language background only. The multilingual groups all performed better than the monolingual group. There was a tendency, nonetheless, for the interpreter groups to achieve higher task scores than the non-interpreter groups. The phonological scores were not reported, but the category scores indicated that the novice interpreters obtained the highest mean score (9.2) followed by the expert interpreters (8.49), the bilingual controls (8.2), and the monolingual controls (7.18). The authors do not report significance levels for these data, so it is not known if this tendency is an actual pattern that might become significant with more power. The tendency is mentioned here because this phenomenon of non-significant findings, but better absolute performance by interpreter groups, can be found often in the literature that purports to show no differences between interpreters and non-interpreters or interpreting students.

Interpreters and non-interpreters also performed a similar cued-recall task in the Signorelli *et al.* (2011) study. In this task, participants silently read word lists and recalled a specified word depending on phonological (word order) or semantic (category) information. Participants read lists of words, six words in length, and were asked to recall the word that came after the cue word in the list (the phonological condition) or the word that belonged to the semantic category of the cue words (the semantic condition). Mean scores were 62.80 and 50.91 for younger and older interpreters, respectively, and 56.73 and 59.90 for younger and older non-interpreters, respectively. No significant group differences manifested between the interpreter and non-interpreter groups, suggesting equal WM skills for these two groups. Younger interpreters, however, showed a trend toward better performance than the other participants, as indicated by a marginally significant interaction of age and profession.

In summary, while a number of studies that report superior performance for interpreters on word-based WM tasks were reported earlier in the chapter, the current section has reminded us that "no difference" findings can also be found in the literature. Indeed, these kinds of findings have been reported in several instances for the same participants for whom significant differences were reported when using different tasks. In the next section, we extend our discussion of a lack of statistical group differences in WM to sentence-based stimulus tasks.

Sentence stimuli supporting parity In addition to tasks using word-list stimuli, performance on two tasks using sentences also failed to find differences in WM performance between interpreters and non-interpreters. Recall that the Köpke and Nespoulous (2006) sentence listening-span task mentioned in the section on interpreter advantage reported that, while the student interpreters performed significantly better than the non-interpreters, the professional interpreters did not. Liu *et al.* (2004) also conducted a listening-span study that included 11 professional interpreters who had at least one year of training and two years of professional experience. The interpreters were compared to two groups of student interpreters. One group of 11 students had a year and a half of simultaneous interpreting training. The other group of 11 students was one month into simultaneous interpreting study. The participants were described as having Mandarin as an L1 and English as an L2 or having native-like proficiency in both languages.

Liu *et al.*'s (2004) phrase-span task is another adaptation of Daneman and Carpenter's (1980) reading-span task. Instead of reading, their participants listened to a series of unrelated spoken English sentences 13 to 16 words in length. Each series consisted of five sets of sentences, beginning with two sentences and progressing to five sentences by an increase of one sentence per series over the course of testing. At the end of each set, the participants wrote down as many of the final words from the sentences as they could remember. The number of final words recalled indicated a participant's phrase span. Liu *et al.* found no significant differences in phrase span across groups. Professionals tended to achieve higher scores than students and the students with more interpreting experience achieved higher scores than those with less experience, however. Mean scores for professional interpreters, advanced students, and beginning students were 3.3, 2.91, and 2.59, respectively. Again, here we see the pattern that, while differences were not significant, the absolute scores were in the direction predicted if experience in interpreting makes a difference.

In summary, the literature on WM in interpreters includes a set of experimental tasks that demonstrates statistically significant superiority of WM in interpreters over interpreting students and non-interpreters (with a single study showing student interpreters having the advantage over the other two groups), while a smaller second set does not. The latter set, however, often shows absolute differences in the direction of interpreter (student or professional) superiority in WM. Thus, one may speculate that the "no difference" findings may reflect a camouflaged effect secondary to the relatively small sample sizes, the range of inter-individual differences among participants and differences in methodology. Moreover, the fact that there were studies in which the same participants either demonstrated group differences or not, depending on the nature of the stimuli and the task (e.g., Köpke & Nespoulous, 2006; Padilla *et al.*, 1995; Signorelli *et al.*, 2011), suggests that task differences are crucial in determining whether group differences will manifest. In the next section we discuss the aspects of tasks across the different studies that may contribute to the differences in outcome across studies.

Why the contradictory findings?

Methodological variation

Procedural differences may account for the discrepant findings across groups. First, we will consider *timing differences* across studies. The free- and final-recall tasks of the Padilla *et al.* (1995) study include a delay in recall, for example. Thus, they do not depend as heavily on phonological information or WM as the immediate repetition involved in the other span tasks described. Indeed, this procedural difference may even contribute to the discrepancy within the Padilla *et al.* study. Recall that a significant group difference was obtained in immediate unsuppressed recall of digits but not in delayed unsuppressed recall of words.

Similarly, *interstimulus-interval differences* may also account for the difference in the free-recall findings between Padilla *et al.* (1995), who presented lists of 16 words, and Köpke and Nespoulous (2006), who presented lists of 12 words. The time delay for the Padilla *et al.* stimuli (3000 milliseconds) was more than twice that of Köpke and Nespoulous (1250 ms) (Köpke & Signorelli, 2011). *Manner of recall* is another delay concern that may have contributed to the discrepancy. In sentence-based tasks, those studies that had participants recall information orally (i.e., Christoffels *et al.*, 2006; Köpke and Nespoulous, 2006; Signorelli *et al.*, 2011) reported group differences; those that had participants write out their responses (i.e., Liu *et al.*, 2004 and Tzou *et al.*, 2011) did not, presumably, since writing may add to the delay for later items recalled. Differences in *scoring and administration* may also give rise to inconsistency (see Köpke & Nespoulous, 2006; Köpke & Signorelli, 2011). Some researchers scored and credited mean list performance (e.g., Köpke & Nespoulous, 2006; Liu *et al.*, 2004; Padilla *et al.*, 1995). Others credited total number of words recalled (e.g., Christoffels *et al.*, 2006; Signorelli *et al.*, 2011). Köpke and Signorelli (2011) pointed out that the latter measure may be more sensitive.

Written versus auditory stimuli

If we look at the results in the literature in terms of the nature of the stimulus, performance patterns emerge. As can be seen if we break down the information in Figure 4.2 into Figures 4.3 and 4.4, tasks with written sentences show a clear advantage for interpreters. Of the four studies that included such stimuli, all evidenced statistically superior performance by interpreters (Padilla *et al.*, 1995; Christoffels *et al.*, 2006; Köpke & Nespoulous, 2006; and Signorelli *et al.*, 2011). What is interesting, of course, is that the sentence-reading tasks show such consistent superiority for the interpreters, while the task of being an interpreter involves no reading; input is all auditory. Some – perhaps most – interpreters take on translation work from written documents to complement their interpreting jobs. However, in such translation work, presumably, WM would not be stressed as one can always refer back to the materials one has worked on previously and review the manner in which one has translated them.

116 *Signorelli & Obler*

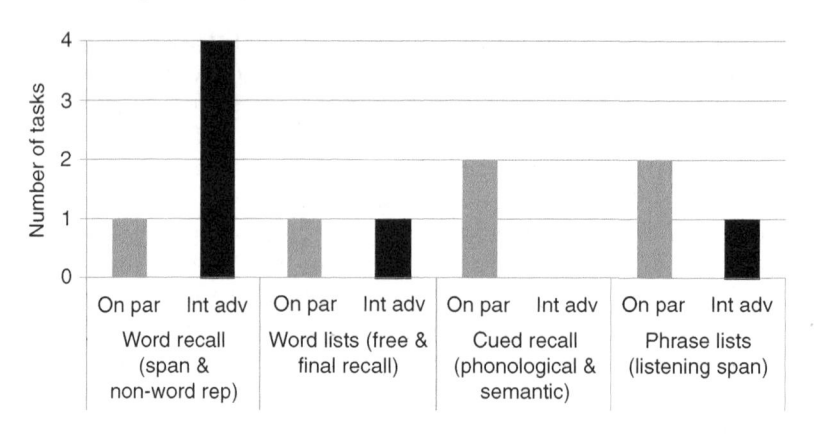

Figure 4.3 WM in interpreters vs. non-interpreters: auditory stimuli across the literature

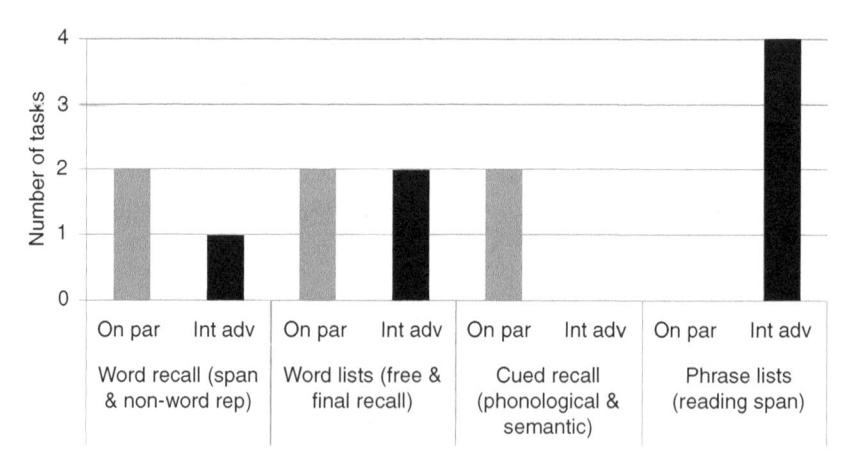

Figure 4.4 WM in interpreters vs. non-interpreters: print stimuli across the literature

Note: Int adv stands for Interpreter Advantage.

In any event, it is then curious that written single-word stimuli show a different pattern from written sentences in the direction of parity between interpreters and non-interpreters. Of the nine tasks that used printed-word stimuli, only three found that interpreters outperformed non-interpreters. This included the Padilla *et al.* (1995) free- and final-recall tasks under the condition of articulation suppression. The remaining six tasks, despite having absolute scores for interpreters in the direction of superiority, did not show statistically significant differences between interpreters and non-interpreters. These tasks included Chincotta and Underwood's (1998) digit-span tasks in both normal and articulation-suppression conditions, Padilla *et al.*'s (1995) free and final recall in normal (non-suppressed) conditions, and Signorelli *et al.*'s (2011) phonological and semantic cued-recall tasks.

Spoken sentences, like written words and unlike written sentences, reveal a pattern of parity between interpreters and non-interpreters. The two studies that used spoken-sentence stimuli mostly showed no statistical differences between interpreters and non-interpreters: this includes the listening-span task from Liu *et al.* (2004) and – for professional interpreters only – the listening-span task from Köpke and Nespoulous (2006). Because listening span is closer to the task that interpreters must use in their professional lives, it is surprising that it does not reveal WM differences between the interpreters and the groups to which they are compared. This may arise because single sentences are not the unit of the working interpreter; rather, extended prior context must be taken into account while interpreting a given sentence.

Spoken-word stimuli, however, revealed a pattern toward interpreter superiority, though not as strongly as printed sentences. Of the nine tasks that used spoken-word stimuli, four did not achieve statistical differences. Two of these, however, report absolute scores in the direction of interpreter superiority. These included the word-span, free-recall without articulation suppression, and the two cued-recall tasks from Köpke and Nespoulous's (2006) study. The remaining five spoken-word tasks evidenced statistically superior performance by interpreters. These included the digit-span tasks in Darò and Fabbro (1994), Padilla *et al.* (1995), and Tzou *et al.* (2011), the non-word repetition task in Signorelli *et al.* (2011), and the free-recall task in articulation suppression for student but not for professional interpreters (Köpke & Nespoulous, 2006).

In summary, interpreters tend to outperform non-interpreters with printed sentences and spoken words. The tendency toward parity seems to emerge in tasks with spoken sentences and written words. While these patterns are relatively clear, why they have unfolded this way is less so. There are, apparently, other factors contributing to the findings that we discuss in the following sections. In the section that follows, we focus on semantic aspects of the stimuli, most particularly, semantic weight.

Semantic weight of the stimulus

The nature of word-list stimuli in regard to their semantic characteristics and consequent cognitive processing outside WM should also be considered when attempting to account for varied findings in the literature. This is particularly important, for example, for the contradiction within the Padilla *et al.* (1995) study (i.e., significantly longer spans for interpreters than non-interpreters with words, but not digits). Assistance from long-term memory via stronger semantic relations among word stimuli that belong to a large, open set of options, compared to digits that come from a small, closed set of options, might also have contributed to the disparity.

Word stimuli have a greater number of semantic associations in long-term memory to facilitate recall relative to digits and non-words. The literature shows that in incidental or delayed recall, such as the free-recall task used in the Padilla *et al.* (1995) study, information is better recalled where salient semantic connections can be made compared to where few or no overt connections exist (e.g., Kroll & Stewart, 1994). This may explain why no group differences manifested with the word stimuli in the Padilla *et al.* study. Performance for the non-interpreter groups under normal as opposed to suppression conditions may have been facilitated by semantic connections, which may have resulted in a performance on par with that of the interpreters in the normal condition. The contribution from the semantic associations may have camouflaged a difference in phonological WM between non-interpreters and interpreters. Support from semantic information may not have persisted in the suppression condition where we saw a stronger WM performance in the interpreter group relative to that in the non-interpreters. This suggests the locus of superior performance for interpreters lies in the phonological loop.

Signorelli *et al.*'s (2011) findings with non-word repetition speak to the semantic weight issues in a different way. Having no semantic meaning, non-words in this study followed the phonological rules of English. The content of what interpreters interpret often involves proper names that do not have translation equivalents and contain essentially only phonological information, akin to non-words. It is possible that practice repeating proper names as part of their professional work may have given interpreters an advantage in non-word repetition, since, arguably, many proper names one hears are novel, and, thus, must be processed as non-words. If this is the case, one can see how it could result in this task being relatively practiced by the interpreters, more so than in the other groups, and might thus account for their enhanced performance in that study. That this task yields significant differences between interpreters and non-interpreters provides more evidence that the phonological loop, obligatory for the non-word repetition task, is a potential locus of WM superiority.

Small participant populations

Many of the studies surveyed here had small participant groups (i.e., ranging from 5 to 40 with a mean of 13). A small number (N) of participants may not yield sufficiently strong statistical power and may therefore compromise external validity. This presence of a small N is important to note since individual performance varied, presumably in all the studies, and there was a tendency for higher scores with increased levels of interpreting experience relative to less or no simultaneous interpreting experience across the reported studies. These tendencies might have become statistically significant had the groups been larger. Nonetheless, as Köpke and Signorelli (2011) note, lack of statistical strength need not be an issue since, in some instances, statistical superiority for interpreters was evident. Qualitative differences across participants, such as interpreting experience, they argue, may be more important than the quantitative ones when considering the contradictory results in the literature. Indeed, Liu *et al.* (2004) tested effect size because of their small group sizes. Finding that only 2 percent of the variability could be accounted for by group differences, the authors proposed that WM differences did not exist among their 12 participants.

Limited background information

Participant heterogeneity may have contributed to the varied findings. Consider the limited background information provided in many studies regarding language history. Pertinent information to collect and control for would include the manner in which languages were acquired, the order of language acquisition, the nature and degree of language use, and the phonological, orthographic, and morpho-syntactic nature of the languages that the participants know. The likely heterogeneity of multilingual participant groups may exacerbate the problems of a small N present in most studies.

Collecting such information is also important because these variables can influence language proficiency. Ascertaining proficiency is important because competency in a particular language influences WM performance in that language. We know, for example, that WM capacity measured by non-word repetition is related to proficiency as measured by vocabulary knowledge in the language of testing (Thorn & Gathercole, 2001). The importance of the proficiency issue regarding interpreters has also been demonstrated. Recall that the findings in the Christoffels *et al.* (2006) study revealed significant differences between interpreters and non-interpreters in sentence-span tasks when performing in their second language (L2), but not their first language (L1), despite high L2 proficiency in both groups. We see the need for assessing and reporting proficiency even more when we consider Tzou et al.'s (2011) findings. Their first- and second-year student interpreters and non-interpreters were subdivided into equally and not-equally proficient groups based on their performance on a self-rating scale and their reading speed. They found that the equally proficient participants performed significantly better than not-equally proficient participants on both their digit and reading-span tasks.

Experience and expertise

Moser-Mercer (2007) has shown that as interpreters move from novice to more expert status, the challenges in the interpreting process change. This sets interpreting experience as a potential locus for the conflict in the literature regarding whether or not interpreters have better WM than non-interpreters. The range of interpreting experience reported in the WM/interpreter literature ranges greatly both within and across studies. Some authors report experience in hours, while others report experience in terms of years, and many only report a general level of professional status (e.g., "second-year student," "professional"). Studies are difficult to compare as a result. Köpke and Nespoulous (2006) also suggest that interpreters, relative to non-interpreters, may have other skills that give them an advantage in various short-term memory tasks. They suggested interpreters may, for example, also be highly skilled readers (arguably accounting for their better reading-span performance), be trained in consecutive interpreting, which would exercise their short-term memory, and, perhaps WM, and may be exceptionally good at problem solving, either through experience in the field, or through self-selection into the profession.

Cross-linguistic differences

Cross-linguistic differences are reported in WM tasks and may be another locus for the discrepancies in the literature. Memory span, as mentioned, is sensitive to word length. We see this, for example, with Welsh-dominant bilinguals, who show greater digit-span performance in English, which has shorter digit names, than in Welsh, which has longer digit names (Ellis & Hennelly, 1980). This suggestion is supported in the cross-linguistic differences seen in the Darò and Fabbro

(1994) study mentioned earlier, in which Group A, who performed the task in Italian, had a slightly lower span than Group B, who performed the task in English, despite all being Italian-dominant speakers. Italian digits have more syllables than their English counterparts, so it is not surprising that Daró and Fabbro's results are similar to those of Ellis and Hennelly. When one considers the wide range of languages in which these memory experiments were run (e.g., Dutch, English, French, Italian, and Mandarin), in this relatively small subset of studies, cross-linguistic factors become a viable locus for the discrepancies that one sees.

First versus second language performance

The language of testing is a natural area to search for sources of discrepancy in the literature. Four of the eight studies reviewed here ran participants in both their first and second languages. Two ran participants in L1 and the remaining two ran participants in L2. Nonetheless, testing in L1 versus L2 did not seem to affect memory performance differentially across interpreter and non-interpreter groups in span tasks. Of the span studies that tested participants in both L1 and L2, three of the four found interpreters to be superior to control groups in both languages (i.e., Christoffels *et al.*, 2006; Daró & Fabbro, 1994; Tzou *et al.*, 2011). The fourth study (i.e., Chincotta & Underwood, 1998) found interpreters and non-interpreters to have comparable skills, also in both languages.

Free-recall results are less clear regarding L1 versus L2 issues. Köpke and Nespoulous (2006), for example, tested only in L1 and found interpreter superiority under articulation suppression. Padilla *et al.* (1995) also only found group differences under articulation suppression, but did not report the language of assessment, unfortunately. The results of the sentence stimuli are also less clear than word-based tasks for forming a consensus on the L1 versus L2 issue. Köpke and Nespoulous tested listening span in L1 and found mixed results, with novice interpreters having a statistically superior performance to non-interpreters. The higher absolute scores for the professional interpreters over non-interpreters were not statistically significant. Liu *et al.* (2004) tested only in L2 and found no difference between interpreters and student interpreters in their listening-span task. Christoffels *et al.* (2006) tested reading span in both L1 and L2 and found interpreter superiority in both cases. Thus, in these free-recall studies, a confusing range of possible outcomes vis-à-vis WM in first and second languages is represented.

In summary, with respect to methodological variables, a variety of factors, including small group sizes, group heterogeneity, the varied nature of stimuli and stimulus presentation modes, and the varied language experiences of the participants, may contribute to whether or not interpreters were reported to have better WM skills than non-interpreters.

Overview of the findings

This chapter reviewed the findings in the literature on WM in simultaneous interpreters in order to determine how this type of memory is engaged in bilingualism, and whether individuals whose work life involves such specialized bilingual language processes have better WM, either as a result of years performing the task, or because individuals with good WM choose to enter the field and remain in it. The chapter focused on the conflicting results in the literature regarding whether or not interpreters have better WM skills than non-interpreters in the hope of moving the question toward resolution. Of the 25 tasks considered across the nine articles reviewed here, only 13 indicate a statistically significant interpreter advantage. However, invariably in those studies where no statistical interpreter advantage was found, absolute scores pointed toward interpreter superiority; in no studies did the absolute scores suggest interpreters performed worse than non-interpreters.

First considered were the different components of WM according to Baddeley's (2000) modular model. Recall the relative sparing of phonological or semantic memory in brain-damaged patients, the lack of phonological word-length effects in semantic recall, and evidence of distinct cortical representation for semantic versus phonological processing mentioned earlier. It stands to reason that different studies may have called upon different components of WM to different degrees, which could explain the discrepancy between studies finding superior WM abilities in interpreters over non-interpreters and those reporting none.

We considered tasks addressing memory simply using word stimuli (i.e., word span, non-word repetition). We see an advantage for interpreters in word-based tasks primarily as reflective of the phonological loop. Five of the eight studies assessing immediate word-recall tasks (i.e., span or non-word repetition) show an interpreter advantage. Conversely, we see mixed performance with interpreters and non-interpreters with word-list recall that involves a delay and probably more significant long-term memory support (i.e., free and final recall).

Three of six tasks reviewed reported evidence of interpreter advantages in free and final recall. When semantic and phonological recall were assessed relatively independently in cued recall, none of these four tasks evidenced an interpreter advantage. We then considered tasks involving more complex storage-and-processing via sentence stimuli. We see an ultimate advantage for interpreters in sentence-based tasks that presumably call upon the entire WM system. Five of the six tasks addressing sentence-span showed an interpreter advantage.

In an attempt to make sense of the data, we looked at the experimental outcomes in terms of processing. In regard to auditory stimuli, we see an interpreter advantage in 6 of 12 tasks and equivalent performance in the other 6. In regard to written stimuli, we see an interpreter advantage in 7 of 13 instances and equivalent performance in 6 of the 13. The input modality alone, thus, does not predict WM performance consistently. Instead, task demands on WM seem to play a larger role than modality. The largest area of advantage comes for interpreters with auditory information that is short and immediately recalled as in word/digit span or non-word repetition. The other notable advantage is with print information that is longer and follows a varied delay as in reading span.

At present we can conclude that a weak interpreter advantage exists depending on the nature of the WM task. We have also suggested that methodological factors such as presentation protocols, semantic weight, participant backgrounds, number of participants, and language issues (i.e., cross-linguistic differences, testing in L1 versus L2) have precluded more consistent findings in the literature as a whole. More research controlling for these factors should generate a more definitive picture. Of particular importance would be assessing language proficiency for all participants and interpreting skills for the professional group. Looking at episodic-buffer function and other areas of cognition such as attention and executive function may also give insight into WM differences between interpreters and non-interpreters.

To conclude, a number of studies have found that bilinguals and multilinguals who are involved in simultaneous interpretation have better WM performance than those who are not (or those who are in the very early stages of their training), and no studies have found that professional interpreters perform worse than non-interpreters with similar language histories. Of course, we cannot say that WM, as it has been tested in these studies, is something that all bilinguals and multilinguals have an advantage in, relative to monolinguals, since only Köpke and Nespoulous (2006) included monolingual controls. What we can say is that, precisely because the cognitive-linguistic tasks involved in simultaneous interpretation must engage aspects of WM and give professional interpreters continuous practice with them, bilinguals with high-proficiency language skills who enter this profession and remain in it have – or are able to develop – somewhat exceptional single-word and sentence-based WM skills. Determining how such findings interface with data that suggest that bilinguals and multilinguals have better executive control than monolinguals (summarized in Hilchey & Klein, 2011) is a challenge that remains for future analyses.

REFERENCES

Baddeley, A. D. (2000). The episodic buffer: a new component of working memory? *Trends in Cognitive Sciences*, 4, 417–423.

Chincotta, D., & Underwood, G. (1998). Simultaneous interpreters and the effect of concurrent articulation on immediate memory. *Interpreting*, 3, 1–20.

Christoffels, I., de Groot, A. M. B., & Kroll, J. F. (2006). Memory and language skills in simultaneous interpreters: the role of expertise and language proficiency. *Journal of Memory and Language*, 54, 324–345.

Crosson, B., Rao, S. M., Woodley, S. J., Rose, A. C., Bobholz, J. A., Mayer, A., et al. (1999). Mapping of semantic, phonological and orthographic verbal working memory in normal adults with function magnetic resonance imaging. *Neuropsychology*, 13, 171–187.

Daneman, M., & Carpenter, P. A. (1980). Individual differences in working memory and reading. *Journal of Verbal Learning and Verbal Behavior*, 19, 450–466.

Darò, V. (1994). Non-linguistic factors influencing simultaneous interpretation. In S. Lambert & B. Moser-Mercer (eds.), *Bridging the gap: empirical research in simultaneous interpretation* pp. 249–272. Philadelphia, PA: John Benjamins.

Darò, V., & Fabbro, F. (1994). Verbal memory during simultaneous interpretation: effects of phonological interference. *Applied Linguistics*, 15, 365–381.

Ellis, N. C., & Hennelly, R. A. (1980). A bilingual word-length effect: implications for intelligence testing and the relative ease of mental calculation in Welsh and English. *British Journal of Psychology*, 71, 43–51.

Haarmann, H. J., & Usher, M. (2001). Maintenance of semantic information in capacity-limited item short-term memory. *Psychonomic Bulletin & Review*, 8, 568–578.

Haarmann, H. J., Davelaar, E. J., & Usher, M. (2003). Individual differences in semantic short-term memory capacity and reading comprehension. *Journal of Memory and Language*, 48, 320–345.

Hilchey, M., & Klein, R. (2011). Are there bilingual advantages on nonlinguistic interference tasks? Implications for the plasticity of executive control processes. *Psychonomic Bulletin & Review*, 18, 625–658.

Köpke, B., & Nespoulous, J.-L. (2006). Working memory performance in expert and novice interpreters. *Interpreting*, 8, 1–23.

Köpke, B., & Signorelli, T. M. (2011). Methodological aspects of working memory assessment in simultaneous interpreters. *International Journal of Bilingualism.* doi: 10.1177/1367006911402981.

Kroll, J. F., & Stewart, E. (1994). Category interference in translation and picture naming: evidence for asymmetric connection between bilingual memory representations. *Journal of Memory and Language,* 33, 149–174.

Liu, M., Schallert, D. L., & Carroll, P. J. (2004).Working memory and expertise in simultaneous interpreting. *Interpreting,* 6, 19–42.

Martin, R. C., Shelton, J. R., & Yaffee, L. S. (1994). Language processing and working memory: neuropsychological evidence for separate phonological and semantic capacities. *Journal of Memory and Language,* 33, 83–111.

Moser-Mercer, B. (2007). *Developing expertise in SI: the role of concentration, speed and memory.* Colloquium presented at the Sixth International Symposium on Bilingualism, Hamburg, Germany, June 2007.

Padilla, P., Bajo, M. T., Cañas, J. J., & Padilla, F. (1995). Cognitive processes of memory and simultaneous interpretation. In J. Tommola (ed.), *Topics in interpreting research.* University of Turku.

Signorelli, T. M., Haarmann, H. J., & Obler, L. K. (2011). Working memory in simultaneous interpreters: effects of task and age. *International Journal of Bilingualism.* doi:10.1177/1367006911403200.

Thorn, A. S. C., & Gathercole, S. (2001). Language differences in verbal short-term memory do not exclusively originate in the process of subvocal rehearsal. *Psychonomic Bulletin & Review,* 8, 357–364.

Tzou, Y., Eslami, Z. R., Chen, H., & Vaid, J. (2011). Effect of language proficiency and degree of formal training in simultaneous interpreting on working memory and interpreting performance: evidence from Mandarin–English speakers. *International Journal of Bilingualism.* doi: 10.1177/1367006911403197.

Wagner, R. K., Torgesen, J. K., & Rashotte, C. A. (1999). *The comprehensive test of phonological processing.* Texas: Pro-Ed.

5 Using electrophysiological measures to track the mapping of words to concepts in the bilingual brain: a focus on translation

Janet G. van Hell and Judith F. Kroll

Abstract

A central question in research on the bilingual mental lexicon is how second language (L2) learners map novel L2 word forms onto their respective meanings. For adult L2 learners, there is already extensive vocabulary knowledge in the first language (L1). How is the new information about L2 represented and processed relative to the L1? Which codes are engaged when translating words from one language into the other? Many previous reviews of the literature have considered these issues (e.g., Kroll & de Groot, 2005). Here we focus on a relatively new source of evidence drawn from recent studies using event-related potentials (ERPs). Because ERPs provide sensitive data about the time course of language processing in the brain, they provide a new opportunity to review the enduring debates in the literature concerning the initial mappings of word form to meaning by L2 learners and their consequences for proficient bilingual performance. We first review the theoretical framework that has shaped this debate, focusing primarily on the Revised Hierarchical Model (Kroll & Stewart, 1994). We then consider briefly the behavioral evidence that has been taken in the past literature to adjudicate alternative claims concerning the role of the L1 translation equivalent in processing L2. We then focus our discussion on recent ERP studies that use variants of the translation task to examine the time course over which information about words in each of the bilingual's two languages becomes activated and available. We argue that converging evidence from electrophysiological studies provides a powerful tool for understanding L2 performance in both learners and highly proficient bilinguals and for resolving longstanding controversies in the literature.

During the earliest stages of acquiring a new language, adult second language (L2) learners must first acquire a vocabulary in the L2 (e.g.,

The writing of this chapter was supported in part by NIH Grant HD053146 to Judith Kroll and NSF Grants BCS-0955090 and OISE-0968369 to Judith Kroll and Janet van Hell.

de Groot & van Hell, 2005). Early models of the bilingual lexicon asked how the newly learned L2 vocabulary is then fitted into the lexical/semantic system that exists for words and concepts that are known in the native language, L1 (e.g., Potter *et al.*, 1984). Potter *et al.* (1984) proposed two models that differed in how directly learners might be able to connect new L2 words to their respective meanings. According to the Concept Mediation Model, this process was assumed to be direct and available early in L2 acquisition. In contrast, the Word Association Model characterized the mapping of L2 word forms to meaning as requiring mediation via the L1 translation, such that the meanings associated with L1 translations were assumed to be transferred to the L2. Potter *et al.* reported data supporting direct conceptual processing of words in the L2, even for relatively novice L2 learners. Subsequent research debated this conclusion and suggested that the two alternatives might characterize different stages of L2 proficiency, with the ability to bypass reliance on the L1 translation equivalent increasing as a learner becomes more proficient in the L2 (e.g., Chen & Leung, 1989; Kroll & Curley, 1988).

Kroll and Stewart (1994) proposed the Revised Hierarchical Model (RHM) to accommodate the developmental changes that occur during the initial stages of L2 learning. By effectively integrating the two models proposed by Potter *et al.* (1984), the RHM provided a framework in which the L1 translation equivalent might be engaged under some circumstances, but once individuals acquire proficiency in the L2, direct conceptual processing also becomes possible. The history of these models and the research that has been performed to evaluate the predictions that they make about the trajectory of L2 development has been reviewed extensively in the recent literature (e.g., Kroll & Tokowicz, 2005; Kroll *et al.*, 2010). Our goal in the present chapter is to evaluate a new body of evidence about the mapping of L2 words to concepts that has emerged in the past ten years with the increasing use of the event-related potentials (ERPs) technique to measure brain activity. ERPs are more sensitive to the time course of processing, and particularly to the earliest stages of processing, than the behavioral methods that have historically been the basis upon which models of the bilingual lexicon have been evaluated. In what follows, we first provide a brief review of the theoretical debate and the behavioral evidence surrounding the RHM. We then turn our focus to the recent ERP studies that use variants of the translation task to examine the time course over which information about words in each of the bilingual's two languages becomes activated and available.

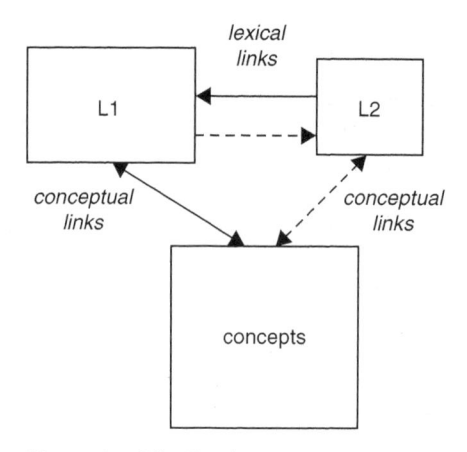

Figure 5.1 The Revised Hierarchical Model

The Revised Hierarchical Model

The RHM is shown in Figure 5.1. The model assumes that there are strong connections between L1 words and their respective concepts. The L2 lexicon is characterized as being smaller and more weakly connected to conceptual information than the L1 lexicon. Critically, the RHM assumes that conceptual information is largely shared across a bilingual's two languages (e.g., Francis, 2005). At the lexical level, there is hypothesized to be an asymmetry in the strength of connections between the two languages. Because L2 is thought to be dependent on L1 mediation during the very earliest stages of L2 learning, there are strong connections from L2 to L1 at the lexical level, but only relatively weak connections from L1 to L2. Over time, there may be feedback that creates a lexical association from L1 to L2, but the L1 will rarely be expected to rely on the L2 for access to meaning. As the individual becomes more proficient in the L2, the RHM assumes that the ability to directly access concepts for L2 words will strengthen, eventually reaching a level of lexical-to-conceptual mappings that is equivalent to that in L1 for bilinguals who are highly proficient and relatively balanced across the two languages.

Kroll and Stewart (1994) initially tested the predictions of the RHM in a translation-production paradigm in which relatively proficient Dutch–English bilinguals were asked to translate words in each direction of translation, from Dutch to English (L1 to L2, forward translation) or from English to Dutch (L2 to L1, backward translation). The materials in the Kroll and Stewart study were presented one at a time but in lists that were either semantically categorized, with each member of a given list drawn from the same semantic category, or randomly mixed. The RHM predicts that the two directions of translation will differ in the degree to which they engage conceptual processing. If there is a strong lexical-level connection from L2 to L1, then translation in that direction should not necessarily require conceptual or semantic processing. In contrast, translation from L1 to L2 will be more likely to engage the meaning of the L1 word because the word-to-concept mappings are stronger for L1 than for L2. Kroll and Stewart found precisely this pattern in translation production. Dutch–English bilinguals were slower to translate from L1 to L2 when the words were presented in the context of semantically categorized lists, whereas the same manipulation had no effect on translation from L2 to L1. They argued that the insensitivity to the semantic manipulation for translation in the backward direction, from L2 to L1, suggested that translation was accomplished at a lexical level alone.

Behavioral evidence for the activation of the L1 translation

In the time since the RHM appeared, there has been mixed support for the predictions of the model, with a debate that has been particularly focused on the issue of whether the L1 translation equivalent is activated when L2 words are processed (see Brysbaert & Duyck, 2010, and Kroll *et al.*, 2010, for a recent summary of the arguments on each side of this debate). Although performance has been examined across a range of comprehension and production tasks in both languages, there are three tasks that have provided the central evidence concerning the role of the L1 translation equivalent in L2 processing: translation production, translation recognition, and translation priming. We first review briefly the behavioral evidence using each of these tasks.

Translation production Potter *et al.* (1984) used a comparison of translation production and picture naming to test the predictions of the Word Association and Concept Mediation Models. They argued that if the Word Association model was correct, then direct access to the translation equivalent would effectively bypass conceptual processing, with the result that translation production would be predicted to be faster than picture naming, a task that necessarily requires conceptual processing to understand the meaning of the pictured object. They found that, if anything, picture naming was faster than translation, and for that reason rejected the Word Association Model in favor of the Concept Mediation Model. In the study by Kroll and Stewart (1994) reviewed above, translation production alone was performed to determine whether translation in each direction was sensitive to a semantic manipulation. They found different results depending on the direction of translation, with evidence for semantic or conceptual processing in only the forward direction of translation, from L1 to L2. The results of these two studies led to different conclusions about translation performance but the data are actually not at odds. The critical comparison for Potter *et al.* (1984) was between picture naming in L2 and translation from L1 to L2. Kroll and Stewart also found that translation from L1 to L2 was conceptually mediated; only translation from L2 to L1, not the focus of the critical comparison in Potter *et al.*, appeared to be lexically mediated.

The translation-production studies that have produced mixed evidence for the RHM's predictions of lexically guided translation performance in the L2 to L1 direction have largely relied on the same research logic as used by Kroll and Stewart (1994). A semantic variable is introduced and manipulated in the context of translation in each of the two directions. The critical question is whether both directions of translation are equally sensitive to the semantic manipulation. If so, the result would suggest that both directions are processed conceptually, contrary to the idea that the translation equivalent in L1 is activated directly when the L2 word is processed. The results of these past studies are reviewed elsewhere (e.g., Kroll & Tokowicz, 2005; Kroll *et al.*, 2010), but in brief, they show that manipulations of variables such as word concreteness or imageability (e.g., de Groot, Dannenburg, & van Hell, 1994), semantic distance (e.g., Duyck & Brysbaert, 2004), and sensitivity to priming by a semantically related picture (e.g., La Heij *et al.*, 1996) affect translation in both directions. In some respects, finding that direct activation of the translation equivalent is not present is not terribly surprising if one considers that most of these studies have examined the performance of relatively proficient bilinguals. The RHM initially proposed that reliance on the L1 translation equivalent in processing the L2 was a strategy that is adopted during early stages of L2 learning; once the ability to process L2 conceptually is in place, the logical need for the L1 translation should be reduced.[1] A more critical test of the role of the translation equivalent is to examine performance developmentally, as learners begin to acquire greater proficiency in using the L2. Because production tasks are notoriously difficult for learners, it is important to have a measure that is comparable for learners at different levels of L2 skill. De Groot (1992) developed a translation recognition task that has been used to examine this issue.

Translation recognition In translation recognition, a word in one of the L2 learner's or bilingual's languages is followed by a word in the other language and the task is to decide whether the second word is the correct translation of the first word. Talamas, Kroll, and Dufour (1999) developed a variant of the translation-recognition task to index sensitivity to the form of the L1 translation equivalent. On half of the trials, the word pairs were not translations but words that were related in form or meaning to the correct translations. For example, some pairs resembled the correct translation in form (e.g., in Spanish and English the pair *hambre–man* would require a "no" response because *hambre* means hunger but resembles the correct translation pair *hombre–man*), whereas other pairs were related in meaning (e.g., *mujer–man* would also require a "no" response because *mujer* means woman). The time to reject these related word pairs as not correct translations was compared to the time to reject word pairs that were completely unrelated to each other. Talamas *et al.* (1999) found that sensitivity to these different types of foil was a function of proficiency. Less-proficient learners were more likely than more-proficient learners to be fooled by words that resembled the form of the translation equivalent. The reverse was true for the semantically related pairs, with greater interference reported for more-proficient than for less-proficient learners.

Although subsequent studies have produced a mixture of evidence regarding the relation between proficiency and semantic interference, for present purposes, the important finding is that differential sensitivity to the form of the translation equivalent has been reported for less-proficient and more-proficient learners (e.g., Ferré, Sánchez-Casas,

---

[1] A question of interest is why the relatively proficient Dutch–English bilinguals tested by Kroll and Stewart (1994) produced asymmetric translation performance given that they were at a similarly high level of proficiency as the bilinguals in the studies that have reported similar conceptual processing in both directions of translation. The reason may be related to the inclusion of relatively low-frequency words in the Kroll and Stewart study (and see de Groot, 1993, for a discussion of word-type effects in translation).

& Guasch, 2006; Sunderman & Kroll, 2006). The result was initially interpreted as support for the RHM in that the hypothesized reliance on the L1 translation appears to be stronger early in L2 learning than later when the ability to directly understand the meaning of L2 words has already developed. As we will see in the discussion of more recent evidence on this approach using ERPs, the pattern of findings is more complicated than the initial behavioral data suggested, with evidence that even relatively proficient bilinguals may activate the translation equivalent in some processing contexts.

Translation priming A third task that has provided important evidence on the availability of the translation equivalent in L2 processing is translation priming. A number of variations of the priming task have been used. A prime word is presented briefly at a duration at which it can be seen clearly or at a very brief duration with a masking stimulus so that the individual is not even aware that a word has been presented. The prime word is then followed at some interval by a target word and typically the task is either to make a lexical decision about the target word (i.e., is the letter string a real word?) or to make a semantic decision (e.g., is the target word a type of animal?). A number of parameters can be manipulated in priming paradigms that potentially affect the degree to which the task indexes automatic processing or deliberate expectations (e.g., see Altarriba & Basnight-Brown, 2007, for a review of recent methodological considerations in these paradigms). For the purpose of the present discussion, a critical observation is that when the prime is masked, there is also no information explicitly available to the participant concerning the language of the prime. A concern that has been voiced about bilingual studies is that there may be effects of expectations (e.g., Grosjean, 2001; Wu & Thierry, 2010b). In the translation-production and recognition tasks reviewed above, the participant is aware that both languages are required to be engaged. If the reason that activation of the translation has been observed in the studies using these tasks is that participants are aware of the requirement to use the other language, then in a masked translation-priming task it may be possible to process the target words in one language alone, without the influence of the other language. As we will see in the priming studies to be discussed and with a great deal of converging evidence from other bilingual paradigms (e.g., van Hell & Dijkstra, 2002), the results of many priming studies now show that there is priming across the bilingual's two languages even when the prime itself is not visible and even when the two languages are structurally distinct, for example, in using different written scripts (e.g., Gollan, Forster, & Frost, 1997; Jiang, 1999).

At issue theoretically is whether there is an asymmetry in the direction of translation priming. If the RHM is correct, then more priming might be predicted from L2 to L1 than from L1 to L2, assuming that there is a direct translation-to-translation link that can be activated. In fact, past translation-priming studies have reported every possible outcome, with more priming from L1 to L2, equal priming in both directions, and more priming from L2 to L1, depending on the task conditions. Duñabeitia *et al.* (2010) reviewed the past translation-priming literature and noted that studies that used lexical decision as the target task have typically reported asymmetrical effects in the two translation directions (e.g., de Groot & Nas, 1991; Dimitropoulou, Duñabeitia, & Carreiras, 2011; Finkbeiner *et al.*, 2004; Gollan *et al.*, 1997; Grainger & Frenk-Mestre, 1998; Jiang, 1999; Jiang & Forster, 2001; Kim & Davis, 2003; Schoonbaert *et al.*, 2009; Voga & Grainger, 2007; Williams, 1994; but see Duyck & Warlop, 2009). Duñabeitia *et al.* (2010) also noted that priming studies that have used semantic categorization tasks have been more likely to observe symmetry across the two directions (e.g., Finkbeiner *et al.*, 2004; Grainger & Frenk-Mestre, 1998; Jiang & Forster, 2001).

Observations of symmetry or asymmetry within behavioral translation-priming studies may not themselves be sufficient to adjudicate between alternative theoretical positions regarding the mapping of form to meaning in bilingual memory. For one thing, like the translation-production studies reviewed above, performance by individuals who are beyond early stages of learning the L2 and are able to access meaning directly for L2 words might be expected to reveal more symmetric patterns of performance. More critically, the time course of processing words in the two languages may be critical. For all L2 learners and for most bilinguals, there is one language that is more dominant than the other. Often it is the native language, but when individuals have been immersed in the L2 for a long period of time, the L2 may become the dominant language (e.g., Heredia, 1997). If processing in the more dominant language is faster than in the less dominant language, then at a fixed duration, there may be more opportunities for the faster language to prime the slower language than the reverse. The likely differences in the time course of processing for the two languages therefore complicate the interpretation of asymmetries in priming. It may not be that the two languages map word forms to meaning in different ways but that they do so over different time frames. Differences in the time course of processing may also interact with the type of processing, making it more or less likely that the weaker of the two languages will access its respective meaning. As we discuss in the section that follows, an advantage of using ERP methods is that it provides a continuous record of the earliest stages of processing.

A critical study by Thierry and Wu Before we discuss in detail the logic of using ERP methods, we describe the results of a study by Thierry and Wu (2007) that reported data that challenged previous interpretations regarding the activation of the translation equivalent by relatively proficient bilinguals. Like the translation-priming studies, Thierry and Wu used a method that did not explicitly require the use of the nontarget language. In their study, highly proficient Chinese–English bilinguals living in the UK, and therefore immersed in their L2, English, performed a semantic-relatedness task. Two words were presented in English and the participant's task was to decide whether the two words were semantically related to one another. Crucially, no Chinese was present. Unbeknownst to the participants, the pairs of English words sometimes had translations in Chinese that shared characters. The presence of shared characters in Chinese, however, was independent of whether the word pair in English was semantically related or not. There were both semantically related and semantically unrelated word pairs in English that contained shared Chinese characters. Thierry and Wu reasoned that if these Chinese–English bilinguals were able to function in English without activating the Chinese translations of the English words, then the presence of the shared Chinese characters in the Chinese translation should have no effect on their performance. They found that there was evidence in the ERP data that the presence of shared characters in the translation modulated the N400 (see next section for detailed information on the N400 and other ERP components), although the bilinguals were unaware of the Chinese translation. A comparison group of monolingual English speakers showed no effects when these shared characters were present. Thierry and Wu concluded that even relatively proficient bilinguals automatically and unconsciously activate the L1 translation equivalents when they process the L2. A later study (Wu & Thierry, 2010a) has shown that it is phonological rather than orthographic information about the L1 translation that is activated.

A recent study by Morford *et al.* (2011), using a behavioral version of the semantic-relatedness task, reported a similar result for a group of deaf readers for whom American Sign Language (ASL) is the L1. The time to judge the semantic relatedness of word pairs in English was affected by whether the translation of the English words in ASL contained similar form elements. The result suggests that deaf readers activate sign translations even when they are reading in English alone and not explicitly required to use ASL. The findings held for highly proficient deaf readers, demonstrating that the co-activation of sign was not due to lack of skill in reading English.

The results of both the Thierry and Wu (2007) and Morford *et al.* (2011) studies create a problem for the debate outlined above concerning the way in which bilinguals and second language learners map word forms to meaning. If the RHM is correct, then only individuals at a relatively early stage of acquiring the L2 should reveal a dependence on the L1 translation equivalent. In both the Thierry and Wu and Morford *et al.* studies, highly proficient bilingual readers revealed activation of the L1 translation equivalent when reading in the L2. These findings thus fail to support the developmental assumption of the RHM that learners access the L1 translation to facilitate understanding the meaning of the L2 word but that once they achieve sufficient proficiency in L2, they can access that meaning directly.

Many previous studies have shown that the process of accessing meaning can occur relatively early in L2 learning and, indeed, that observation has been a focus in the debate over the RHM (e.g., Dufour & Kroll, 1995, and see Kroll *et al.*, 2010, for a discussion of these findings). But the Thierry and Wu (2007) and Morford *et al.* (2011) results suggest that the L1 translation is not simply used as a means to transfer knowledge from L1 to L2 during the earliest stages of L2 acquisition. Instead, it appears to become active even once individuals are able to understand the meanings of L2 words directly. In the theoretical debate surrounding the RHM, those arguing that the predictions of the RHM fail to be supported have relied on the evidence for direct meaning access for L2 words as showing that it is not necessary to activate the L1 translation when processing the L2 (see Brysbaert & Duyck, 2010, for a summary of these arguments). The Thierry and Wu and Morford *et al.* studies provide compelling evidence for the activation of the L1 translation even among highly proficient bilinguals and even among bilinguals who have been immersed in an L2 environment for a long period of time.

In the remainder of this chapter, we first briefly discuss the basic principles of electroencephalograms (EEG)/ERPs in language research. We then focus on how ERP methods can be used to resolve this apparent puzzle about the role of the L1 translation in L2 processing, and how L2 learners and bilinguals map word form to meaning. As we will see, the time course of processing, which may differ for the bilingual's two languages and in distinct ways across different processing tasks, may provide a key to allow us to begin to understand these apparent contradictions within the behavioral literature.

Basic principles of EEGs/ERPs in language research

Electrodes placed in key positions on the scalp can measure variations in electrical activity produced by large populations of brain cells. The recording of voltage variations over time is called the electroencephalogram (EEG). Event-related brain potentials (ERPs) are derived from the EEG through a filtering process, and reflect regularities in electrical brain activity that are time-locked to an external event, like the presentation of a word (see, e.g., Handy 2005; Luck 2005, for excellent introductions to ERP recordings and analyses). Small voltage changes associated with, for example, reading a word are time-locked to the onset of the presentation of the word. These voltage changes make up the ERP signal. ERPs thus provide an on-line, millisecond-by-millisecond record of the brain's electrical activity during language processing. ERPs therefore can be used to index ongoing language-related perceptual and cognitive processes as they unfold over time.

A typical ERP signal consists of a series of positive and negative peaks (termed *components*) related to stimulus processing. ERP components are characterized by polarity, latency, amplitude, topographic scalp distribution, and a functional description of the cognitive processes they are assumed to index. An ERP component has either a positive polarity (positive-going wave, labeled by P), or a negative polarity (negative-going wave, labeled by N). Latency reflects the time course of the ERP signal and includes onset latency (the time at which a component begins), rise time (the time it takes to go from a low value to a high value), peak latency (the time at which a component reaches its peak amplitude), and duration (the length of the component). Components are often labeled according to their polarity and peak amplitude latency (e.g., N400 is a negative-going wave that reaches its peak amplitude around 400 milliseconds after stimulus onset; see Figure 5.2). The relative peak amplitude of a component is assumed to reflect the degree of engagement of the associated cognitive processes. For example, the amplitude of the N400 decreases as the semantic relation between a word and the sentence in which it is embedded increases (e.g., Kutas & Federmeier, 2000). ERP components further have a characteristic topographical scalp distribution. Finally, components are functionally described in terms of the experimental manipulation to which a component is sensitive and the cognitive process(es) the component is assumed to reflect.

Components that have been identified as electrophysiological markers of the cognitive processes underlying word translation are the P200, N250, N400, and Late Positivity Complex (LPC). As we will see below, different variants of translation tasks (i.e., translation priming and

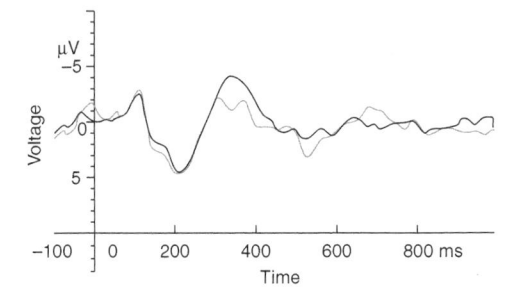

Figure 5.2 An illustration of the N400 component in ERP waveforms

translation recognition) elicit different components, and not all studies observe the same components.

The P200 is a positive-going wave in the 150–275 ms latency range that peaks around 200 to 250 ms after stimulus onset, and often coincides with the onset of the N400. It is distributed mainly over central-frontal and parietal-occipital electrode sites. The functional significance of the P200 is not yet completely understood, but evidence in language research (mostly priming studies) indicates that the P200 may reflect neural processes that occur when a visual input is compared with an expected word (e.g., Federmeier, Mai, & Kutas, 2005).

The N250 is a negative-going waveform in the 150–250 ms latency range that is sensitive to form-level processing (e.g., Holcomb & Grainger, 2006), and has been observed mainly in masked priming studies. The N250 is interpreted as indexing the mapping of sub-lexical form to orthographic representations. Adapting this idea to translation priming, this leads to two options. First, the presentation of a word in one language could rapidly activate its translation in the other language via direct lexical links. Alternatively, translation-priming effects in the N250 may reflect feedback from semantic representations activated by the prime that influence form-level representations during target word processing.

The N400 is a large-amplitude negative-going wave in the 300–500 ms latency range, and peaks around 400 ms after stimulus onset. It is usually largest over central and parietal electrode sites. The N400 indexes the processing of semantic information, for example, relating the meaning of a word to the preceding linguistic context (e.g., Kutas & Federmeier 2000; Kutas & Hillyard 1980; Lau, Phillips, & Poeppel, 2008). It is enhanced, for example, when there is a semantic incongruence (e.g., Kutas & Hillyard, 1980) or when words are difficult to integrate into a given linguistic context (e.g., Van Petten et al., 1999).

The LPC is a late positive-going wave that appears slightly after the N400 time window and extends for several hundred milliseconds. It typically has a broad posterior scalp distribution and, like the N400, is largest over centro-parietal scalp regions. The LPC is believed to reflect sentence-level integration (e.g., Kaan et al., 2000) or re-analysis (e.g., Friederici, 1995), a reconfiguration of stimulus–response mapping (e.g., Moreno, Rodriquez-Fornells, & Laine, 2008), and memory-retrieval processes (e.g., Paller & Kutas, 1992).

One thing to note is that the typical latency and topographic characteristics of ERP components are based on adult speakers who perform a language task in their native language. In bilinguals who process language materials in their L2, slight variations in latency and topographic scalp distribution have been observed. For example, the onset of components, in particular later components like the N400, can be delayed in bilinguals when they are processing in their L2 (e.g., Ardal et al., 1990; Moreno & Kutas, 2005; van Hell & Tokowicz, 2010). A delayed onset is consistent with the idea that for unbalanced bilinguals who are less proficient in their L2 than in L1, processing in L2 is slowed down.

ERP evidence on translation in bilinguals

In the next two sections, we will review ERP studies that have used two variants of the translation task: translation priming and translation recognition.

ERP translation-priming studies

A paradigm that has recently become increasingly popular in the ERP literature on translation is translation priming. In a typical translation-priming study, bilinguals are presented with a target word (e.g., house) that is preceded by a prime in the same language (house–house), its translation (*casa*–house) or an unrelated word (skirt–house or *falda*–house). The primes and targets are typically noncognate words and are presented in the bilingual's two languages, rendering L1–L1 and L2–L2 repetition-priming conditions and L1–L2 and L2–L1 translation-priming conditions. In the translation-priming analysis, the ERP waveform of the target preceded by the translation prime is compared with the waveform of the target preceded by the unrelated prime. A translation-priming effect is obtained when the ERP waveform in a particular time window (e.g., the N250 or N400) is more negative-going (or more positive-going in cases of positive polarity) for targets preceded by unrelated primes than for targets preceded by their translation.

Alvarez, Holcomb, and Grainger (2003) presented native English speakers who were beginning or intermediate learners of Spanish with mixed lists of noncognate L1 and L2 words. To ensure semantic processing, they were instructed to read each word and press a button when a word referred to a body part (on 10% of the trials). The critical words were preceded on the previous trial by the same word (e.g., house–house; within-language repetition-priming trials), their translation (e.g., *casa*–house; translation-priming trials) or an unrelated word. Repetition-priming trials were either L1–L1 or L2–L2. In the translation-priming trials, the prime-target trials were either L1–L2 or L2–L1. The results showed that the amplitude of the N400 was modulated by translation priming, although the reduction in N400 amplitude was smaller in translation priming than in repetition priming. Importantly, the L2–L1 translation-priming effects were larger in the 300–500 ms window (the typical N400 component), and declined in the subsequent 500–700 ms and 700–1000 ms windows. In contrast, the L1–L2 translation-priming effects were small in the N400 time window, and tended to become stronger in the later phase of the LPC window (700–1000 ms). This indicates that translation priming from L1 to L2 has a later time course than translation priming from L2 to L1, which is in line with the RHM. The RHM states that translation priming from L2 to L1 is mostly lexically driven, and translation priming from L1 to L2 is mostly semantically driven. Presentation of an L2 prime automatically activates its L1 translation via the lexical-level connection, and because the L2–L1 lexical link is stronger than the L1–L2 lexical link, L2 words activate their L1 translations more rapidly, and more strongly. Indeed, the L2–L1 translation-priming effect emerged earlier, and was larger, than the L1–L2 translation-priming effect. The L1–L2 translation-priming effect emerged in the later time windows, which may reflect the longer time course of activating semantic representations.

The participants in the Alvarez *et al.* (2003) study were native English speakers who were enrolled in beginning to intermediate courses in Spanish at a university. Their low proficiency in L2 and the developing L2 word-form-to-concept mappings may underlie the translation-priming asymmetry, and the delayed time course of L1–L2 versus L2–L1 translation priming. As predicted by the RHM, an increased L2 proficiency level should reflect more symmetrical patterns of L1–L2 and L2–L1 translation priming. Using the same within-language and between-language repetition paradigm as Alvarez *et al.* (2003), Geyer *et al.* (2011) examined highly proficient Russian–English bilinguals who had emigrated to the USA between the ages of 7 and 16, and were thus immersed in their L2. Geyer *et al.* indeed observed symmetrical effects for L1–L2 and L2–L1 translation priming, in the 300–500 ms and 500–700 ms windows. A direct comparison of the L2–L1 translation-priming patterns of the less-proficient English–Spanish bilinguals in Alvarez *et al.* (2003) and the highly proficient Russian–English bilinguals in Geyer *et al.* (2011) showed that the translation-priming effects emerged later in the highly proficient bilinguals than in the less-proficient bilinguals. This suggests that an increase in L2 proficiency co-occurs with a decrease in the automaticity with which L2 words activate their L1 translation via direct lexical links, possibly because the direct lexical link becomes weaker with increased proficiency, and/or the L2 word-form-to-concept link becomes stronger and more symmetrical to the L1 word-form-to-concept link. Alternatively, the bilinguals tested by Geyer *et al.*, who were immersed in their L2 environment and tested in an L2 context, may have inhibited their L1. The context in which these immersed bilinguals were tested may have produced a more inhibitory pattern for L1, in contrast to L2 speakers tested in an L1 environment (as, e.g., in Alvarez *et al.*, 2003).

The large majority of studies in the emergent literature on neural correlates of translation priming presented words visually. An exception is the auditory word-repetition and translation-priming study by Phillips *et al.* (2006). They presented fairly fluent English–French bilinguals quintets of words via earphones. In the critical conditions, the first four words in each quintet were repetitions of the same word in L1 (e.g., bed, bed, bed, bed) or L2 (*jupe, jupe, jupe, jupe*), followed by a fifth word that was another repetition (e.g., bed), its translation (*lit*), or an unrelated word in the same (sky) or the other language (*ciel*). ERP responses to the fifth word were compared with the ERP responses to the first repetition of the word (word 2, at which the N400 was most attenuated). The L1–L2 translation condition (bed–*lit*) elicited a phonological mismatch negativity (PMN) in the 200–250 ms epoch followed by an N400 in the 350–550 ms epoch and a late posterior positivity between 600 ms and 800 ms. The L2–L1 translation condition (*jupe*–skirt) also elicited a PMN and a late posterior positivity in the 500–600 ms time window, with an earlier onset than in L1–L2 translation. Notably, in contrast to the clear N400 in L1–L2 translation, no N400 was observed in L2–L1 translation. Finally, both the L1–L1 and L2–L2 repetition conditions elicited a PMN and an N400, with the N400 appearing a bit later in L2–L2 repetition than in L1–L1 repetition.

A complicating factor in the interpretation of the translation asymmetry observed by Phillips *et al.* (2006) is that the repeated presentation of the L1 or L2 words, and the 500 ms interval between the presentation of two consecutive words, may have induced translation strategies in the bilinguals long before the critical fifth word, the actual translation, was presented. Likewise, in the translation-priming studies of Alvarez *et al.* (2003) and Geyer *et al.* (2011), the time that elapsed between presentation of the prime and the target (stimulus-onset asynchrony, SOA) was quite long – 2700 ms in Alvarez *et al.* and 3350 ms in Geyer *et al.* Because the primes were clearly visible and the SOAs were long, the translation-priming effects may have been driven by an overt translation strategy (cf. Altarriba & Basnight-Brown, 2007). For example, when participants consciously translate the L2 prime into L1 prior to the presentation of the L1, the ERP measurements actually reflect L1–L1 repetition priming rather than translation priming. Second, it is difficult to tease apart whether the translation-priming effects are driven by word-form factors or semantic factors.

A technique in which the prime is presented very briefly (e.g., 50 ms) and masked (e.g., by hashes) prevents overt translation of the prime. Moreover, as proposed by Holcomb and Grainger (2006), masking the prime and using ERPs enables a more precise tracking of the time course of component lexical processes (earlier effects) and semantic processes (later effects) in priming. More specifically, Holcomb and Grainger (2006) argue that the N250 reflects early lexical processes in which prelexical orthographic representations are mapped onto orthographic representations. The N400 indexes semantic integration (Kutas & Hillyard, 1980) and a form–meaning interface in which lexical forms are mapped onto their semantic representations (Holcomb & Grainger, 2006), so a modulation of the N400 would signify the activation of semantic codes and word-form-to-concept mappings. Applying this logic to the RHM, L2–L1 translation priming should be reflected in a modulation of the N250, at least in less-proficient bilinguals whose L2 to L1 lexical links are strong and who are still developing their L2 word-form-to-concept link. L1–L2 translation priming, on the other hand, should engage that activation of semantic information in both less-proficient and highly proficient bilinguals, which would be reflected in a modulation of the N400.[2]

---

[2] To a certain extent, each of the components may reflect a combination of form and semantic influences, but it can be expected that lexical-level effects will be greater on the N250, and semantic-level effects will be greater on the N400.

Using the masked translation-priming technique with an SOA of 67 ms, Midgley, Holcomb, and Grainger (2009) presented fairly proficient French–English bilinguals with a target word in L1 or in L2, preceded by the same word (repetition priming), its translation (translation priming), or an unrelated prime. Participants were instructed to rapidly press a button when a word referred to an animal. Both L1–L2 and L2–L1 translation priming produced an N400 effect, although the N400 in L2–L1 translation priming was not typical (negative-going at posterior sites, but reversed positive-going at frontal sites). Midgley et al. (2009) also observed a modulation of the N250 in L1–L2 translation priming, but not in L2–L1 translation priming.[3] As argued by the authors, this may suggest a semantic influence early in processing in L1–L2 translation priming that was reflected in the N250 component and peaked around 300 ms post-target onset. The absence of an L2–L1 translation-priming effect in the N250 is puzzling, and differs from the L2–L1 translation priming observed in the 300–500 ms windows in the unmasked priming studies by Alvarez et al. (2003) and Geyer et al. (2011). A possible account is that the bilinguals, all late learners who were less proficient in L2 than in L1, needed more time to fully process the briefly presented primes in their L2. The fact that L2–L1 translation-priming effects were observed in the later N400 time window confirms that the bilinguals were slower and less efficient in processing L2 primes.

Following this line of argumentation, Midgley et al. (2009) predicted that with a longer L2 prime duration (and a longer SOA), L2–L1 translation-priming effects should emerge in the N250 time window. This prediction was tested by Schoonbaert et al. (2010), who presented English–French bilinguals who were fairly proficient in their L2 French with L1 targets preceded by their L2 translations or unrelated words, or vice versa. Participants were asked to perform a lexical decision on the targets (and filler pseudo-words). The prime duration was 100 ms and the SOA was 120 ms (in contrast to the 50 ms and 67 ms durations used

---

[3] Chauncey, Grainger, and Holcomb (2008) used a similar masked priming procedure to Midgley et al. (2009), with a prime duration of 50 ms and 100 ms. The study was framed as a language-switching study, ERPs were time-locked to the prime (rather than to the target as in Midgley et al.), and the language-switched (translation) trials were compared with non-switched (within-language repetition) trials (rather than to unrelated trials as in Midgley et al.). French–English bilinguals who were moderately proficient in English showed a language-switch-related modulation in the N250 in the L1–L2 direction, but not in the L2–L1 direction, both with 50 ms and 100 ms prime duration, a pattern that parallels Midgley et al.'s translation-priming findings. In the N400 region, switching effects were found for both L1–L2 and L2–L1 switching directions, in both prime duration conditions.

in Midgley *et al.*, 2009). In the L2–L1 translation-priming condition, a modulation of the N250 was observed, followed by an N400 effect (both in the 300–400 and 400–500 ms windows) and a post-N400 effect in the 500–600 ms window. The ERP pattern in L1–L2 translation priming was largely comparable to that of L2–L1 translation priming. A combined analysis of both translation directions yielded a subtle asymmetry in the N250, in that the N250 effect was larger in the L2–L1 direction. The analysis also showed a larger, and more sustained, N400 effect (in the 400–500 ms and 500–600 ms windows) in L1–L2 translation priming than in L2–L1 translation priming, which is likely to be related to a slower processing of L2 words, and thus an N400 latency shift for these words.

Schoonbaert *et al.*'s (2010) study indicates that robust L2–L1 translation-priming effects can be obtained in masked priming with a somewhat longer prime duration, allowing bilinguals who are less proficient in their L2 sufficient time to process the L2 word. The translation asymmetry observed in the N250 window, with larger N250 effects in L2–L1 translation, shows that the asymmetry observed in the unmasked priming studies can also be observed when the prime is masked. Assuming that the N250 reflects lexical-level processes (as suggested by Holcomb & Grainger, 2006), it demonstrates that L2 primes activate their L1 translations more rapidly than L1 primes activate their L2 translations. This corroborates the asymmetry in the strength of the lexical links between words in L2 and L1, with L2–L1 links being stronger than L1–L2 links, in less-proficient bilinguals, as proposed by the RHM. In fact, the RHM predicts that the L2–L1 priming effects will be most pronounced in the N250 window, and the L1–L2 priming effects most pronounced in the N400 window. This is exactly the pattern found by Schoonbaert *et al.* (2010) and supports Midgley *et al.*'s (2009) conjecture that unbalanced bilinguals need more time to process the prime for L2–L1 priming to occur.

The masked and unmasked translation-priming studies discussed so far used noncognate translations to prevent form overlap between prime–target trials from driving the translation-priming effects. These studies tested bilinguals whose two languages shared the same alphabetic script (e.g., French and English) or had a Cyrillic and Latin script (e.g., Russian and English). The most extreme case that enables a test of how primes are processed with minimal interference from target orthography is created by examining the performance of bilinguals whose two languages have a completely different script (e.g., Japanese characters and English letters). As argued by Hoshino *et al.* (2010), the magnitude of translation-priming effects depends on how well orthographic, phonological, and semantic information extracted from the prime can be integrated with orthographic, phonological, and semantic information extracted from the target. When the prime and target have a different script, the co-activation of orthography will not only be minimal, but different scripts also provide a strong bottom-up cue as to which language the prime belongs to, which will further reduce co-activation of lexical information. Cross-script translation priming thus creates an ideal testing ground for studying early semantic influences in bilingual lexical processing.

Hoshino *et al.* (2010) presented relatively proficient Japanese–English bilinguals, immersed in the USA in an L2 English environment, with target words in L1 Japanese or in L2 English, in blocked lists. The targets were preceded by a masked prime, presented for 50 ms (SOA 80 ms), that was either a repetition of the target (repetition priming), a translation of the target (translation priming), or an unrelated word. The bilinguals were instructed to read the words and press a button when they detected a word that referred to a body part (go/no-go semantic categorization). For L1–L2 translation priming, a significant N250 effect was obtained, followed by a significant N400 effect; at the anterior sites, there was also evidence of a very early effect in the 100–200 ms epoch. In contrast, no L2–L1 translation-priming effect was observed in any of the time windows. Repetition-priming effects were obtained for both L1 and L2 targets, in the N250 and N400 time windows. Hoshino *et al.* argued that it is unlikely that the L1–L2 translation-priming effect reflected an automatic activation of the L2 translation of the L1 prime at the lexical level: this should have resulted in larger L2–L1 than L1–L2 priming effects, and the opposite pattern was obtained. Rather, they interpreted the L1–L2 translation-priming effects in the N250 as signifying that L1 primes rapidly activate their semantic representations, and this activation feeds back and influences lexical-level representations of the L2 target. The L1 primes modulated ERP responses to L2 targets throughout the N250 and N400 time windows. The absence of translation-priming effects from L2 to L1 may reflect the bilinguals' relatively slow processing of L2 prime words that were presented for 50 ms.

The masked translation studies discussed so far tested unbalanced, successive bilinguals who were less proficient in their L2 than in their L1, and who learned their L2 at school after the age of seven or older. This raises the question of to what extent the previous findings are specific to unbalanced, successive bilinguals, or whether they also generalize to bilinguals with more balanced proficiency across the two languages. Previous behavioral studies on translation production suggest that unbalanced bilinguals who are strongly dominant in the L1 are likely to produce a translation asymmetry, with faster translation from L2 to L1 than from L1 to L2, whereas more proficient or balanced bilinguals are more likely to produce similar translation performance in the two directions (e.g., Kroll *et al.*, 2002).

To examine the consequence of balanced bilingualism for ERP performance on a masked translation-priming study, Duñabeitia *et al.* (2010) tested highly proficient simultaneous Basque–Spanish bilinguals, who were native speakers in each of the languages and had a balanced use of both languages on a daily basis. They were presented with Basque and Spanish words (in two different blocks), preceded by identical primes (e.g., *cuento–cuento* [tale]), translation primes (*ipuin–cuento*), or unrelated primes in the same (*huelga–cuento* [*huelga*: strike]), or different (*antza–cuento*) language as the target. Primes were masked and presented for 50 ms, and participants were instructed to read the words and detect words (by pressing a button) that referred to animal names (go/no-go semantic categorization task). The proficient bilinguals' ERP data showed a significant N400 effect that was symmetrical for L1–L2 and L2–L1 translation. No translation-priming effects were observed in the N250. The observed translation symmetry in the highly proficient Basque–Spanish bilinguals replicates the symmetrical pattern observed in the highly proficient Russian–English bilinguals in Geyer *et al.*'s (2011) unmasked priming study. Together, these findings suggest that in highly fluent bilinguals, the neural correlates of L2 form-to-concept mappings are symmetrical to those of L1 form-to-concept mappings.

ERP translation-priming studies: wrap-up One question this review of ERP translation-priming studies raises pertains to the instructions participants received to ensure they read the stimuli attentively. Some studies asked participants to perform a lexical decision on the target word (Geyer *et al.*, 2011; Schoonbaert *et al.*, 2010), whereas other studies asked participants to make a semantic categorization and decide whether or not the target word referred to a body part (Alvarez *et al.*, 2003) or to an animal (Duñabeitia *et al.*, 2010; Hoshino *et al.*, 2010; Midgley *et al.*, 2009). The lexical-decision and semantic-decision tasks make different demands on the activation of orthographic, phonological, and semantic knowledge. For example, semantic information will be more strongly involved in a semantic decision on the target word compared to deciding whether a letter string is a word or not. In the behavioral literature, as discussed above, translation-priming studies that used a semantic-decision task tended to find symmetrical translation effects, whereas studies using a lexical-decision task typically found asymmetrical translation effects. This suggests that semantic decision recruits both L1 word-to-concept mappings and L2 word-to-concept mappings, whereas lexical decision recruits mainly L1 word-to-concept mappings.

Can the translation-priming studies using ERP methodology be interpreted along similar lines? Not really. The four studies using a semantic-decision task observed quite different translation-priming patterns. Duñabeitia *et al.* (2010) found symmetrical translation-priming effects in the N400 in highly proficient Basque–Spanish bilinguals, whereas Hoshino *et al.* (2010), testing fairly fluent Japanese–English bilinguals, observed L1–L2 translation-priming effects in the N250 and N400 but found no effects in L2–L1 translation priming. Midgley *et al.* (2009) observed symmetrical translation priming in the N400, but only L1–L2 translation priming was observed in the N250. Finally, Alvarez *et al.* (2003), testing beginning-intermediate L1 English learners of L2 Spanish, observed both L1–L2 and L2–L1 priming effects, but L1–L2 translation priming had a later time course than L2–L1 translation priming. The two studies that asked participants to perform a lexical-decision task observed symmetrical L1–L2 and L2–L1 translation-priming effects in highly proficient Russian–English bilinguals (Geyer *et al.*, 2011) and in fairly proficient English–French bilinguals (Schoonbaert *et al.*, 2010), although the bilinguals in the latter study showed a larger N250 effect in the L2–L1 direction, and a more sustained N400 effect in L1–L2 priming than in L2–L1 priming.

These variable ERP patterns reflect the large variability across electrophysiological studies of translation priming in terms of methodology (including masked versus unmasked presentation of the prime, prime duration, task instructions that emphasize semantics or word-form codes, mixed versus blocked presentation of the L1 and L2 targets), and the participants (variations in L2 proficiency, age of first exposure to the L2, language learning history, L2 immersion). Such variation is not uncommon in the emergent literature of studies on bilingual processing using ERPs (see, e.g., review studies by Kotz, 2009; Moreno *et al.*, 2008; van Hell & Tokowicz, 2010; van Hell & Witteman, 2009). This suggests that more systematic studies are needed, taking into account and possibly controlling for the factors outlined here, before we can draw any firm conclusions. It also shows that insights into the time course of translation priming obtained using ERPs add novel and important evidence to the reaction-time and accuracy data obtained in behavioral translation-priming studies.

One important factor that has been largely overlooked in both the behavioral and the ERP literature (but see Guasch *et al.*, 2011) pertains to the degree of meaning similarity between a word in one language and its translation. The implicit assumption in noncognate-translation-priming studies is that the meanings of translation equivalents are similar, and that translation equivalents provide the closest possible semantic relation between two different word forms (see, e.g., Duñabeitia *et al.*, 2010; Midgley *et al.*, 2009). As argued by Duñabeitia *et al.* (2010), assuming that an N400 effect reflects how well orthographic, phonological, and semantic representations activated by the prime are integrated with orthographic, phonological, and semantic representations activated when reading (or hearing) the target, no differences are to be expected between repetition priming and translation priming. But is it legitimate to assume that the meanings of the target in one language and its translation prime are identical, as in the target and its repetition prime? Several behavioral (e.g., Degani, Prior, & Tokowicz, 2011; Laxén & Lavaur, 2010; Tokowicz *et al.*, 2002; van Hell & de Groot, 1998a) and neuroimaging (Illes *et al.*, 1999) studies suggest that the semantic representations of two translations do not always overlap completely, at least in bilinguals with different levels of proficiency in their two languages, or in certain word types. For example, van Hell and de Groot (1998a) asked Dutch–English bilinguals to perform a word-association task twice on the same list of words (nouns and verbs that varied in concreteness and cognate status), once in the language of the stimuli (within-language) and once in the other language (between-language). It appeared that the within- and between-language associations for concrete words and for cognates were more often translations of one another than those for abstract words and noncognates, and nouns evoked more translations than verbs. This suggests that lexical and conceptual representations may be more similar for some types of words (e.g., concrete cognate nouns like apple–*appel*) than for others (e.g., abstract noncognate nouns like truth–*waarheid*).

A recent behavioral translation- and semantic-priming study, in which the degree of semantic relatedness between prime–target pairs was manipulated, provides further evidence that semantic overlap affects priming (Guasch *et al.*, 2011). Guasch *et al.* presented highly proficient Catalan–Spanish bilinguals with prime–target pairs that were either translations (*ruc–burro* [donkey]), very closely related (*ruc–caballo* [horse]), closely related (*ruc–oso* [bear]), or unrelated. Primes and targets were presented in L1 and L2, and vice versa, and the bilinguals performed a lexical-decision task or a semantic-decision task on the target words. In both language directions, and in both tasks, the degree of semantic overlap modulated the magnitude of the priming effects: priming effects were largest in the translation pairs, somewhat smaller in the closely semantically related pairs, and smallest in the semantically related pairs.

In their group of highly proficient bilinguals (they refer to these bilinguals as "multiple L1" bilinguals), Duñabeitia *et al.* (2010) found that the N400 translation-priming and repetition-priming effects were basically identical, which indeed hints at complete semantic overlap of translations. However, other translation-priming studies using less-proficient L2 speakers typically observed smaller and less robust translation-priming effects than repetition-priming effects, even in the case of L2–L2 repetition priming (Alvarez *et al.*, 2003; Geyer *et al.*, 2011; Hoshino *et al.*, 2010). This suggests that the implicit assumption that within-language repetition priming is comparable to between-language translation priming in the recruitment of semantic information may not hold for bilinguals who are less proficient in L2 than in L1.

ERP translation-recognition studies

In the masked and unmasked translation-priming studies, the bilinguals were instructed to read the words and to perform a lexical decision on the target, or to decide whether the target referred to a body part or to a living creature. They were never instructed to make a translation decision, or even to relate words from the two languages in a meaningful way. One could argue that the evidence emanating from the translation-priming studies informs the component processes involved in word recognition, which is a first component of word translation, but does not capture all the processes involved in word translation. Only a handful of electrophysiological studies have examined word translation under conditions in which bilinguals are instructed to make an explicit decision on whether an L1 and an L2 word are translations or not. In the first published ERP study on translation recognition, Vigil-Colet, Pérez-Ollé, and García-Albea (2000) studied highly proficient Catalan–Spanish and Spanish–Catalan bilinguals who performed a translation-recognition task in which correct and incorrect translation pairs were presented in both L1–L2 and L2–L1 translation directions. The first word was presented for 500 ms, and after a random interval of 1000–2000 ms, the second word was presented for 500 ms. Vigil-Colet *et al.* found that the P300–P600 complex was involved in translation recognition and concluded that these components may be viewed as indexes of stimulus relevance and activation in short-term memory.

Vigil-Colet et al. (2000) framed their study in the memory literature and focused on P300–P600 components that index short-term memory processes. This study remains largely silent on the specific ERP components, like the N400, that were studied in the later published translation-priming studies. In a recent translation-recognition study using ERPs, Palmer, van Hooff, and Havelka (2010) focused more directly on lexical and semantic processing and the RHM. Palmer et al. hypothesized that the N400 effect should be larger in L2–L1 translation recognition than in L1–L2 translation recognition. They argued that when an L2 word precedes its L1 translation, the L2 word should rapidly activate the L1 word via the relatively strong L2–L1 lexical link, even before the L1 word is actually presented. If indeed the L1 word is the correct translation (in the correct-translation trials), the pre-activation of the L1 word's lexical and semantic representations should facilitate the lexical-semantic integration process, which should reduce the N400 amplitude in response to the L1 word. However, if the L1 word is the incorrect translation, a large N400 inflection is predicted due to violation of expectancy. The resulting N400 effect (in which the correct and incorrect translation conditions are contrasted) should be large in L2–L1 translation. In the case of L1–L2 translation recognition, the L1 word does not rapidly activate its L2 translation because translation occurs via the slower conceptual links. When the L2 translation is presented, only the shared semantic representation has been pre-activated by the L1 word, which will lead to a reduced N400 amplitude when the correct L2 translation is presented, but to a lesser extent than in L2–L1 translation. Presentation of the incorrect L2 translation will elicit an N400, but this N400 will be smaller than in L2–L1 translation because expectancy violation will be smaller. Therefore, the N400 effect in L1–L2 translation is predicted to be smaller than in L2–L1 translation.

Palmer et al. (2010) tested Spanish–English (Experiment 1) and English–Spanish (Experiment 2) bilinguals with a rather wide range of L2 proficiency levels and age of first exposure to L2; the Spanish–English bilinguals were immersed in their L2, and the English–Spanish bilinguals were immersed in their L1. They were presented with a word in L1 followed by a word in L2, or vice versa, some of which were correct translations and some of which were not. Half of the words had low imageability ratings and half had high imageability ratings. The first word was presented for 500 ms, and after a blank screen of 300 ms the second word was presented, with a resulting SOA of 800 ms. In both groups of bilinguals, L2–L1 translation elicited a larger N400 effect than L1–L2 translation. In the L2 non-immersed bilinguals, but not in the L2 immersed bilinguals, a similar asymmetry was observed in the reaction-time data, such that L2–L1 translation was faster than L1–L2 translation. In the ERP data, concreteness did not affect the N400 (although concrete translations were recognized faster and more accurately in the behavioral data in the L2 immersed but not in the L2 non-immersed bilinguals) and concreteness did not modulate the translation asymmetry observed in the ERP data. The larger N400 effect in L2–L1 than in L1–L2 translation supports the asymmetry assumption in the RHM.

In the ERP evidence in the Vigil-Colet et al. (2000) and Palmer et al. (2010) studies, it is difficult to tease apart lexical and semantic factors involved in translation recognition. Two recent studies explored the neural correlates of lexical and semantic interference effects in translation recognition, employing the lexical and semantic distractor manipulation that has been successfully used in behavioral studies (e.g., Comesaña et al., 2009; Ferré et al., 2006; Sunderman & Kroll, 2006; Talamas et al., 1999). Guo et al. (in press) compared ERP and behavioral performance in a translation-recognition task performed in the L2 to L1 direction with highly proficient Chinese–English bilinguals immersed in the L2 in the USA. When the L1 word was not the correct translation, it was either related to the correct translation by sharing phonology with the translation, similar in meaning to the correct translation, or completely unrelated. In a first experiment, Guo et al. found evidence for sensitivity to both types of distractor in both the behavioral and the ERP data. However, the time course of activation revealed by the ERP record distinguished responses to the distractors related in form to the translation from those that were semantically related to the translation. Early in processing, there was a P200 for the translation form distractors in contrast to the N400 that was observed for the semantically related distractors. For both types of distractor, there was an LPC effect from 500–700 ms that presumably reflected the mapping of stimulus processing onto a decision, although again the pattern was distinct for the two types of distractor.

At one level, the results of Guo et al. (in press) using the translation recognition paradigm replicated the main features of Thierry and Wu's (2007) results. Highly proficient Chinese–English bilinguals immersed in a predominantly English-speaking environment produced evidence that they activated the Chinese translation equivalent. However, the two studies, although using different paradigms, were also similar in another respect in that they both used relatively long SOAs between the presentation of the first and second words. In the Guo et al. study, the SOA was 750 ms and in the Thierry and Wu study the SOA ranged from 1000 ms to 1200 ms. Guo *et al.* reasoned that the long SOA may have allowed or encouraged access to the translation equivalent for these proficient bilinguals. In a second experiment, they replicated the same distractor conditions in the translation-recognition task with a matched group of Chinese–English bilinguals but with the SOA between the L2 and L1 words reduced to 300 ms. Under these short-SOA conditions, there was again evidence for a strong effect for the semantic distractors but a marked reduction in the sensitivity to the translation distractors. The pattern of results suggests that direct access to the L1 translation equivalent of the L2 word may depend on whether the task conditions provide sufficient time and opportunity to engage the translation (cf. Schoonbaert *et al.*, 2010). The fact that sensitivity to the meaning of the L2 word is not affected by the timing to the same extent suggests that for highly proficient bilinguals, the translation of the L2 word may be activated once the meaning of the word has been accessed.

All studies discussed so far examined adult bilinguals or L2 learners. However, many bilinguals have learned their L2 during childhood, often in a classroom, but remarkably few experimental studies have examined the initial stages of developing L2 lexical-semantic knowledge in *child* classroom learners (but see Brenders, van Hell, & Dijkstra, 2011, under review; Comesaña *et al.*, 2009; Poarch & van Hell, 2012). Using the translation-recognition paradigm, Brenders, van Hell, and Dijkstra (under review) examined Dutch classroom learners of L2 English in fifth and sixth grade of elementary school (after 5 and 16 months of instruction, respectively) and adult proficient Dutch–English bilinguals. Following the critical manipulations in the Talamas *et al.* (1999) study, participants were presented with correct L2–L1 translation words (e.g., chair–*stoel*), semantic distractor words (chair–*kast* [closet]), word-form distractor words (chair–*stoep* [sidewalk]), or unrelated control words (chair–*fiets* [bike]). The L2 word was presented for 350 ms, followed by a blank screen for 300 ms, after which the L1 word was presented for 350 ms. Participants were instructed to delay their "yes" or "no" response until a warning cue was presented (at variable time intervals to prevent contamination of the EEG by motor artifacts). The most important finding was that, for both beginning L2 learners and proficient bilinguals, the ERP analyses yielded an N400 effect for semantic distractor pairs relative to incorrect control pairs. Moreover, the N400 was less negative-going for the word-form distractors than for incorrect controls in the fifth-grade beginning learners, but more negative-going in the sixth-grade beginning learners and proficient bilinguals. The reaction-time and accuracy data, collected in a parallel behavioral experiment, mimicked the ERP data.

The RHM proposes a shift in translation from reliance on lexical links to reliance on conceptual links as L2 proficiency increases. The ERP and behavioral data of the beginning L2 learners tested by Brenders *et al.* (under review) suggest that even at an early stage in L2 learning, these classroom learners activate semantic information during the word-recognition task. This finding adds to accumulating evidence that, under certain conditions, L2 learners in an early stage of L2 learning activate semantic information, and employ L2 word-to-concept mappings (cf. Kroll *et al.*, 2010). One such condition appears to be the context in which L2 learning takes place, in particular the semantic richness of the L2 learning situation (cf. Trofimovich & McDonough, 2011). L2 English elementary-school instruction methods used in Dutch schools typically teach novel words in semantically rich and meaningful contexts, using learning situations enriched by pictures and real-life situations. These are optimal conditions for fostering L2 word-form-to-concept mappings. In contrast, adult beginning learners who learn their L2 at university often learn L2 vocabulary by connecting the novel word to its translation. This word–word learning method boosts lexical-level links. The suggestion that the conditions in which L2 words are learned affect the strength of L2 word-form-to-concept mappings is corroborated by a recent study by Comesaña *et al.* (2009). They taught Spanish-speaking children (with no knowledge of Basque) L2 Basque words via either L2 picture-association learning or L2–L1 word-association learning, and later tested the children using a translation-recognition task in which they were presented with semantically related or unrelated word pairs as the critical incorrect translation pairs. In L2 picture-association learning, but not in L2–L1 word-association learning, a significant semantic interference effect was observed, after just one vocabulary-learning session. The observation of semantic effects in an early stage of L2 learning parallels Brenders *et al.*'s (under review) findings, and indicates that the use of pictures might have stimulated the development of L2 word-to-concept mappings. A recent neurocognitive L2 learning study showed that L2 word retrieval engaged different cortical structures depending on how these L2 words had been learned (via written L1 translations or in a context-rich real-life situation; Jeong *et al.*, 2010). Variations in learning strategy may therefore have a profound influence on the neural underpinnings of lexical and conceptual links in second language learners and bilinguals.

ERP evidence on translation and the Revised Hierarchical Model: concluding remarks

Since the initial word-translation studies were published in the 1980s and 1990s and the first models were proposed to capture the lexical and conceptual links engaged in word translation (i.e., the Word Association and Concept Mediation Models, and their combination in the RHM), numerous behavioral and ERP studies have been published that together provide a wealth of insight into the codes that are engaged when translating words from one language to the other, and the time course of accessing form and meaning in two languages. The present review of behavioral and ERP studies indicates that the majority of evidence can be captured with the basic assumptions of the RHM, provided that two qualifications are made with respect to the original model proposed about 20 years ago (Kroll & Stewart, 1994).

First, a general pattern that emerges from the ERP studies reviewed in this chapter is that L2 to L1 lexical links tend to be stronger than L1 to L2 lexical links, in line with the original RHM. Unlike the initial proposal, however, the L2–L1 lexical links do not decay as L2 proficiency increases. Rather, not only beginning L2 learners but also relatively proficient bilinguals seem to employ this L2–L1 lexical-level link, and activate the L1 equivalent when processing a word in the L2 (e.g., Alvarez *et al.*, 2003; Geyer *et al.*, 2011; Morford *et al.*, 2011; Schoonbaert *et al.*, 2010; Thierry & Wu, 2007), particularly in situations when L2 language processing is challenging. The current behavioral and ERP evidence also seriously challenges recent claims that lexical-level L2–L1 connections do not exist (Brysbaert & Duyck, 2010). Rather, the co-activation and translation of L2 words and their L1 equivalents appear to be a fundamental phenomenon in bilingual processing. The critical question is not so much whether the L1 equivalent is activated when reading or hearing words in the L2, but, rather, how the L1 is used at different stages of L2 learning and in different language-processing contexts.

A second important component of the RHM pertains to L2 word-form-to-concept mappings, and the conceptual links between L2 words and their meanings. In the initial 1994 version of the RHM, this link was assumed to develop with increased L2 proficiency. Behavioral evidence suggests that moderately proficient L2 learners can directly access L2 word meanings (Dufour & Kroll, 1995; see Kroll *et al.*, 2010 for further discussion), but recent studies on child learners indicate that child beginning L2 learners activate L2 word meanings in a very early stage of L2 learning (Brenders *et al.*, under review; Comesaña *et al.*, 2009). This activation of L2 word meaning in this early stage of L2 learning seems to be boosted by the context-rich and meaningful L2 learning environment in which these children are embedded.

To conclude, the currently available ERP and behavioral evidence on how L2 learners and bilinguals exploit lexical and conceptual links indicates that a hallmark of proficient language use is the ability to fully exploit lexical and conceptual links depending on linguistic and contextual task demands, the difficulty of the language materials the bilingual perceives or produces, and the situational context of language learning and language use. The high end of bilingual processing may be a bilingual whose L1–L2 and L2–L1 processing is fully symmetrical, as in the Basque–Spanish bilinguals tested by Duñabeitia *et al.* (2010). Until this stage is reached, L2 learners' and less proficient bilinguals' processing may be characterized by asymmetries in L1–L2 and L2–L1 processing, along the lines reviewed in this chapter. Future research may delineate conditions that are associated with such asymmetries.

One such line of future research may explore the role of L2 immersion, and how the component processes of translation differ for L2 learners and bilinguals immersed in an L2 environment (e.g., Geyer *et al.*, 2011; Hoshino *et al.*, 2010; Thierry & Wu, 2007) as compared to bilinguals who are tested in the L1 environment (e.g., Alvarez *et al.*, 2003; Midgley *et al.*, 2009; Schoonbaert *et al.*, 2010). In the past decade, many studies have examined how L2 proficiency and age of acquisition modulates L2 processing, but the influence of L2 immersion remained largely unexplored. As alluded to above, the surprising finding that L2–L1 translation-priming effects emerged later in highly proficient Russian–English bilinguals (Geyer *et al.*, 2011) than in less-proficient English–Spanish bilinguals (Alvarez *et al.*, 2003) may be related to the fact that the highly proficient bilinguals may have inhibited their L1 while immersed in an L2 environment. A recent behavioral study by Linck, Kroll, and Sunderman (2009) indeed showed that translation-recognition performance among L2 learners was modulated by conditions of language immersion. When English learners of Spanish at an intermediate level of proficiency had classroom L2 experience only, they produced significant behavioral interference in translation recognition for distractors that resembled the form of the translation and also for distractors that were semantically related. However, when English learners of Spanish at the same intermediate level were immersed in a study-abroad program in Spain, the effect for the translation distractors was eliminated but the semantic effects were strong. Together with other evidence in that study, Linck *et al.* argued that the L1 appears to have been inhibited in the L2 immersion environment.

A final suggestion we make for future research is to explore the electrophysiological correlates of translation production. Behavioral studies on translation production opened the field and led to important insights into the role of lexical and conceptual information in L1–L2 and L2–L1 translation (de Groot, 1992; de Groot *et al.*, 1994; Kroll & Stewart, 1994; La Heij *et al.*, 1996; Potter *et al.*, 1984; van Hell & de Groot, 1998b), but ERP evidence on the time course of component processes involved in translation production, and possible differences between L1–L2 vs. L2–L1 translation production is currently lacking.

REFERENCES

Altarriba, J., & Basnight-Brown, D. M. (2007). Methodological considerations in performing semantic and translation-priming experiments across languages. *Behavior Research Methods*, 39, 1–18.

Alvarez, R. P., Holcomb, P. J., & Grainger, J. (2003). Accessing word meaning in two languages: an event-related brain potential study of beginning bilinguals. *Brain and Language*, 87, 290–304.

Ardal, S., Donald, M. W., Meuter, R., Muldrew, S., & Luce, M. (1990). Brain responses to semantic incongruity in bilinguals. *Brain and Language*, 39, 187–205.

Brenders, P., van Hell, J. G., & Dijkstra, T. (2011). Word recognition in child second language learners: evidence from cognates and false friends. *Journal of Experimental Child Psychology*, 109, 383–396.

(under review). *The development of lexical and conceptual processing in second language learners: electrophysiological and behavioral studies.*

Brysbaert, M., & Duyck, W. (2010). Is it time to leave behind the Revised Hierarchical Model of bilingual language processing after fifteen years of service? *Bilingualism: Language and Cognition*, 13, 359–371.

Chauncey, K., Grainger, J., & Holcomb, P. J. (2008). Code-switching effects in bilingual word recognition: a masked priming study with event-related potentials. *Brain and Language*, 105, 161–174.

Chen, H.-C., & Leung, Y.-S. (1989). Patterns of lexical processing in a non-native language. *Journal of Experimental Psychology: Learning, Memory, and Cognition*, 15, 316–325.

Comesaña, M., Perea, M., Piñeiro, A., & Fraga, I. (2009). Vocabulary teaching strategies and conceptual representations of words in L2 in children: evidence with novice learners. *Journal of Experimental Child Psychology*, 104, 22–33.

Degani, T., Prior, A., & Tokowicz, N. (2011). Bidirectional transfer: the effect of sharing a translation. *Journal of Cognitive Psychology*, 23, 18–28.

de Groot, A. M. B. (1992). Determinants of word translation. *Journal of Experimental Psychology: Learning, Memory, and Cognition*, 18, 1001–1018.

(1993). Word-type effects in bilingual processing tasks: support for a mixed-representational system. In R. Schreuder & B. Weltens (eds.), *The bilingual lexicon* (pp. 27–51). Amsterdam: John Benjamins.

de Groot, A. M., & van Hell, J. G. (2005). The learning of foreign language vocabulary. In J. F. Kroll & A. M. B. de Groot (eds.), *Handbook of bilingualism: psycholinguistic approaches* (pp. 9–29). New York, NY.

de Groot, A. M. B., & Nas, G. L. J. (1991). Lexical representation of cognates and noncognates in compound bilinguals. *Journal of Memory and Language*, 30, 90–123.

de Groot, A. M. B., Dannenburg, L., & van Hell, J. G. (1994). Forward and backward word translation by bilinguals. *Journal of Memory and Language*, 33, 600–629.

Dimitropoulou, M., Duñabeitia, J. A., & Carreiras, M. (2011). Masked translation priming effects with low proficient bilinguals. *Memory & Cognition*, 39, 260–275.

Dufour, R., & Kroll, J. F. (1995). Matching words to concepts in two languages: a test of the concept mediation model of bilingual representation. *Memory & Cognition*, 23, 166–180.

Duñabeitia, J. A., Dimitropoulou, M., Uribe-Etxebarria, O., Laka, I., & Carreiras, M. (2010). Electrophysiological correlates of the masked translation priming effect with highly proficient simultaneous bilinguals. *Brain Research*, 1359, 142–154.

Duyck, W., & Brysbaert, M. (2004). Forward and backward number translation requires conceptual mediation in both balanced and unbalanced bilinguals. *Journal of Experimental Psychology: Human Perception and Performance*, 30, 889–906.

Duyck, W., & Warlop, N. (2009). Translation priming between the native language and a second language: new evidence from Dutch–English bilinguals. *Experimental Psychology*, 56, 173–179.

Federmeier, K. D., Mai, H., & Kutas, M. (2005). Both sides get the point: hemispheric sensitivities to sentential constraint. *Memory & Cognition*, 33, 871–886.

Ferré, P., Sánchez-Casas, R., & Guasch, M. (2006). Can a horse be a donkey? Semantic and form interference effects in translation recognition in early and late proficient and nonproficient Spanish-Catalan bilinguals. *Language Learning*, 56, 571–608.

Finkbeiner, M., Forster, K., Nicol, J., & Nakamura, K. (2004). The role of polysemy in masked semantic and translation priming. *Journal of Memory and Language*, 51, 1–22.

Francis, W. S. (2005). Bilingual semantic and conceptual representation. In J. F. Kroll & A. M. B. de Groot (eds.), *Handbook of bilingualism: psycholinguistic approaches* (pp. 251–267). New York: Oxford University Press.

Friederici, A. (1995). The time course of syntactic activation during language processing: a model based on neuropsychological and neurophysiological data. *Brain and Language*, 50, 259–281.

Geyer, A., Holcomb, P. J., Midgley, K. J., & Grainger, J. (2011). Processing words in two languages: an event-related brain potential study of proficient bilinguals. *Journal of Neurolinguistics*, 24, 338–351.

Gollan, T., Forster, K. L., & Frost, R. (1997). Translation priming with different scripts: masked priming with cognates and noncognates in Hebrew–English bilinguals. *Journal of Experimental Psychology: Learning, Memory, and Cognition*, 23, 1122–1139.

Grainger, J., & Frenck-Mestre, C. (1998). Masked priming by translation equivalents in bilinguals. *Language and Cognitive Processes*, 13, 601–623.

Grosjean, F. (2001). The bilingual's language modes. In J. Nicol (ed.), *One mind, two languages: bilingual language processing* (pp. 1–22). Malden, MA: Blackwell.

Guasch, M., Sánchez-Casas, R., Ferré, P., & García-Albea, J. (2011). Effects of the degree of meaning similarity on cross-language semantic priming in highly proficient bilinguals. *Journal of Cognitive Psychology*, 23, 942–961.

Guo, T., Misra, M., Tam, J. W., & Kroll, J. F. (in press). On the time course of accessing meaning in a second language: an electrophysiological investigation of translation recognition.

Handy, T. C. (2005). *Event-related potentials. A methods handbook*. Cambridge, MA: MIT Press.

Heredia, R. R. (1997). Bilingual memory and hierarchical models: a case for language dominance. *Current Directions in Psychological Science*, 6, 34–39.

Holcomb, P. J., & Grainger, J. (2006). On the time course of visual word recognition: an event-related potential investigation using masked repetition priming. *Journal of Cognitive Neuroscience*, 18, 1631–1643.

Hoshino, N., Midgley, K. J., Holcomb, P. J., & Grainger, J. (2010). An ERP investigation of masked cross-script translation priming. *Brain Research*, 1344, 159–172.

Illes, J., Francis, W. S., Desmond, J. E., Gabrieli, J. D., Glover, G. H., Poldrack, R., et al. (1999). Convergent cortical representation of semantic processing in bilinguals. *Brain and Language*, 70, 347–363.

Jeong, J., Sugiura, M., Sassa, Y., Wakusawa, K., Horie, K., Sato, S., et al. (2010). Learning second language vocabulary: neural dissociation of situation-based learning and text-based learning. *NeuroImage*, 50, 802–809.

Jiang, N. (1999). Testing processing explanations for the asymmetry in masked cross-language priming. *Bilingualism: Language and Cognition*, 2, 59–75.

Jiang, N., & Forster, K. I. (2001). Cross-language priming asymmetries in lexical decision and episodic recognition. *Journal of Memory and Language*, 44, 32–51.

Kaan, E., Harris, A., Gibson, E., & Holcomb, P. J. (2000). The P600 as an index of integration difficulty. *Language and Cognitive Processes*, 15, 159–201.

Kim, J., & Davis, C. (2003). Task effects in masked cross-script translation and phonological priming. *Journal of Memory and Language*, 49, 484–499.

Kotz, S. A. (2009). A critical review of ERP and fMRI evidence on L2 syntactic processing. *Brain and Language*, 109, 68–74.

Kroll, J. F., & Curley, J. (1988). Lexical memory in novice bilinguals: the role of concepts in retrieving second language words. In M. Gruneberg,

P. Morris, & R. Sykes (eds.), *Practical aspects of memory* (Vol. 2, pp. 389–395). London: John Wiley & Sons.

Kroll, J. F., & de Groot, A. M. B. (eds.) (2005). *Handbook of bilingualism: psycholinguistic approaches.* New York: Oxford University Press.

Kroll, J. F., & Stewart, E. (1994). Category interference in translation and picture naming: evidence for asymmetric connections between bilingual memory representations. *Journal of Memory and Language*, 33, 149–174.

Kroll, J. F., & Tokowicz, N. (2005). Models of bilingual representation and processing. In J. F. Kroll & A. M. B. de Groot (eds.). *Handbook of bilingualism: psycholinguistic approaches* (pp. 531–553). New York: Oxford University Press.

Kroll, J. F., Michael, E., Tokowicz, N., & Dufour, R. (2002). The development of lexical fluency in a second language. *Second Language Research*, 18, 137–171.

Kroll, J. F., van Hell, J. G., Tokowicz, N., & Green, D. W. (2010). The Revised Hierarchical Model: a critical review and assessment. *Bilingualism: Language and Cognition*, 13, 373–381.

Kutas, M., & Federmeier, K. D. (2000). Electrophysiology reveals semantic memory use in language comprehension. *Trends in Cognitive Neuroscience*, 4, 463–470.

Kutas, M., & Hillyard, S. A. (1980). Reading senseless sentences: brain potentials reflect semantic incongruity. *Science*, 207, 203–205.

La Heij, W., Hooglander, A., Kerling, R., & van der Velden, E. (1996). Nonverbal context effects in forward and backward translation: evidence for concept mediation. *Journal of Memory and Language*, 35, 648–665.

Lau, E. R., Phillips, C., & Poeppel, D. (2008). A cortical network for semantics: (de)constructing the N400. *Nature Neuroscience*, 9, 920–933.

Laxén, J., & Lavaur, J. M. (2010). The role of semantics in translation recognition: effects of number of translations, dominance of translations and semantic relatedness of multiple translations. *Bilingualism: Language and Cognition*, 13, 157–183.

Linck, J. A., Kroll, J. F., & Sunderman, G. (2009). Losing access to the native language while immersed in a second language: evidence for the role of inhibition in second language learning. *Psychological Science*, 20, 1507–1515.

Luck, S. J. (2005). *An introduction to the event-related potential technique.* Cambridge, MA: MIT Press.

Midgley, K. J., Holcomb, P. J., & Grainger, J. (2009). Masked repetition and translation priming in second language learners: a window on the time-course of form and meaning activation using ERPs. *Psychophysiology*, 46, 551–565.

Moreno, E., & Kutas, M. (2005). Processing semantic anomalies in two languages: an electrophysiological exploration in both languages of Spanish–English bilinguals. *Cognitive Brain Research*, 22, 205–220.

Moreno, E. M., Rodriquez-Fornells, A., & Laine, M. (2008). Event-related potentials (ERPs) in the study of bilingual processing. *Journal of Neurolinguistics*, 21, 477–508.

Morford, J. P., Wilkinson, E., Villwock, A., Piñar, P., & Kroll, J. F. (2011). When deaf signers read English: do written words activate their sign translations? *Cognition*, 118, 286–292.

Paller, K. A., & Kutas, M. (1992). Brain potentials during memory retrieval provide neurophysiological support for the distinction between conscious recollection and priming. *Journal of Cognitive Neuroscience*, 4, 375–391.

Palmer, S. D., van Hooff, J. C., & Havelka, J. (2010). Language representation and processing in fluent bilinguals: electrophysiological evidence for asymmetric mapping in bilingual memory. *Neuropsychologia*, 48, 1426–1437.

Phillips, N. A., Klein, D., Mercier, J., & De Boysson, C. (2006). ERP measures of auditory word repetition and translation priming in bilinguals. *Brain Research*, 1125, 116–131.

Poarch, G. J., & van Hell, J. G. (2012). Cross-language activation in children's speech production: evidence from second language learners, bilinguals, and trilinguals. *Journal of Experimental Child Psychology*, 111, 419–438.

Potter, M. C., So, K.-F., Von Eckardt, B., & Feldman, L. B. (1984). Lexical and conceptual representation in beginning and more proficient bilinguals. *Journal of Verbal Learning and Verbal Behavior*, 23, 23–38.

Schoonbaert, S., Duyck, W., Brysbaert, M., & Hartsuiker, R. J. (2009). Semantic and translation priming from a first language to a second and back: making sense of the findings. *Memory and Cognition*, 37, 569–586.

Schoonbaert, S., Holcomb, P. J., Grainger, J., & Hartsuiker, R. J. (2010). Testing asymmetries in noncognate translation priming: evidence from RTs and ERPs. *Psychophysiology*, 48, 74–81.

Sunderman, G., & Kroll, J. F. (2006). First language activation during second language lexical processing: an investigation of lexical form meaning and grammatical class. *Studies in Second Language Acquisition*, 28, 387–422.

Talamas, A., Kroll, J. F., & Dufour, R. (1999). Form related errors in second language learning: a preliminary stage in the acquisition of L2 vocabulary. *Bilingualism: Language and Cognition*, 2, 45–58.

Thierry, G., & Wu, Y. J. (2007). Brain potential reveal unconscious translation during foreign-language comprehension. *Proceedings of the National Academy of Sciences*, 104, 12530–12535.

Tokowicz, N., Kroll, J. F., de Groot, A. M. B., & van Hell, J. G. (2002). Number-of-translation norms for Dutch–English translation pairs: a new tool for examining language production. *Behavior Research Methods, Instruments, & Computers*, 34, 435–451.

Trofimovich, P., & McDonough, K. (eds.). (2011). *Insights from psycholinguistics: applying priming research to L2 learning and teaching*. Amsterdam: John Benjamins.

van Hell, J. G., & Dijkstra, T. (2002). Foreign language knowledge can influence native language performance in exclusively native contexts. *Psychonomic Bulletin & Review*, 9, 780–789.

van Hell, J. G., & de Groot, A. M. B. (1998a). Conceptual representation in bilingual memory: effects of concreteness and cognate status in word association. *Bilingualism: Language and Cognition*, 1, 193–211.

(1998b). Disentangling context availability and concreteness in lexical decision and word translation. *The Quarterly Journal of Experimental Psychology*, 49A, 41–63.
van Hell, J. G., & Tokowicz, N. (2010). Event-related brain potentials and second language learning: syntactic processing in late L2 learners at different L2 proficiency levels. *Second Language Research*, 26(1), 43–74.
van Hell, J. G., & Witteman, M. J. (2009). The neurocognition of switching between languages: a review of electrophysiological studies. In L. Isurin, D. Winford, & K. de Bot (eds.), *Multidisciplinary approaches to code switching* (pp. 53–84). Amsterdam/Philadelphia: John Benjamins.
Van Petten, C., Coulson, S., Rubin, S., Plante, E., & Parks, M. (1999). Time course of identification and semantic integration in spoken language. *Journal of Experimental Psychology: Learning, Memory, and Cognition*, 25, 394–417.
Vigil-Colet, A., Pérez-Ollé, J., & García-Albea, J. E. (2000). The role of the P300 component in a translation-recognition task. *Psicothema*, 12(4), 605–614.
Voga, M., & Grainger, J. (2007). Cognate status and cross-script translation priming. *Memory & Cognition*, 35, 938–952.
Williams, J. N. (1994). The relationship between word meanings in the first and second language: evidence for a common, but restricted, semantic code. *European Journal of Cognitive Psychology*, 6, 195–220.
Wu, Y. J., & Thierry, G. (2010a). Chinese–English bilinguals reading English hear Chinese. *The Journal of Neuroscience*, 30, 7646–7651.
(2010b). Investigating bilingual processing: the neglected role of language processing contexts. *Frontiers in Language Sciences*, 1, 178.

6 Age effects in L2 learning: comparing child and adult learners' performance on tests of implicit and explicit memory

Pavel Trofimovich, Sandra Martin-Chang, and Kyle Levesque

Abstract

In this chapter, we first review several cognitive explanations for age effects in second (L2) language learning, particularly those that relate to different aspects of human memory. We then report the results of a study that compares the performance of age-matched groups of children and adults (native speakers and L2 learners) on explicit and implicit tests of memory of English words read under two conditions (story vs. list). Overall, the obtained findings showed no essential differences in memory performance between 11–13-year-old children and 17–26-year-old adults learning English as their L2. More strikingly, the L2 learners' performance on tests of explicit and implicit memory was very similar to the performance of age-matched native English-speaking children and adults. We discuss contributions of explicit and implicit memory to child–adult differences in L2 learning.

For over half a century, the field of language acquisition has grappled with the "sensitive-periods controversy" (Long, 2007, p. 43). Penfield and Roberts (1959) were among the first to propose that in order for a child to learn a language to nativelike mastery, exposure to a language must occur within a certain developmental "window," described as a critical or a sensitive period. This idea was later taken up by Lenneberg (1967), who speculated that a critical period for language, which was biologically determined through brain maturation, ended around the age of puberty. The critical/sensitive period for language learning, of the kind

This project was supported by Social Sciences and Humanities Research Council of Canada (SSHRC) and Fonds québécois de la recherche sur la société et la culture grants to Pavel Trofimovich and to Sandra Martin-Chang. The authors would like to thank David Bertrand, Robin Grumet, Kathryn MacFadden-Willard, and Fernanda Soler for their help with all aspects of this study, and Jeanette Altarriba, Ludmila Isurin, and Sarita Kennedy for their helpful comments on an earlier version of this chapter.

proposed by Lenneberg, thus involves a certain biologically determined period of sensitivity to language followed by a decline in the capacity to learn it (see Bornstein, 1987, for more on critical/sensitive periods).

A wealth of evidence has been amassed in both first (L1) and second (L2) language literature to support the basic assumption underlying the notion of a critical/sensitive period – that learning a language beyond early childhood appears to result in often incomplete, non-nativelike mastery of the language. For instance, cases of L1 deprivation in early childhood due to severe abuse or profound hearing loss, such as Genie and Chelsea (e.g., Curtiss, 1977, 1988), and patterns of sign language learning by deaf individuals (e.g., Newport, 1988) point to the conclusion that full acquisition of some L1 skills (particularly, grammar) is especially hard, if not impossible, beyond early childhood. Similarly, there is ample evidence in L2 literature that children, while often initially slower at L2 learning, eventually outperform adults on a variety of language tasks, and that even the most successful adult learners are seldom fully nativelike in their L2 (e.g., Long, 2007).

At the heart of the sensitive-periods controversy is whether L2 "age effects" are determined by a biologically driven critical/sensitive period or instead arise as a consequence of other factors. Some researchers, like Lenneberg, support the notion of a biologically determined critical/sensitive period for L2 learning. For example, Pulvermüller and Schumann (1994) attribute older children's and adults' diminishing ability to learn an L2 to a gradual decline in neuronal plasticity in specific areas of the brain (for discussion of other neurobiological processes linked to language development, see Jacobs, 1988; Neville, Mills, & Lawson, 1992). Others, however, refute the existence of a biologically determined critical/sensitive period, instead linking age effects to a variety of social-educational factors (e.g., Jia & Aaronson, 2003; Flege, Yeni-Komshian, & Liu, 1999; Moyer, 1999) or cognitive variables (e.g., Hakuta, Bialystok, & Wiley, 2003). Still others, for example, hypothesize that age effects arise as a consequence of the act of prior learning itself, and are not necessarily due to age-bound neurobiological limitations alone. According to this view, older learners' difficulties in L2 learning may be traceable to age-based developmental processes that render speech perception and production more specialized for the processing of L1 input (Bever, 1981), or to a loss of perceptual sensitivities due to older learners' extensive prior experience with their L1 (McCandliss et al., 2002).

An examination of the literature on child–adult differences in L2 learning reveals a number of plausible interpretations of age effects, including those with neurobiological, linguistic, social, attitudinal, experiential, and cognitive underpinnings. It may not be possible, therefore, to give full justice to the complexity of the issue in the confines of a brief chapter (for reviews, see Birdsong, 2009; DeKeyser, 2012; DeKeyser & Larson-Hall, 2005; Montrul, 2008; Muñoz, 2006). Instead, in keeping with the overall focus of the present volume, our goal is to discuss possible contributions of *memory* to age effects in L2 learning. To attain this objective, we first review several cognitive explanations for age effects, particularly those that relate to different aspects of human memory. We then report the results of a study that compares the performance of age-matched groups of children (L1 and L2) and adults (L1 and L2) on explicit and implicit tests of memory of English words read under two conditions. We conclude by discussing contributions of explicit and implicit memory to child–adult differences in L2 learning.

Cognitive and memory-based explanations of age effects

One cognitive explanation of L2 age effects relates to differential involvement of cognitive processing mechanisms in childhood and adulthood due to general ageing (Bialystok & Hakuta, 1999; Hakuta et al., 2003). The assumption underlying this view is that such cognitive functions as memory, attention, speed of processing, and various kinds of cognitive control (e.g., ability to shift between tasks or choose between two competing response sets) deteriorate across the lifespan of an individual as part of general age-bound cognitive decline (Craik & Bialystok, 2008). The proponents of this position cite evidence from a number of studies, including analyses of large-scale census data (Chiswick & Miller, 2008; Hakuta et al., 2003), which indicate that the ability to learn an L2 declines steadily across the lifespan, without the abrupt discontinuities typical of a critical/sensitive period (see Stevens, 2004, for criticisms). Although the claim that general cognitive ageing is responsible for the decline of L2 learning ability across the lifespan is certainly very appealing, there is currently little direct evidence suggesting that differences in cognitive abilities between younger children, older children, and adults determine their eventual L2 learning outcomes.

Another cognitive explanation for age effects invokes quantitative differences in children's and adults' cognitive processing capacity. Known as the "less is more" hypothesis (Newport, 1990), this view holds that children's usually smaller cognitive processing capacity, as compared to that of adults, can actually aid children in L2 learning. According to this hypothesis, children, precisely because they have a narrow processing "window," are able to pay attention to smaller units of language available in the input, to extract relevant information from this input, and to use this information to aid subsequent language processing. By contrast, adults are worse at doing so because their fully developed processing capacity encourages them to process language input holistically, often missing critical form–meaning relationships (Elman, 1993; Kareev, Lieberman, & Lev, 1997; Kersten & Earles, 2001, but see Rohde & Plaut, 1999). In support of this explanation of age effects, Cochran, McDonald, and Parault (1999), for example, showed that adults who were taught some expressions in American Sign Language while performing a concurrent task that limited their processing capacity were better able to apply the learned grammatical patterns to novel contexts than those who were exposed to such expressions without a concurrent task. Although results like these are certainly intriguing, again, there is currently no direct evidence linking younger children's processing limitations to their eventual L2 success.

Another memory-based account of age effects in L2 learning concerns child–adult differences in the involvement of procedural and declarative memory. Ullman (2001, 2005) proposed that the processing and learning of the L1 is subserved by two memory systems: declarative memory responsible for the learning of form–meaning relationships stored in the lexicon and procedural memory responsible for the learning of grammar (see also Paradis, 2009). According to Ullman, the information stored in declarative memory is generally explicit (open to conscious awareness), whereas procedural memory is responsible for implicit learning (learning without awareness). Ullman hypothesized that L2 age effects reflect a diminished role of procedural memory in L2 learning by adults. In other words, the learning associated with the procedural memory system is sensitive to critical-period effects, but declarative memory stays relatively constant (and in fact appears to improve) throughout development. As a result, adult learners tend to rely on the declarative memory system in learning most aspects of the L2, including those that are normally learned through this memory system (lexicon) and those that are typically learned procedurally (grammar).

There are several studies that have provided some (albeit indirect) evidence that differential involvement of declarative and procedural memory in child versus adult L2 learning is linked to learners' L2 attainment. Harley and Hart (1997) showed that a measure of analytical ability (from Pimsleur's Language Aptitude Battery) was the only significant predictor of L2 proficiency for learners who started L2 instruction in grade 7. In a similar vein, DeKeyser (2000) reported a non-significant correlation between a measure of grammatical sensitivity (based on the Words in Sentences subtest of Carroll and Sapon's Modern Language Aptitude Test) and grammaticality judgment scores for early L2 learners but a significant association between these two measures for late L2 learners (for similar evidence, see Abrahamsson & Hyltenstam, 2008; DeKeyser, Alfi-Shabtay, & Ravid, 2010). If analytical ability and grammatical sensitivity (i.e., the capacity to recognize the grammatical functions of words in sentences) are interpreted as being related to declarative/explicit memory functions, then one interpretation of these findings is that adolescent and adult L2 learners mostly rely on analytical (i.e., declarative/explicit) learning mechanisms, whereas children have access to procedural (implicit) learning mechanisms (DeKeyser, 2000; DeKeyser & Larson-Hall, 2005). In fact, based on this evidence, DeKeyser (2012) recently suggested that the core questions to guide current and future research on L2 age effects are "whether there is a specific period of decline in the ability for *implicit* language learning, and whether any such decline is due to maturational factors" (p. 446, emphasis added). Because implicit memory underlies at least some aspects of implicit learning (Buchner & Wippich, 1998; Kihlstrom, Dorfman, & Park, 2007), an important goal of future research is to clarify the roles of implicit and explicit memory in L2 learning.

Explicit and implicit memory in L1 processing and learning

Before addressing the issue of child–adult differences in the involvement of explicit and implicit memory in L2 learning, it is first important to understand how explicit memory is different from implicit memory and how both kinds of memory are involved in child and adult L1 processing and learning. According to Schacter (1992), explicit memory refers to "intentional or conscious recollection of prior experiences" while implicit memory describes "changes in performance or behavior that are produced by prior experience on tests that do not require any intentional or conscious recollection" (p. 244). Explicit memory is typically measured using "traditional" memory tasks (e.g., recall, recognition) which involve asking participants overtly to remember previously encountered information, such as words, objects, and events. Implicit memory, on the other hand, is frequently assessed using tasks that make no overt link to a previous experience. When performing such tasks (e.g., identifying degraded words or completing word stems, such as completing *ele__* with *elephant* or *elevator*) participants do not realize that their memories for prior events are being accessed, yet their performance on implicit tasks is affected by these memories.

Current L1 literature shows clear dissociations between participants' performance on tests of explicit and implicit memory. The first dissociation between explicit and implicit memory is experimental, most clearly seen within the transfer-appropriate processing (TAP) framework of memory. Originating in experimental observations by Morris, Bransford, and Franks (1977), the TAP framework postulates that human memory performance is determined by the nature of the processing operations involved in learning and subsequent testing episodes (Roediger & McDermott, 1993). In essence, memory performance is best when the processing operations involved in learning are reinstated at test (e.g., asking a participant to memorize a list of words in Phase 1 and explicitly recall them in Phase 2). When viewed within the TAP framework, memory tests are discussed with respect to the processing operations which they incur. Two kinds of processing operations are usually targeted in TAP: conceptual processing, which includes a focus on meaningful, semantic information (e.g., appropriateness of a word to a sentence frame), and perceptual processing, which involves analysis of surface-level, form-related information (e.g., type of print, rhyming of words, or loudness of the speech signal).

The typical experimental dissociation between explicit and implicit memory is related to the extent to which a memory test draws on conceptual and/or perceptual processing. Explicit tests of memory (such as recall and recognition) primarily involve conceptual processing, and are thus more influenced by conceptual than perceptual processing at the time of learning. The reverse is true for implicit tests of memory (such as identification and word-stem completion) because these tests primarily involve perceptual processing. Therefore, results on these tests are more influenced by perceptual than conceptual processing at the time of learning. Thus, for example, emphasizing semantic relationships among individual words in a word learning task, as opposed to their orthographic or phonological relationships, should have a greater impact on explicit recall. In contrast, emphasizing orthographic or phonological relationships among individual words, as opposed to focusing on their semantic relationships, should have a greater impact on implicit word-stem completion. This experimental dissociation between explicit and implicit memory has been documented for both L1 adults (Roediger & McDermott, 1993) and L1 children (McFarland, Duncan, & Bruno, 1983).

The second dissociation between explicit and implicit memory is developmental. Performance on explicit memory tests tends to improve from childhood to early adulthood (e.g., Komatsu, Naito, & Fuke, 1996; Perez, Peynircioğlu, & Blaxton, 1998), probably as a result of greater use of recall strategies, increasing knowledge base, and the development of meta-memory in older children (Pressley & Schneider, 1997). After reaching a certain level in early adulthood, performance on explicit memory tests then tends to decline gradually in late adulthood, possibly as part of general cognitive ageing (Light & Singh, 1987). In contrast, performance on implicit memory tests tends to stay constant throughout an individual's lifespan, from early childhood to late adulthood (Komatsu *et al.*, 1996; Perez *et al.*, 1998).

The current study

One conclusion to be drawn from the review of existing literature on L2 age effects is that there is an increased interest in cognitive, memory-based explanations for child–adult differences in L2 learning. However, what is largely missing from this literature are direct comparisons of child and adult L2 learners' performance on different memory tasks, including tests of explicit and implicit memory. Such comparisons have the potential not only to establish that there are differences in the involvement of explicit and implicit memory in L2 learning, but also to eventually help link such differences to patterns of children's and adults' ultimate L2 attainment. As a first step in accomplishing this goal, the current study compared the performance of native English children and adults as well as native French child and adult learners of English on tests of surprise recall (an explicit memory task) and word-stem completion (an implicit memory task).

Our first objective was to test for an experimental dissociation between explicit and implicit memory, based on the principles of the TAP framework. To address this objective, all participants were tested on explicit and implicit memory tasks following two learning conditions: reading words in context (as part of a story) and in isolation (in a word list). If explicit and implicit memory are dissociable based on an experimental processing manipulation (reading words in context vs. in isolation), then we would expect better performance on explicit recall in the context condition than in the isolation condition, and better performance on implicit stem completion in the isolation condition than in the context condition. Both predictions are based on the TAP principles, namely, that experience with words in context (increased conceptual processing) should have a greater impact on explicit recall, whereas experience with words in isolation (increased perceptual processing) should have a greater impact on implicit stem completion. Our main interest here was to determine whether there would be any difference in the performance of L2 children and adults, as compared to the performance of age-matched L1 children and adults, which would speak to potential differences in the involvement of explicit and implicit memory in L2 learning.

Our second objective was to test for a developmental dissociation between explicit and implicit memory. If explicit and implicit memory are dissociable based on participants' age, then we would expect adults to outperform children on explicit recall, and both children and adults to perform similarly on implicit stem completion. These predictions are based on previous developmental work on explicit and implicit memory suggesting that performance on tests of explicit memory should improve with age but that performance on tests of implicit memory should remain stable. Again, our main concern here was to document any similarities or differences in the performance of L2 children and adults, especially in relation to the performance of age-matched L1 children and adults, which would reveal potential differences in the involvement of explicit and implicit memory in L2 learning.

Method

Participants A total of 88 children and adults were recruited from the Montreal area. They included 45 native English speakers and 43 native French speakers. The samples of English and French participants were further subdivided into two groups according to their age. The two groups of native English speakers consisted of 21 children (15 girls, 6 boys) between the ages of 10 and 13 ($M = 11.2$, $SD = 1.0$) and 24 young adults (12 women, 12 men) between the ages of 18 and 35 ($M = 23.1$, $SD = 4.2$). All children came from monolingual English homes located in predominantly English-speaking areas of Montreal and attended English-medium schools. All young adults were undergraduate students at an English-speaking university. Although most native English speakers reported some experience with French (Quebec is a French-speaking province of Canada), they represented the population of language speakers who learned English as their first language and spoke it natively.

The two groups of native French speakers included 20 children (5 girls, 15 boys) between the ages of 11 and 13 ($M = 11.8$, $SD = 0.7$) and 23 young adults (14 women, 9 men) between the ages of 17 and 26

($M = 19.7$, $SD = 2.3$).[1] These participants had been exposed to French since birth and had been raised in monolingual French homes. At the time of the study, all the children were attending a secondary school in French and learning English as part of regular L2 instruction. Using a 9-point scale (1 = *extremely poor*, 9 = *extremely fluent*), the children self-rated their proficiency in French ($M = 8.0$, $SD = 0.7$) higher than in English ($M = 5.6$, $SD = 1.2$). They also estimated that they used French on average 88 percent ($SD = 8.5$) and English about 16 percent ($SD = 6.3$) of the time daily. Similarly, all the adults were enrolled in a French-medium junior college and attended English courses as part of L2 instruction. They also self-rated their proficiency in French ($M = 8.6$, $SD = 0.5$) higher than in English ($M = 7.0$, $SD = 0.8$), and estimated their daily use of French and English at a mean of 84 percent ($SD = 15.8$) and 27 percent ($SD = 16.2$), respectively.

Because the participants differed in their experiences with English and were likely to vary in their English proficiency, the reading subtest of the Wide Range Achievement Test (WRAT-3, Wilkinson, 1993) was administered to estimate the participants' English reading ability and to ensure that the English children and the French participants possessed the skills necessary to complete the reading tasks successfully. The reading subtest consists of 42 individual words of increasing difficulty that participants are asked to read aloud. The reading scores (summarized in Table 6.1) were submitted to a 2 × 2 (age × native language) analysis of variance (ANOVA), which yielded a significant main effect of age, $F(1, 84) = 53.87$, $p < 0.0001$, a significant main effect of language, $F(1, 84) = 17.58$, $p < 0.0001$, and a significant two-way interaction, $F(1, 84) = 34.20$, $p < 0.0001$. Pairwise comparisons carried out to explore the significant interaction revealed that the English adults scored significantly higher than the remaining three groups ($p < 0.0001$), and that these three groups did not differ in their reading ability ($p > 0.05$). These findings showed that all participant groups demonstrated a reasonable level of reading ability in English but that there were developmental differences in reading ability between the participant groups.[2]

---

[1] Unfortunately, the sample in the current study made it impossible to match the English and French speakers by gender across the two age groups. While we suspect that this had little effect on our results, future studies should attempt to, as far as possible, match English and French speakers for gender so that any differences could be attributed to their language status with greater confidence.

[2] Although at first glance it may appear counterintuitive that the French children would demonstrate comparable reading ability to the English children, this finding is likely to be specific to the reading task used here. Easy words featured on the WRAT-3 reading ability subtest (e.g., *animal, felt, finger, tree*) were probably easy for both L1 and

Table 6.1 *Mean reading ability (WRAT-3) and working memory (WJ-III) scores for the four participant groups (standard deviations in parentheses)*

Group	Reading ability (WRAT-3)	Working memory (WJ-III)
English children	25.16 (3.61)	13.90 (2.72)
English adults	35.75 (3.63)	21.00 (4.44)
French children	25.85 (4.64)	15.05 (2.52)
French adults	27.13 (3.56)	17.61 (3.27)

In addition to a test of reading ability, the numbers-reversed test from the Woodcock Johnson III Tests of Cognitive Abilities (WJ-III, Woodcock, McGrew, & Mather, 2001) was administered to all participants in their L1 in order to estimate possible differences in working-memory capacity. This test requires participants to hold increasingly difficult sequences of numbers in their short-term memory (for up to 8 digits in total) while attempting to reverse the original number sequence. The working memory scores (summarized for each group in Table 6.1) were submitted to a similar 2 × 2 ANOVA that yielded a significant main effect of age, $F(1, 84) = 44.70$, $p < 0.0001$, and a significant two-way interaction, $F(1, 84) = 9.87$, $p = 0.002$, with no significant main effect of native language, $F(1, 84) = 2.42$, $p = 0.12$. Pairwise comparisons revealed that the English adults scored significantly higher than the French adults, $t(45) = 2.97$, $p = 0.005$, and that both adult groups scored significantly higher than both groups of children ($p < 0.007$), which did not differ from each other ($p > 0.05$). These findings overall showed age- and language-based differences in working memory capacity between participant groups. The implications of these findings are discussed below in relation to the main findings.

Materials All participants were exposed to target words in two experimental reading conditions: in context and in isolation. To achieve this, a total of 40 target words (e.g., *child, heart, minute, scare, sticks, whistle, tiptoe*) were selected from existing materials described in Martin-Chang and Levy (2005) and organized into four mutually

L2 children, whereas hard words (e.g., *discretionary, egregious, omniscient, disingenuous*) were equally hard for both groups.

exclusive sets of 10 target words. The four sets were matched for mean word length (5.7, 6.1, 5.9, and 5.8 characters) and mean word frequency (3.6, 3.6, 3.2, and 3.5 log-based frequency per million), as estimated through the SUBTLEX$_{US}$ corpus of spoken American English (Brysbaert & New, 2009). For the context condition, the first two sets were separately embedded into one short story (*First Class*), resulting in two versions of the same story. The remaining two sets were integrated into another short story (*Halloween*), similarly yielding two story versions. Within a story, each target word was repeated twice, for a total of 20 (2 × 10) target word exposures. The stories ranged between 558 and 582 words in length and between grade 3.6 and grade 4.1 level of reading difficulty for native speakers of English (as analyzed by the Flesch-Kincaid formula). For the isolation condition, the ten target words in each set were shown twice, presented one at a time in random order on a computer screen and read aloud.

In order to measure the involvement of explicit and implicit memory, a surprise explicit recall test and an implicit word-stem completion test were included in this study. The explicit recall task required participants to recall verbally as many of the target words as possible. Verbal recall was deemed more appropriate than written recall considering that English-speaking children and all French-speaking participants were likely to have had less experience with writing in English, which might have inadvertently hindered their performance on this task. Verbal recall also ensured that the participants did not receive additional orthographic exposure to any target words outside of the contextual and isolated reading conditions.

The word-stem completion task is an implicit memory task that requires participants to quickly generate a response based on the first letters of a word (the stem). None of the target words began with a prefix, and each stem could potentially be completed with a number of words, including single- and multi-morphemic words. The task included a total of 30 stems, 20 of which were derived from the target words presented in context and in isolation (i.e., words that were read aloud by the participant) as well as an additional 10 stems from a "control" set of target words (i.e., words that were not seen by participants). Similar to previous studies (Martin-Chang & Levesque, 2011), word stems included the first three letters of the target words (e.g., *tea__* for *teacher*). The order of the reading conditions (context-isolation, isolation-context) was counterbalanced across participants, and the four target sets appeared equally often in the context, isolation, and control conditions.

Procedure Individual testing was carried out by trained experimenters in a quiet room at the participants' school/university or at an alternative location, such as their home or the home of a friend. The entire testing session lasted approximately 25 minutes. Without divulging the memory component of the study, the participants were informed that the general purpose of the investigation was to understand how children learn to read. However, in order to acknowledge the perceived simplicity of the tasks, the participants were also told that their participation would assist in establishing a baseline score for comparison purposes. All participants were asked to direct their full attention to the activities and perform to the best of their abilities. The tasks occurred in the following order: WRAT-3 reading test, exposure conditions (context and isolation), surprise explicit recall, numbers reversed, implicit word-stem completion, and (for all French-speaking participants) vocabulary knowledge test.

For the WRAT-3 reading test, the participants were presented with 42 words of increasing difficulty and asked to read the words aloud, from left to right down the page, to the best of their ability. The testing sessions were not audio recorded. During the task, the experimenter recorded the participants' answers on a separate score sheet and provided no feedback as to the accuracy of their responses. The task ended when participants read ten consecutive items incorrectly or read all the words on the page. For consistency in scoring, each experimenter was trained with regard to the correct pronunciation of the words (e.g., *terpsichorean*). In order to reduce scoring bias against the French participants, each experimenter was also instructed to disregard phonological substitutions commonly found in French-accented English speech (e.g., production of /ð/ as /d/, /h/ deletion and epenthesis). For scoring purposes, one point was given for every word read correctly; in order to be awarded a point, it was required that the entire word was read accurately in accordance with the word's conventional pronunciation.

Next, the participants were exposed to a total of 20 target words through two experimental conditions: in context and in isolation. Words presented in context were read within a short story. A shared reading procedure was employed whereby the experimenter read the majority of the story and the participants read only the 20 words (10 targets × 2 exposures). The participants were asked to follow along with their finger as the reading took place. This was done to replicate the procedure typically followed with children. In addition, this procedure prevented the participants from fixating on the target words for an extended period of time. Paying attention to the story was further stressed as the participants were informed that they would be asked comprehension questions following the completion of the passage. One yes–no question was asked orally after the story had been read; this question did not contain any target words. The stories were typed in Times New Roman size 14 font and printed on 8½ × 11 white paper. All target words were bolded and underlined to make them noticeable from the surrounding print.

Words read in isolation were presented individually at the center of a computer screen. The participants were asked to read the words aloud to the best of their ability as they appeared on the screen. Before seeing the actual target words, the participants were shown two examples (*dog*, *bird*) to familiarize them with the procedure. The target words, written in Times New Roman size 66 font and displayed at the center of the screen, were presented twice in random order, resulting in 20 (2 × 10) exposures. Each target word appeared on the screen for a total of 2 seconds, followed by a 2 seconds delay during which a fixation point was displayed in the middle of the screen. On the rare occasion that a target word was read incorrectly, the experimenter promptly provided the correct pronunciation. The participants successfully incorporated the experimenter's feedback and corrected their responses on the subsequent encounter with a misread target word. Reading accuracy was thus at ceiling during the second target word exposure in both conditions for all participant groups.

Immediately following both exposure conditions, a surprise explicit memory task was administered. The participants were asked to recall verbally as many of the target words as possible from those that were read previously in a story and in a list. They were also informed that this task was not subject to a time limit and that no penalty would be incurred for incorrect guesses. Upon completing the task, the participants were asked if they had been aware of the study's memory component or otherwise had known to remember the target words that were being read. The answer to these questions was "no" for all participants.

Next, the participants completed the WJ-III numbers-reversed test (Woodcock *et al.*, 2001). The experimenter read aloud a string of numbers of increasing length (e.g., *2...8...4*) at the rate of approximately one digit per second, and the participants were asked to repeat them aloud in reverse order (e.g., *4...8...2*). The participants were provided with two examples before beginning the task. The test continued until the three highest-numbered items in a group were answered incorrectly. A total score was then calculated by summing all correct responses.

The native French speakers (children and adults) performed this task in French to obtain an estimate of working memory capacity that was independent of L2 skill.

Following the working memory task, the implicit word-stem completion test was administered. In this test, the participants saw 30 word stems presented individually in random order for a period of 10 s each. The stems were written in Times New Roman size 66 font and were shown in the middle of a computer screen. The participants were asked to complete each stem with as many words as possible during the allotted 10 s period. They were informed that the stems varied in level of difficulty, but that each item could potentially be answered with multiple correct responses, except names of people or places. Two sample items (*not__* and *lan__*) along with several possible answers (e.g., *nothing, notebook; language, land*) were provided with the instructions to the task. Participants generated their answers orally while the experimenter recorded them verbatim on a separate score sheet.

Finally, at the end of the testing session, the native French speakers completed a word knowledge test in order to determine whether they were familiar with the target words. The participants were asked to translate each target English word into French or to leave the response blank if the word was unknown. This task was self-paced, and the participants were given a simple example (mother–*mère*) before starting the test.

Data analysis

The primary measures in this study were proportion of target words recalled in the explicit recall task and the proportion of target word stems completed in the implicit word-stem completion task. These measures were calculated separately in each encoding condition (context vs. isolation). In the recall task, the scores were computed by summing the number of target words remembered correctly from each exposure condition. In the word-stem completion task, the scores were computed by summing all responses for stems completed correctly with a previously read target word. Notably, although participants generated several words for each stem during the allotted time, targets were only scored as correct if they were generated as the first response. Additional scoring criteria were identical in both tasks. Singular–plural differences with nouns (e.g., target *sticks* = response *stick*) were accepted as correct responses. However, inflected and derived forms and other non-exact matches between the targets and the responses were considered wrong (e.g., target *broke* ≠ response *broken*; target *realize* ≠ response *realization*).

This strict criterion was adopted in order to ensure consistent scoring procedures across conditions.

The final proportion scores were derived by dividing the summed scores by the total number of target words in each condition. Because the native French speakers may not have known some target words prior to the experiment, the total number of target words for each native French participant was adjusted by excluding previously unknown words (as revealed through the word knowledge test). Unknown words (those that were translated into French incorrectly or not translated at all) accounted for about six words per child (SD = 4.9) and about two words per adult (SD = 2.2), out of a total of 40 target words.

Results

For all statistical tests, the alpha level for significance was set at 0.05. All correlations were based on two-tailed distributions.

Explicit recall Before examining the relationship between the participants' age and their performance on the explicit recall task, we first compared the rate of false recall (i.e., words that the participants mistakenly recalled as having been encountered earlier) between the four participant groups. The goal of this analysis was to ensure that the participants had not demonstrated any obvious biases in recalling words encountered in context and in isolation. In the context condition, false recall rates ranged between a mean of 0.7 and 1.2 words. In the isolation condition, false recall rates were comparable, the means ranging between 0.4 and 1.3 words. The number of falsely recalled words for each participant was submitted to a mixed three-way ANOVA with age (child, adult) and native language (English, French) as between-subject factors and exposure condition (context, isolation) as a within-subject factor. This ANOVA yielded no significant main effects or interactions, $F(1, 84) < 2.78$, $p > 0.10$, suggesting that no participant group demonstrated any obvious bias in recalling non-target words from the two exposure conditions.

In the following analysis, we compared the proportion of the target words correctly recalled by the four participant groups. For this analysis, we submitted the participants' recall scores to a similar three-way ANOVA, which yielded a significant main effect of exposure condition, $F(1, 84) = 7.13$, $p = 0.009$, and a marginally significant main effect of age, $F(1, 84) = 3.23$, $p = 0.07$, with no other significant main effects or interactions ($p > 0.05$). This pattern of findings suggested that all participants, regardless of their L1 or age, recalled more words previously

Table 6.2 *Mean proportion of explicit recall for the four participant groups as a function of exposure condition (standard deviations in parentheses)*

Group	Exposure condition	
	Context	Isolation
English children	0.26 (0.15)	0.37 (.013)
English adults	0.34 (0.18)	0.42 (0.21)
French children	0.35 (0.12)	0.37 (0.21)
French adults	0.36 (0.16)	0.43 (0.19)

read in isolation than in context, and that overall there was a marginally significant trend for adults to recall more words than for children. Mean proportions of explicit recall are shown in Table 6.2 and the obtained pattern of findings is depicted graphically in Figure 6.1.

The next analysis sought to determine whether there was a relationship between the participants' explicit recall and their reading ability (as measured through the WRAT-3 reading ability subtest) and their working memory capacity (as measured through the WJ-III numbers-reversed task). To accomplish this, we computed Pearson correlation coefficients between the participants' recall scores (separately for each exposure condition) and their reading ability and working memory scores. These analyses yielded no significant relationships either for the entire sample of participants or for subsets of participants grouped by age and native language ($p > 0.05$). This finding suggested that the participants' explicit recall was not significantly related to their reading ability or their working memory capacity.

Implicit word stem completion Previous research has demonstrated that comparing participants' performance between several treatment conditions on implicit memory tests may depend, at least in part, on having comparable baseline performance rates (Chapman et al., 1994). A baseline performance rate refers here to response rates for "control" materials (i.e., words not previously read by participants in context or isolation). Therefore, in the first analysis, we compared the word-stem completion rates for control words between the four participant groups. Proportions of completed word stems for control words were uniform across the groups of participants and ranged between a mean of 0.19 and one of 0.21. These rates were submitted

Age effects in L2 learning 177

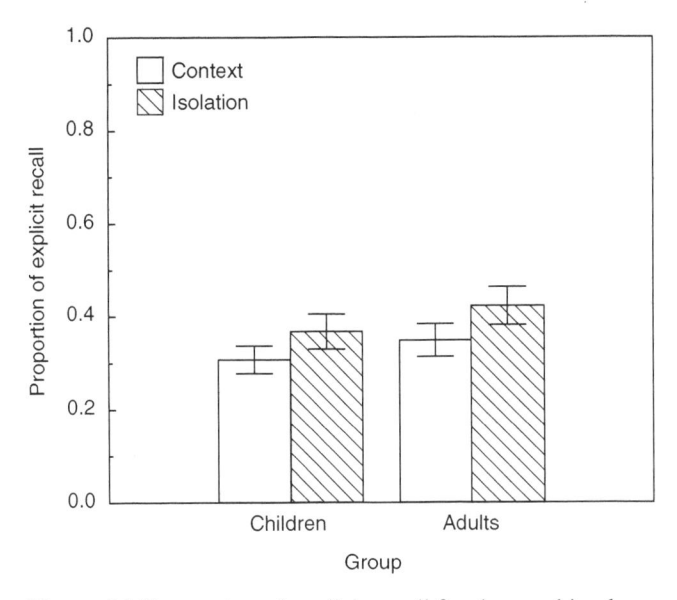

Figure 6.1 Proportion of explicit recall for the combined groups of native English and French children and native English and French adults as a function of exposure condition (context vs. isolation)

to a 2 × 2 (age × native language) ANOVA that yielded no significant main effects or interaction, $F(1, 84) < 0.26$, $p > 0.61$, suggesting that baseline performance rates were statistically comparable. It appears, then, that the participants were equally likely to complete word stems for previously unread words, regardless of their age or native language.

In the next analysis, we compared the proportion of stems completed correctly with a previously read target word. We submitted the participants' stem completion scores to a mixed three-way ANOVA with age (child, adult) and native language (English, French) as between-subject factors and exposure condition (context, isolation) as a within-subject factor. This ANOVA yielded a significant main effect of exposure condition, $F(1, 84) = 36.50$, $p < 0.0001$, and a significant main effect of native language, $F(1, 84) = 17.59$, $p < 0.0001$, with no other significant main effects or interactions ($p > 0.05$). This pattern of findings suggested that all participants, regardless of their native language or age, responded with more words previously read in isolation than in context, a finding that was identical to the memory performance on the explicit recall task. These results also indicated that overall, the native French participants completed more word stems correctly (regardless of the

Table 6.3 *Mean proportion of implicit word-stem completion for the four participant groups as a function of exposure condition (standard deviations in parentheses)*

Group	Exposure condition	
	Context	Isolation
English children	0.30 (0.11)	0.44 (0.15)
English adults	0.33 (0.14)	0.45 (0.17)
French children	0.44 (0.15)	0.57 (0.20)
French adults	0.43 (0.18)	0.53 (0.14)

exposure condition) than the native English participants did. Mean proportions of implicit word-stem completion are shown in Table 6.3, and the obtained pattern of findings is depicted graphically in Figure 6.2.

In the final analysis, we examined whether the participants' word-stem completion was related to their reading ability and their working-memory capacity. As in the previous analysis of explicit recall scores, we computed Pearson correlation coefficients between the participants' word-stem completion scores (separately for each exposure condition) and their reading ability and working memory scores. These analyses revealed a moderate negative association between implicit memory performance in the isolation condition and reading ability, but only for the group of native English adults, $r(23) = -0.54$, $p = 0.007$. This finding suggested that those native English adults who showed higher reading ability on the WRAT-3 reading subtest were also those who demonstrated lower word-stem completion rates on the implicit memory task in the isolation condition.

Discussion

The main goal of the study was to provide direct comparisons of child and adult L2 learners' performance on tests of explicit and implicit memory, in order to investigate the involvement of explicit and implicit memory in L2 processing. Overall, the obtained findings showed no essential differences in memory performance between 11–13-year-old children and 17–26-year-old adults learning English as their L2. More strikingly, the L2 learners' performance on tests of explicit and implicit memory was very similar to the performance of age-matched native English-speaking children and adults.

Age effects in L2 learning   179

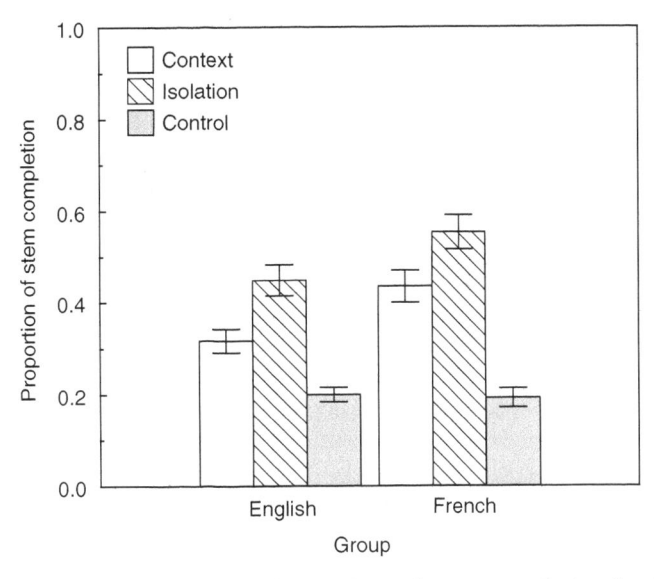

Figure 6.2 Proportion of implicit word-stem completion for the combined groups of native English children and adults and native French children and adults as a function of exposure condition (context vs. isolation vs. control)

Experimental dissociation between explicit and implicit memory

The first objective of this study was to investigate the experimental dissociation between explicit and implicit memory. Our findings provide partial support for a TAP account of memory for words read in different contexts. In line with our predictions, words read in isolation were used more frequently to complete word stems than words read in stories. This suggests that words read in isolation may activate more perceptual processes than words read in meaningful contexts. However, in contrast to our expectations, reading words in isolation (cf. Figures 6.1 and 6.2) also enhanced explicit recall. The superior recall of "list" items is at odds with the large body of literature showing that words read in isolation are disadvantaged on tests of explicit memory in comparison to words read in other kinds of meaningful contexts, such as antonym pairs, passages, scrambled, and coherent texts (e.g., Martin-Chang & Levesque, 2011; Masson & MacLeod, 2000). This finding raises the question of why the words read in context were remembered more poorly than the words read in isolation.

One plausible explanation for this finding is that some participants (e.g., children or L2 learners) were less sensitive than others to contextual information that determines the strength of explicit recall (Lorsbach & Reimer, 2008). However, the findings from the recall task were robust and held regardless of the participants' age and L1 status. Another possibility is that poor readers or readers with smaller working memory, compared to good readers or readers with larger memory capacity, adopted a single-word focus during reading (Faulkner & Levy, 1999), which interfered with contextual processing of stories. However, this explanation is contradicted by the results of the correlational analyses, which revealed no association between the participants' recall performance and their reading ability or working memory capacity.

There are also several methodological explanations for this finding. It is likely that the precise nature of contextual reading influenced the results on the surprise recall task. The contextual reading condition in this study involved a shared reading procedure whereby the experimenter read the majority of the story and the participants read only the target words (which were bolded and underlined to make them stand out from the surrounding text). If the strength of explicit recall, at least in part, depends on the degree of contextual binding of words in context, then it is likely that the target words presented in stories were not processed in as much of a conceptually oriented manner as they could have been. For example, Masson and MacLeod (2000) argued that readers must be "capable of and oriented toward text comprehension" (p. 1096) for contextual binding to occur. In this study, however, the participants may have been listening to the stories with an increased focus on individual words, and their orientation toward the comprehension of the story as a whole may have been obstructed. Clearly, this possibility needs to be explored further by using contextual conditions that do not make target words highly distinctive or that involve participants reading entire stories.

Still another methodological explanation concerns the order of task elements in the experimental procedure. The target words were presented twice in each experimental condition and the surprise recall task occurred immediately (i.e., with no delay between exposure and explicit recall). Ongoing replication projects with L1 speakers have pointed toward a three-way (condition × recency × repetition) interaction, whereby words seen in isolation, more than once, immediately before the surprise recall task are advantaged during explicit recall. Therefore, it is possible that words seen immediately before recall task were still in the participants' short-term memory when they were asked to recall them. Although the target words were also read twice in the context condition, they were separated by large sections of text, which may be at least one reason why an equivalent boost in explicit memory was not observed when words were read in context before the recall task. This interesting possibility needs to be explored further before firm conclusions can be reached.

Developmental dissociation between explicit and implicit memory

The second objective of this study was to test for a developmental dissociation between explicit and implicit memory. Overall, our findings supported this dissociation. The results from the explicit recall task revealed a marginally significant trend for the adult participants to recall more words than the child participants, regardless of their L1. This finding adds to the extensive literature showing improvements in participants' performance on explicit tests of memory over time as a result of developmental changes in encoding and retrieval strategies (e.g., Pressley & Schneider, 1997). This finding is also in line with earlier findings reported by Levesque (2010), who used identical tasks with younger L1 children and found robust age effects for explicit memory, with a group of 7–9-year-old children performing more poorly than a group of young adults. On the other hand, the results from the implicit word-stem completion task revealed no differences in performance between children and adults, regardless of their L1, which is in agreement with the literature on developmental invariance of implicit memory (Komatsu *et al.*, 1996; Perez *et al.*, 1998). This finding supports the idea that a memory system beyond explicit awareness is available early in development and remains relatively stable across the lifespan.

One intriguing finding of this study was that, overall, the L2 participants showed superior performance compared to the L1 participants on the implicit word-stem completion task (see Figure 6.2). This result held regardless of the reading condition and the participants' age. At least one possible explanation for this finding is that L2 learners approached word reading as a potential word learning opportunity, relying mostly on orthographic (perceptual) information to encode L2 words. A similar strategy is used by young children who are faced with an unknown or difficult word: they will first attempt to decode it according to its perceptual (e.g., orthographic) configuration and only then will they rely on surrounding context (if available) to help resolve the decoding ambiguity (e.g., Nation & Snowling, 1998). It is possible that both L2 children and adults engaged in a predominantly perceptual (orthographic) processing of words in both conditions. Therefore, it is not surprising that such enhanced perceptual processing benefited the L2 participants on the word-stem completion task, a test driven by perceptual processing. The significant negative association between implicit memory performance in the isolation condition and reading ability obtained for the native English adults is compatible with this explanation. In a sense, only the native English adults with high reading ability possess the skill that allows them to read isolated words holistically without heavy reliance on perceptual, data-driven, orthographic decoding strategies. As a result of this decreased perceptual processing, these readers tend to perform more poorly on perceptually driven memory tasks than readers with a weaker reading ability.

Explicit and implicit memory and L2 age effects

The current study was conceptualized within a broader area of research on age effects in L2 learning and was motivated by an increased interest in cognitive, memory-based explanations for child–adult differences in L2 learning. The study's main aim was to test claims that child and adult L2 learners might differ in their performance on tests of explicit and implicit memory, which could provide at least one explanation for age effects in L2 learning. Essentially, claims such as these posit that child–adult differences in L2 learning arise due to a developmental shift from implicit to explicit learning processes, which result in children learning the L2 implicitly while adults engage in explicit learning (Bley-Vroman, 2009; DeKeyser, 2000, 2012). Contrary to these proposals, in this study we found little evidence that 11–13-year-old children and 17–26-year-old adults differ with respect to their performance on tests of explicit and implicit memory for L2 words. More importantly, there was no age-based decline in implicit memory performance; in fact, the L2 learners, compared to the L1 speakers, exhibited superior performance on the test of implicit memory. Taken together, these findings suggest that, at least in the context of this study, child and adult L2 learners' implicit memory performance with respect to L2 words is comparable and developmentally stable. These findings are also in full agreement with evidence that adult L2 learners demonstrate such implicit memory effects as auditory priming (enhanced processing of previously heard spoken L2 words) and syntactic priming (increased accuracy in production of previously used L2 structures), which are typically interpreted in terms of implicit learning (see McDonough & Trofimovich, 2008; Trofimovich & McDonough, 2011).

Of course, our findings cannot (and should not) be interpreted as unequivocally challenging the idea that differences in explicit and implicit learning underlie L2 age effects. First, while clearly relevant to the constructs of explicit and implicit learning, explicit and implicit memory are concepts that are distinct from these constructs (Buchner & Wippich, 1998; Kihlstrom et al., 2007). For instance, Shanks (2003) provides a "traditional" definition of implicit learning as "learning which takes place incidentally, in the absence of deliberate hypothesis-testing strategies, and which yields a knowledge base that is inaccessible to consciousness" (p. 11) and acknowledges that both claims central to this definition (minimal demands of attention and lack of awareness) are far from being settled in the research literature. Even less clear is how implicit memory, which is typically defined in relation to particular memory tasks (e.g., Schacter, 1992), relates to implicit learning (for a review of L2 implicit memory research, see DeKeyser, 2003; Ellis, 2005; Robinson, 2010).

It is also possible that a potential shift from reliance on implicit to reliance on explicit memory structures occurs in a different developmental time frame, not captured within this study, that such a shift is dependent on the context of learning (e.g., classroom vs. naturalistic), or that different aspects of the L2 (e.g., vocabulary vs. grammar or pronunciation) vary in the extent to which they are susceptible to such a shift (DeKeyser, 2003). Clearly, these issues need to be addressed in future research. Finally, the findings of the current study have little to say about the issue of ultimate L2 attainment, in the sense that it is unclear how similarities in L2 child and adult learners' performance on tests of explicit and implicit memory relate to their eventual success in L2 learning. Carefully designed cross-sectional research or, better yet, longitudinal studies, could eventually link children's and adults' memory performance to patterns of their ultimate L2 attainment. In the meantime, the quest for viable explanations of child–adult differences in L2 learning is still on, and cognitive explanations of such differences, including those based on different aspects of human memory function, provide appealing alternatives to a variety of neurobiological, experiential, linguistic, and social accounts of age-based differences in L2 learning.

REFERENCES

Abrahamsson, N., & Hyltenstam, K. (2008). The robustness of aptitude effects in near-native second language acquisition. *Studies in Second Language Acquisition*, 30, 481–509.

Bever, T. G. (1981). Normal acquisition processes explain the critical period for language learning. In K. C. Diller (ed.), *Individual differences and universals in language learning aptitude* (pp. 176–198). London: Newbury.

Bialystok, E., & Hakuta, K. (1999). Confounded age: linguistic and cognitive factors in age differences for second language acquisition. In D. Birdsong (ed.), *Second language acquisition and the critical period hypothesis* (pp. 161–181). Mahwah, NJ: Lawrence Erlbaum.

Birdsong, D. (2009). Age and the end state of second language acquisition. In T. Bhatia & W. Ritchie (eds.), *The new handbook of second language acquisition* (pp. 401–424). Bingley: Emerald.

Bley-Vroman, R. (2009). The evolving context of the fundamental difference hypothesis. *Studies in Second Language Acquisition*, 31, 175–198.

Bornstein, M. H. (1987). Sensitive period in development: definition, existence, utility, and meaning. In M. H. Bornstein (ed.), *Sensitive periods in development* (pp. 3–17). Hillsdale, NJ: Lawrence Erlbaum.

Brysbaert, M., & New, B. (2009). Moving beyond Kučera and Francis: a critical evaluation of current word frequency norms and the introduction of a new and improved word frequency measure for American English. *Behavior Research Methods*, 41, 977–990.

Buchner, A., & Wippich, W. (1998). Differences and commonalities between implicit learning and implicit memory. In M. A. Stadler & P. A. Frensch (eds.), *Handbook of implicit learning* (pp. 3–46). Thousand Oaks, CA: Sage.

Chapman, L. J., Chapman, J. P., Curran, T. E., & Miller, M. B. (1994). Do children and the elderly show heightened semantic priming? How to answer the question. *Developmental Review*, 14, 159–185.

Chiswick, B. R., & Miller, P. W. (2008). A test of the critical period hypothesis for language learning. *Journal of Multilingual and Multicultural Development*, 29, 16–29.

Cochran, B. P., McDonald, J. L., & Parault, S. J. (1999). Too smart for their own good: the disadvantage of a superior processing capacity for adult language learners. *Journal of Memory and Language*, 41, 30–58.

Craik, F. I. M., & Bialystok, E. (2008). Lifespan cognitive development: the roles of representation and control. In F. I. M. Craik & T. A. Salthouse (eds.), *The handbook of aging and cognition* (pp. 557–601). New York: Psychology Press.

Curtiss, S. (1977). *Genie: a psycholinguistic study of a modern-day "wild child."* New York: Academic Press.

(1988). Abnormal language acquisition and grammar: evidence for modularity of language. In L. M. Hyman & C. N. Li (eds.), *Language, speech, and mind: studies in honour of Victoria A. Fromkin* (pp. 81–102). London: Routledge.

DeKeyser, R. M. (2000). The robustness of critical period effects in second language acquisition. *Studies in Second Language Acquisition*, 22, 499–533.

(2003). Implicit and explicit learning. In C. J. Doughty & M. H. Long (eds.), *Handbook of second language acquisition* (pp. 313–348). Malden, MA: Blackwell.

(2012). Age effects in second language learning. In S. Gass & A. Mackey (eds.), *Handbook of second language acquisition* (pp. 442–460). London: Routledge.

DeKeyser, R. M., & Larson-Hall, J. (2005). What does the critical period really mean? In J. F. Kroll & A. M. B. de Groot (eds.), *Handbook of bilingualism: psycholinguistic approaches* (pp. 89–108). Oxford University Press.

DeKeyser, R. M., Alfi-Shabtay, I., & Ravid, D. (2010). Cross-linguistic evidence for the nature of age effects in second language acquisition. *Applied Psycholinguistics*, 31, 413–438.

Ellis, N. C. (2005). At the interface: dynamic interactions of explicit and implicit language knowledge. *Studies in Second Language Acquisition*, 27, 305–352.

Elman, J. L. (1993). Learning and development in natural networks: the importance of starting small. *Cognition*, 48, 71–99.

Faulkner, H. J., & Levy, B. A. (1999). Fluent and nonfluent forms of transfer in reading: words and their message. *Psychonomic Bulletin & Review*, 6, 111–116.

Flege, J. E., Yeni-Komshian, G. H., & Liu, S. (1999). Age constraints on second language acquisition. *Journal of Memory and Language*, 41, 78–104.

Hakuta, K., Bialystok, E., & Wiley, E. (2003). Critical evidence: a test of the critical-period hypothesis for second language acquisition. *Psychological Science*, 14, 31–38.

Harley, B., & Hart, D. (1997). Language aptitude and second language proficiency in classroom learners of different starting ages. *Studies in Second Language Acquisition*, 19, 379–400.

Jacobs, B. (1988). Neurobiological differentiation of primary and secondary language acquisition. *Studies in Second Language Acquisition*, 10, 303–337.

Jia, G., & Aaronson, D. (2003). A longitudinal study of Chinese children and adolescents learning English in the United States. *Applied Psycholinguistics*, 24, 131–161.

Kareev, Y., Lieberman, I., & Lev, M. (1997). Through a narrow window: sample size and the perception of correlation. *Journal of Experimental Psychology: General*, 126, 278–287.

Kersten, A. W., & Earles, J. L. (2001). Less really is more for adults learning a miniature artificial language. *Journal of Memory and Language*, 44, 250–273.

Kihlstrom, J. F., Dorfman, J., & Park, L. (2007). Implicit and explicit memory and learning. In M. Velmans & S. Schneider (eds.), *The Blackwell companion to consciousness* (pp. 525–539). Malden, MA: Blackwell.

Komatsu, S., Naito, M., & Fuke, T. (1996). Age-related and intelligence-related differences in implicit memory: effects of generation on a word-fragment completion test. *Journal of Experimental Child Psychology*, 62, 151–172.

Lenneberg, E. H. (1967). *Biological foundations of language*. New York: Wiley.

Levesque, K. (2010). *How do children process words in stories? Differential semantic and perceptual processing of words read in context and isolation.* Unpublished MA thesis. Concordia University, Montreal, Canada.

Light, L. L., & Singh, A. (1987). Implicit and explicit memory in young and older adults. *Journal of Experimental Psychology: Learning, Memory, and Cognition*, 13, 531–541.

Long, M. H. (2007). *Problems in SLA*. Mahwah, NJ: Lawrence Erlbaum.
Lorsbach, T. C., & Reimer, J. F. (2008). Context processing and cognitive control in children and young adults. *The Journal of Genetic Psychology*, 169, 34–50.
Martin-Chang, S. L., & Levy, B. A. (2005). Fluency transfer: differential gains in reading speed and accuracy following isolated word and context training. *Reading and Writing*, 18, 343–376.
Martin-Chang, S. L. & Levesque, K., (2010). Taken out of context: differential processing in contextual and isolated-word reading. *Journal of Research in Reading*. doi:10.1111/j.1467-9817.2011.01506.x
Masson, M. E. J., & MacLeod, C. M. (2000). Taking the "text" out of context effects in repetition priming of word identification. *Memory and Cognition*, 28, 1090–1097.
McCandliss, B. D., Fiez, J. A., Protopapas, A., Conway, M., & McClelland, J. L. (2002). Success and failure in teaching the r-l contrast to Japanese adults: predictions of a Hebbian model of plasticity and stabilization in spoken language perception. *Cognitive, Affective, and Behavioral Neuroscience*, 2, 89–108.
McDonough, K., & Trofimovich, P. (2008). *Using priming methods in second language research*. New York: Routledge.
McFarland, C. E. Jr., Duncan, E., & Bruno, J. M. (1983). Developmental aspects of the generation effect. *Journal of Experimental Child Psychology*, 36, 413–428.
Montrul, S. A. (2008). *Incomplete acquisition in bilingualism: re-examining the age factor*. Amsterdam: John Benjamins.
Morris, C. D., Bransford, J. D., & Franks, J. J. (1977). Levels of processing versus transfer appropriate processing. *Journal of Verbal Learning and Verbal Behavior*, 16, 519–533.
Moyer, A. (1999). Ultimate attainment in L2 phonology: the critical factors of age, motivation, and instruction. *Studies in Second Language Acquisition*, 21, 81–108.
Muñoz, C. (ed.). (2006). *Age and the rate of foreign language learning*. Clevedon: Multilingual Matters.
Nation, K., & Snowling, M. J. (1998). Individual differences in contextual facilitation: evidence from dyslexia and poor reading comprehension. *Child Development*, 69, 996–1011.
Neville, H. J., Mills, D. L., & Lawson, D. S. (1992). Fractionating language: different subsystems with different sensitive periods. *Cerebral Cortex*, 2, 244–258.
Newport, E. L. (1988). Constraints on learning and their role in language acquisition: studies of the acquisition of American Sign Language. *Language Science*, 10, 147–172.
 (1990). Maturational constraints on language learning. *Cognitive Science*, 14, 11–28.
Paradis, M. (2009). *Declarative and procedural determinants of second languages*. Amsterdam: John Benjamins.

Penfield, W., & Roberts, L. (1959). *Speech and brain-mechanisms.* Princeton University Press.
Perez, L. A., Peynircioğlu, Z. F., & Blaxton, T. A. (1998). Developmental differences in implicit and explicit memory performance. *Journal of Experimental Child Psychology*, 70, 167–185.
Pressley, M., & Schneider, W. (1997). *Introduction to memory: development during childhood and adolescence.* Mahwah, NJ: Lawrence Erlbaum.
Pulvermüller, F., & Schumann, J. H. (1994). Neurobiological mechanisms of language acquisition. *Language Learning*, 44, 681–734.
Robinson, P. (2010). Implicit artificial grammar and incidental natural second language learning: how comparable are they? *Language Learning*, 60, 245–263.
Roediger, H. L., & McDermott, K. B. (1993). Implicit memory in normal human subjects. In F. Boller & J. Grafman (eds.), *Handbook of neuropsychology* (vol. 8, pp. 63–131). Amsterdam: Elsevier.
Rohde, D. L. T., & Plaut, D. C. (1999). Language acquisition in the absence of explicit negative evidence: how important is starting small? *Cognition*, 72, 67–109.
Schacter, D. L. (1992). Priming and multiple memory systems: perceptual mechanisms of implicit memory. *Journal of Cognitive Neuroscience*, 4, 244–256.
Shanks, D. R. (2003). Attention and awareness in "implicit" sequence learning. In L. Jiménez (ed.), *Attention and implicit learning* (pp. 11–42). Amsterdam: John Benjamins.
Stevens, G. (2004). Using census data to test the critical-period hypothesis for second-language acquisition. *Psychological Science*, 15, 215–216.
Trofimovich, P., & McDonough, K. (eds.). (2011). *Applying priming methods to L2 learning, teaching and research: insights from psycholinguistics.* Amsterdam: John Benjamins.
Ullman, M. T. (2001). The neural basis of lexicon and grammar in first and second language: the declarative/procedural model. *Bilingualism: Language and Cognition*, 4, 105–122.
  (2005). A cognitive neuroscience perspective on second language acquisition: the declarative/procedural model. In C. Sanz (ed.), *Mind and context in adult second language acquisition* (pp. 141–178). Washington, DC: Georgetown University Press.
Wilkinson, G. S. (1993). *The Wide Range Achievement Test – Third Edition.* Wilmington, DE: Wide Rang Inc.
Woodcock, R., McGrew, K. S., & Mather, N. (2001). *Woodcock-Johnson III – Tests of Cognitive Abilities.* Chicago, IL: Riverside Publishing Company.

7 Bilingualism, language, and aging

Mira Goral

Abstract

Older adults often complain about age-related changes, including difficulty retrieving words during language production and comprehending complex sentences during language processing. Research data, coming primarily from studies with monolingual individuals, corroborate the self-reported age-related language changes. For users of two or more languages, little is known about whether both languages show comparable age-related changes or whether, as anecdotal evidence suggests, the first language might show more resistance to change than later-acquired languages. Also controversial is to what degree age-related cognitive decline in domains such as inhibition, switching, and alternating attention, accounts for the observed age-related language changes and whether these cognitive changes are attenuated in aging multilinguals. Indeed, recent research evidence suggests that multilingualism contributes to cognitive reserve that has been shown to delay age-related decline in specific cognitive skills, including switching and control abilities. Theories and data concerning this potential advantage of multilinguals and the challenging task of assessing the two (or more) languages of older multilinguals are discussed.

This chapter reviews language and cognitive changes associated with aging and the manifestation of such changes in bilingual older adults. First, language changes associated with healthy aging, informed primarily by studies with monolingual adults, are summarized. Then, data from the few studies with bilingual older adults are presented. Such studies have focused primarily on how age affects lexical-retrieval skills, whereas additional domains have rarely been examined. Then, a summary of cognitive changes in older age is provided, based on studies with monolingual individuals followed by those conducted with healthy bilinguals and with bilinguals with progressive neurological disease. The potential relations between language and other cognitive changes in aging are discussed. Finally, the proposal that older bilinguals have an advantage over their monolingual peers is reviewed. This chapter demonstrates that the study of language and cognitive changes associated with bilingual aging contributes not only to our understanding of language and cognitive processing in individuals who use multiple languages but also helps answer broader questions concerning the relationship between language and cognition.

Age-related language decline in monolinguals and bilinguals

Age-related language decline in monolinguals

Amid the physiological and neurological decline accompanying the process of aging, language skills remain relatively intact and some even improve with age (Goral, 2004; Wingfield & Stine-Morrow, 2000). Nevertheless, neurologically healthy older people often complain about changes in their language abilities, primarily their name recall and their processing of spoken language in certain listening conditions. Research studies with older individuals corroborate these complaints, confirming that two language domains that present difficulty for older adults in experimental settings are lexical retrieval for production and auditory comprehension of complex material. In laboratory naming tests, older adults typically produce target names of objects, actions, and people less often than younger adults. Such age-related lower performance on picture-naming tests has been documented primarily with monolingual individuals, in cross-sectional as well as longitudinal studies (e.g., Albert, Heller, & Milberg, 1988; Ardila & Rosselli, 1989; Barresi *et al.*, 2000; Borod, Goodglass, & Kaplan, 1980; Connor *et al.*, 2004; Goulet, Ska, & Kahn, 1994; Le Dorze & Durocher, 1992; MacKay *et al.*, 2002; Nicholas *et al.*, 1985; Ramsay *et al.*, 1999; Thuillard-Colombo & Assal, 1992; Welch *et al.*, 1996).

Three types of findings converge to suggest that the difficulty is with the retrieval of the target name rather than a loss of lexical items. The first is the finding that on vocabulary tests that require recognition rather than retrieval of words older adults perform as well as or better than younger adults (e.g., Béland & Lecours, 1990; Goral *et al.*, 2007). The second is the increased success in word retrieval that older adults experience once they are provided with the first sounds of the target word (e.g., Au *et al.*, 1995; Conner *et al.*, 2011). For example, in the Boston Naming Test (BNT; Kaplan, Goodglass, & Weintraub, 1983), used extensively with individuals with aphasia and in studies with healthy older adults, participants are presented with 60 line drawings of progressively infrequent objects (e.g., Item 1 is "bed"; Item 49 is "asparagus") and are asked to name the object depicted in the drawing. Semantic cues (e.g., "it is a vegetable") followed by phonemic cues ("as...") are provided as needed. Research studies show that accuracy of older participants increases when the first phonemes of the target response are provided. Consistently, a third finding is an age-related increased prevalence of tip-of-the-tongue states, in which people feel that they know the word they are attempting to produce and often can retrieve partial phonological information about it (e.g., number of syllables, initial phoneme), but cannot retrieve the full form for production (Burke et al., 1991).

Whereas some retrieval difficulties may start early – in individuals' fourth or fifth decades – the most obvious decline has been associated with individuals who are 70 or over. However, a direct relationship between age and retrieval performance has not always been demonstrated, and great inter-individual variability, along with confounding variables, such as formal education and gender, characterize the results (e.g., Kempler, 2005; Tsang & Lee, 2001; Zec et al., 2007).

In addition to word-retrieval deficits, older adults have been found to demonstrate increased difficulty in comprehending auditorily presented complex materials (e.g., Federmeier, Kutas, & Schul, 2010; Obler et al., 1991; Stine-Morrow, Ryan, & Leonard, 2000; Wingfield, 1999; Wingfield & Stine-Morrow, 2000), particularly when the materials do not include the typical redundancy associated with human communication (e.g., under noisy conditions, when context is reduced). For example, complex sentence structures (such as center-embedded sentences) are typically more challenging than simple structures (e.g., Waters & Caplan, 2001) and fast presentation conditions are typically more difficult than presentation at normal rates (e.g., Peelle & Wingfield, 2005). Here too, great inter-individual variability has been demonstrated and age alone does not always predict performance (e.g., Goral et al., 2011; Grossman et al., 2002; Wingfield & Grossman, 2006). Researchers have suggested that, in addition to the possibility that language processing per se declines in older age, extra-linguistic changes may account for language performance differences, as discussed below.

Age-related language decline in bilinguals

From studies with young adults we know that testing bilingual individuals and comparing them to monolinguals may be challenging. Conceptually, it has been argued that bilinguals cannot be regarded as comparable to two monolinguals in one mind (e.g., Grosjean, 1998) and that a direct comparison between language performance of bilinguals and monolinguals may be misguided. Furthermore, testing bilingual participants in one or both of their languages on a variety of language tests has demonstrated that, as may be expected, language proficiency affects performance. But even in highly proficient bilinguals and those who grew up in their L2 environment, scores obtained for bilingual participants have been found to differ from those obtained for monolingual individuals. Specific to the lexical-retrieval domain, bilingual speakers typically name fewer pictures correctly, may have more tip-of-the-tongue states, and generate fewer words on list-generation (known also as verbal fluency) tasks than expected on the basis of monolingual norms (e.g., Gollan & Acenas, 2004; Gollan & Brown, 2006; Gollan *et al.*, 2007; Kohnert, Hernandez, & Bates, 1998; Roberts *et al.*, 2002). Indeed, even when bilinguals are tested in their better, dominant language, they may differ from monolinguals performing the same task.

For example, Kohnert *et al.* (1998) have shown that first language (L1) speakers of Spanish who were early learners of English and had received most of their education in English maintained high proficiency in both languages and scored higher on the BNT in English than in Spanish, but their scores in English were nevertheless lower than the monolingual norm. Similarly, verbal-fluency results have been reported to differ for monolingual and bilingual speakers (e.g., Kempler, Teng, & Dick, 1998; Sandoval *et al.*, 2010); specifically, bilingual participants typically generate fewer items that start with the target sound or that belong to the target semantic category than do monolingual participants.

At least two, potentially co-existing, reasons may explain these differences in performance between monolinguals and bilinguals. First, such differences may reflect smaller vocabularies and lower proficiency among the bilinguals being tested. Second, the lower performance observed for bilinguals may be associated with processes of competition between their two languages. Sandoval *et al.* (2010) set out to examine the effects of bilingualism on verbal fluency and to test possible accounts for these effects. The authors compared the performance of young monolingual English speakers and English-dominant, Spanish–English bilingual speakers matched for age (mean = 20) and education (mean = 14) on fluency tasks using a series of letter pairs (e.g., "fa") and semantic categories (e.g., "types of clothing"). They found that their bilingual participants produced fewer correct responses (in English) than the monolingual participants in both the semantic and letter tasks. The bilinguals also produced more low-frequency words than the monolinguals, mainly in the semantic task, and were slower to produce the first word as well as subsequent words than the monolinguals in both tasks. When the authors compared retrieval in the dominant versus the non-dominant language of the bilinguals, they found – consistent with the proficiency reported by the participants – more correct responses in English than in Spanish. They also found that the bilinguals were slower to produce the words in their non-dominant language than in their dominant language. Furthermore, the difference in performance between the bilingual and monolingual participants was evident in the initial time segments of the task rather than toward the end of each trial. A difference in the last time segment in each trial would have been consistent with the reduced-vocabulary account of lower performance. The authors therefore interpreted their results as evidence for retrieval interference between the two languages. This finding suggests that not only proficiency in each language, but also competition between the two languages affects bilinguals' scores.

Because most studies that have documented age-related language differences have been conducted with monolingual individuals, relatively little is known about language changes associated with typical aging in bilingual and multilingual individuals. Recently, a few naming studies with bilinguals have included older participants, but – in keeping with Grosjean's (1998) notion – did not compare the older bilinguals directly to monolingual peers. Hernandez and Kohnert (1999) examined performance of a younger group and an older group of Spanish–English bilinguals on the BNT and found that there were no differences between the two age groups in their accuracy scores. The older bilinguals, however, were slower and made more naming errors than the younger bilinguals in mixed versus blocked language conditions. These findings can be taken as evidence for a dissociation between aging and linguistic and cognitive skills, as discussed below. Gollan et al. (2007) asked older bilinguals to complete the BNT once in each of their two languages and found that the balanced bilinguals – those with relatively equal scores in both languages – scored higher when correct responses were counted regardless of the language in which they were produced compared to the number of correct responses produced in each language separately. The scores of the unbalanced bilinguals did not differ in the two scoring approaches. The finding of higher scores in the "composite scoring" has been previously reported for younger bilingual adults (Kohnert et al., 1998). Testing age-related language changes in older bilinguals, at least for balanced bilinguals, may therefore be more accurate if responses in both languages are considered.

Rosselli *et al.* (2000) did compare performance of older bilingual speakers to that of age-matched monolingual speakers on the BNT and on two additional language abilities: sentence-repetition and verbal-fluency tasks. Participants were Spanish–English bilinguals, as well as monolingual English speakers and monolingual Spanish speakers, between the ages of 50 and 84. The results demonstrated that there was no difference between the bilinguals and the monolinguals on either the sentence-repetition task or the phonemic-fluency task. In addition, the difference between the bilinguals and the monolinguals in accuracy on the BNT did not reach significance. By contrast, the bilinguals produced fewer words than the monolinguals in the semantic-fluency task in both English and Spanish. Consistent with Gollan and her colleagues (Gollan *et al.*, 2007; Sandoval *et al.*, 2010), Rosselli *et al.* (2000) interpreted the results as evidence for the role of interference between the two languages in performance. In this case, a semantic-fluency task is more likely to foster the activation of both languages than a phonemic-fluency task, in which language-specific lexemes are directly retrieved.

To date, evidence regarding the effect of age on language skills of older bilinguals and multilinguals in each of their two or more languages and for parallel versus differential performance in the two or more languages in older age is lacking. One study that examined naming performance in the dominant and non-dominant languages of young and old bilingual speakers focused primarily on the effect of language mixing and switching (Gollan & Ferreira, 2009). The authors reported more errors and longer latencies in the less-dominant language for all their participants as well as more errors and longer latencies for the older as compared to the younger adults. However, age-related differences in accuracy and speed of responses were not evident for the balanced bilinguals – those with strong Spanish skills – compared to the English-dominant bilinguals. Whereas the authors further discussed the switching behavior of their participants and compared required and voluntary switching, they did not address differential effects of age on performance in each of the two languages of their older bilingual participants.

In a recent study, Goral and colleagues (Goral, Spiro, & Obler, in preparation) examined naming performance of healthy older bilinguals in both their languages. Naming performance of 120 Spanish–English community-dwelling adults was measured by the administration of two types of lexical-retrieval task: the BNT and semantic word generation ("animal," "clothing") in both Spanish and English. Results for

78 individuals between the ages of 50 and 83, who had a Mini-Mental Status Examination (MMSE; Folstein, Folstein, & McHugh, 1975) score of 27 (out of 30) and higher and at least 40 percent accuracy on both the English and Spanish versions of the BNT, revealed that age correlated with lexical-retrieval performance in English, L2, but not in Spanish, L1. Furthermore, a regression analysis revealed that number of years of education, number of years of living in an English-speaking country, and self-rated language proficiency significantly predicted performance in both languages; by contrast, older age predicted lower performance only in English. The authors note that the participants varied in their relative current language proficiency in their L1 and L2; yet neither English nor Spanish proficiency correlated with age, suggesting that proficiency could not account for the age effect found for the English naming scores. Furthermore, age correlated significantly with the total number of years lived in an English-speaking country and both variables emerged as significant predictors for English performance. By contrast, only length of stay in an English-speaking country – but not age – predicted lower performance in Spanish. These findings suggest that there may be a differential effect of age on language skills in bilinguals, affecting abilities in the second language earlier than those in the first language.

This differential effect of age on the second language of older bilinguals is consistent with findings from another domain, namely, the study of bilingual individuals who experience dementia. Language is one domain that is typically impaired in dementia, particularly in primary progressive aphasia and in dementia of the Alzheimer's type. For example, people with dementia of the Alzheimer's type often experience anomia, that is, difficulty with word retrieval, and as a result, their language production is characterized by semantic paraphasia and empty speech (e.g., Kemper & Altman, 2009; Ober, 2002). They may also show difficulty maintaining discourse coherence and comprehending complex discourse (e.g., Kempler, 2005; Welland, Lubinski, & Higginbotham, 2002). People who are diagnosed with primary progressive aphasia demonstrate impairment in their language skills prior to impairment in other cognitive domains (Mesulam, 2003). Difficulties include anomia, slowed speech production in the non-fluent type, and degraded semantic representation in the fluent type. Researchers have proposed that at least in part, language difficulty associated with dementia may be due to cognitive impairments in domains such as memory and processing speed (e.g., Bayles *et al.*, 1991; Kempler & Goral, 2008).

Existing data regarding relative performance in the two languages of older bilinguals with dementia show a mixed pattern of results.

Whereas some studies have reported greater preservation of L1 skills (Mendez et al., 1999; Mendez, Saghafi, & Clark, 2004), at least two studies have reported comparable impairment in both languages (Hernández et al., 2007; Meguro et al., 2003) and another has found relatively greater impairment in the more dominant language (Gollan et al., 2010).

Mendez et al. (2004) reported two cases of differential impairment associated with dementia, both favoring L1. One was an English–Spanish–German trilingual speaker, whose naming and word comprehension deficits appeared greater in Spanish and German than in his L1 English. Another was a trilingual who spoke Spanish, English, and Polish and whose progressive difficulty with word retrieval and word comprehension was worse in Polish (L3), better in English (L2), and best, although also impaired, in Spanish, his L1. Meguro et al. (2003), by contrast, reported on four Japanese–Portuguese bilinguals who developed dementia and demonstrated comparable naming impairment in both languages. Comparable impairment in the two languages was also reported for a Catalan–Spanish bilingual woman with dementia of the Alzheimer's type (Hernández et al., 2007). In her naming performance, the participant demonstrated greater difficulty with noun retrieval than with verb retrieval, even when the stimuli were matched on a variety of variables, including frequency, length, and cognate status. The disproportionate difficulty with noun production was evident in both her languages. Her performance was highly accurate for both word categories on tests that measured word comprehension in both languages. Finally, Gollan et al. (2010) reported on BNT data from 29 Spanish–English bilinguals diagnosed with probable dementia of the Alzheimer's type, demonstrating greater impairment in the participants' more-dominant – albeit not necessarily their first-acquired – language. Specifically, the patients' scores in their dominant language (English for 16 participants, Spanish for 13) differed from those of 42 matched healthy controls, whereas smaller differences were noted when scores in the non-dominant language were compared.

Consistent with those studies that found better-preserved skills in L1 than in other languages of bilingual and multilingual individuals, reports demonstrate that some (although not all) individuals with dementia switch to their L1 even when their interlocutors do not understand or speak that language (De Santi et al., 1990; Friedland & Miller, 1999; Mendez et al., 1999). These studies concur with anecdotal reports of bilingual individuals with dementia (and some elderly neurologically healthy individuals) favoring their L1. This L1 preference may be accounted for by the Regression Hypothesis, that is, the assumption that older individuals revert to their first-learned and more dominant language (Ardila & Ramos, 2008). McMurtray, Saito, and Nakamoto (2009) further argued that the regression to L1 use may be an early indicator of the development of dementia. They reviewed two patients who were proficient bilinguals and regular users of both their languages (Japanese and English). Both patients demonstrated decreased use of L2 and a shift to predominant use of L1 preceding the development of cognitive impairment later diagnosed as dementia.

An alternative account for inappropriate language choice is inefficient or impaired language control processes. This hypothesis has been put forward to explain pathological switching and selective language impairment in bilingual aphasia (Green, 1998; Green & Abutalebi, 2008) but can be extended to account for patterns of differential language use in bilingual individuals with dementia. Cognitive control as it pertains to bilingual performance is relevant to the discussion concerning the relationship between language and other cognitive abilities, addressed in the following sections.

Age-related cognitive decline in monolinguals and bilinguals

Age-related cognitive changes, such as reduced working memory capacity, impaired inhibition mechanisms, and difficulty with novel tasks have been extensively documented (e.g., Caplan & Waters, 1999; Craik & Salthouse, 2008; Drag & Bieliauskas, 2009; Kemper & Kemtes, 1999; Park et al., 2002; Salthouse, 2010). It is therefore possible that the age-related language changes in monolingual and bilingual adults and the differential performance in the languages of older bilinguals summarized above are not primarily linguistic in origin, but rather are rooted in extra-linguistic cognitive changes (e.g., Obler et al., 2011). Whereas a comprehensive discussion of the relations between language and cognition is beyond the scope of this chapter, two areas of research are of immediate interest here. One pertains to underlying cognitive mechanisms that have been proposed to explain age-related language changes (and language performance generally) (e.g., Gollan & Brown, 2006; Hasher & Zacks, 1988; Just & Carpenter, 1992; King & Just, 1991; Salthouse, 1988; Waters & Caplan, 2001). The other relates to the potential superior abilities of bilinguals in specific cognitive domains, such as attention control. First, the main findings of age-related cognitive changes are summarized, followed by a discussion of cognitive disadvantages and advantages of bilingualism.

Age-related cognitive decline in monolinguals

Several cognitive domains have been associated with age-related decline, including certain aspects of memory (e.g., working memory), cognitive speed, and attention. For example, lower performance of older as compared to younger adults has been documented on a variety of commonly used neuropsychological tests, including the Wisconsin Card Sorting Test (e.g., Rhodes, 2004), working-memory-span tests (e.g., Park *et al.*, 2002; Wingfield *et al.*, 1988), the Trail Making Test (e.g., Salthouse & Fristoe, 1995), the Simon Test (Bialystok *et al.*, 2004; Van der Lubbe & Verleger, 2002), and the Stroop Task (e.g., Van der Elst *et al.*, 2006; West & Alain, 2000), as well as a number of experimental tasks (e.g., Mata, von Helversen, & Rieskamp, 2010; Salthouse *et al.*, 1998; Taconnat *et al.*, 2009, to name a few). In the Stroop Task (Stroop, 1935), participants are presented with color words printed in different ink colors. Participants are first instructed to read the words (automatic condition) and in a second condition (interference condition) to name the color of the ink. The task requires the inhibition of automatically activated word reading in conditions in which the word is the name of one color (e.g., "blue") but is printed in a different color ink (e.g., yellow). Findings suggest that older adults are less successful than younger adults in inhibiting the automatically activated word reading. For example, Van der Elst *et al.* (2006) examined Stroop performance in a large sample of Dutch speakers ranging in age from 24 to 81 and found that – consistent with previous results – age was a significant predictor of both time and accuracy measures.

Performance on the tests used in such studies may rely not only on the specific domain targeted (e.g., inhibition), but also on higher skills that have been collectively termed executive function (EF) and include a variety of interacting abilities, such as attention-switching control, decision making, and planning (e.g., Band, Riddernikhof, & Segalowitz, 2002; Greenwood, 2000; Miyake, 2001). These higher cognitive skills may all contribute to performance on any complex cognitive task. However, testing the individual contribution of each specific domain has proved difficult (Ashendorf & McCaffrey, 2008; Borella, Carretti, & De Beni, 2008; Miyake *et al.*, 2000). As in the language domain, here too, great inter-individual variability characterizes the findings (e.g., Ghisletta, McArdle, & Lindenberger, 2006; Raz, 2009).

The declining language and other cognitive abilities reported for older individuals raise the question as to whether language decline accompanies cognitive decline or results from it. It is possible that difficulty with processing complex spoken language, for example, is associated primarily with deficient working memory and inhibition abilities rather than with a linguistic deficit. Similarly, verbal-fluency tasks may test not only lexical abilities but also cognitive skills, such as use of strategies and monitoring abilities (e.g., Troyer, 2000). Confrontation naming tests may tap a primarily linguistic ability, although here, too, one can argue that the contrasting trajectories of vocabulary scores (increasing with age) and word-retrieval scores (decreasing with age) can be accounted for by underlying extra-linguistic cognitive abilities, such as selection and inhibition (e.g., Kavé, Samuel-Enoch, & Adiv, 2009).

Age-related cognitive decline and bilingualism

Two potentially conflicting sets of results have been addressed in the literature on cognitive aging and bilingualism: one demonstrating lower performance of bilinguals as compared to their monolingual peers, the other highlighting superior performance by bilinguals in specific domains.

Although only a handful of studies directly addressing cognitive skills in older bilinguals can be found in the literature, reports demonstrate that, as found with language tests, there are cognitive tests that reveal a disadvantage for bilinguals as compared to monolinguals (e.g., Ardila et al., 2000; Fernandes et al., 2007). For example, Fernandes et al. (2007) presented monolingual and bilingual younger (mean age = 20) and older adults (mean age = 70) with lists of semantically related words in different conditions, with and without interference. The bilingual participants were identified based on questionnaire data and spoke a wide range of languages; testing was conducted only in English. The authors found a main effect of age and a main effect of language group, indicating that older participants recalled fewer words than younger participants and that bilingual participants recalled fewer words than monolingual participants. By contrast, there was no significant difference in the effect of interference on correct recall between monolingual and bilingual participants. Bilinguals and monolinguals also did not differ in their performance on a digit-span task. The authors hypothesized that the lower scores of the bilinguals on the recall test were due to their lexical, rather than cognitive abilities.

Lower scores of bilinguals on normative tests in English, as well as on tests translated into other languages, could be, in part, due to language-specific differences, because variations in word length, semantic relations, cultural associations, and level of proficiency can interact with performance (e.g., Ardila, 2003, 2007; Kempler et al., 1998; Manly, 2008; Yoon et al., 2004). Whereas normative data from bilinguals on many neuropsychological tests are not currently available, researchers have begun in recent years to emphasize the need to establish norms for bilingual participants on such tests (Acevedo et al., 2009; Ardila, 2007; Mungas et al., 2000; Ostrosky-Solís et al., 2007). Perhaps particularly lacking are data from older bilingual individuals (see Ardila, 2003; Goral, 2004).

Lower scores achieved by older bilinguals on language tests (e.g., naming tests) may reflect retrieval difficulties associated with aging (in one or both of their languages) or compromised performance associated with bilingualism – due to the fact that bilinguals' vocabularies in each of their languages are less comprehensive than those of monolinguals or due to processes of inter-language interference and competition. In addition, bilinguals who regularly use one language more than the other may experience a language shift (Heredia & Altarriba, 2001) and changes associated with language attrition (e.g., Goral et al., 2008; Köpke et al., 2007); that is, a decreased ability in a language that is being used less often (typically L1), as use and proficiency in another language (typically L2) increases. These potentially co-existing processes may be difficult to dissociate. Evidence from switching tasks suggests that even if older bilinguals perform well in each of their languages, they experience greater difficulty than younger bilinguals when the task requires switching between their languages (e.g., Hernandez & Kohnert, 1999). This is consistent with the assumption that declining cognitive skills may affect language performance in older bilingual people.

Furthermore, declining cognitive skills, such as decreased inhibition and selection skills and other decreased EF abilities, can account for bilingual language behaviors associated with dementia. Specifically, appropriate language selection and language switching is likely to rely on intact attention and switching control processes. Moreover, if we accept theories that suggest that for bilinguals and multilinguals all their languages are active at all times (e.g., de Groot, Delmaar, & Lupker, 2000; Kroll et al., 2008), good inhibition skills would be needed to alternate between the languages, inhibiting the unselected one(s) (e.g., Green, 1998; Meuter & Allport, 1999; Kroll, Bobb, & Wodniecka, 2006). Compromised inhibition skills may lead to a need for a long-term suppression of one of the languages, to avoid the otherwise typical co-activation of both languages and alternating inhibition of one. A regression to using one language only, reported above, can be explained by such long-term suppression, although this does not explain why L1 specifically would be favored. Whether L1 is indeed favored in such cases or just appears to be as a result of a reporting bias, needs to be determined.

In contrast to the disadvantages summarized above, recent studies that examined performance of older bilinguals on cognitive tasks have focused on the potential advantage that bilingualism offers. Findings from these studies demonstrate that bilingualism interacts with age-related cognitive changes. For example, Bialystok and her colleagues found that older bilingual adults performed better than older monolingual adults and similar to younger monolingual and bilingual individuals on a task that required suppressing irrelevant information while attending to task-relevant information (Bialystok et al., 2004; Bialystok et al., 2009). In a series of experiments, Bialystok and her colleagues (2004) compared performance of younger and older monolingual and bilingual speakers on the Simon Test. In this test, a red or blue square appears on the right or the left of a computer screen and participants are asked to press the left shift key or the right shift key when they see a red or blue square, respectively. Half the trials are congruent, that is, the square is presented on the same side as the target response key, and half of the trials are incongruent, the square being presented on the opposite side. Monolingual and bilingual participants who performed similarly on memory, intelligence, and vocabulary tests differed in their performance on the Simon Test. Namely, the bilingual participants demonstrated a smaller Simon effect, that is, smaller response-time differences between congruent and incongruent conditions, than did the monolinguals. Moreover, there were greater age differences between the monolingual older and younger groups than between the two bilingual age groups.

Additional studies have corroborated the finding that bilinguals have an advantage over monolinguals in tasks that require conflict resolution using executive control (Costa, Hernández, & Sebastián-Gallés, 2008; Wodniecka et al., 2010). Several of these studies have used versions of the Stroop Task in which automatically activated information needs to be suppressed in order to complete the task successfully. Results demonstrated a reduced Stroop interference effect in bilingual speakers as compared to monolinguals (Bialystok, Craik, & Luk, 2008; Hernández et al., 2010; Zied et al., 2004). For example, Hernández et al. (2010) employed a version of the Stroop Task that did not involve word stimuli. They found that their 42 Catalan–Spanish bilinguals were faster than 42 Spanish monolingual young adults, showed a reduced Stroop interference effect, and enjoyed a facilitation effect. In a second, visual-attention-to-cues experiment, bilinguals did not perform differently from monolinguals. The authors interpreted their results to suggest that bilingualism affects specific cognitive abilities – specifically executive control – but not others, such as attention-orientation processes. Zied *et al.* (2004) showed that older participants who were proficient Arabic–French bilinguals demonstrated smaller interference effects on the Stroop Task than less-proficient older bilinguals, suggesting that proficient bilinguals are particularly good at inhibiting competing information.

However, recent attempts to replicate the bilingual advantage have not been successful, leaving the question open for further study. For example, Kousaie and Phillips (2012) examined performance on the Stroop Task of four participant groups: younger (mean age = 23) and older (mean age = 69) monolinguals, and younger (mean age = 24) and older (mean age = 72) highly proficient bilingual (English–French) participants. In contrast to previous studies, their bilingual participants were not immigrants and were matched to the monolingual individuals in terms of socio-cultural variables. The authors found no bilingual advantage; they reported a significant age effect, with the younger participants demonstrating faster responses than the older ones, but no effect of language group or interaction between age and language group.

The potential cognitive advantage associated with bilingual older adults is consistent with findings from bilingual children (e.g., Bialystok, 2001; Bialystok *et al.*, 2004; Rosenblum & Pinker, 1983). Studies comparing the cognitive abilities of monolingual and bilingual children are characterized by a history of contradictory findings, yet recent, rigorous experiments have demonstrated that in selected domains, bilingual children outperform their monolingual peers. For example, Bialystok analyzed her own work as well as the work of others and found that when monolingual and bilingual children were compared on language tasks that required various levels of analysis, knowledge, and metalinguistic awareness, neither group consistently outperformed the other. By contrast, on all tasks that required control of attention, such as attending to selected elements while ignoring others, bilingual children showed a consistent advantage (e.g., counting words in sentences versus counting words in strings; judging grammaticality of anomalous sentences versus judging grammaticality of incorrect but meaningful sentences; the Simon Test) (e.g., Bialystok, 2001). Bialystok suggests that the common element of studies and tasks in which bilingual children demonstrate an advantage over monolingual children is not control over knowledge or metalinguistic abilities, but rather a specific cognitive process, namely, control of attention. It can be hypothesized that this ability to direct attention only to specific aspects of the information or the task at hand is particularly developed in bilingual individuals who need to exercise such skills daily, selecting the appropriate language of conversation and inhibiting and activating selective language systems as they toggle between their languages.

Support for the superior control abilities of older bilinguals may also be found in evidence from bilingual individuals with dementia. Whereas the reports on dementia in bilinguals summarized above demonstrate the potential consequences of cognitive impairment on language performance, recent studies demonstrate that the manifestation of dementia-related cognitive changes may be delayed in multilinguals as compared to monolinguals. Bialystok, Craik, and Freedman (2007) examined the medical records of 184 individuals with dementia and classified each person as a monolingual (n = 91) or a bilingual (n = 93). The bilinguals varied in their age of L2 learning and in the languages they spoke (there were 25 different first languages among the participants). The authors found that the age of onset of dementia symptoms – as determined by family report during the initial neurological assessment – of the bilingual speakers was significantly later (4.1 years) than that of the monolinguals. The authors proposed that constant use of two (or more) languages may have the type of effect identified as cognitive reserve (e.g., Stern et al., 1999; Stern, 2009). The concept of cognitive reserve can account for the differential onset and rate of cognitive decline associated with older individuals who have had higher versus lower levels of education, occupation, and socialization. Further support for the relationship between bilingualism and reserve can be found in the results reported by Kavé and her colleagues (Kavé et al., 2008). In a study that reviewed interviews collected from over 800 individuals who were 75 or older and examined the relations between the number of languages spoken and a number of additional demographic variables and performance on a mental-state screening test, these authors found a relation between the number of languages spoken and cognitive skills. That is, those who reported speaking multiple languages performed better than those who reported speaking only two languages (there were no monolingual individuals in their sample).

Conclusions

Bilingual older people experience decreasing language abilities, similar to those documented for monolingual older people. However, age-related language changes in bilinguals may develop late and may affect one language while sparing another. These selective effects may result from processes of language attrition or may reflect decreased abilities to inhibit and activate the languages. Indeed, it is possible that age-related cognitive decline underlies language changes evident in older adulthood generally and in older bilinguals specifically. Furthermore, there is research evidence suggesting that, on selected cognitive skills, bilinguals may have an advantage over their monolingual peers. Studies with healthy bilingual older individuals have demonstrated better performance of bilingual older adults on tasks that require attention switching and executive control, and studies with neurologically impaired individuals demonstrated delayed cognitive decline in bilinguals as compared to monolinguals. These advantages may be attributed to the lifelong use of two languages and the continuous practice of selective activation and inhibition. It is noted, however, that a bilingual advantage is not always found. The mechanisms that underlie this potential advantage for bilinguals are fertile ground for further research. Whether language and other cognitive skills change in unison or demonstrate independent trajectories also remains to be examined.

REFERENCES

Acevedo, A., Krueger, K. R., Navarro, E., Ortiz, F., Manly, J. J., Padilla-Velez, M. M., et al. (2009). The Spanish translation and adaptation of the Uniform Data Set of the National Institute on Aging Alzheimer's Disease Centers. *Alzheimer Disease and Associated Disorders*, 23, 102–109.

Albert, M. S., Heller, H. S., & Milberg, W. (1988). Changes in naming ability with age. *Psychology and Aging*, 3, 173–178.

Ardila, A. (2003). Language representation and working memory with bilinguals. *Journal of Communication Disorders*, 36, 233–240.

(2007). Toward the development of a cross-linguistic naming test. *Archives of Clinical Neuropsychology*, 22, 297–307.

Ardila, A., & Ramos, E. (2008). Normal and abnormal aging in bilinguals. *Dementia and Neuropsychologia*, 2, 242–247.

Ardila, A., & Rosselli, M. (1989). Neuropsychological characteristics of normal aging. *Developmental Neuropsychology*, 5, 307–320.

Ardila, A., Rosselli, M., Ostrosky-Solis, F., Marcos, J., Granda, G., & Soto, M. (2000). Syntactic comprehension verbal memory and calculation abilities in Spanish–English bilinguals. *Applied Neuropsychology*, 7, 3–16.

Ashendorf, L., & McCaffrey, R. J. (2008). Exploring age-related decline on the Wisconsin Card Sorting Test. *The Clinical Neuropsychologist*, 22, 262–272.

Au, R., Joung, P., Nicholas, M., Obler, L. K., Kass, R., & Albert, M. L. (1995). Naming ability across the adult life span. *Aging and Cognition*, 2, 300–311.

Band, G. P. H., Riddernikhof, K. R., & Segalowitz, S. (2002). Explaining neurocognitive aging: is one factor enough? *Brain and Cognition*, 49, 259–267.

Barresi, B., Nicholas, M., Connor, L. T., Obler, L. K., & Albert, M. L. (2000). Semantic degradation and lexical access in age-related naming failures. *Aging, Neuropsychology, and Cognition*, 7, 169–178.

Bayles, K. A., Tomoeda, C. K., Kaszniak, A. W., & Trosset, M. W. (1991). Alzheimer's disease effects on semantic memory: loss of structure or impaired processing? *Journal of Cognitive Neuroscience*, 3, 166–182.

Béland, R., & Lecours, A. R. (1990). The aphasia battery: a subset of normative data in relation to age and school education. *Aphasiology*, 4, 439–462.

Bialystok, E. (2001). Metalinguistic aspects of bilingual processing. *Annual Review of Applied Linguistics*, 21, 169–181.

Bialystok, E., Craik, F. I. M., Klein, R., & Viswanathan, M. (2004). Bilingualism, aging, and cognitive control: evidence from the Simon task. *Psychology and Aging*, 19(2), 290–303.

Bialystok, E., Craik, F. I. M., & Freedman, M. (2007). Bilingualism as a protection against the onset of symptoms of dementia. *Neuropsychologia*, 45, 459–464.

Bialystok, E., Craik, F. I. M., & Luk, G. (2008). Cognitive control and lexical access in younger and older bilinguals. *Journal of Experimental Psychology: Learning, Memory and Cognition*, 34, 859–873.

Bialystok, E., Craik, F. I. M., Green, D. W., & Gollan, T. H. (2009). Bilingual minds. *Psychological Science in the Public Interest*, 10(3), 89–129.

Borella, E., Carretti, B., & De Beni, R. (2008). Working memory and inhibition across the adult life-span. *Acta Psychologica*, 128, 33–44.

Borod, J. C., Goodglass, H., & Kaplan, E. (1980). Normative data on the Boston Diagnostic Aphasia Examination, Parietal Lobe Battery, and the Boston Naming Test. *Journal of Clinical Neuropsychology*, 2, 209–215.

Burke, D. M., MacKay, D. G., Worthley, J. B., & Wade, E. D. (1991). On the tip of the tongue: what causes word-finding failure in young and older adults. *Journal of Memory and Language*, 30, 542–579.

Caplan, D., & Waters, G. S. (1999). Verbal working memory and sentence comprehension. *Behavioral and Brain Sciences*, 22, 77–126.

Conner, P. S., Hyun, J., O'Connor-Wells, B., Anema, I., Goral, M., Monéreau-Merry, M., et al. (2011). Age-related differences in idiom production in adulthood. *Clinical Linguistics and Phonetics*, 25(10), 899–912.

Connor, L. T., Spiro, A. III, Obler, L. K., & Albert, M. L. (2004). Change in object naming ability during adulthood. *Journal of Gerontology: Psychological Sciences*, 59(5), 203–209.

Costa, A., Hernández, M., & Sebastián-Gallés, N. (2008). Bilingualism aids conflict resolution: evidence from the ANT task. *Cognition*, 106, 59–86.

Craik, F. I. M., & Salthouse, T. A. (eds.) (2008). *Handbook of aging and cognition* (3rd edn). New York: Psychology Press.

de Groot, A. M. B., Delmaar, P., & Lupker, S. (2000). The processing of interlexical homographs in translation recognition and lexical decision: support for non-selective access to bilingual memory. *Quarterly Journal of Experimental Psychology*, 53(2), 397–428.

De Santi, S., Obler, L. K., Sabo-Abrahamson, H., & Goldberger, J. (1990). Discourse abilities and deficits in multilingual dementia. In Y. Joanette & H. H. Brownell (eds.), *Discourse ability and brain damage: theoretical and empirical perspectives* (pp. 224–235). New York: Springer.

Drag, M. A., & Bieliauskas, L. A. (2009). Contemporary review 2009: cognitive aging. *Journal of Geriatric Psychiatry and Neurology*, 23(2), 75–93.

Federmeier, K. D., Kutas, M., & Schul, R. (2010). Age-related and individual differences in the use of prediction during language comprehension. *Brain and Language*, 115, 149–161.

Fernandes, M. A., Craik, F. I. M., Bialystok, E., & Kreuger, S. (2007). Effects of bilingualism, aging, and semantic relatedness on memory under divided attention. *Canadian Journal of Experimental Psychology*, 61, 128–141.

Folstein, M. F., Folstein, S. E., & McHugh, P. R. (1975). "Mini-Mental State": a practical method for grading the cognitive state of patients for the clinician. *Journal of Psychiatric Research*, 12, 189–198.

Friedland, D., & Miller, N. (1999). Language mixing in bilingual speakers with Alzheimer's dementia: a conversation analysis approach. *Aphasiology*, 13, 427–444.

Ghisletta, P., McArdle, J. J., & Lindenberger, U. (2006). Longitudinal cognition-survival relations in old and very old age: 13-year data from the Berlin Aging Study. *European Psychologist*, 11(3), 204–223.

Gollan, T. H., & Acenas, L. A. (2004). What is a TOT? Cognate and translation effects on tip-of-the-tongue states in Spanish-English and Tagalog–English bilinguals. *Journal of Experimental Psychology: Learning, Memory, and Cognition*, 30, 246–269.

Gollan, T. H., & Brown, A. S. (2006). From tip-of-the-tongue (TOT) data to theoretical implications in two steps: when more TOTs means better retrieval. *Journal of Experimental Psychology: General*, 135, 462–483.

Gollan, T. H., & Ferreira, V. S. (2009). Should I stay or should I switch? A cost-benefit analysis of voluntary language switching in young and aging bilinguals. *Journal of Experimental Psychology: Learning, Memory & Cognition*, 35, 640–665.

Gollan, T. H., Fennema-Notestine, C., Montoya, R. I., & Jernigan, T. L. (2007). The bilingual effect on Boston Naming Test performance. *The Journal of the International Neuropsychological Society*, 13, 197–208.

Gollan, T. H., Salmon, D. P., Montoya, R. I., & da Pena, E. (2010). Accessibility of the nondominant language in picture naming: a counterintuitive effect of dementia on bilingual language production. *Neuropsychologia*, 48, 1356–1366.

Goral, M. (2004). First-language decline in healthy aging: implications for attrition in bilingualism. *Journal of Neurolinguistics*, 17, 31–52.

Goral, M., Spiro, A. III, Albert, M. L., Obler, L. K., & Connor, L. (2007). Change in lexical-retrieval skills in adulthood. *The Mental Lexicon*, 2(2), 215–238.

Goral, M., Libben, G., Obler, L. K., Jarema, G., & Ohayon, K. (2008). Lexical attrition in younger and older bilingual adults. *Clinical Linguistics and Phonetics*, 22, 509–522.

Goral, M., Clark-Cotton, M. R., Spiro, A. III, Obler, L. K., Verkuilen, J., & Albert, M. L. (2011). The contribution of set shifting and working memory to sentence processing in older adults. *Experimental Aging Research*, 37, 516–538.

Goral, M., Spiro, A. III., & Obler, L. K. (in preparation). The relations between language and cognitive changes in older bilingual and monolingual adults.
Goulet, P., Ska, B., & Kahn, H. J. (1994). Is there a decline in picture naming with advancing age? *Journal of Speech and Hearing Research*, 37, 629–644.
Green, D. W. (1998). Mental control of the bilingual lexico-semantic system. *Bilingualism: Language and Cognition*, 1, 67–81.
Green, D. W., & Abutalebi, J. (2008). Understanding the link between bilingual aphasia and language control. *Journal of Neurolinguistics*, 21, 558–576.
Greenwood, P. M. (2000). The frontal aging hypothesis evaluated. *Journal of the International Neuropsychological Society*, 6, 705–726.
Grosjean, F. (1998). Studying bilinguals: methodological and conceptual issues. *Bilingualism: Language and Cognition*, 1, 131–149.
Grossman, M., Cooke, A., DeVita, C., Alsop, D., Detre, J., Chen, W., et al. (2002). Age-related changes in working memory during sentence comprehension: an fMRI study. *NeuroImage*, 15, 302–318.
Hasher, L., & Zacks, R. T. (1988). Working memory, comprehension, and aging: a review and a new view. In G. H. Bower (ed.), *The psychology of learning and motivation* (pp. 193–225). San Diego, CA: Academic Press.
Heredia, R. R., & Altarriba, J. (2001). Bilingual language mixing: why do bilinguals code-switch? *Current Directions in Psychological Science*, 10, 164–168.
Hernandez, A. E., & Kohnert, K. J. (1999). Aging and language switching in bilinguals. *Aging, Neuropsychology, and Cognition*, 6(2), 69–83.
Hernández, M., Costa, A., Sebastián-Gallés, N., Juncadella, M., & Reñe, R. (2007). The organisation of nouns and verbs in bilingual speakers: a case of bilingual grammatical category-specific deficit. *Journal of Neurolinguistics*, 20, 285–305.
Hernández, M., Costa, A., Fuentes, L. J., Vivas, A. B., & Sebastián-Gallés, N. (2010). The impact of bilingualism on the executive control and orienting networks of attention. *Bilingualism: Language and Cognition*, 13, 315–325.
Just, M. A., & Carpenter, P. A. (1992). A capacity theory of comprehension: individual differences in working memory. *Psychological Review*, 99, 122–149.
Kaplan, E., Goodglass, H., & Weintraub, S. (1983). *The Boston Naming Test*. Philadelphia: Lea & Febiger.
Kavé, G., Eyal, N., Shorek, A., & Cohen-Mansfield, J., (2008). Multilingualism and cognitive state in the oldest old. *Psychology & Aging*, 23(1), 70–78.
Kavé, G., Samuel-Enoch, K., & Adiv, S. (2009). The association between age and the frequency of nouns selected for production. *Psychology and Aging*, 24, 17–27.
Kemper, S., & Altman, L. J. P. (2009). Dementia and language. In P. R. Hof & C. V. Mobbs (eds.), *Handbook of the neuroscience of aging* (pp. 293–298). London: Elsevier.
Kemper, S., & Kemtes, K. A. (1999). Limitations on syntactic processing. In S. Kemper & R. Kliegl (eds.) *Constraints on language: aging, grammar, and memory* (pp. 79–106). Boston: Kluwer Academic Publishers.

Kempler, D. (2005). *Neurocognitive disorders in aging.* Thousand Oaks, CA: Sage.

Kempler, D., & Goral, M. (2008). Language and dementia: neuropsychological aspects. *Annual Review of Applied Linguistics,* 28, 1–18.

Kempler, D., Teng, E., & Dick, M. (1998). The effects of age, education, and ethnicity on verbal fluency. *Journal of the International Neuropsychological Society,* 4(6), 531–538.

King, J., & Just, M. A. (1991). Individual differences in syntactic processing: the role of working memory. *Journal of Memory and Language,* 30, 580–602.

Kohnert, K. J., Hernandez, A. E., & Bates, E. (1998). Bilingual performance on the Boston Naming Test: preliminary norms in Spanish and English. *Brain and Language,* 65, 422–440.

Köpke, B., Schmid, M. S., Keijzer, M. C. J., & Dostert, S. (2007). *Language attrition: theoretical perspectives.* Amsterdam: John Benjamins.

Kousaie, S., & Phillips, N. A. (2012). Aging and bilingualism: absence of a 'bilingual advantage' in Stroop interference in a non-immigrant sample. *The Quarterly Journal of Experimental Psychology,* 65(2), 356–369.

Kroll, J. F., Bobb, S. C., & Wodniecka, Z. (2006). Language selectivity is the exception, not the rule: arguments against a fixed locus of language selection in bilingual speech. *Bilingualism: Language and Cognition,* 9, 119–135.

Kroll, J. F., Bobb, S. C., Misra, M., & Taomei, G. (2008). Language selection in bilingual speech: evidence for inhibitory processes. *Acta Psychologica,* 128, 416–430.

Le Dorze, G., & Durocher, J. (1992). The effects of age, educational level, and stimulus length on naming in normal subjects. *Journal of Speech-Language Pathology and Audiology,* 16, 21–29.

MacKay, A. J., Connor, L. T., Albert, M. L., & Obler, L. K. (2002). Noun and verb retrieval in healthy aging. *Journal of the International Neuropsychological Society,* 8, 764–770.

Manly, J. (2008). Critical issues in cultural neuropsychology: profit from diversity. *Neuropsychological Review,* 18, 179–183.

Mata, R., von Helversen, B., & Rieskamp, J. (2010). Learning to choose: cognitive aging and strategy selection in decision making. *Psychology and Aging,* 25, 299–309.

McMurtray, A., Saito, E., & Nakamoto, B. (2009). Language preference and development of dementia among bilingual individuals. *Hawaii Medical Journal,* 68, 223–226.

Meguro, K., Senaha, M., Caramelli, P., Ishizaki, J., Chubacci, R., Meguro, M., et al. (2003). Language deterioration in four Japanese-Portuguese bilingual patients with Alzheimer's disease: a trans-cultural study of Japanese elderly immigrants in Brazil. *Psychogeriatrics,* 3, 63–68.

Mendez, M. F., Perryman, K. M., Pontón, M. O., & Cummings, J. L. (1999). Bilingualism and dementia. *Journal of Neuropsychiatry and Clinical Neuroscience,* 11, 411–412.

Mendez, M. F., Saghafi, S., & Clark, D. G. (2004). Semantic dementia in multilingual patients. *Journal of Neuropsychiatry and Clinical Neuroscience,* 16, 381.

Mesulam M. M. (2003). Primary progressive aphasia–a language-based dementia. *New England Journal of Medicine*, 349, 1535–1542.

Meuter, R. F. I., & Allport, A. (1999). Bilingual language switching in naming: asymmetrical costs of language selection. *Journal of Memory and Language*, 40, 25–40.

Miyake, A. (2001). Individual differences in working memory. Introduction to the special section. *Journal of Experimental Psychology*, 130(2), 163–168.

Miyake, A., Friedman, N. P., Emerson, M. J., Witzki, A. H., Howerter, A., & Wager, T. (2000). The unity and diversity of executive functions and their contributions to complex 'frontal lobe' tasks: a latent variable analysis. *Cognitive Psychology*, 41, 49–100.

Mungas, D., Reed, B. R., Marshall, S. C., & Gonzalez, H. M. (2000). Development of psychometrically matched English and Spanish language neuropsychological tests for older persons. *Neuropsychology*, 2, 209–223.

Nicholas, M., Obler, L. K., Albert, M., & Goodglass, H. (1985). Lexical retrieval in healthy aging. *Cortex*, 21, 595–606.

Ober, B. A. (2002). TR and non-RT methodology for semantic priming research with Alzheimer's disease patients: a critical review. *Journal of Clinical and Experimental Neuropsychology*, 24, 883–912.

Obler, L. K., Fein, D., Nicholas, M., & Albert, M. L. (1991). Auditory comprehension and aging: decline in syntactic processing. *Applied Psycholinguistics*, 12, 433–452.

Obler, L. K., Albert, M. L., Spiro, A. III, Goral, M., Rykhlevskaia, E., Hyun, J., et al. (2011). Language changes associated with aging. In M. L. Albert & J. E. Knoefel (eds.), *Clinical neurology of aging* (3rd edn) (pp. 485–493). New York: Oxford University Press.

Ostrosky-Solís, F., Gómez-Pérez, Ma. E., Matute, E., Rosselli, M., Ardila, A., & Pineda, D. (2007). NEUROPSI Attention and Memory: a neuropsychological test battery in Spanish with norms by age and educational level. *Applied Neuropsychology*, 14, 156–170.

Park, D. C., Lautenschlager, G., Hedden, T., Davidson, N., Smith, A. D., & Smith, P. (2002). Models of visuospatial and verbal memory across the adult life span. *Psychology and Aging*, 17, 299–320.

Peelle, J. E., & Wingfield, A. (2005). Dissociations in perceptual learning revealed by adult age differences in adaptation to time-compressed speech. *Journal of Experimental Psychology: Human Perception and Performance*, 31(6), 1315–1330.

Ramsay, C. B., Nicholas, M., Au, R., Obler, L. K., & Albert, M. L. (1999). Verb naming in normal aging. *Applied Neuropsychology*, 6, 57–67.

Raz, N. (2009). Decline and compensation in aging brain and cognition: promises and constraints. *Neuropsychological Review*, 19, 411–414.

Rhodes, G. M. (2004). Age-related differences in performance on the Wisconsin Card Sorting Test: a meta-analytic review. *Psychology and Aging*, 19, 482–494.

Roberts, P., Garcia, L. J., Desrochers, A., & Hernandez, D. (2002). English performance of proficient bilingual adults on the Boston Naming Test. *Aphasiology*, 16, 635–645.

Rosenblum, T., & Pinker, S. A. (1983). Word magic revisited: monolingual and bilingual children's understanding of the word-object relationship. *Child Development*, 54, 773–780.

Rosselli, M., Ardila, A., Araujo, K., Weeks, V. A., Caracciolo, V., Padilla, M., et al. (2000). Verbal fluency and repetition skills in healthy older Spanish-English bilinguals. *Applied Neuropsychology*, 7, 17–24.

Salthouse, T. A. (1988). Resource-reduction interpretation of cognitive aging. *Developmental Review*, 8, 238–272.

(2010). *Major issues in cognitive aging*. New York: Oxford University Press.

Salthouse, T. A., & Fristoe, N. M. (1995). A process analysis of adult age effects on a computer-administered trail making test. *Neuropsychology*, 9, 518–528.

Salthouse, T., Fristoe, N., McGuthry, K. E., & Hambrick, D. Z. (1998). Relation of task switching to speed, age and fluid intelligence. *Psychology and Aging*, 13, 445–461.

Sandoval, T. C., Gollan, T. H., Ferreira, V. S., & Salmon, D. P. (2010). What causes the bilingual disadvantage in verbal fluency: the dual-task analogy. *Bilingualism: Language and Cognition*, 13, 231–252.

Stern, Y. (2009). Cognitive reserve. *Neuropsychologia*, 47(10), 2015–2028.

Stern, Y., Albert, S., Tang, M. X., & Tsai, W. Y. (1999). Rate of memory decline in AD is related to education and occupation: cognitive reserve? *Neurology*, 53, 1942–1947.

Stine-Morrow, E. A. L., Ryan, S., & Leonard, S. (2000). Age differences in on-line syntactic processing. *Experimental Aging Research*, 26, 315–322.

Stroop, J. R. (1935). Studies of interference in serial verbal reactions. *Journal of Experimental Psychology*, 18, 643–662.

Taconnat, L., Raz, N., Toczé, C., Bouazzaoui, B., Sauzéon, H., Fay, S., et al. (2009). Ageing and organisation strategies in free recall: the role of cognitive flexibility. *European Journal of Cognitive Psychology*, 21, 347–365.

Thuillard-Colombo, F., & Assal, G. (1992). Adaptation française du test de dénomination de Boston. Versions abrégées. *Revue Européene de Psychologie Appliquée*, 42, 67–71.

Troyer, A. K. (2000). Normative data for clustering and switching on verbal fluency tasks. *Journal of Clinical and Experimental Neuropsychology*, 22, 370–378.

Tsang, H.-L., & Lee, T. M. C. (2001). The effect of ageing on confrontational naming ability. *Archives of Clinical Neuropsychology*, 18, 81–89.

Van der Elst, W., Van Boxtel, M. P. J., Van Breukelen, G. J. P., & Jolles, J. (2006). The Stroop color-word test: influence of age, sex, and education; and normative data for a large sample across the adult age range. *Assessment*, 13, 62–79.

Van der Lubbe, R. H. V., & Verleger, R. (2002). Aging and the Simon task. *Psychophysiology*, 39, 100–110.

Waters, G. S., & Caplan, D. (2001). Age, working memory, and on-line syntactic processing in sentence comprehension. *Psychology and Aging*, 16, 128–144.

Welch, L. W., Doineau, D., Johnson, S., & King, D. (1996). Educational and gender normative data for the Boston Naming Test in a group of older adults. *Brain and Language*, 53, 260–266.

Welland, R. J., Lubinski, R., & Higginbotham, D. J. (2002). Discourse comprehension test performance of elders with dementia of the Alzheimer type. *Journal of Speech, Language & Hearing Research*, 45, 1175–1187.

West, R., & Alain, C. (2000). Age-related decline in inhibitory control contributes to the increased Stroop effect observed in older adults. *Psychophysiology*, 37, 179–189.

Wingfield, A. (1999). Comprehending spoken questions: effects of cognitive and sensory change in adult aging. In N. Schwarz, D. C. Park, B. Knauper & S. Sudman (eds.), *Cognition, aging, and self-reports* (pp. 201–229). Philadelphia, PA: Psychology Press.

Wingfield, A., & Grossman, M. (2006). Language and the aging brain: patterns of neural compensation revealed by functional brain imaging. *Journal of Neurophysiology*, 96(6), 2830–2839.

Wingfield, A., & Stine-Morrow, E. A. L. (2000). Language and speech. In F. I. M. Craik & T. A. Salthouse (eds.) *The handbook of aging and cognition* (pp. 359–416). Mahwah, NJ: Lawrence Erlbaum Associates.

Wingfield, A., Stine, E. A. L., Lahar, C. J., & Aberdeen, J. S. (1988). Does the capacity of working memory change with age? *Experimental Aging Research*, 14(2–3), 103–107.

Wodniecka, Z., Craik, F. I. M., Luo, L., & Bialystok, E. (2010). Does bilingualism help memory? Competing effects of verbal ability and executive control. *International Journal of Bilingual Education and Bilingualism*, 13, 575–595.

Yoon, C., Feinberg, F, Hu, P., Hall, A., Hedden, T., Chen, H.-Y. M., et al. (2004). Category norms as a function of culture and age: comparisons of item responses to 105 categories by American and Chinese adults. *Psychology and Aging*, 19(3), 379–393.

Zec, R., Burkett, N. R., Markwell, S. J., & Larsen, D. L. (2007). A cross-sectional study of the effects of age, education, and gender on the Boston Naming Test. *Clinical Neuropsychologist*, 21(4), 587–616.

Zied, K. M., Phillipe, A., Karine, P., Valerie, H.-T., Ghislaine, A., Arnaud, R., et al. (2004). Bilingualism and adult differences in inhibitory mechanisms: evidence from a bilingual Stroop task. *Brain and Cognition*, 54, 254–256.

8 Crossovers and codeswitching in the investigation of immigrant autobiographical memory

Carmit Altman, Robert W. Schrauf, and Joel Walters

Abstract

Using a cue-word paradigm from autobiographical memory, we report on an investigation of bilingual memory and codeswitching among immigrant adults. The aims of the chapter are threefold: (1) to analyze the relationship between language and memory among bilingual immigrants via same language and crossover memories (memories which were cued in one language yet retrieved in the other language the bilingual knows); (2) to examine the extent to which immigration influences classical memory patterns; and (3) to find out whether behavioral evidence – codeswitching – exists to support immigrants' self-reported memory retrieval of crossover memories. Twelve English–Hebrew bilingual immigrants aged 64–79 were asked to retrieve specific memories to cue words in separate first language (L1) and second language (L2) sessions. Following retrieval of memories, participants were asked to report the decade of the memory event and the language in which the memory came to them. Results replicated Schrauf and Rubin (1998, 2000), showing evidence for a reminiscence bump (a higher than expected number of memories during the 10–30 age period) and a trend toward an immigration bump in bilinguals who immigrated at a later age. Overall, 40 percent of the memories recalled were "crossovers" (i.e., memories in a language that differed from the language of the experimental session and cue word). In an attempt to find behavioral correlates for "crossover" judgments, narratives from selected memories were examined for the extent of within-utterance bilingual codeswitching. Narratives elicited for selected memories revealed more codeswitching in crossover memories, showing evidence for a consistency between reported memories and bilingual language behavior.

The present chapter reports on a study of bilingual autobiographical memory, focusing on the effect of bilinguals' two languages on memory retrieval and the effect of immigration on the reminiscence bump (RB), in autobiographical memory (Schrauf & Rubin, 1998, 2000).

Specifically, the study characterizes effects of immigration on the recall of autobiographical memories among English–Hebrew immigrants to Israel, first in terms of their influence on RB data and then in terms of two laboratory measures of bilingual processing: crossover memories and codeswitching. Crossover memories involve the metalinguistic report by the participant of his or her awareness of the language of retrieval, and codeswitching refers to occasions when participants switch from one language to the other during the oral narration of their memories. By examining patterns of crossover memories and codeswitching, we attempt to get at some of the uniquely bilingual aspects of autobiographical memory.

Bilingual speech involves the alternate use of two languages by the same speaker, within a single utterance, across speaking turns, from topic to topic, setting to setting, and listener to listener. Bilinguals acquire their languages in a wide variety of contexts and attain a highly variable range of proficiencies. Simultaneous and sequential child bilinguals, hotel desk clerks, and hospital intake nurses, students on study abroad programs, foreign workers, and immigrants all lay claim to some form of bilingualism. Mature adults in their 60s and 70s have personal memories that include monolingual as well as bilingual events. Retrieval of these events can occur in one, the other, or both languages of their linguistic repertoire. The narratives that reflect someone's life story may be recounted in a single language or peppered with bilingual codeswitching, one of the linguistic phenomena which makes a bilingual unique. The brief review below first presents some background on autobiographical memory and immigration effects in that paradigm. In particular, we focus on what has been called the RB, retrieval of large numbers of memories during the 10–30 age period (Rubin & Schulkind, 1997). Several explanations for the RB are given, one of which is preferred as an account for the effects of immigration on the RB. In the next section, the notion of crossover memories – those memories reported to be retrieved in a language different from the experimental session – is introduced as a means to examine the language of retrieval. The last section describes relevant research on codeswitching, presented here as a behavioral correlate of crossover memories.

Reminiscence bump and immigration effects

In a cognitively and psychologically healthy person, the distribution of memories across the lifespan shows three components (Conway & Rubin, 1993; Rubin & Schulkind, 1997). Infantile amnesia has been

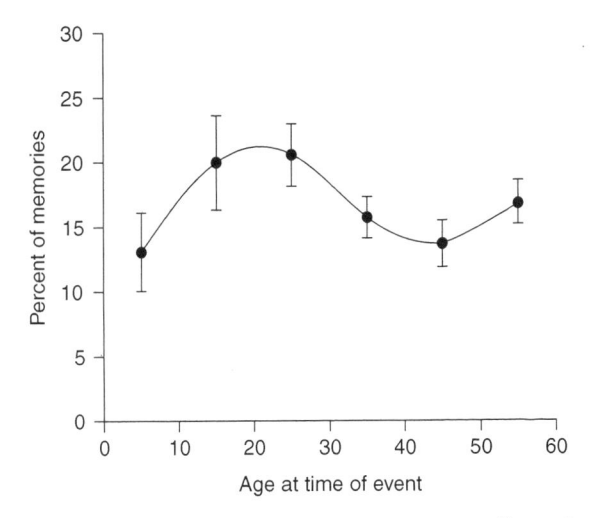

[Figure: graph showing percent of memories vs age at time of event, with a peak around age 20-25]

Figure 8.1 Distribution of memories in monolingual mature adults

suggested as a way to characterize memories for events prior to the age of 3–4; these memories are not generally accessible to adult recall (e.g., Nelson, 1993). At the other end of the memory spectrum, there is robust evidence for enhanced memory of recent events – termed *the recency effect* (Rubin, 1982). Finally, the *reminiscence bump* describes recall of a larger than expected number of vivid and important memories from the 10–30 age period of life (Rubin & Schulkind, 1997). Figure 8.1 graphically depicts the reminiscence bump.

Three possible explanations have been suggested for the reminiscence bump. A maturational account suggests that cognitive capacities are at their optimum from ages 10–30, and as such, one remembers more events from that period (Cerella, 1985; Rubin, Rahal, & Poon, 1998). A social development account maintains that more events are recalled from the 10–30 age period because this is when an individual's personal and social identity is formed and one's self-narrative is constructed (Fitzgerald, 1988). Finally, a cognitive mechanisms account suggests that during young adulthood, a person goes through a period of rapid change followed by a period of relative stability (Rubin *et al.*, 1998). The contrast between change and stability offers optimal conditions for remembering and later recall. Based on the cognitive mechanisms approach, Schrauf and Rubin (1998) maintain that early adulthood is similar to immigration in that both involve a period of rapid change followed by relative stability. Thus, the cognitive mechanisms account provides a plausible explanation for the effect of immigration on the recall of memories, usually observed as a kind of second reminiscence bump at the time of immigration.

Crossover memories

Many studies of autobiographical memory have employed a cue-word technique for eliciting autobiographical memories with adult bilinguals (Bugelski, 1977; Larsen et al., 2002; Marian & Neisser 1997, 2000; Matsumoto & Stanny, 2006; Otoya, 1987; Schrauf & Rubin, 1998, 2000). Bugelski (1977) asked 22 Spanish–English bilingual adults to report their first thoughts in response to 20 common words during three age periods: 1–15, 16–30, and 30+. The procedure was conducted first in Spanish and a month later in English. Results showed that thoughts recalled in response to English cue words were associated with later time periods than those in Spanish. Similarly, Otoya (1987) studied 40 Spanish–English bilingual students, half of whom were monocultural (most born in the USA) and half bicultural (immigration from ages 7–18). Participants were asked to think of three memories up to the age of 8 and another two memories from the age of 14+. Then they were asked to recall personal memories for 10 words from each language (six of which were translation equivalents). Results showed that monocultural participants reported earlier memories than bicultural bilinguals, and Otoya (1987) concluded that cognitive consequences of migration accounted for these differences.

Marian and Neisser (1997) presented 20 Russian–English bilinguals with 16 Russian–English pairs of cue words constructed from translation equivalents. Participants were asked to associate autobiographical memories with the cue words and later asked to specify the date of the memories. On average, memories cued in Russian were dated earlier than memories cued in English. This study also reported that the language of retrieval matched the language at the time of the event. In a subsequent study, Marian and Neisser (2000) presented 16 Russian–English pairs of translation-equivalent prompts to 24 Russian–English bilingual university students. Participants were asked to associate autobiographical memories with the cue-word prompts, to date the memories, and to indicate the language at the time of the event. Participants were instructed not to codeswitch and to respond "only in the language appropriate for that part" of the experiment, since the authors' purpose was to arrive at language-specific recall. Results showed that the cues in a given language tended to facilitate retrieval of events that had occurred in that same language. Similarly, Matsumoto and Stanny (2006) found that Japanese–English bilinguals recalled more and earlier memories when presented with a Japanese (L1) cue. Furthermore, access to autobiographical memory was optimized when there was congruity between the language of the cue and the language of encoding. Schrauf and Rubin (1998) investigated the distribution of autobiographical memories in mature Spanish–English bilinguals (ages 61–69) who had immigrated to the United States during adulthood (ages 20–35). They examined the effects of immigration, a major cultural and linguistic transition, on the retrieval of autobiographical memories. The lexical cueing technique (Crovitz & Schiffman, 1974; Galton, 1879) was used and their assumption was that the retrieval of personal memories would be influenced by the language of the cue word, that is, cue words in the L1 would trigger earlier memories and cue words in L2 would be associated with memories from the period after immigration. Schrauf and Rubin's (1998) findings showed no cue-word effects with mature adults, in contrast to Marian and Neisser's (2000) findings with university students. In addition, Schrauf and Rubin (1998, 2000) asked participants to indicate the "language in which the memory came to them" in order to ascertain whether each cue word would trigger a crossover memory. Their findings indicated that crossover memories, which amounted to 20 percent in their 1998 study and 25 percent in their 2000 study, generated more English (L2) crossovers after immigration and more Spanish (L1) crossover memories before immigration.

The cueing methodology was also used by Larsen et al. (2002), who examined Polish immigrants in Denmark. The study consisted of two groups of participants over the age of 50: (1) "early" immigrants, who were 24 years old at the time of immigration, and (2) "late" immigrants, who were 34 when immigrating. Both groups recalled more autobiographical memories in Polish (L1) for the decades before immigration and more memories in Danish (L2) for the decades after immigration. Crossover memories lend credence to the notion that some of the bilingual's memories are language specific (Schrauf & Rubin, 2000). These authors maintain that memories of bilinguals may be stored in one or the other language in some enduring fashion. Their findings show that the notion of "memory in words" appeared clear to bilinguals, and that they were able to rate the degree to which particular memories "came to them in words." This was independent of the other rated features (e.g., a sense of reliving, sensory detail, emotionality, and rehearsal) that the memory might be associated with. In an effort to provide behavioral support for "reported recall" in autobiographical memory, we introduce here the phenomenon of bilingual codeswitching.

Codeswitching

One noticeable feature in the speech of many bilinguals is the phenomenon of codeswitching (CS). CS refers to alternation of one or more languages in the discourse of people who share more than a single language. CS research has followed two largely independent tracks, one structural/linguistic, another functional/sociolinguistic. Proposals such as Poplack's (1980) equivalence and bound morpheme constraints, Sankoff's (2002) mathematical model of bilingual discourse, and generative approaches to CS (e.g., MacSwan, 1999, 2005; Myers-Scotton, 2005) all focus on how to represent the structural constituents of two grammars. MacSwan (2005) suggests that research on CS might best be conceptualized as the study of how linguistic subsystems interact in bilinguals "such that morphological and phonological coding of a lexical item is possible in some syntactic contexts and not in others" (MacSwan, 2005, p. 5). In this work, CS is considered a distinctly bilingual phenomenon that is demonstrated by the speaker's language behavior. CS from this perspective is concerned with the representation of lexical categories and syntactic relations in bilingual speech and in the switch points between L1 and L2. Functional approaches to CS, in contrast, have focused on language use and the social motivations that underlie the phenomenon. Among the most prominent "functions" of CS are: setting, participants, and topic (e.g., Gardner-Chloros, Charles, & Cheshire, 2000; Zentella, 1997). Pragmatically, CS has been shown to express focus, emphasis, clarification, contrast, and the like (Zentella, 1997). Early on, Genesee (1980) observed that bilinguals may recognize the psychological and social purposes of CS. Walters (2005) synthesizes structural and functional approaches to CS in a model of sociopragmatic and psycholinguistic processing based on literature from a wide range of studies (e.g., Clyne, 2003; Grosjean, 1995; Myers-Scotton, 2005; Zentella, 1997).

The frequency of CS ranges from 5–25 percent of the utterances in corpora from a variety of studies involving natural speech. Focus on surface-level switching has led to a distinction between lexical CS and CS of larger segments of speech (Paradis & Nicoladis, 2007), where lexical switches, in particular nouns and noun phrases, range from 14–70 percent. Zentella (1997) reported that 14 percent of codeswitches in a corpus of children and adults were lexical codeswitches of nouns. Stephens (1986) stated that 31 percent of the codeswitches in his data were noun-related; and Iluz-Cohen and Walters (in press) found that 70 percent of English–Hebrew preschool children's codeswitches were lexical. These studies reported far more CS than what Paradis and Nicoladis (2007) found in their study of French–English bilingual children, where lexical CS rates were under 3 percent.

In summary, the reminiscence bump during the 10–30 age period and effects due to the cognitive and linguistic changes characteristic of immigration are not specific to bilingual processing. Crossover memories, however, are unique to bilinguals, but they represent metalinguistic or reported language use. Thus, a more elaborated narrative of the memory, its setting, participants, and details may provide more insight into language specifics and the bilingual processes of autobiographical memory. To examine this possibility, we elicited longer narratives about specific memories in order to gain further entry to the event, looking at CS as a way to tap into other bilingual features of autobiographical memory.

Predictions

Robust evidence for a **reminiscence bump** between the ages of 10 and 30 in comparison to other decades of the lifespan (Rubin & Schulkind, 1997) led us to predict more memories for the reminiscence bump period for both L1 and L2 sessions. In line with previous research concerning **crossover memories** (Schrauf & Rubin 1998, 2000), it was hypothesized that same-language memories would be more numerous than crossover memories, but that there would be a substantial number of crossover memories, and these would be more abundant for L2 (Hebrew) sessions/cue words than for L1 (English) sessions/cue words. We also predicted that there would be more bilingual language use in the form of intrasentential **CS** for crossover memories than for same-language memories.

Method

Participants

Twelve mature adult bilinguals, six men and six women, whose ages ranged from 64 to 79, took part in the study. Participants were recruited by personal contacts with faculty members from Bar Ilan University. All participants agreed to participate in the study voluntarily, and prior to the interviews, each participant was asked to sign a consent form.

Participants were native speakers of English who were exposed either exclusively or predominantly to English (L1) from infancy through early adulthood. All participants reported having learned Hebrew (L2) during adulthood. Following data collection, two native Hebrew speakers evaluated the English–Hebrew bilingual participants' L2 vocabulary, grammar and fluency on a scale from 1-10 based on the memories participants provided; results were 7.87, 7.70, and 7.75, respectively. All participants had immigrated to Israel from an English-speaking country (USA or UK) during adulthood, mostly for religious or ideological reasons. The mean age of immigration was 31.5 and the range was from age 21 to 46. The individual ages of immigration were 21, 22, 23, 27, 27, 29, 33, 34, 37, 39, 40, and 46. Two potential participants were dropped from the study because they could not respond fluently in Hebrew.

Procedure and materials

All participants took part in two sessions, one in each language, either in their homes or in the university, using the cue-word technique employed by Schrauf and Rubin (1998) with stimulus words selected from Rubin (1980). The first session was conducted in L2 and the second session in L1. The first session was held in the less-preferred language as a way of ensuring that the participant was able to sustain a conversation in L2. The second session, conducted by the same bilingual interviewer, took place from one to two weeks after the first session and involved the same procedure. It should be noted that the cues were provided in the language of the session such that in the L1 session, L1 cues were presented, and in the L2 session, L2 cues were shown. At the end of the second session, participants were asked to complete a language background questionnaire. Each session lasted approximately 90 minutes with the exception of one participant, whose sessions each lasted four hours due to the length of his responses to the cue words and the narratives produced. All sessions were recorded on a Sony MP3 Player for digital recording and transferred electronically for transcription.

Instructions Procedures were based in part on Schrauf and Rubin's (1998, 2000) tasks related to retrieval of specific memories and in part on actual language behavior in the form of narratives related to specific events recalled. During the first session, conducted in L2, participants were asked to look, in sequence, at each of 16 cue words and briefly talk about a concrete and specific memory for each word.

To ensure that the participant understood the instructions to recall a memory that occurred "at one particular place or time," s/he was first given examples of different memories that would be possible responses to the cue word "bicycle." For example, participants were told that, upon hearing the word "bicycle," a person might recall the first time he or she learned how to ride a bicycle with his or her father holding the handlebars. This is an event that occurred at a particular place and time. In contrast, they were told that "riding my bicycle home from school" would not specify a unique time or place. Three more examples from different life periods were provided so that participants would not be influenced to recall memories from a specific time period. Participants then engaged in two to three practice trials prior to the beginning of the experiment. For each memory, the participant was asked to report the language of that memory. This report allowed us to classify memories as same-language or crossover memories depending on whether the reported language was the same as the language of the experimental session (*same language*) or different from the experimental session (*crossover*). After all 16 cue words had been responded to, each participant was asked to go back and provide dates for each of the memories.

The present research also sought to examine actual bilingual language behavior. Thus, after a participant completed the cue-word procedure, the interviewer chose one memory from each of the decades of the lifespan and asked the participant to provide a longer and more detailed oral narrative about that memory. Events were chosen by the interviewer to cover a range of time intervals for each language, a balance of L1/L2 retrievals, and a balance of both same-language and crossover memories. Approximately nine narratives were elicited from each participant in each session. The CS data were based on narratives, where participants were asked to describe "anything else remembered about the specific memory." In order to achieve a balance among the different experimental conditions, the narratives were elicited from memories chosen both on the basis of the decade in which they took place and on the language in which they were retrieved.

Data analyses

The following components of bilingual autobiographical memory in the two language sessions were examined:

(1) Reminiscence bump: measured by comparing the age of total memories in the 10–30 age period versus the decades immediately before and after the 10–30 age period.
(2) Immigration effect: measured by the rise in numbers of memories in the five years before and after the individuals' age at immigration.

(3) Same-language versus crossover memories: comparing metalinguistic judgments of memory retrieval, as either a match of language of session and judged language of retrieval (same) or a disjunction between language of session and judged language of retrieval (crossover).

(4) Codeswitched language behavior: codeswitches were counted for each instance in which the participant switched from the language of the session to the other language. For example, in the sentence, *I went to the* **makolet** *[grocery store] yesterday* one instance of CS in the English session was counted. That is, the speaker codeswitched once from the language of the session (English) to the other language (Hebrew).

Recall data were analyzed with parametric and non-parametric statistical procedures (ANOVA, chi-square, and z-scores). Narrative data were transcribed and coded for CS.

Results and discussion

Three aspects of bilingual autobiographical memory are reported here. First, we present data on the reminiscence bump and the effects of immigration for the twelve English–Hebrew bilingual participants. Next, we provide a detailed analysis of same-language and crossover memories. Finally, we examine the extent of CS in the oral narratives in order to assess whether the reported language of retrieval in crossover memories is supported by actual language behavior.

Reminiscence bump and immigration effects

A total of 384 memories were elicited from the 12 English–Hebrew (E–H) bilinguals (12 participants × 2 languages × 16 cue words). Of these, 41 memories were excluded since they were not specific enough regarding time and place, or participants refused to talk about the cue word (e.g., grief). This yielded a total of 343 memories. In order to adjust for age differences and since reminiscence-bump patterns were clearer for older participants (over age 70) than among those in their early and mid 60s, only memories up to age 60 were included. Figure 8.2 depicts the mean number of memories for each decade across the lifespan. The figure illustrates the findings from all 12 participants and combines data from both L1 and L2 language sessions.

The data from these English–Hebrew bilingual adults replicate Schrauf and Rubin's (1998, 2000) findings, showing clear evidence

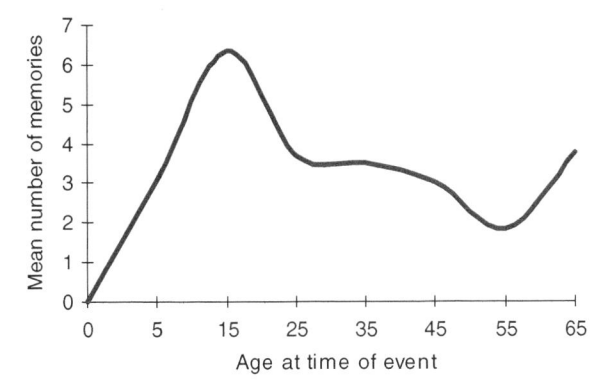

[Figure: graph showing mean number of memories vs age at time of event, with peak around age 15]

Figure 8.2 Distribution of memories across the lifespan from both English and Hebrew sessions for English–Hebrew participants

for a reminiscence bump during the 10–30 age period, as indicated by the salient peak during this time interval. Mean recall of memories for these two decades was 4.66 (SD = 1.52). Memories recalled during the age periods surrounding the reminiscence bump (0–10 and 30–40) averaged 3.06 (SD = 1.62). Z-scores comparing numbers of memories for the two decades surrounding the reminiscence bump (0–10 and 30–40) and the two decades of the reminiscence bump (10–20 and 20–30) showed that the number of memories was significantly higher for the reminiscence bump period (z = 2.91, p < 0.01). Although the histogram suggests a smaller rise during the 30–40 year decade, this effect was not significant. Figures 8.3a and 8.3b present recall of memories for English (L1) and Hebrew (L2), respectively, across the six age intervals.

In both figures, a reminiscence bump and another smaller rise are visible. The reminiscence bump appears at the age of 15 in Figures 8.3a and 8.3b. The later bump appears in L1 around age 45 and in L2 around age 35. The reason for this difference may be the different nature of L1 and L2 recall. Individual data indicate that all 12 participants showed a rise in memories for the 10–30 age periods in the L1 session and 11 of the 12 participants showed a rise for the same period for memories in the L2 sessions.

In order to clarify immigration effects, participants were divided into two groups: (a) earlier immigrants (n = 6): those who immigrated *before* age 30; and (b) later immigrants (n = 6): those who immigrated *after* age 30. The earlier immigrants arrived in Israel at a mean age of 24.83 (SD = 3.25), while the later immigrants arrived at a mean age

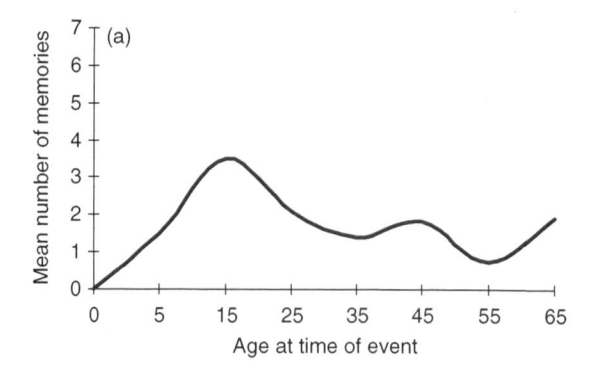

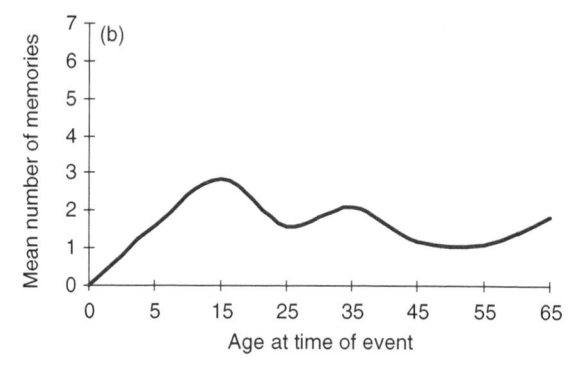

Figure 8.3 Distribution of memories during the English (a) and Hebrew (b) sessions for 12 English–Hebrew adult bilinguals

of 38.16 (SD = 4.70). Findings for these two subgroups can be seen in Figures 8.4a and 8.4b.

The graphs in Figures 8.4a and 8.4b are similar in that both present a robust reminiscence bump; however, they show a distinct difference in the period beyond age 30. Earlier immigrants (Figure 8.4a) show no noticeable rise in the number of memories (immigration effect), since mean age of immigration (M = 24.83) falls within the reminiscence bump decades (10–30). In contrast, later immigrants show a rise in memories during the 35–45 age period, which may be due to the immigration experience. In the case of earlier immigrants, the overlap between the two memory components (reminiscence bump and immigration effect) does not allow us to determine the cause of the rise of memories (Figure 8.4a), but in the case of later immigrants for whom the traditional bump precedes immigration, the effect is notable.

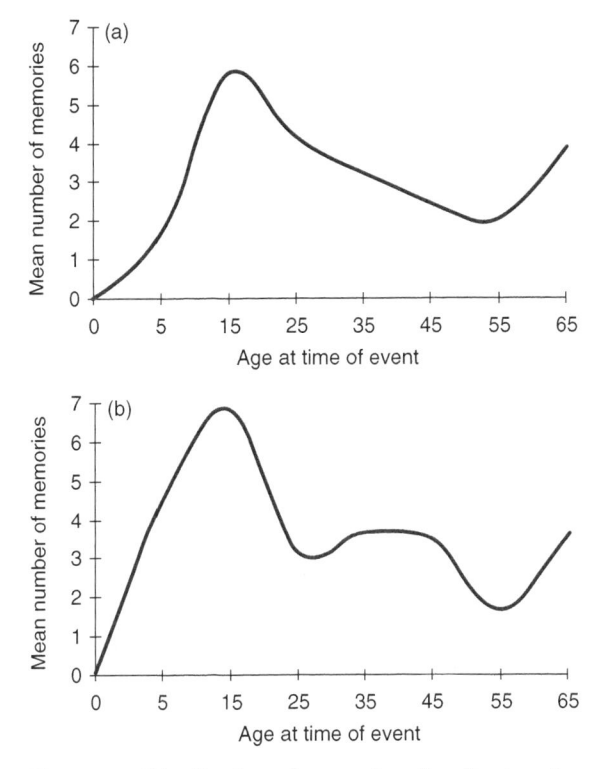

Figure 8.4 Distribution of memories of earlier immigrants/arrival prior to age 30 (a) and later immigrants/arrival after age 30 (b)

A closer look at the relative influence of L1 vs. L2 on the distribution of memories of the different age-at-immigration groups is called for in order to further understand the higher number of memories surrounding the immigration period. Figures 8.5a and 8.5b present the memories in the English (L1) session for the earlier immigrants (age-at-immigration = 21–29) and for the later immigrants (age-at-immigration = 33–46). Figure 8.6a and 8.6b present the memories in the Hebrew (L2) session for the earlier immigrants and for the later immigrants, respectively.

All four figures show a reminiscence bump during the 10–20 age period. More specifically, Figures 8.5a and 8.6a, which present the data from the earlier immigrants, show reminiscence bumps and less pronounced immigration effects, whereas Figures 8.5b and 8.6b, which display data from the later immigrants, show reminiscence bumps and more pronounced immigration effects. Nevertheless, the figures representing

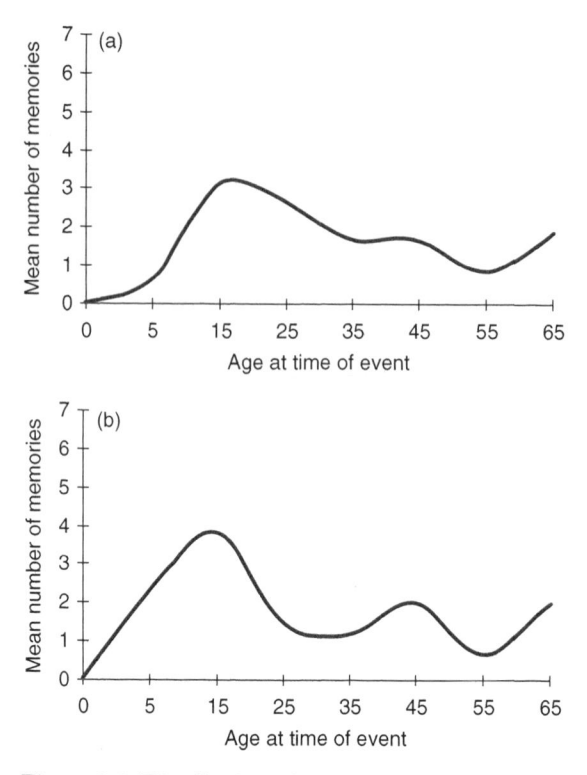

Figure 8.5 Distribution of memories in English for English–Hebrew bilinguals who immigrated before age 30 (a) and for those who immigrated after age 30 (b)

the distribution of L1 memories (8.5a and b) suggest an immigration bump during the 40–50 age period, while the figures representing the distribution of L2 memories (8.6a and b) suggest a possible immigration effect during the 30–40 age period, coinciding with the mean age of immigration, 31.5. However, a chi-square analysis comparing L1 and L2 memories across the decades shows no significant differences between the earlier and later immigrants in this regard ($p > 0.05$).

The division into earlier and later immigrants was intended to sharpen the differences between the groups, but important individual differences in age of immigration may have masked the group differences as they were defined here. Individual data for later immigrants in L1 revealed that four out of six participants showed a distinct rise in number of memories immediately following immigration, while the other two showed a 6–10 year delay from the immigration age to the rise

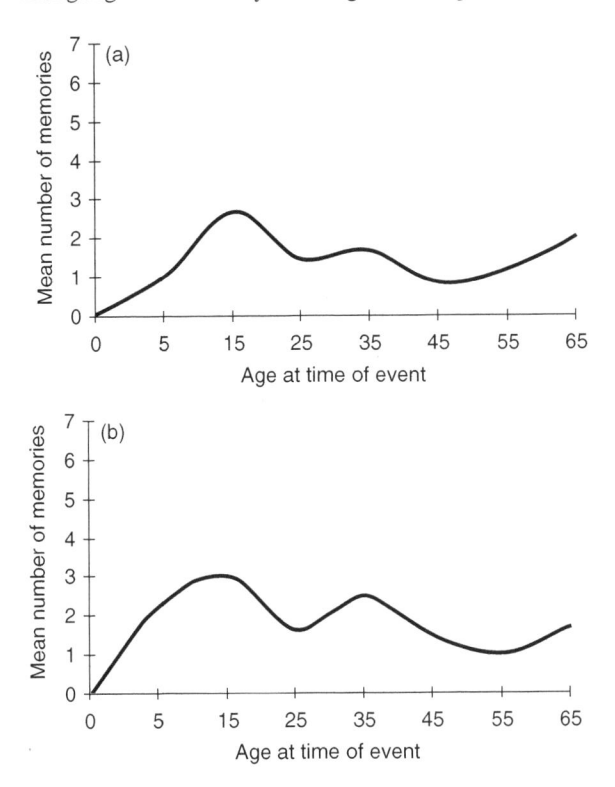

Language and memory in bilingual immigrants 225

Figure 8.6 Distribution of memories in Hebrew for English–Hebrew bilinguals who immigrated before age 30 (a) and for those who immigrated after age 30 (b)

in the number of memories. In L2, two participants exhibited an immediate rise in memories very close (two years) to their age of immigration, another two participants showed no rise, and two others showed a decline in the number of memories. For the earlier immigrants, five of the six participants showed a pattern similar to that of the later immigrants (i.e., an immediate rise or a delay of 8–10 years between age of immigration and the rise in the number of memories), the sixth participant showed no systematic pattern. In L2, five participants exhibited a higher number of memories immediately following immigration.

The generalization from individual data analyses is that immigration effects emerge immediately after immigration or with a delay of 6–10 years following immigration in both L1 and L2. More specifically, L1 memories showed clearer evidence of immigration effects while the L2 picture was more complex. These patterns may be related to immigration being a

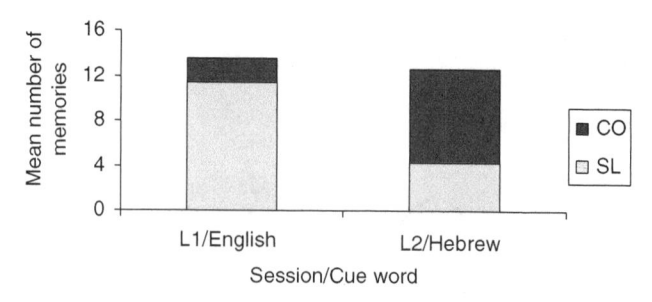

Note: CO = Crossover Memories; SL = Same-Language Memories.

Figure 8.7 Mean number of same-language and crossover memories in L1 and L2 sessions/cue words among English–Hebrew bilinguals

time of rapid change followed by a period of relative stability, as proposed by Schrauf and Rubin (1998). Future research should examine participants who immigrated prior to and following the reminiscence-bump period in order to better see the influence of immigration on the distribution of memories. It would also be useful to indicate how well these different immigrants integrated into society as a way of gaining further insight into their native language and L1 memory patterns.

In conclusion, in response to the prediction dealing with the role of L1 and L2 in autobiographical memory and immigration influence, we can see that the reminiscence bump appears in both L1 and L2 sessions. In addition, it appears that there are more memories forming an additional bump in the 40–50 age period in L1 and a bump in the 30–40 age period in L2. Dividing the 12 participants into earlier and later immigrants shows this pattern but, given the individual variation, these findings need further clarification.

Crossover and same-language memories

This section examines the relationship between same-language and crossover memories. In Figure 8.7, same-language memories, those which were reported to be retrieved in the same language as the session/cue words (L1 to L1 and L2 to L2), are compared with crossover memories, those reported to be retrieved in the bilingual's "other" language during a particular session (L1 to L2 and L2 to L1).

In general, there were more crossovers than same-language memories in L2 sessions/cue words and more same-language than crossover memories in L1. In addition, participants reported retrieval of significantly more L1 memories in the L1 (English) sessions ($M = 11.75$, $SD = 2.39$)

than L2 memories in the L2 (Hebrew) session ($M = 4.25$, $SD = 3.70$). A chi-square analysis showed that this difference was significant ($\chi^2 = 88.85$, $Phi = 0.52$, $p < 0.001$). In the L2 sessions, there were significantly more CO (Crossover Memories) than in the L1 sessions. More specifically, participants recalled relatively more L1/English memories in L2/Hebrew sessions ($M = 8.41$, $SD = 3.70$) than L2/Hebrew memories in L1/English sessions ($M = 2.08$, $SD = 2.57$). A chi-square analysis showed that participants recalled more same-language memories in L1 (English) sessions and more crossover memories in the L2 (Hebrew) sessions ($\chi^2 = 88.85$, $Phi = 0.52$, $p < 0.001$). The most straightforward interpretation for both the same-language and crossover findings is based on the fact that L1 is the more proficient and preferred language of the participants, even in L2 sessions. Psycholinguistically, the crossovers are evidence for activation of both languages. Despite the fact that the participant was instructed and cued in one language, s/he reported memories from the other language, evidence that traces of language cues remain in long-term, autobiographical memory. In a study of lexical activation, Schwartz and Kroll (2006) concluded that "cross-language alternatives" are active at all stages of processing. In making this argument elsewhere, Kroll and colleagues (Kroll et al., 2008) distinguish L1 from L2 processing. L1 is claimed to be more proficient and "faster" and thus less susceptible to L2 influence. This state may be what led to same-language memories in the present study. L2 is argued to involve more cross-language interaction. It is this state which led to the crossover memories in the present study.

Crossover memories, however, are based on a participant's reported language use, a metalinguistic measure of the retrieval language. In order to get a more explicitly behavioral perspective on autobiographical memory, we examined another indicator, one involving actual language use, by asking participants to provide longer narratives for a selection of their crossover and same-language memories. These narratives were expected to provide us with two additional facets of information. By asking for a more detailed description of a particular memory, we hoped to get closer to the encoding stage of memory. Also, by looking at CS, we were able to look at one of the unique aspects of bilingualism, this one based on actual language use.

Codeswitching in same-language and crossover memories

In this section, we examine instances of CS in same-language and crossover memories. For this analysis, we counted each instance of CS in which the participant switched from the language of the session

Table 8.1 *Frequency and proportion of codeswitching in same-language and crossover memories for L1 and L2 sessions*

Memory type	Language of session	Frequency of CS	Total words	Proportion of CS	SD
Same-language	L2	47	3,871	0.012	0.018
memories	L1	168	12,801	0.013	0.016
Crossover	L2	137	8,097	0.016	0.049
memories	L1	65	2,825	0.023	0.022
Totals		417	27,594	0.015	0.026

to the other language. For example, in an utterance produced in the English session in which a Hebrew word was inserted, one instance of CS in the English session was counted: *I went to the **makolet** [grocery store] yesterday*. Similarly, there is one instance of CS in the Hebrew utterance *haya tamid kaxa me' axore ha [it was always like that behind the] ... **in the back of her mind***.

An attempt was made to balance the number of narratives for L1 and L2 memories. A total of 229 narratives were elicited and transcribed: 114 in English (L1) and 115 in Hebrew (L2). The findings for frequency and proportion of CS are presented in Table 8.1. Following Paradis and Nicoladis (2007) and Iluz-Cohen and Walters (2011), the proportion of instances of CS was calculated as a function of the total number of words produced. It should be noted that CS across individuals ranged from 3–67 instances.

We predicted that narratives for crossover memories would involve more instances of CS, showing a consistency between metalinguistic reports of retrieval and actual CS behavior. The mean proportion of CS instances was submitted to a 2 × 2 ANOVA for memory type (same-language/crossovers) and session language (L1/L2), yielding a significant main effect for memory type, ($F(1, 225) = 13.06$, $p < 0.001$). The main effect for session language and the interaction term were not significant ($F < 1$). This finding confirms the hypothesis predicting more CS in crossover memories, thus validating participants' metalinguistic judgments (COs) with behavioral evidence (CS).

General discussion

The present study took an established paradigm in autobiographical memory and combined it with two linguistic phenomena uniquely linked to bilingualism – crossover memories and CS, in order to examine bilingual phenomena in relation to immigration effects in memory patterns across the lifespan. The study first replicated findings of a reminiscence bump in autobiographical memory in both L1 and L2 in the 10–30 age period. This finding will be discussed in light of previous findings on the role of language in autobiographical memory. Second, modest immigration effects were found in the form of an "immigration bump" for later immigrants, those who immigrated after age 30. Finally, both indicators of bilingual processing, crossover memories and CS, emerged as relevant in bilingual memory.

Language and autobiographical memory

The autobiographical memory paradigm has been used with Spanish–English (Schrauf & Rubin, 1998, 2000), Russian–English (Marian & Neisser, 1997), and here, with English–Hebrew participants. In terms of autobiographical memory patterns, findings are largely similar. The results here replicate Schrauf and Rubin's (1998) finding of a reminiscence bump for retrieval of memories from ages 10–30. In the present study, differences emerged in the distribution of memories across the lifespan and, overall, more memories were recalled in L1/English, the pre-immigration language. This finding also supports Schrauf and Rubin's (2000) conclusion that the language of encoding for events prior to immigration was Spanish, since participants lived in a Spanish-speaking country and spoke only Spanish there. It also lends indirect support to Marian and Neisser's (1997) findings that memories that were cued in L1/Russian were dated earlier than those cued in L2/English.

The salient reminiscence bump in the 10–30 age decades was found for both L1 and L2 sessions, raising the question as to whether the reminiscence bump in *bilingual* autobiographical memory patterns exists in both languages or is carried over from L1. A closer look at recall across the lifespan shows differences between L1 and L2 sessions, with a more pronounced reminiscence bump in L1 (Figure 8.3a) and a somewhat different structure beyond this period in L2 (Figure 8.3b). These differences may be due to stronger connections between memory and language in L1. The participants in the present study lived in English-speaking enclaves and exhibited high maintenance of L1/English. This is a plausible reason for transfer of the L1 reminiscence bump to L2 sessions. Furthermore, the sociolinguistic vitality of English in Israel also contributes to linguistic stability for these bilinguals across time. These factors may have been what led to the differences (see below) between the present study and those of Schrauf and Rubin (1998, 2000), where the participants were more balanced bilinguals, lived in less enclaved linguistic environments and, thus, produced fewer crossover memories.

Immigration and autobiographical memory

The finding that later immigrants (those who arrived after the age of 30) showed a more pronounced rise in the distribution of their memories following immigration than earlier immigrants (those who immigrated prior to age 30) further indicates that memory-recall patterns across the lifespan are sensitive to significant life changes such as immigration. This finding parallels Rubin *et al.*'s (1998) "cognitive mechanisms account" for the reminiscence bump. These authors suggested that a period of change followed by a period of relative stability optimizes recall. Immigration is clearly a good candidate for such a change.

Age of immigration is related to the question of whether memories increase as a result of changes in stability during and following immigration. When age of immigration *coincides* with another period of change in stability (life changes during adolescence and early adulthood), it is difficult to differentiate between the reminiscence bump and an immigration effect. When immigration takes place *after* the reminiscence-bump period, the immigration effect can be discerned on its own. Thus, the findings here are influenced by methodological limitations regarding the age of immigration of the earlier immigrants. Future research should take this issue as well as individual patterns of immigration and recall into account.

Crossover memories

The present findings showed a total of 40 percent crossovers for English and Hebrew sessions. This result was somewhat higher than Schrauf and Rubin (2000), who reported 25 percent crossovers from their Spanish–English bilinguals. Moreover, both studies showed more crossovers from L2 to L1 than from L1 to L2 (twice as many in Schrauf and Rubin, three-and-a-half times as many in the present study). Two complementary explanations, one individual and one sociolinguistic, may help account for the higher number of crossovers in L2/Hebrew in the present study in comparison to the data from Schrauf and Rubin's (1998, 2000) Spanish–English bilinguals. In terms of individual bilingualism, the language preference and proficiency of the participants in the present study was probably more tilted to L1/English than Schrauf and Rubin's (1998) more balanced bilinguals. In sociolinguistic terms, the vitality of English both as an agent of ethnolinguistic identity and in Israeli society at large, may also have contributed to the large number of crossover memories from L2/Hebrew to L1/English. Thus, in order to disentangle individual proficiency differences from sociolinguistic factors, one would need data from different contexts where English is L2, or conversely, data from the same context (the USA) but from speakers of different L1s.

Codeswitching

The finding of more instances of CS in crossover memories first and foremost provides behavioral evidence for self-reported language of retrieval data, both of which afford insight into bilingual memory. CS provides evidence that when one retrieves memories in another language, there may be some activation of that language. This activation shows up in language performance even though the speaker unconsciously knows that this other language is not what is expected of him/her. In terms of the directionality of CS, we were surprised to find that the difference between CS from L1 to L2 and CS from L2 to L1 was not statistically significant. We assumed that our English-dominant bilingual participants would CS more from L2 to L1, primarily due to lexical gaps and retrieval difficulties. The results showed that lexical gaps existed from L2 to L1, but there were more L2 cultural words and phrases used in L1 (e.g., *shuk* "open market," *aliyah* "immigration"), which may indicate that these bilinguals were in different stages of cultural integration. The frequency of CS alone cannot explain the various uses and types of CS. Thus, further research is needed in order to understand the motivation for CS in L1 and L2.

Methodological considerations

The central question in the field of bilingual autobiographical memory has been the extent to which memories are encoded in a particular language. When an experimental participant is asked to identify the language of the last utterance of a codeswitched conversation or mixed text, content information always overrides the language of the text (e.g., Berkowitz, 1984; Horiba, 1996). Similarly, Francis (1999) points out that memory for language, like verbatim memory, decays faster in comparison to memory for content. Another way of phrasing this paradox is: given that memory for language is not even strong in short-term memory, how can we expect long-term episodic autobiographical memory to recover information that may have disappeared within moments of an event?

Retrieval reports in this and other bilingual autobiographical memory studies cannot respond to Miller's (1981) call for contiguity between the cognitive event and the experimental measurement. Autobiographical memory does not lend itself to this kind of experimentation, and one has to rely on other techniques. As Schrauf and Durazo-Arvizu (2006) point out, neither the assumption that "the language spoken at the time of the memory" (Schrauf & Rubin, 2000, p. 621) nor the participant's report of the language in which the memory came to them (Marian & Neisser, 2000) can account for recoding effects. That is, whenever a bilingual retrieves the memory and re-tells the story (effectively reconstructing it), the language of that re-telling may result in a linguistic recoding of all or portions of the memory trace. Thus, when the participant is asked to identify the retrieval language, it is possible, even likely, that contextual information such as the setting, topic, and participants in the memory influence the decision, and the participant really has no direct access to the language of encoding.

The recall task used here, that is, retrieval of the language of a particular autobiographical memory, falls squarely in what has been criticized as "reproductive" as opposed to "functional" memory (Anderson, 1996; Glenberg, 1997). As such, the task lacks a specific goal. Rather, it fits into the class of tasks described by Small and Nusbaum (2004) as metalinguistic, unnatural, and artificial, which involve a complex of cognitive processes including motor activity, working memory, and attention. Retrieval of the language of a memory is an attempt to identify the language of an event. It does not focus directly on the event itself (unless, of course, it is a language event like how one learned to pronounce vowels in words with a silent 'e'). Nor does it involve language use. Nevertheless, it may include memory for the people, place, and activities at the time of the memory as well as their reconstruction over the participant's lifetime. As Schrauf and Durazo-Arvizu (2006) point out, when asked to identify the language of the memory, a respondent may in fact rely on any of the higher order schemata that organize the memory (place, people, lifetime period, other linked events, *or* the language of the memory). Thus, on the one hand, self-reported recall of the language of memory involves a complex integral of information; and on the other, it is a unitary, "reproductive" measure, much like stating the date or time of a memory. This combination of diffuse judgment and the reconstructed aspects of autobiographical memory are claimed here to account for the relatively large number of crossover memories in general and in L2 sessions in particular. Moreover, the issues raised here motivated the inclusion of CS data as a behavioral correlate of self-reported language data.

Concluding note

The findings in the present study were colored by strong preferences for English, the language of birth, proficiency, and prestige for the US/UK immigrant participants. Despite the overall importance of language dominance in the findings, the two uniquely bilingual measures in the study, crossover memories and CS in narratives, each contributed insights for the developing field of bilingual autobiographical memory in mature adults.

REFERENCES

Anderson, N. H. (1996). *A functional theory of cognition*. Mahwah, NJ: Lawrence Erlbaum Associates.

Berkowitz, R. (1984). Recognition memory for input language in nonfluent bilinguals. *Revue Roumaine de Linguistique: Cahiers de Linguistique Théorique et Appliquee*, 21, 119–130.

Bugelski, B. R. (1977). Imagery and verbal behavior. *Journal of Mental Imagery*, 1, 9–52.

Cerella, J. (1985). Information processing rates in the elderly. *Psychological Bulletin*, 98, 67–83.

Clyne, M. (2003). *Dynamics of language contact*. Cambridge University Press.

Conway, M. A., & Rubin, D. C. (1993). The structure of autobiographical memory. In A. E. Collins, S. E. Gathercole, M. A. Conway, & P. E. Morris (eds.), *Theories of memory* (pp. 103–137). Hove: Erlbaum.

Crovitz, H. F., & Schiffman, H. (1974). Frequency of episodic memories as a function of their age. *Bulletin of the Psychonomic Society*, 4, 517–518.

Fitzgerald, J. M. (1988). Vivid memories and the reminiscence bump phenomenon: the role of a self narrative. *Human Development*, 31, 261–273.

Francis, W. S. (1999). Cognitive integration of language and memory in bilinguals: semantic representation. *Psychological Bulletin*, 125(2), 193–222.

Galton, F. (1879). Psychometric experiments. *Brain*, 2, 149–162.

Gardner-Chloros, P., Charles, R., & Cheshire, J. (2000). Parallel patterns? A comparison of monolingual speech and bilingual codeswitching discourse. *Journal of Pragmatics*, 32, 1305–1341.

Genesee, F. 1980. *The social psychological significance of code switching for children*. ERIC Document ED200024.

Glenberg, A. M. (1997). What memory is for. *Behavioral and Brain Sciences*, 20(1), 1–55.

Grosjean, F. (1995). A psycholinguistic approach to codeswitching: the recognition of quest words by bilinguals. In L. Milroy & P. Muysken (eds.) *One speaker, two languages: cross-disciplinary perspectives on codeswitching*. Cambridge University Press.

Horiba, Y. (1996). Comprehension processes in L2 reading. *Studies in Second Language Acquisition*, 18(4), 433–473.

Iluz-Cohen, P., & Walters, J. (2011). Telling stories in two languages: narratives of bilingual preschool children with typical and impaired language. *Bilingualism: Language and Cognition*, 15, 1–17.

Kroll, J. F., Bobb, S. C., Misra, M., & Guo, T. (2008). Language selection in bilingual speech: evidence for inhibitory processes. *Acta Psychologica*, 128, 416–430.

Larsen, S., Schrauf, R. W., Fromholt, P., & Rubin, D. C. (2002). Inner speech and bilingual autobiographical memory: a Polish-Danish cross-cultural study. *Memory*, 10, 45–54.

MacSwan, J. (1999). *A minimalist approach to intrasentential code switching*. New York: Garland.

(2005). Codeswitching and generative grammar: a critique of the MLF Model and some remarks on "modified minimalism." *Bilingualism: Language and Cognition*, 8(1), 1–22.

Marian, V., & Neisser, U. (1997). *Autobiographical memory in bilinguals*. Poster session presented at the 38th Annual Meeting of the Psychonomic Society, Philadelphia, PA.

(2000). Language-dependent recall of autobiographical memories. *Journal of Experimental Psychology*, 129(3), 361–368.

Matsumoto, A., & Stanny, C. J. (2006). Language dependent access to autobiographical memory in Japanese–English bilinguals and US monolinguals. *Memory*, 14, 378–390.

Miller, G. A. (1981). Trends and debates in cognitive psychology. *Cognition*, 10, 215–225.

Myers-Scotton, C. (2005). *Multiple voices: an introduction to bilingualism*. London: Blackwell.

Nelson, K. (1993). Explaining the emergence of autobiographical memory in early childhood. In A. F. Collins, S. E. Gathercole, M. A. Conway, & P. E. Morris (eds.), *Theories of memory* (pp. 355–385). Hove: Erlbaum.

Otoya, M. T. (1987). *A study of personal memories of bilinguals: the role of culture and language in memory encoding recall*. Unpublished doctoral dissertation, Harvard University, Cambridge, MA.

Paradis, J., & Nicoladis, E. (2007). The influence of dominance and sociolinguistic context on bilingual preschoolers' language choice. *The International Journal of Bilingual Education and Bilingualism*, 10(3), 277–297.

Poplack, S. (1980). Sometimes I'll start a sentence in Spanish y termino en Español: toward a typology of code-switching. *Linguistics*, 18, 581–618.

Rubin, D. C. (1980). 51 properties of 125 words: a unit analysis of verbal behavior. *Journal of Verbal Learning and Verbal Behavior*, 19, 736–755.

(1982). On the retention function for autobiographical memory. *Journal of Verbal Learning and Verbal Behavior*, 21, 21–38.

Rubin, D. C., & Schulkind, M. D. (1997). The distribution of autobiographical memories across the lifespan. *Memory & Cognition*, 25, 859–866.

Rubin, D. C., Rahal T. A., & Poon, L. W. (1998). Things learnt in early adulthood are remembered best. *Memory & Cognition*, 26(1), 3–19.

Sankoff, D. (2002). *A mathematical model for the production of bilingual discourse.* Paper presented at the Second University of Vigo International Symposium on Bilingualism, Vigo, Galicia, Spain.

Schrauf, R. W., & Durazo-Arvizu, R. (2006). Bilingual autobiographical memory and emotion: theory and methods. In Pavlenko, A. (ed.). *Bilingual minds: emotional experience, expression, and representation* (pp. 284–311). Clevedon: Multilingual Matters Ltd.

Schrauf, R. W., & Rubin, D. C. (1998). Bilingual autobiographical memory in older adult immigrants: a test of cognitive explanations of the reminiscence bump and the linguistic encoding of memories. *Journal of Memory and Language*, 39(3), 437–457.

(2000). Internal languages of retrieval: the bilingual encoding of memories for the personal past. *Memory & Cognition*, 28(4), 616–623.

Schwartz, A. I., & Kroll, J. F. (2006). Bilingual lexical activation in sentence context. *Journal of Memory and Language*, 55, 197–212.

Small, S. L., & Nusbaum, H. C. (2004). On the neurobiological investigation of language understanding in context, *Brain and Language*, 89(2), 300–311.

Stephens, D. A. (1986). *Linguistic aspects of code-switching among Spanish/English bilingual children.* Ph.D. thesis, University of Arizona.

Walters, J. (2005). *Bilingualism: the sociopragmatic-psycholinguistic interface.* Mahwah, NJ: Lawrence Erlbaum Associates.

Zentella, A. C. (1997). *Growing up bilingual: Puerto Rican children in New York.* Malden, MA: Blackwell.

9 Linguistic relativity and bilingualism

Panos Athanasopoulos and Fraibet Aveledo

Abstract

If our native language affects our thinking, can learning a new language restructure our mental representations of reality and the world? The current chapter will attempt to answer that question, drawing on recent empirical evidence from a variety of research domains. We consider a range of variables that may modulate bilingual cognition and conceptualization, and we discuss the ways in which the ongoing investigation of the bilingual mind from a relativistic perspective has significantly added to our knowledge of how bilinguals mentally represent categories in their mind.

This chapter will examine the idea that bilinguals may have a unique perspective of the world, dissimilar to that of monolinguals, as a result of speaking languages with different concepts. The theoretical basis of this new line of research is rooted in one of the most debated theories in cognitive science, namely the Linguistic Relativity Hypothesis (LRH), also known as the Sapir-Whorf hypothesis after its originators in the twentieth century, Edward Sapir and Benjamin Lee Whorf (Sapir, 1949; Whorf, 1956). Sapir and Whorf contended that while we all see the same objective reality, we nonetheless interpret and classify it differently, based on the categories made available in our language. A full historical account of the hypothesis falls outside the scope of this chapter and can be found in numerous volumes and articles, some specifically related to bilingualism (see e.g., Pavlenko, 2011). Suffice to mention that the hypothesis generated a lot of interest in its early days, but then fell out of favour as modular theories of the mind began to develop in the 1960s through to the 1990s. While studies sporadically appeared during that period (see e.g., Kay & Kempton, 1984), it was not until the early to mid 90s that the hypothesis enjoyed a revival, particularly in the fields of cognitive and experimental psychology and, more recently, mainstream linguistics.

Several scholars, such as Lucy (1992a, 1992b), Levinson (1996), and Slobin (1996), among others, provided a theoretical and methodological framework in which it is possible to operationalize the Whorfian question using modern cognitive theories that place the experimental method at the heart of the hypothesis, emphasizing the need to implement both linguistic and non-linguistic cognitive paradigms (see e.g., Lucy, 1997, and Casasanto, 2008, for reviews). More recently, advances in the field of cognitive neuroscience (the science of how the brain works when we think) have made it possible to investigate the neural correlates of language effects on cognition, thus providing tangible evidence for Whorfian effects in the human brain (see Regier & Kay, 2009, for a recent review). While not all of the available evidence supports the hypothesis (see e.g., Tse & Altarriba, 2008, among others), at least nowadays the hypothesis has become a core area of investigation into the human mind and brain.

During the past decade, this interest has expanded to the field of bilingualism, and researchers have begun to investigate the possible effects of learning, knowing, and using a second or foreign language on thinking and reasoning. The main purpose of the current chapter is to provide a state-of-the-art synthesis of this research, starting with early attempts to bring together the fields of bilingualism and linguistic relativity, and to systematize their relationship in a clear theoretical and methodological framework. We will then focus on empirical investigations in the research domains of colour perception, grammatical number and object categorization, and grammatical aspect and motion event conceptualization. We focus on the first two domains because they are the most extensively researched to date and thus offer us the first glimpses of how a mind with two languages may view the world. We focus on the third domain because it may lead to new directions in the investigation of bilingual cognition, focusing on more complex linguistic constructs (compared to colour terms and grammatical number) and less concrete perceptual categories (compared to colour and objects). It is particularly important to consider effects of language on bilingual cognition in a variety of different domains, because effects and phenomena observed in one domain may not necessarily apply to another perceptual or linguistic domain (see Gentner & Boroditsky, 2001, for a discussion of domain-specific effects in linguistic relativity research, and Pavlenko, 2011, for a similar discussion focusing on bilingual cognition; see also Boroditsky, Schmidt, & Phillips, 2003; Kousta, Vinson, & Vigliocco, 2008; Forbes *et al.*, 2009; and Kurinski & Sera, 2011, for research on grammatical gender, a domain which, for reasons of space, will not be covered in this chapter). Subsequently the chapter will discuss some of the factors underpinning bilingual cognition in light of the available empirical evidence, in order to see to what extent different types of variables may affect the way bilinguals behave in cognitive tasks, and what this tells us about the organization of the bilingual mind in general. Finally, the chapter will briefly consider the precise role of memory in effects of language on cognition, and discuss ongoing research that explores this phenomenon in the context of bilingualism.

Early discussions of linguistic relativity and bilingualism

Some of the early discussions on linguistic relativity and bilingualism are rooted in arguments that the bilingual person is not two monolinguals in the same body, but a unique language user with a complete language system (Grosjean, 1982, 1989, 1992, 1998) and the related view that the second language (L2) user is an independent speaker/hearer/thinker rather than an imperfect version of a monolingual native-speaker ideal (Cook, 1991, 1992, 1999, 2003). Although these scholars were not overtly writing about linguistic relativity per se, their ideas about the mind of the bilingual person were aligned with the growing trends of the time to posit bilinguals as the population par excellence for the operationalization of the hypothesis in the experimental arena. For example, Hunt and Agnoli (1991) argued that bilinguals may have unique representations of the world as a result of going back and forth between two different ways of conceptualizing reality. Would bilingual mental representations then depend on the language in which they were tested? Would bilinguals transfer concepts of one language to the other? Would bilinguals appraise social situations differently as a result of the specific devices their languages use to codify social distinctions? What would the overall psychological consequences of bilingualism be? All of these questions have nowadays developed into empirical programmes of research. For example, effects of language-of-experiment instructions on bilingual cognitive performance have been investigated in a variety of domains (see e.g., Athanasopoulos, 2007, and Boroditsky, Ham, & Ramscar, 2002), and it has now been established that transfer may occur at the conceptual level (see e.g., Jarvis & Pavlenko, 2008). Additionally, research has extensively considered the effects of bilingualism on social perception, with particular emphasis on language emotionality (see e.g., Wierzbicka, 2004, and Pavlenko, 2006), and there is now ample research on the general psychological consequences of using two languages (see Bialystok, 2009, for a review).

Building on Hunt and Agnoli (1991), Green (1998) attempted to propose a theoretical account of linguistic relativity and bilingualism in accordance with Levelt's (1989) model of language production. His analysis, starting from the assumptions of how a message is built based on lexical concepts and how these lexical concepts are accessed, drives him to the conclusion that conceptualization (the process in Levelt's model that selects information from the world to verbalize a message) must be language specific. This has implications for bilingual speakers, who must then have different concepts for each language. In assuming this view, Green (1998) stresses that it is important to take into consideration several dynamic variables that bear on the bilingual person's thinking processes, such as proficiency in their languages, and the fact that bilinguals may use their languages differentially on different occasions and for varying purposes. Green (1998) made another important distinction regarding the nature of the effects of bilingualism on cognition. He distinguished between general and language-specific effects. The former relate to general cognitive processes such as metalinguistic awareness and selective attention. As mentioned earlier, there is now an abundance of evidence to suggest that bilingualism enhances these general cognitive skills in the individual, and may even offset symptoms of dementia and other neurodegenerative diseases (Bialystok, 2009). In relation to language-specific effects on cognition, Green (1998) asserts that these stem from specific grammatical and lexical features of languages, and concern higher level cognitive processing such as reasoning and categorization. Those kinds of effects are most relevant to linguistic relativity research. Green (1998) goes on to provide a methodological blueprint for how research in this domain may proceed. He considers the neo-Whorfian experimental approaches of scholars like John Lucy (1992b) and advocates the use of these paradigms in the study of bilingual cognition (see also Pavlenko, 1999). The following sections describe how this research has materialized in the past decade or so.

Colour and bilingual cognition

Early studies in this area focused on the semantics of colour. The main aim was to ascertain whether bilinguals displayed different usage of colour terms in either of their languages compared to monolinguals, and whether a 'semantic shift' had occurred in where bilinguals placed the best example (prototype) of particular colour terms on a colour chart. For example, Ervin (1961), Caskey-Sirmons and Hickerson (1977), and Andrews (1994) showed that bilinguals shifted the boundaries and the prototypes of their native colour categories towards those of monolingual speakers of their L2, prompting some researchers to claim that 'the worldview of bilinguals, whatever their first language, comes to resemble, to some degree, that of monolingual speakers of their second' (Caskey-Sirmons and Hickerson, 1977, p. 365). One study has also shown that bilinguals may select unique colour prototypes that are neither similar nor 'in-between' those of monolingual speakers of either language (Athanasopoulos, 2009). Zollinger (1988) showed that Japanese children living in Germany used some colour terms from the first language (L1) less frequently than Japanese children living in Japan. Jameson and Alvarado (2003) found that bilingual speakers whose L1 (Vietnamese) has fewer colour terms than their L2 (English) tended to modify their colour-naming behaviour according to the distinctions made in their L2, suggesting that bilinguals use whichever system is maximally informative.

More recent studies in the domain of colour have focused on non-linguistic cognitive processing such as categorization and perception. Based on recent evidence that these processes can be biased by the way in which a language encodes colour terms (see Regier & Kay, 2009, for a review), a series of studies by Athanasopoulos and colleagues asked how bilingual speakers would perceive the spectrum when their two languages differ in how they encode colour. Athanasopoulos (2009) investigated this question in native speakers of Greek who were also L2 users of English. Greek uses two distinct terms to refer to light and dark shades of the blue area of colour space. Athanasopoulos (2009) asked Greek–English bilinguals and English monolinguals to judge the similarity between light-blue and dark-blue colour squares. Results showed that bilingual speakers who had lived in the L2-speaking country (UK) for more than two years shifted towards the L2 norm in their perception of colour. More importantly, the study showed that bilinguals' similarity judgements were closely linked with the availability of the relevant terms in the mental lexicon, derived via a task that asked participants to list all the colour names they could think of. Those bilinguals that tended to place their native colour terms for the two blue shades lower down the list also judged light and dark blue stimuli as more similar to one another, like English monolinguals.

Athanasopoulos et al. (2011) extended the investigation of bilingual colour cognition to Japanese speakers of L2 English. Japanese, like Greek, distinguishes between two shades of blue, light and dark. The study investigated how late Japanese–English bilinguals with a high level of proficiency in the L2 (English) discriminate dark and light blue stimuli. The results confirmed the prediction that bilinguals would differ from both monolingual groups, with their behaviour falling between the two, but they also showed that the degree to which bilinguals resembled the L2 monolingual group depended on the frequency of language use. Those bilinguals that tended to use their L2 more frequently than their L1 were also the ones more likely to discriminate less between light and dark blue. This seems to indicate that the cognitive system remains dynamic and flexible even when an advanced level of proficiency has been reached in the L2.

Some recent studies have shifted the investigation of bilingual colour perception to a more biologically grounded arena through the use of neurophysiological techniques like event-related brain potentials (ERPs). Thierry et al. (2009) and Athanasopoulos et al. (2010) adapted a visual oddball paradigm where Greek and English speakers were instructed to attend to a target square (probability 20%) in a stream of circles (probability 80%), some of which varied in luminance (standard circles: probability 70%, deviant circles: probability 10%). In two blocks standards and deviants were either light or dark blue, and in two other blocks they were light or dark green. The participants' brain electrical activity was monitored while they were exposed to these series of stimuli. The main analysis focused on an ERP component called visual mismatch negativity (vMMN), a marker considered automatic and unconscious, since it requires no dedicated attention, and occurring between 170 and 220 milliseconds post-stimulus (Czigler, Balazs, & Winkler, 2002; Winkler, 2005). Results showed a vMMN effect of similar magnitude for blue and green standard–deviant contrasts in native speakers of English who do not make a lexical distinction between light and dark blue. Greek participants, on the other hand, displayed greater vMMN modulations for the blue rather than the green standard–deviant contrast, consistent with their language's partition of the blue area of the colour spectrum into a lighter shade (*ghalazio*) and a darker shade (*ble*). The researchers further carried out a re-analysis of the results of their study, splitting the Greek participants into two groups, based on their length of residence in the UK: short stay (mean = 7.2 months, range 5–12 months) and long stay (mean = 42.6 months, range 1.5–5 years). This new analysis showed that length of stay is an important factor in neurophysiological changes in bilinguals. Short-stay bilinguals displayed more sensitivity to the light/dark blue contrast than long-stay bilinguals, as evidenced by a larger vMMN modulation in the former group. Interestingly, language proficiency per se did not seem to exert an influence on the neurophysiological changes exhibited by bilinguals. The authors concluded that their findings can be explained through Casasanto's (2008) assumption that learning a language implies the strengthening of associations between words and their referents in the real world. When an individual comes into contact with a new language and culture, new associations are formed, and, crucially, the strength of the old associations may be readjusted.

Grammatical number and bilingual cognition

Studies in this area focus on the grammatical instantiation of number in the nominal system of a language, and whether that has any effect on non-linguistic categorization of countable and non-countable objects. These studies commonly take as their starting ground Lucy's seminal study in 1992, which showed that the grammatical difference in the way English and Yucatec encode plural marking in [+/- animate] and [+/- discrete] nouns affects the way speakers attend to similarities and differences in the number/amount of different types of entities. Athanasopoulos (2006) adapted Lucy's (1992b) study and extended it to monolingual speakers of Japanese and English, and Japanese–English bilinguals. Japanese is a language that shares the same features reported in Yucatec. That is, nouns considered [+animate, +discrete] can be optionally marked for plural (these are nouns typically referring to humans and animals). On the other hand, [-animate, +discrete] nouns (e.g., a spoon, an apple), as well as [-animate, -discrete] nouns (e.g., sand, water) do not take plural marking and instead, in order to express countability, these nouns are externally modified by a numeral and a unitizer, which is called a classifier. By contrast, in English only [-animate, -discrete] nouns are externally modified by means of a numeral and a unitizer. On the other hand, [-animate, +discrete] nouns usually take obligatory plural marking (via a plural morpheme).

Assuming that Lucy's (1992b) classification is correct, Athanasopoulos (2006) predicted that monolingual speakers of English would attend more to changes in the number of countable objects than monolingual speakers of Japanese in a picture similarity judgement task, since the crucial grammatical difference between the languages concerns [-animate, +discrete] (i.e., countable) nouns. The results bore out this prediction, and furthermore showed that Japanese speakers who knew English at an advanced level behaved more like English monolinguals than Japanese monolinguals in their similarity judgements. Japanese speakers who knew English at an intermediate level behaved more like Japanese monolinguals, although minor shifts toward the English monolingual pattern were observed, suggesting that changes in cognition could occur in learners who have not yet reached an advanced level of proficiency in the L2.

Cook et al. (2006) examined the relationship between grammatical number marking and classification of objects based on either shape or material properties. Previous research by Lucy (1992b) and Imai and Gentner (1997) showed that speakers of English are more likely to classify objects based on common shape rather than common material, whereas speakers of classifier languages like Yucatec and Japanese may show the reverse tendency. According to Lucy (1992b) and Imai and Gentner (1997), this cognitive difference may be an effect of the syntactic differences between the two languages. That is, the lack of a syntactic distinction between mass and count nouns in Japanese makes speakers of this language pay more attention to the item's material. On the other hand, speakers of English, who need to distinguish between mass and count nouns in order to assign numerals or unitizers, pay more attention to the shape of the items. Following the methodology of Imai and Gentner (1997), Cook et al. (2006) asked Japanese speakers who were English L2 users to extend the novel name of an object to another object based on either common shape or common material properties. The results showed that Japanese speakers with the longest period of living in an English-speaking country showed a pattern of categorization that was between that reported by Imai and Gentner (1997) for English and Japanese monolinguals. The preference for shape increased with the period of living in the L2 country.

Athanasopoulos' (2007) study sought to disentangle the possible influences of L2 proficiency, length of stay in the L2-speaking country, and the language used for task instructions (L1 or L2) on the changing cognitive state of the L2 user. The study also investigated preferences previously observed in English and Japanese speakers in relation to the categorization of objects according to shape and material. Athanasopoulos (2007) asked how these differences between Japanese and English may influence Japanese–English bilinguals. What is the relative influence of language proficiency and length of stay? Do bilinguals show two separate cognitive representations of the concepts, each utilized according to the language of task instructions, or are cognitive changes of a deeper nature, such that bilinguals may shift their cognitive patterns even when instructed in the L1? In a non-verbal similarity judgement task, Athanasopoulos (2007) replicated previous findings from Imai and Mazuka (2003) and Lucy and Gaskins (2003), and in a multiple regression analysis found that L2 proficiency was the best predictor of the degree to which bilinguals shift towards the L2 pattern. Therefore, the higher the proficiency, the higher the similarity with English monolinguals, regardless of how long bilinguals had previously lived in the L2-speaking country, and regardless of the language used for task instructions. Similar findings were obtained in a follow-up study by Athanasopoulos and Kasai (2008), who found that cognitive preferences may shift towards the L2 even in bilinguals who had never lived in the L2-speaking country before, but who were very advanced speakers of the L2.

Motion events and thinking for speaking in bilinguals

The majority of studies in this area have focused on the conceptualization of motion events during speech production. As such, these studies have very little to say about non-linguistic cognition and linguistic relativity, but they do offer a theoretical basis upon which further studies may develop. Many of the existing studies take Slobin's (1996, 2003) 'thinking-for-speaking' hypothesis as their general theoretical backdrop. A full theoretical account of this hypothesis falls outside the scope of this chapter, but in brief terms the hypothesis assumes that speakers are bound by the available expressions in their language when they wish to communicate a concept, and as such must select language-specific ways of conceptualizing reality when speaking. While the hypothesis does not make any assumptions regarding cognitive processing beyond the linguistic level, it shares a lot of common ground with the linguistic relativity hypothesis, inasmuch as both theories take as their basic tenet the existence of linguistic diversity (i.e., the fact that concepts are language specific). The studies that we review in this section are relevant for linguistic relativity because they delineate a theoretically informed account of how languages may vary in how they express motion that could serve as a pivot for further studies focusing on non-linguistic motion event cognition.

One set of studies has focused on differences between languages that do and do not express grammatically aspect and its relation to the conceptualization of goal-oriented motion events. Recent studies in this area have shown that speakers of aspect languages (e.g., Arabic, English, Russian) tend to exclude endpoints when describing dynamic goal-oriented stimuli (e.g., an agent moving towards an endpoint), focusing instead on the internal temporal perspective of the event. On the other hand, speakers of non-aspect languages such as Norwegian or German display a tendency to defocus the ongoingness of the action and instead focus on the endpoints in their verbal descriptions (see Schmiedtová, von Stutterheim, & Carroll, 2011, for a recent review).

A recent study by Bylund and Jarvis (2011) operationalized these cross-linguistic differences within the theoretical framework of the Conceptual Transfer Hypothesis (CTH), which assumes that speakers of different languages can have different patterns of conceptualization and, in bilinguals and second language learners, the patterns from one language can be transferred to the other language. This concept, according to the authors, differs from the LRH in a few important ways. First, not all the conceptual differences found in speakers must be caused by particular characteristics of their language's grammar, thus presumably allowing for the influence of extra-linguistic biological or sociocultural factors on bilingual cognition. Second, the CTH supposes that the effect of language on cognition is produced only when communication is taking place, (i.e., during language processing), and in this respect it is more similar to Slobin's thinking-for-speaking hypothesis.

The authors tested the CTH by analyzing the relation between grammatical aspect and the conceptualization of endpoint versus ongoingness in goal-oriented motion events in bilinguals. Based on assumptions made in cognitive grammar (Langacker, 2008), Bylund and Jarvis (2011) postulated that aspect is a language element that interacts in interesting ways with the distinction between an immediate temporal scope (focusing only on the ongoing action of an event) and a maximal temporal scope (focusing on the holistic properties of the event, including its endpoints). When grammatical aspect is absent in a language, a verb does not distinguish between these two viewing frames. Consequently, the whole event, endpoint included, appears within the temporal scope. When an aspect marker is used, an immediate temporal viewing frame is imposed and the endpoints are excluded. Bylund and Jarvis (2011) explored the dynamic nature of the relationship between aspect and viewing frames of reference in Spanish–Swedish bilinguals. Spanish is a language that marks aspect grammatically on the main verb of a sentence, while Swedish is a non-aspect language that utilizes extra-grammatical lexical or pragmatic devices to convey aspectual properties of events. The specific aim of the study was to test whether Spanish–Swedish bilinguals would deviate from the L1 norm (which promotes an immediate viewing frame and defocuses endpoints) as a result of being in a linguistic environment (Swedish) that promotes a maximal viewing frame.

The researchers asked their participants to watch videos showing different degrees of goal-oriented motion events. Participants had to describe the scenes in Spanish (their L1). Results showed that the bilinguals behaved differently from Spanish monolinguals. First, bilingual speakers produced more endpoints in motion events and simple verb forms than Spanish monolinguals. Proficiency in L1, measured through the ability to identify grammatical aspect errors in a grammaticality judgement test, was the best predictor of endpoint encoding:

the lower the L1 proficiency of the bilingual speaker, the higher his/her endpoint encoding frequencies. Age of onset of L2 acquisition was also a significant factor that correlated with endpoint encoding in L1. That is, the later the speaker started to acquire Swedish, the lower her/his endpoint encoding frequencies.

Flecken (2011) investigated effects of grammatical aspect on verbal encoding in early bilingual speakers of Dutch (an aspect language) and German (a non-aspect language). Flecken's (2011) main question was what would be the preferred option for these early and simultaneous bilinguals in terms of endpoint encoding. Twelve simultaneous bilinguals were compared with 19 Dutch monolinguals and 19 German monolinguals. Participants had to describe a set of video clips focusing on the question *what is happening*? Additionally, their eye movements were recorded with eye-tracking equipment before and during the description task in order to study their planning and organization of the content that was going to be expressed. The results showed that bilinguals displayed patterns of language use that were dissimilar to either monolingual norm. Specifically, these early bilinguals frequently used the progressive form in Dutch, but they also tended to combine progressive aspect with the mention of endpoints, a combination that is not at all frequent in monolingual Dutch speakers. The eye-tracking analysis demonstrated that bilinguals also allocated attention differently from the monolingual groups. Bilinguals tended to look earlier and for longer periods to the action than to the agent of the event, and this correlated with a high frequency of use of progressive forms, showing that there is a tight link between frequency of use of specific linguistic features and attention allocation to specific aspects of a dynamic event.

Factors underpinning bilingual cognition and conceptualization

The findings to date show that learning and using a second language may have profound consequences for cognition. Generally, bilinguals are shown to display two main types of cognitive pattern: (1) they may approximate native speakers of their L1 or L2, but (2) more frequently, they may display cognitive patterns that are in between those of monolingual speakers of either language. Importantly, studies also show that these patterns are flexible and may change with increasing L2 expertise, or under specific experimental conditions. Because of the dynamic and multi-varied nature of bilingualism, Jarvis and Pavlenko (2008) and Athanasopoulos (2011) stress the importance of considering variables that pertain to language expertise and knowledge itself, as well as variables that have more to do with the sociocultural environment and context where L2 acquisition may take place. In this section, we review some of these variables in the light of the empirical evidence discussed earlier, in an attempt to gain a clearer view of the factors that underpin bilingual cognitive behaviour.

Many studies show a shift in cognitive patterns in bilinguals with an advanced level of L2 proficiency while bilinguals with intermediate L2 proficiency continue to exhibit L1-like cognitive patterns (although the beginning of a shift is still noticeable, see e.g., Athanasopoulos, 2006). Studies have also focused on the link between specific linguistic constructs and bilingual cognition. For example, Athanasopoulos (2007) used a grammaticality judgement task to measure participants' knowledge of grammatical number marking in English. This score was then combined with the score obtained in a general proficiency test (the Oxford Quick Placement Test, 2001) to create a composite L2 proficiency index for each participant. This score significantly predicted each L2 user's degree of cognitive shift towards L2-based patterns. Athanasopoulos and Kasai (2008) measured knowledge of grammatical number marking by asking participants to orally describe a picture containing various objects. They found a significant correlation between the score elicited in this task and their participants' shift in cognitive preferences towards the L2. Athanasopoulos (2009) found that attrition of L1 colour terms for blue in lexical memory correlated significantly with a weakening of the light/dark blue distinction in Greek–English bilinguals. Bylund and Jarvis (2011) found that decreasing L1 proficiency correlated significantly with increasingly L2-like conceptualization patterns in Spanish–Swedish bilinguals.

Some studies have focused on possible maturational constraints on bilingual cognition, either because of a biologically determined 'sensitive' period for language acquisition, or as a result of gradual decline of general learning mechanisms throughout the lifespan. For this reason, the influence of this variable may not be directly observable, but instead it may be a mediating variable in the relationship between language proficiency and degree of cognitive restructuring. For example, Athanasopoulos and Kasai (2008) found that both specific L2 proficiency and age of L2 acquisition could predict L2 cognitive shift, but at the same time the two predicting variables also correlated with each other. In a subsequent analysis, the effect of specific L2 proficiency on cognitive shift remained even when taking into account age of L2 acquisition, while the effect of age of L2 acquisition was abolished when taking into account specific L2 proficiency. On the other hand, a study by Boroditsky (2001) on time concepts in Chinese–English bilinguals found a strong effect of age of L2 acquisition on the degree of cognitive shift towards the L2, while length of exposure to English played no role whatsoever. Bylund and Jarvis (2011) found that age of onset of L2 acquisition could independently predict the degree to which conceptualization patterns remained L1-like or had shifted towards the L2.

Aside from language proficiency and age of acquisition, the degree to which an individual uses their second language may often depend on the interactional context and the degree of immersion in a specific community or country. Increasing the opportunity to use the language due to these factors may in turn increase expertise in the particular language and may potentially provide the individual with target-like examples of specific linguistic features. For example, the study by Athanasopoulos *et al.* (2011) showed a significant effect of frequency of language use, such that the more frequently individuals used their L2, the more their cognitive patterns shifted away from the L1 towards the L2. The effect remained even after controlling for variables such as proficiency, age of acquisition, and length of stay in the L2-speaking country. Flecken's (2011) study showed a link between frequency of use of specific grammatical features and attention allocation to dynamic scenes.

In the context of evaluating perceptual distinctions, an L2 setting (e.g., receiving experiment instructions in the L2 by a native speaker of the L2) may promote a cognitive pattern that resembles that of monolingual speakers of the L2. This is precisely what was found by Boroditsky *et al.* (2002) in their study of action events in Indonesian–English bilinguals. Those bilinguals who were instructed in the L2 showed a more L2-based cognitive pattern than bilinguals tested in their L1. However, the study also showed that L2 users who received instructions in the L1 did not show a completely L1-based cognitive pattern, but were between monolingual speakers of either language. Athanasopoulos (2007) also varied the language of task instructions but found no significant difference. Both L1-instructed and L2-instructed L2 users displayed cognitive patterns that were between those of monolingual speakers of either language.

Living in the country where the second language is spoken as a native language may promote and induce in the individual an inclination, conscious or unconscious, to emulate the linguistic and, crucially, the non-linguistic behaviour of the target-language community. Cook *et al.* (2006), for example, found no between-group significant difference when they split their bilinguals by general L2 proficiency, but they did find a significant difference when bilinguals were split by length of stay in the L2 country. Athanasopoulos (2007) found a significant relationship between length of stay and L2 cognitive shift, but the effect disappeared when L2 proficiency was taken into account. Athanasopoulos (2009) found independent effects of both lexical memory and length of stay on colour similarity judgements, suggesting that both factors may influence cognition, while Athanasopoulos *et al.* (2010) found that length of stay correlated significantly with changes in neural correlates of colour perception. It appears, however, that living in the L2-speaking country is a sufficient but not necessary condition for bilingual cognitive shift. Athanasopoulos and Kasai (2008) found effects of L2 on cognition in bilinguals who had not previously lived in the L2-speaking country. This finding is corroborated by studies by Brown and Gullberg (2008, 2011) on gesture behaviour in Japanese–English bilinguals, which demonstrate evidence of shift towards the L2 gesture pattern even in bilinguals who had never lived in the L2-speaking country before.

The role of memory in linguistically mediated thinking

What is the cognitive mechanism by which lexical and grammatical patterns may influence cognitive processing of colours, objects, and events? The empirical evidence to date points to memory processes, and specifically working memory, as being central in the way language affects cognition. The language-as-strategy hypothesis (Gennari *et al.*, 2002) predicts that language is employed on-line to facilitate performance in cognitively demanding situations, where a participant is likely to use information drawn from their linguistic classifications to make a judgement. Gennari *et al.* (2002) carried out a similarity judgement task of motion events in English and Spanish speakers (English tends to emphasize the manner of motion, while Spanish tends to emphasize the path of motion). Differences between groups were found, but, crucially, these differences were abolished under a verbal-shadowing condition, where participants were asked to inspect the scenes while repeating a nonsense syllable (thus occupying the phonological loop). According to the authors, the absence of the linguistic relativity effect in the verbal-shadowing condition suggests that language is employed strategically to hold events in memory while performing the task.

Results from studies in other cognitive domains like colour are also compatible with this hypothesis. These studies show that, in the absence of any experimental manipulations, participants will rely on language as a default strategy to solve simple mental tasks. For example, when participants are required to judge whether two colours are same or different as quickly and as accurately as they can, cognitive differences between speakers of different languages are found, and indeed exacerbated as the difficulty of the task increases (i.e., by decreasing the perceptual distance between stimuli, Winawer et al., 2007). These differences are abolished under verbal-interference conditions, for example, when participants have to repeat a nonsense syllable or rehearse covertly a string of digits (Roberson & Davidoff, 2000; Winawer et al., 2007). These findings are consistent with accounts that non-linguistic cognitive processes such as memory are linguistically mediated (Baddeley, 2003), and they show that language is indeed used as a tool for carrying out mental tasks that involve memory.

The role of memory in linguistic relativity effects in bilinguals seems to be in need of further exploration. In what is essentially ongoing research as part of a wider exploration of representation of motion events in bilingual cognition, Bylund, Athanasopoulos, and Damjanovic (2011) reported data from 80 English learners of German as a second language that were given a memory-based triads matching task. In this task, participants were asked to match a target scene with an intermediate degree of endpoint orientation with two alternative scenes with low and high degree of endpoint orientation, respectively (German promotes endpoint encoding while English highlights ongoingness, see relevant section earlier in the chapter). Results showed that, when compared to monolingual English speakers, the learners of German were more prone to base their similarity judgements on endpoint saliency rather than ongoingness. Moreover, it was found that this strategy became more pronounced as L2 proficiency increased. These findings suggest that native-language event cognition patterns may be restructured through additional language learning, but further confirmation is needed through a verbal-shadowing task of the memory processes that may be involved in the manifestation of the observed effects.

Conclusions

In conclusion, we have attempted to synthesize some of the available evidence on the relationship between the linguistic relativity hypothesis and bilingualism. We first focused on the theoretical attempts that called for research on bilingualism through the viewpoint of linguistic relativity. We then reviewed studies in three domains, namely colour, number, and motion, because they are among the most well-researched areas and offer much information about cognitive processing in the bilingual mind (in the case of colour and number), but also about processes of thinking for speaking (in the case of motion), which are in a sense related to relativistic enquiries of the human mind. We subsequently considered some of the variables that studies show may modulate bilingual cognition, and we showed that both linguistic and extra-linguistic variables may interact with the dynamic and flexible state of the bilingual mind. Finally, we speculated on the role of memory in the observed relativistic effects in a variety of domains, concluding that more research is needed to understand the nature of those effects in bilinguals.

The emerging field of linguistic relativity and bilingualism provides a glimpse of the nature of bilingual mental representations, which are usually neglected in mainstream models of bilingual cognition. For example, one of the most prominent models of bilingual cognitive architecture proposed by Kroll (1993) and Kroll and de Groot (1997) focuses mostly on lexical access rather than conceptual representation, and assumes that the bilinguals' languages are equivalent at the conceptual level. The studies on linguistic relativity and bilingualism clearly show that this cannot be the case. Bilinguals appear to have a much more complex conceptual organization than previously thought, and may exhibit behaviour that is unlike that of their monolingual peers, depending on several dynamic variables such as proficiency, cultural immersion, and frequency of language use, and potentially many others. In this light, L2 learning implies not only mapping words onto pre-existing concepts, as has been traditionally assumed in models of lexical retrieval and conceptual access, but also creating new concepts by either internalizing concepts that are specific to the L2, or by merging existing concepts with new ones. Any model of bilingual cognition that fails to take this into account is bound to provide an incomplete and ultimately erroneous picture of the mind with two languages.

Research is still in its early stages, but the ongoing investigation of the bilingual mind from a relativistic perspective has yielded fruitful and informative results that bear on our knowledge of how bilinguals see the world. Future enquiries will elucidate further the precise role of specific linguistic, biological, and sociocultural factors on bilingual cognition, as well as the extent of the effects in different perceptual domains, and thus be in a better position to delve more into the cognitive mechanisms involved in conceptual restructuring during the process of second and foreign language learning.

REFERENCES

Andrews, D. (1994). The Russian color categories *sinij* and *goluboj*: an experimental analysis of their interpretation in the standard and emigré languages. *Journal of Slavic Linguistics*, 2, 9–28.

Athanasopoulos, P. (2006). Effects of the grammatical representation of number on cognition in bilinguals. *Bilingualism: Language and Cognition*, 9, 89–96.
  (2007). Interaction between grammatical categories and cognition in bilinguals: the role of proficiency, cultural immersion, and language of instruction. *Language and Cognitive Processes*, 22, 689–699.
  (2009). Cognitive representation of color in bilinguals: the case of Greek blues. *Bilingualism: Language and Cognition*, 12, 83–95.
  (2011). Cognitive restructuring in bilingualism. In A. Pavlenko (ed.), *Thinking and speaking in two languages* (pp. 29–65). Bristol: Multilingual Matters.
Athanasopoulos, P., & Kasai, C. (2008). Language and thought in bilinguals: the case of grammatical number and nonverbal classification preferences. *Applied Psycholinguistics*, 29, 105–121.
Athanasopoulos, P., Dering, B., Wiggett, A., Kuipers, J. R., & Thierry, G. (2010). Perceptual shift in bilingualism: brain potentials reveal plasticity in pre-attentive colour perception. *Cognition*, 116, 437–443.
Athanasopoulos, P., Damjanovic, L., Krajciova, A., & Sasaki, M. (2011). Representation of colour concepts in bilingual cognition: the case of Japanese blues. *Bilingualism: Language and Cognition*, 14, 9–17.
Baddeley, A. (2003). Working memory: looking back and looking forward. *Nature Reviews Neuroscience*, 4, 829–839.
Bialystok, E. (2009). Bilingualism: the good, the bad, and the indifferent. *Bilingualism: Language and Cognition*, 12, 3–11.
Boroditsky, L. (2001). Does language shape thought? English and Mandarin speakers' conceptions of time. *Cognitive Psychology*, 43, 1–22.
Boroditsky, L., Ham, W., & Ramscar, M. (2002). What is universal about event perception? Comparing English and Indonesian speakers. *Proceedings of the 24th Annual Meeting of the Cognitive Science Society*. Fairfax, VA.
Boroditsky, L., Schmidt, L., & Phillips, W. (2003). Sex, syntax, and semantics. In D. Gentner & S. Goldin-Meadow (eds.), *Language in mind: advances in the study of language and thought* (pp. 61–79). Cambridge, MA: MIT Press.
Brown, A., & Gullberg, M. (2008). Bidirectional crosslinguistic influence in L1–L2 encoding of Manner in speech and gesture: a study of Japanese speakers of English. *Studies in Second Language Acquisition*, 30, 225–251.
  (2011). Bidirectional cross-linguistic influence in event conceptualization? Expressions of path among Japanese learners of English. *Bilingualism: Language and Cognition*, 14, 79–94.
Bylund, E., & Jarvis, S. (2011). L2 effects on L1 event conceptualization. *Bilingualism: Language and Cognition*, 14, 47–59.
Bylund, E., Athanasopoulos, P., & Damjanovic, L. (2011). Does learning a new language change the way you think about events? Evidence from English learners of German. Paper presented at the *12th Conference of the International Pragmatics Association*, 3–8 July, Manchester, UK.
Casasanto, D. (2008). Who's afraid of the Big Bad Whorf? Cross-linguistic differences in temporal language and thought. *Language Learning*, 58, 63–79.

Caskey-Sirmons, L., & Hickerson, N. (1977). Semantic shift and bilingualism: variation in the color terms of five languages. *Anthropological Linguistics*, 19, 358–367.
Cook, V. (1991). The poverty-of-the-stimulus argument and multi-competence. *Second Language Research*, 7, 103–117.
  (1992). Evidence for multicompetence. *Language Learning*, 42, 557–591.
  (1999). Going beyond the native speaker in language teaching. *TESOL Quarterly*, 33, 185–209.
  (2003). The changing L1 in the L2 user's mind. In V. Cook (ed.), *Effects of the second language on the first* (pp. 1–18). Clevedon: Multilingual Matters.
Cook, V., Bassetti, B., Kasai, C., Sasaki, M., & Takahashi, J. (2006). Do bilinguals have different concepts? The case of shape and material in Japanese L2 users of English. *International Journal of Bilingualism*, 10, 137–152.
Czigler, I., Balazs, L., & Winkler, I. (2002). Memory-based detection of task-irrelevant visual changes. *Psychophysiology*, 39, 869–873.
Ervin, S. (1961). Semantic shift in bilingualism. *American Journal of Psychology*, 74, 233–241.
Flecken, M. (2011). Event conceptualization by early Dutch–German bilinguals: insights from linguistic and eye-tracking data. *Bilingualism: Language and Cognition*, 14, 61–77.
Forbes, J. N., Poulin-Dubois, D., Rivero, M. R., & Sera, M. (2009). Grammatical gender affects bilinguals' conceptual gender: implications for linguistic relativity and decision making. *The Open Applied Linguistics Journal*, 1, 68–76.
Gennari, S., Sloman, S., Malt, B., & Fitch, W. (2002). Motion events in language and cognition. *Cognition*, 83, 49–79.
Gentner, D., & Boroditsky, L. (2001). Individuation, relativity, and early word learning. In M. Bowerman & S. C. Levinson (eds.), *Language acquisition and conceptual development* (pp. 215–256). Cambridge University Press.
Green, D. (1998). Bilingualism and thought. *Psychologica Belgica*, 38, 253–278.
Grosjean, F. (1982). *Life with two languages: an introduction to bilingualism*. Cambridge University Press.
  (1989). Neurolinguists, beware! The bilingual is not two monolinguals in one person. *Brain and Language*, 36, 3–15.
  (1992). Another view of bilingualism. In R. Harris (ed.), *Cognitive processing in bilinguals* (pp. 51–62). Amsterdam: North Holland.
  (1998). Studying bilinguals: methodological and conceptual issues. *Bilingualism: Language and Cognition*, 1, 131–149.
Hunt, E., & Agnoli, F. (1991). The Whorfian hypothesis: a cognitive psychology perspective. *Psychological Review*, 98, 377–389.
Imai, M., & Gentner, D. (1997). A crosslinguistic study of early word meaning: universal ontology and linguistic influence. *Cognition*, 62, 169–200.
Imai, M., & Mazuka, R. (2003). Re-evaluating linguistic relativity: language-specific categories and the role of universal ontological knowledge in the construal of individuation. In D. Gentner & S. Goldin-Meadow

(eds.), *Language in mind: advances in the study of language and thought* (pp. 429–464). Cambridge, MA: MIT Press.

Jameson, K. A., & Alvarado, N. (2003). Differences in color naming and color salience in Vietnamese and English. *Color Research & Application*, 28, 113–138.

Jarvis, S., & Pavlenko, A. (2008). *Crosslinguistic influence in language and cognition*. New York: Routledge.

Kay, P., & Kempton, W. (1984). What is the Sapir-Whorf hypothesis? *American Anthropologist*, 86, 65–79.

Koustá, S. T., Vinson, D. P., & Vigliocco, G. (2008). Investigating linguistic relativity through bilingualism: the case of grammatical gender. *Journal of Experimental Psychology: Learning, Memory & Cognition*, 34, 843–858.

Kroll, J. (1993). Accessing conceptual representations for words in a second language. In R. Schreuder & B. Weltens (eds.), *The bilingual lexicon* (pp. 53–81). Amsterdam: John Benjamins.

Kroll, J., & de Groot, A. M. B. (1997). Lexical and conceptual memory in the bilingual: mapping form to meaning in two languages. In A. M. B. de Groot & J. Kroll (eds.), *Tutorials in bilingualism: psycholinguistic perspectives* (pp. 169–199). Mahwah, NJ: Lawrence Erlbaum.

Kurinski, E., & Sera, M. D. (2011). Does learning Spanish grammatical gender change English-speaking adults' categorization of inanimate objects? *Bilingualism: Language and Cognition*, 14, 203–220.

Langacker, R. (2008). *Cognitive grammar: a basic introduction*. New York: Oxford University Press.

Levelt, W. J. M. (1989). *Speaking: from intention to articulation*. Cambridge, MA: MIT Press.

Levinson, S. C. (1996). Relativity in spatial conception and description. In J. J. Gumperz & S. C. Levinson (eds.), *Rethinking linguistic relativity* (pp. 177–202). Cambridge University Press.

Lucy, J. A. (1992a). *Language diversity and thought: a reformulation of the linguistic relativity hypothesis*. Cambridge University Press.

(1992b). *Grammatical categories and cognition. A case study of the linguistic relativity hypothesis*. Cambridge University Press.

(1997). Linguistic relativity. *Annual Review of Anthropology*, 26, 291–312.

Lucy, J. A., & Gaskins, S. (2003). Interaction of language type and referent type in the development of nonverbal classification preferences. In D. Gentner & S. Goldin-Meadow (eds.), *Language in mind: advances in the study of language and thought* (pp. 465–492). Cambridge, MA: MIT Press.

Pavlenko, A. (1999). New approaches to concepts in bilingual memory. *Bilingualism: Language and Cognition*, 2, 209–230.

(2006). *Bilingual minds: emotional experience, expression, and representation*. Clevedon: Multilingual Matters.

(2011). *Thinking and speaking in two languages*. Bristol: Multilingual Matters.

Quick Placement Test. (2001). Oxford University Press.

Regier, T., & Kay, P. (2009). Language, thought and color: Whorf was half right. *Trends in Cognitive Sciences*, 13, 439–446.

Roberson, D., & Davidoff, J. (2000). The categorical perception of colours and facial expressions: the effect of verbal interference. *Memory & Cognition*, 28, 977–986.

Sapir, E. (1949). *Selected writings in language, culture and personality* (D. Mandelbaum, ed.). Berkeley, CA: University of California Press.

Schmiedtová, B., von Stutterheim, Ch., & Carroll, M. (2011). Implications of language-specific patterns in event construal of advanced L2 speakers. In A. Pavlenko (ed.), *Thinking and speaking in two languages* (pp. 66–107). Bristol: Multilingual Matters.

Slobin, D. I. (1996). From "thought and language" to "thinking for speaking." In J. J. Gumperz & S. C. Levinson (eds.), *Rethinking linguistic relativity* (pp. 70–96). Cambridge University Press.

  (2003). Language and thought online: cognitive consequences of linguistic relativity. In D. Gentner & S. Goldin-Meadow (eds.), *Language in mind: advances in the study of language and thought* (pp. 157–191). Cambridge, MA: MIT Press.

Thierry, G., Athanasopoulos, P., Wiggett, A., Dering, B., & Kuipers, J. (2009). Unconscious effects of language-specific terminology on pre-attentive colour perception. *Proceedings of the National Academy of Sciences*, 106, 4567–4570.

Tse, C.-S., & Altarriba, J. (2008). Evidence against linguistic relativity in Chinese and English: a case study of spatial and temporal metaphors. *Journal of Cognition and Culture*, 8, 335–357.

Whorf, B. L. (1956). *Language, thought, and reality: selected writings of Benjamin Lee Whorf* (J. B. Carroll, ed.). Cambridge, MA: MIT Press.

Wierzbicka, A. (2004). Bilingual lives, bilingual experience. *Journal of Multilingual and Multicultural Development*, 25, 94–104.

Winawer, J., Witthoft, N., Frank, M. C., Wu, L., Wade, A. R., & Boroditsky, L. (2007). Russian blues reveal effects of language on colour discrimination. *Proceedings of the National Academy of Sciences*, 104, 7780–7785.

Winkler, I. (2005). Preattentive binding of auditory and visual stimulus features. *Journal of Cognitive Neuroscience*, 17, 320–339.

Zollinger, H. (1988). Categorical color perception: influence of cultural factors on the differentiation of primary and derived basic color terms in color naming by Japanese children. *Vision Research*, 28, 1379–1382.

10 Testing effects for novel word learning in Chinese–English bilinguals

Chi-Shing Tse and Xiaoping Pu

Abstract

The current study explored the influence of individuals' language proficiency on the observed benefit of repeated testing when they learned Swahili–English word pairs. Sixty Chinese–English bilinguals learned 40 Swahili–English word pairs for a subsequent Swahili cued-recall test given one week later. In the acquisition phase, participants acquired 20 pairs via repeated study and the other 20 via repeated testing, where they were instructed to give the English translation equivalent in response to its corresponding Swahili word. After about a week, participants were given a Swahili cued-recall test for all 40 pairs. Their first language (Chinese) and second language (English) proficiency were estimated by their grades on the Hong Kong Certificate of Education Examination and the Hong Kong Advanced Level Examination. The Shipley vocabulary subscale (1940) was also used to estimate participants' English proficiency. The results showed an overall testing effect; that is, English words were better recalled when the pairs were acquired via repeated testing than when they were acquired by repeated study. The effect was larger for those with higher English proficiency, which can be interpreted in the context of Kroll and Stewart's (1994) Revised Hierarchical Model of bilingual memory. The limitations of the current study and future directions are discussed.

Vocabulary learning is one of the most important topics in second language acquisition (see e.g., Nation, 2001, for a review). The advantage of repeated testing over repeated study in vocabulary learning has been reported in several memory and instruction studies, most of which involved the learning of vocabulary in a language that was novel to the participants (e.g., Karpicke & Roediger, 2008). However, no published study has investigated how participants' language proficiency

---

This research was supported by Faculty and Departmental Supportive Fund, The Chinese University of Hong Kong. We thank Jeanette Altarriba and Ludmila Isurin for their comments on an earlier version of this chapter and Thomas Cheung and Candy Leung for their help with data collection.

could influence the effectiveness of this strategy in vocabulary learning, nor has the benefit of repeated testing been examined using a bilingual population, which may have implications for the structures and processes of bilingual memory. In the current study, we examined the effects of Chinese–English bilinguals' first (L1) and second language (L2) proficiency on their learning of paired associates – L2 words and their corresponding translation equivalents in the Swahili language "L3."[1] Bilinguals acquired Swahili–English word pairs via repeated testing or repeated study, and then performed a final Swahili cued-recall test around a week later. Relative to repeated study, repeated testing has been found in the published memory literature to enhance long-term retention, which is hereafter called the *testing effect*. We replicated this effect and found that it could be modulated by the bilinguals' L2 proficiency. Before elaborating upon the details of this study, we provide an overview of the literature on vocabulary learning and the testing effect, describe Kroll and Stewart's (1994) Revised Hierarchical Model (RHM) of bilingual memory, and speculate how this model would predict the influence of bilinguals' L1 and L2 proficiency on the learning of vocabulary in a totally unknown language ("L3").

Vocabulary knowledge and vocabulary learning strategies

Words are building blocks of verbal communication, and vocabulary knowledge plays an essential role in text comprehension (e.g., Brisbois, 1995; Elgort & Nation, 2010; Hu & Nation, 2000; Nation, 2006, 2007). According to Nation (2001), vocabulary knowledge can be classified as receptive or productive, which refers to the ability to recognize word meaning in listening or reading *or* to use a word in speaking or writing, respectively. Receptive vocabulary develops more quickly and is twice as large as productive vocabulary in language development (e.g., Marton, 1977). This may reflect how different kinds of vocabulary knowledge are used (e.g., Melka, 1997). A test of productive vocabulary knowledge involves learners producing the L2 translation equivalent in response to an L1 word, whereas a test of receptive vocabulary knowledge involves learners producing the L1 translation equivalent in response to an L2 word (see e.g., de Groot & Keijzer, 2000 and Webb, 2008, for a further discussion of the productive–receptive distinction).

---

[1] The quotation marks suggest that from the bilinguals' perspective, these L3 vocabulary items are actually more similar to nonwords than to words in a new language.

The cued-recall tests in the current study were all receptive because our participants were given an "L3" word cue and asked to recall their L2 translation equivalents.

As noted in Nation (2008, see also Daller, Milton, & Treffers-Daller, 2007; Jiang, 2004, for other conceptualizations of L2 vocabulary learning), vocabulary learning involves four strands: meaning-focused inputs, meaning-focused outputs, language-focused learning, and fluency development. The meaning-focused inputs and outputs are related to receptive (Krashen, 1985) and productive vocabulary knowledge (Swain, 2005), respectively. These two strands of vocabulary learning are often developed via instructional methods like communication activities, such as listening to stories and writing a passage. Language-focused learning can be done via direct teaching, intensive reading, and training in vocabulary learning strategies. When learners acquire a certain degree of knowledge in one language, they can develop their fluency by practicing receptive and productive vocabulary knowledge and thus improving the automaticity of access to and control over the existing vocabulary (see also Daller et al., 2007). Given that the cued-recall test used in the current study involved the recall of L2 translation equivalents in response to "L3" word cues, it should be classified as a form of language-focused learning.

Several ways have been proposed to categorize vocabulary learning strategies (e.g., Barcroft, 2009; Elgort & Nation, 2010; Fan, 2003; Gu & Johnson, 1996; Schmitt, 1997; see also Nation, 2001, for a comprehensive review). Nation (2007) classified vocabulary learning strategies by the sources (e.g., using contextual information to understand the word meaning) and processes of forming vocabulary knowledge (e.g., noticing, retrieving, and generating). Schmitt (1997) divided 50 vocabulary learning strategies into two groups: incidental vs. intentional learning (but see Paribakht & Wesche, 1999, for an argument that vocabulary learning should be viewed as an incidental vs. intentional continuum, rather than purely incidental or intentional). Incidental learning, such as guessing from context to infer the novel word meaning in extensive reading, underscores the importance of meaningful contexts (e.g., DeKeyser, 1998; Dupuy & Krashen, 1993). When dealing with unknown words in a text, learners may use the contextual information to guess their meaning and in turn acquire these words after encountering them repeatedly in various contexts (e.g., Nagy, Herman, & Anderson, 1985; Paribakht & Wesche, 1999). In contrast to incidental learning, intentional learning refers to learners intentionally acquiring words, such as memorizing a list of new words by rote. This may involve the repeated retrieval of the form and meaning of the novel words (e.g., Coady, 1997; Elgort & Nation, 2010; Hulstijn, 2001; Nation, 2007). Research has shown that naturalistic, incidental usage-based learning is not sufficient to acquire L2 vocabulary (Cobb & Horst, 2004; Ellis, 2008; Laufer, 2005) and needs to be supplemented by deliberate form-focused learning (e.g., Elgort & Nation, 2010). For example, Prince (1996) showed that translation-based L2 vocabulary learning was more effective than learning L2 vocabulary in sentential contexts. Hulstijn (2001, see also Elgort, 2011) found that learners could remember the vocabulary items acquired through intentional learning for a longer time than those acquired through incidental learning. Nation (2008) also argued that incidental learning via extensive reading may direct learners' attention to text comprehension rather than to learning specific words in the text. This may not be an efficient way to learn new vocabulary because a substantial amount of input is required to allow learners opportunities to encounter the same set of vocabulary items over and over again. In short, an incidental learning strategy on its own seems not to be adequate for learning vocabulary in a foreign language.

Regarding the effectiveness of intentional vocabulary learning strategies, studies using self-reported questionnaires revealed the relationship between vocabulary proficiency and strategy use (e.g., Ahmed, 1989; Barcroft, 2009; Fan, 2003; Gu & Johnson, 1996; Schmitt, 1997). For example, Lawson and Hogben (1996) reported positive correlations between word recall and simple rehearsal, orthographic and phonological similarity, paraphrase, and mnemonic aid. Schmitt (1997) reported that "mechanical" strategies such as memorization, note taking, and repetition are used more often than strategies that involve deep processing such as guessing, imagery, and the keyword technique (cf. Atkinson & Raugh, 1975). Other than strategy use, other learner-internal factors like metacognitive belief, motivation, and attitudes, as well as learner-external factors like socioeconomic status, cultural context, and educational setting, can influence foreign vocabulary learning (e.g., Tseng & Schmitt, 2008). For instance, O'Malley *et al.* (1985) reported that, unlike Western students, Asian students were more efficient at using rote memorization strategies than strategies like imagery to learn vocabulary. The current study contrasted the effectiveness between two intentional strategies, repeated study vs. repeated testing, on vocabulary learning in a paired-associate paradigm.

Testing effect and paired-associate vocabulary learning

Tests have often been regarded as a way of measuring learning, rather than as a method to facilitate learning. While preparing for an exam, most students choose to repeatedly read their notes or textbooks rather than engage in self-testing (e.g., Karpicke, Butler, & Roediger, 2009; Kornell & Bjork, 2007). However, many studies have reported a *testing effect* – the advantage in long-term retention for materials that are repeatedly tested over those that are repeatedly studied during the retention interval (see Delaney, Verkoeijen, & Spirgel, 2010; Roediger & Karpicke, 2006; Rohrer & Pashler, 2010, for reviews). The robust benefit of testing on memory has been obtained with study materials including paired associates (e.g., Carrier & Pashler, 1992), pictures (e.g., Wheeler & Roediger, 1992), general knowledge facts (e.g., McDaniel & Fisher, 1991), and textbook passages (e.g., Agarwal *et al.*, 2008). Repeated testing has also been shown to produce benefits in free recall (e.g., Karpicke & Roediger, 2007; Tulving, 1967), cued recall (e.g., Carpenter, Pashler, & Vul, 2006), and episodic recognition (e.g., Glover, 1989). The testing effect has been demonstrated in young college students (e.g., Karpicke & Roediger, 2008), children (e.g., Gates, 1917), medical students (e.g., Larsen, Butler, & Roediger, 2009), healthy older adults (e.g., Tse, Balota, & Roediger, 2010), and even patients with multiple sclerosis (e.g., Sumowski, Chiaravalloti, & DeLuca, 2010).

The benefit of repeated testing, which has been revitalized by Roediger, Pashler, and their colleagues in the memory literature, has also been reported in some vocabulary learning studies. For example, Baddeley (1990, see also Nation, 2001) demonstrated the positive role of retrieval in vocabulary learning for building up form–meaning mappings. The repeated testing strategy has been implemented in some computer-assisted language learning devices (e.g., Chen & Chung, 2008; Kwon *et al.*, 2010). Nation (2008) also suggested that learners should be given repeated opportunities for increasingly spaced retrieval of each newly learned vocabulary. However, even though some reported that spaced retrieval has a positive effect on long-term L2 vocabulary learning (e.g., Bahrick *et al.*, 1993), they did not compare the effect of repeated study vs. testing on vocabulary acquisition. In the following paragraphs, we summarize the findings of three vocabulary learning studies that directly examined the testing effect: Royer (1973), McNamara and Healy (1995), and Barcroft (2007).

In Royer (1973), the repeated testing group learned 20 Turkish–English word pairs in the first trial and then used the same set of 20

Turkish cue words to self-test themselves regarding their English translation equivalents on subsequent trials, whereas the repeated study group were given the same amount of time but were instructed to study the Turkish–English word pairs only. Immediately after the acquisition phase, both groups were asked to recall the English translation equivalents in response to L2 Turkish words, so this was a receptive L2 vocabulary test. Royer showed that the repeated testing group performed better than the repeated study group, suggesting that relative to repeated study, repeated testing enhanced L2 vocabulary learning when tested immediately.

McNamara and Healy (1995) had two groups of participants (referred to as a read group and a generate group) learn the association between nonwords and their corresponding English "translation equivalents." All participants first learned the English–nonword pairs. Then, given English word cues, participants in the read group were instructed to copy their corresponding target nonwords, while those in the generate group were instructed to recall them. Both groups were given an immediate as well as a one-week-delayed cued-recall test in which they needed to recall nonwords in response to their English counterparts, so it was a productive L2 vocabulary test. The testing effect occurred: those in the generate group performed better than those in the read group in both immediate and delayed tests.

Finally, using picture–L2 pairs rather than word pairs, Barcroft (2007) manipulated the repeated study and repeated testing conditions within participants, rather than between participants as in other studies. In the acquisition phase, participants were given the same amount of time to read or recall the L2 word in response to a picture cue. The final picture-cued recall tests were given immediately, two days later, and one week later. Barcroft reported the testing effect, regardless of the retention interval.

However, none of these three studies took into account their participants' L1 and L2 proficiency. As elaborated next, based on Kroll and Stewart's (1994) RHM of bilingual memory, the testing effect might be modulated by participants' L1/L2 proficiency. These hypotheses were tested in the current study.

Bilingual memory models

While bilingual memory models have more often been used to explain bilingual lexical processing rather than bilingual memory processing, their premises could be extended to account for the current findings, including the effect of repeated testing on vocabulary acquisition.

Bilingual memory models can be categorized into two groups based on whether the representations of the two languages' translation equivalents are stored in a shared (single-coded) or separate (dual-coded) memory system(s). Single-code theories suggest that the representations of translation equivalents in two languages are all stored as supralinguistic, abstract codes that are independent of the language in which the words occur (Francis, 1999). Given that these codes contain word meaning, these theories predict that L1 words should prime their L2 translation equivalents, and vice versa. For example, when Spanish–English bilinguals read the word *blue*, their subsequent recognition of *azul* (blue in Spanish) should be facilitated because both of them are represented in common codes (see Altarriba & Basnight-Brown, 2007, for a review). In contrast, dual-code theories assume that L1 and L2 translation equivalents are stored separately in their lexicons, with associative links between them for coordinating concepts in the two systems (Francis, 1999). These theories predict that semantic priming may not occur between two languages, although evidence for this has been mixed (e.g., Chen & Ng, 1989; Scarborough, Gerard, & Cortese, 1984). In order to reconcile these two theories, some researchers adopt a hybrid approach, assuming that L1 and L2 translation equivalents are stored in their lexicons, which are also connected to a non-language-specific conceptual store. The lexicons store the linguistic features of encoded memory, whereas the conceptual store contains the knowledge about word meaning (e.g., Heredia, 1997; Kroll & Stewart, 1994).

Word Association Model and Concept Mediation Model

The Word Association Model suggests that new words in the L2 lexicon are directly associated with words in the L1 lexicon, which is in turn connected to the conceptual store. There is no conceptual link between the L2 lexicon and the conceptual store (Potter *et al.*, 1984). To process an L2 word, bilinguals should translate it into L1 via the L1 → L2 link, and then retrieve its meaning from the conceptual store. In contrast, the Concept Mediation Model argues that the L2 and L1 lexicons are connected directly and independently to the conceptual store (Potter *et al.*, 1984). Because these two models assume that the words in lexicons are stored separately from the concepts, the lexical properties of a word cannot influence the organization of the concepts, and vice versa. Potter *et al.* performed two experiments, L1 → L2 word translation and picture naming in L2, to test the above models. Assume that a picture is retrieved via a link connected to the conceptual store, the Word Association Model predicted that L1 → L2 word translation would be faster than picture naming in L2 as a shorter path is involved in the former task. The Concept Mediation Model predicted that there would be no difference between the two tasks because the processing of L2 words need not involve the L1 lexicon. Potter *et al.* found that the two tasks did yield equivalent reaction times, thereby providing support for the Concept Mediation Model.

The Revised Hierarchical Model

Kroll and Stewart (1994) elaborated the Concept Mediation Model with the following modifications. First, they added lexical links between the two lexicons in order to account for translation priming effects across the languages. Second, they varied the size of the L1 and L2 lexicons to demonstrate the difference in the vocabulary sizes between L1 and L2 for emerging bilinguals. Third, they assigned differential strengths to each link (i.e., L1 → L2) to depict the ease of language switching. For example, it is more difficult to translate words from L1 to L2 than the other way round because of the weak L1 → L2 link. This RHM is a hybrid of the Concept Mediation Model (i.e., two lexicons are individually connected with the conceptual store via conceptual links) and the Word Association Model (i.e., two lexicons are connected with each other via bidirectional lexical links). Kroll and Stewart's RHM (see Kroll, Sumutka, & Schwartz, 2005, for a review) predicted a difference in language processing between fluent and less-fluent bilinguals, assuming that a bilingual has a larger L1 lexicon than L2 lexicon. The conceptual link for L1 (L1 ↔ concept) is also stronger than the conceptual link for L2 (L2 ↔ concept). Depending on the size of the L2 lexicon and the strength of its conceptual links, language abilities at different stages of L2 acquisition could be predicted. In the early stage of L2 acquisition, bilinguals have to associate every new L2 word that they learn with its L1 translation, so L1 and L2 lexicons should be closely connected with each other. However, the L2 → L1 link is stronger than the L1 → L2 link due to translation asymmetry: bilinguals translate the words from L2 to L1 more often than the other way round. As bilinguals at this stage learn novel concepts more often via their L1 than their L2, L1 conceptual links should be stronger than L2 conceptual links.

How could this RHM explain L2 vocabulary learning? As noted in Altarriba and Mathis (1997, see also Altarriba & Knickerbocker, 2011), when bilinguals access the meaning of a new L2 vocabulary, they shift their focus from its lexical characteristics, such as linking "dog" to "狗" (dog in Chinese), to the concept represented by that word, such as

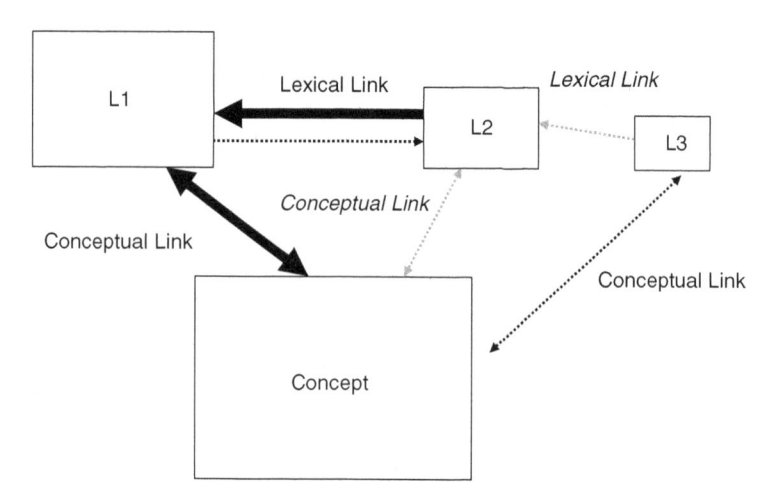

Note. The conceptual link highlighted in gray reflects bilinguals' L2 proficiency. The lexical link highlighted in gray determined bilinguals' final recall performance in the current study.

Figure 10.1 Modified Revised Hierarchical Model of bilingual memory

linking "dog" to the *dog* concept. At first, the meaning of L2 words is only indirectly connected to the L2 lexicon via the L1 lexicon. Hence, bilinguals have to translate from L2 to L1 to determine the meaning of these L2 words. With repeated exposure, a direct link could be built between the L2 words and the conceptual store. By then, L2 → L1 translation could then be unnecessary to determine meaning.

What happens when bilinguals learn to associate their L2 words with "L3" words? To depict this point, a modified RHM is sketched in Figure 10.1. When bilinguals receive the "L3"–L2 word pairs, they could access the meaning of an "L3" word via an "L3" → L2 link (e.g., linking *mbwa* [dog in Swahili] to "dog"). This is especially true when bilinguals anticipate that they will need to recall the L2 words in response to the "L3" words (as in the current study). Hence, they may focus on building the "L3" → L2 link. This learning process might depend on the strength of the L2 conceptual link. For those bilinguals who are proficient in L2, L2 conceptual links could guide access to the concept and in turn facilitate the strengthening of the "L3" → L2 link. However, those who are not proficient in L2 may rely more on the L1 conceptual link and in turn slow down the build-up of the "L3" → L2 link. As the vocabulary learning task requires bilinguals to respond with L2 words to the "L3" words without necessarily the retrieval of their corresponding L1 translation equivalents, it is unlikely that they would build up the "L3" → L1 links. To avoid cluttering, the "L3" → L1 link was not drawn in Figure 10.1. Regarding the difference between repeated study and repeated testing, retrieving an item could alter one's pre-existing knowledge by strengthening the encoding process (Roediger & Guynn, 1996; Roediger & Karpicke, 2006). Hence, one could expect that the more frequently bilinguals retrieve the L2 via an "L3" → L2 link, the stronger the "L3" → L2 link could be. In contrast, repeated study may not strengthen the "L3" → L2 link to the same degree as repeated testing. In addition, this might be the case only for bilinguals with high L2 proficiency because those with low L2 proficiency might need to allocate resources to access the concept via the L1 conceptual link, thus making it less likely that the "L3" → L2 link could be strengthened to the same extent as for the bilinguals with high L2 proficiency who can retrieve the concept via the L2 conceptual link more easily. However, one could also argue that bilinguals did not necessarily access the conceptual store when they learned the "L3"–L2 word pairs. The cued-recall task only required them to build and strengthen the "L3" → L2 link in the acquisition phase and retrieve the L2 words in response to their corresponding "L3" words in the final recall test. If this were the case, the testing effect would be the same regardless of bilinguals' L1/L2 proficiency. The current study was designed to test these two hypotheses.

The present study

Although many of the previous testing-effect studies involved unfamiliar foreign-language vocabulary in their paired-associate stimuli (e.g., Swahili in Karpicke & Roediger, 2008), no study has examined whether the benefit of repeated testing in vocabulary learning could be modulated by participants' language proficency. In the present study, we address this issue by using Swahili–English word pairs as study materials as none of our Chinese–English bilingual participants are familiar with this African language, as was confirmed by a pre-screening procedure prior to their participation in the experiment. The participants were instructed to learn the association between Swahili and English words because they would be asked later to recall the English translation equivalent corresponding to each Swahili word cue. In the 12 study-trial (S) or memory-test-trial (T) cycles during the acquisition phase, college-student participants acquired half of the Swahili–English word pairs via repeated study (in a S-S-S-T-S-S-S-T-S-S-S-T sequence – 9 study trials + 3 memory-test trials), and half via repeated testing (in a S-T-S-T-S-T-S-T-S-T-S-T sequence – 6 study trials + 6 memory test trials). Following other testing-effect studies that involved foreign vocabulary (e.g., Karpicke & Roediger, 2008), we used a one-week retention interval; that is, participants were asked to perform a final cued-recall test after a week for all 40 Swahili–English word pairs that had been acquired through repeated study or repeated testing. We did not use the typical S-T-T-T-S-T-T-T-S-T-T-T sequence (i.e., 3 study trials + 9 memory test trials) in the acquisition phase (see e.g., Karpicke & Roediger, 2007) because in our pilot test this manipulation yielded substantially lower cumulative recall performance at the end of the acquisition phase, prehaps due to the absence of frequent corrective feedback across multiple memory-test trials, which might have led to participants making higher intrusion errors and in turn counteracting the benefit of repeated testing in their recall performance (see Tse et al., 2010, for a discussion based on older adults' data).

By manipulating the repeated study and repeated testing condition within participants (following e.g., Kang, McDermott, & Roediger, 2007; McDaniel, Roediger, & McDermott, 2007; Tse et al., 2010; Weinstein, McDermott, & Roediger, 2010), we could obtain the testing effect; that is, better performance for the pairs that were acquired via repeated testing, relative to those that were acquired via repeated study, and examine how it might be modulated by bilinguals' L1 and L2 proficiency, which could be quantified by (a) their self-reported grades on standardized university entrance examinations, and (b) estimation via a computerized 40-item vocabulary subscale test on the Shipley Institute of Living Scale (Shipley, 1940; Zachary, 1992). The full Shipley scale was devised to provide a quick measure of intellectual functioning, and contains vocabulary knowledge (reliability coefficient = 0.87) and abstract thinking (reliability coefficient = 0.89) subscales. In the current study, we administered the vocabulary subscale, and participants' vocabulary knowledge was estimated using raw Shipley scores (see Yap et al., 2008; Yap, Tse, & Balota, 2009, for other studies that used this test to quantify participants' English vocabulary knowledge). Despite its age, this test continues to be widely used by researchers and it has been shown to correlate highly with most standard intelligence tests (see Zachary, Paulson, & Gorsuch, 1985, for a review).

Method

Participants

Sixty Chinese–English bilingual undergraduates at the Chinese University of Hong Kong who reported normal or corrected-to-normal vision participated for monetary compensation. An equal number of participants received each of the counterbalancing lists. Participants provided their informed consents at the start of the study and reported their ages (*Mean* = 20.82, *Standard Deviation* = 1.63), their Chinese (L1) and English (L2) grades on the Hong Kong Certificate of Education Examination (HKCEE, taken in Grade 11) and on the Hong Kong Advanced Level Examination (HKALE, taken in Grade 13). These two were the standardized public university entrance examinations in Hong Kong. The grades were converted as follows: E = 1, D = 2, C = 3, B = 4, A = 5 (grade E is the pass grade on the examination). These were regarded as self-reported ratings of their L1 proficiency (M = 3.62, SD = 1.15 for HKCEE; M = 2.67, SD = 1.11 for HKALE) and L2 proficiency (M = 3.53, SD = 0.97 for HKCEE; M = 2.62, SD = 1.01 for HKALE). On average and based on these ratings, our participants were fluent bilinguals because their L1 and L2 proficiencies were statistically equivalent (p > 0.45 in both). To measure participants' L2 proficiency, we had them complete the Shipley vocabulary subscale (1940) after the acquisition phase, which showed that their mean vocabulary age was 14.90 (SD = 1.20).

Materials and design

A pool of 175 Swahili–English word pairs was constructed, some of which were from Nelson and Dunlosky (1994), and some were constructed by translating the category exemplars in Van Overschelde, Rawson, and Dunlosky (2004) using http://translate.google.com/. To make sure that (a) participants knew the meaning of all the English words used in the current study, and (b) the perceived difficulty of the Swahili–English word pairs was evenly distributed across two sets of stimuli, and was relatively low to avoid a ceiling effect, we conducted a norming study with another group of 32 Chinese–English bilinguals. These participants were instructed to give a familiarity rating on a 5-point scale to each of 175 English words and an ease-of-learning rating on a 5-point scale to each of 175 Swahili–English word pairs. The two rating tasks were blocked and counterbalanced between participants. All English words and Swahili–English word pairs were randomly presented. Based on the rating data, we chose 40 Swahili–English word pairs in which all English words were higher than 4.5 in familiarity rating and all pairs were lower than 2.3 in ease-of-learning rating. These 40 pairs were divided into two sets of 20. The assignment of stimuli to repeated study and repeated testing conditions was counterbalanced across participants. For half of the participants, Set A was used in the repeated study condition and Set B in the repeated testing condition, and for the other half, the assignment was reversed. Table 10.1 lists mean statistics of

Table 10.1 *Mean statistics for the lexical characteristics of Swahili–English word pairs in Set A and Set B*

	Set A Mean	Set A SD	Set B Mean	Set B SD	Difference? p
Word length	4.90	1.12	4.75	1.52	0.72
Log HAL word frequency	9.24	1.43	9.33	1.24	0.84
Lexical decision RT	605.60	51.97	606.76	39.11	0.94
Naming RT	599.02	42.84	601.78	39.74	0.83
Lexical decision accuracy	0.98	0.02	0.98	0.02	0.67
Naming accuracy	1.00	0.01	0.99	0.02	0.08
Word concreteness	5.96	0.33	6.08	0.44	0.33
English word familiarity rating	4.86	0.12	4.90	0.08	0.18
Swahili–English word pair ease-of-learning rating	1.93	0.17	1.85	0.12	0.08

Note: The "Difference?" column lists the *p* value of the independent-sample *t* test for each of the lexical characteristics for Set A and Set B. As shown, none of them approached statistical significance. Other than word concreteness, English word familarity rating, and ease-of-learning rating for Swahili–English word pairs, all mean values of the lexical characteristics were from Balota *et al.*'s (2007) English Lexicon Project. HAL = Hyperspace Analogue to Language; SD = Standard Deviation; RT = Reaction Time.

lexical characteristics, normed ease-of-learning and normed familiarity ratings for English words for all Swahili–English word pairs. The full set of stimuli is listed in Table 10.2.

Procedure

PC-compatible laptop computers running E-prime software (Schneider, Eschman, & Zuccolotto, 2001) were used to control stimulus presentation and to collect data. Participants were tested in groups of one to three in a quiet room while seated comfortably in front of a computer monitor. All stimuli were presented in white lowercase letters, using Courier New 18-point bold font, at the center of the screen and participants' responses were made on a computer keyboard.

At the beginning of the experiment, participants were informed that they would study a list of Swahili (i.e., an African language) words,

Table 10.2 *Experimental stimuli*

Set A				Set B			
Swahili	English	Swahili	English	Swahili	English	Swahili	English
ndizi	banana	farasi	horse	pombe	beer	kaburi	grave
kitabu	book	ziwa	lake	mashua	boat	kofia	hat
fagio	broom	tumbili	monkey	ndugu	brother	godoro	mattress
ndoo	bucket	chungwa	orange	siagi	butter	kipanya	mouse
nafaka	corn	sumu	poison	zulia	carpet	kitunguu	onion
kaa	crab	viazi	potato	ngombe	cow	nguruwe	pig
tabibu	doctor	mwamba	rock	pazia	curtain	malkia	queen
yai	egg	kiatu	shoe	mbwa	dog	hariri	silk
bustani	garden	theluji	snow	jicho	eye	nyanya	tomato
bunduki	gun	dirisha	window	chakula	food	ukuta	wall

together with their English translations and would be tested for their ability to recall the English translations in response to their respective Swahili words. There were study and memory-test trials in this acquisition phase. In a *study* trial, a Swahili–English word pair, with two line spacings inserted between the two words, was presented for 5 s. In a *memory-test* trial, a Swahili word stayed on the screen until the participants typed in their answer for its corresponding English translations. Their typed responses appeared on the screen. A 500 ms blank screen was inserted between each trial. With an emphasis on the importance of spelling their answers correctly, we allowed our participants to use the BACKSPACE key to correct their responses. After they finished typing their answer, they pressed the ENTER key to continue. No corrective feedback was provided throughout the experiment. They were instructed to come up with an English translation for every single Swahili word cue and encouraged to guess if they were not sure about the answer. This instruction was given in order to increase the opportunities for participants to make extra-list and intra-list intrusion errors, thus increasing the difficulty of this vocabulary-learning task. The participants were reminded that the study and memory-test trials would be interleaved with each other. There were 12 cycles of study/memory test trials. In each cycle, each of the 40 Swahili–English word pairs was presented either as a study trial or a memory-test trial. No pair was dropped from the cycles in the acquisition phase, unlike some recent studies (e.g., Karpicke & Roediger, 2008). Half of the 40 Swahili–English word pairs (the repeated study condition) appeared in the S-**S**-S-T-S-**S**-S-T-S-**S**-S-T sequence, whereas the other half (the repeated testing condition) appeared in the S-T-S-T-S-T-S-T-S-T-S-T sequence. Thus, in the 2nd, 6th, and 10th cycles, half of the pairs were presented as study trials and half memory-test trials. After all study and memory-test trials, a self-paced break was given before the next cycle proceeded. Within each cycle, all study and/or memory-test trials were randomly intermixed.

After about a one-week retention interval, participants were given the final cued-recall test, in which the procedure was identical to the memory-test trial during the acquisition phase, except that participants were now tested for all 40 Swahili–English word pairs learned in either repeated study or repeated testing conditions. After the participants finished this final cued-recall test, they were given the vocabulary subscales in Shipley (1940).

Results

Unless otherwise specified, the significance level was set at 0.05. The effect sizes of F and t are represented by η_p^2 and Cohen's d, respectively. The typed response was scored as correct when it was spelled correctly or matched with the grammatically derived forms of the answer (e.g., recalling *games* for *game*). As the counterbalancing of the stimuli (Set A vs. B) for the repeated study and repeated testing conditions did not interact with any variable in the following analyses (all Fs < 1), this factor was not considered any further. We performed exploratory factor analyses on various participants' L1 and L2 proficiency measures to extract the factor scores that represent their L1 and L2 proficiencies. For L1 proficiency, the factor loadings of the Chinese grade in HKALE and the Chinese grade in HKCEE were 0.89 and 0.89, respectively, which accounted for 79 percent of the variance across these two measures. For L2 proficiency, the factor loadings of the English grade in HKALE, the English grade in HKCEE, and Shipley's vocabulary subscale were 0.89, 0.79, and 0.80, respectively, which accounted for 68 percent of the variance across these three measures.

Acquisition phase Figure 10.2 shows the cumulative proportion of Swahili–English word pairs recalled during the acquisition phase as a function of repeated study and repeated testing conditions. For the pairs in the repeated study condition, participants received the cued-recall test in the 4th, 8th, and 12th cycles, whereas for the pairs in the repeated testing condition, they received the test in the 2nd, 4th, 6th, 8th, 10th, and 12th cycles. Hence, only the data from the 4th, 8th and 12th cycles could be analyzed as a function of the two

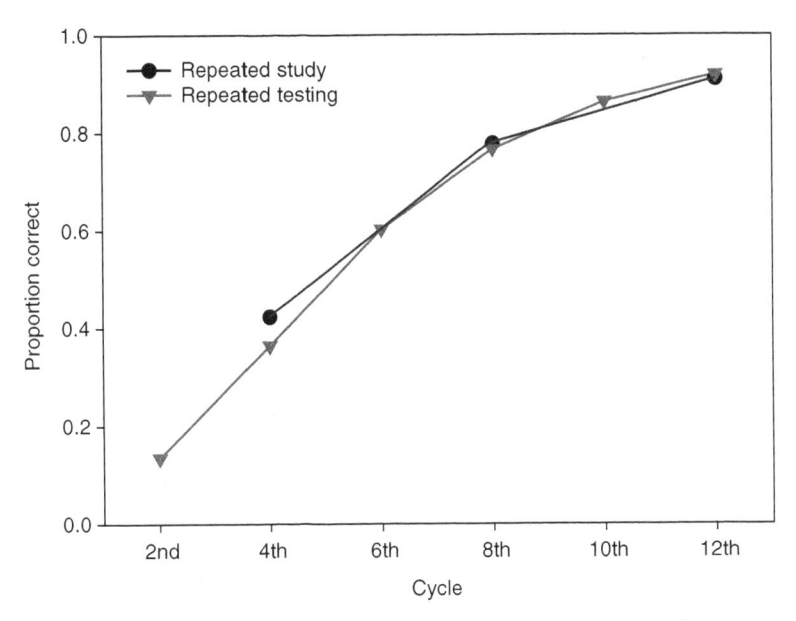

Figure 10.2 Mean proportion of Swahili–English word pairs recalled in repeated study and repeated testing conditions across the 12 cycles in the acquisition phase

learning conditions. We conducted a 2 (Condition) × 3 (Cycle: 4th, 8th, and 12th) repeated-measures analysis of variance (ANOVA), using a Greenhouse-Geisser correction for the potential violation of sphericity. The main effects of Cycle and Condition and their interaction were all significant [$F(1.49, 87.68) = 395.89$, $MSE = 0.03$, $\eta_p^2 = 0.87$; $F(1,59) = 4.67$, $MSE = 0.01$, $\eta_p^2 = 0.07$; and $F(1.86, 109.58) = 7.85$, $MSE = 0.01$, $\eta_p^2 = 0.12$, respectively]. However, the difference between repeated study and repeated testing conditions was significant only in the 4th cycle [0.42 vs. 0.36, $t(59) = 3.75$, $d = 0.69$], but not in the 8th [0.78 vs. 0.77, $t(59) = 0.85$, $d = 0.16$] or 12th cycle [0.91 vs. 0.92, $t(59) = 0.76$, $d = 0.14$]. More importantly, the absence of any difference in the last (12th) cycle means that the extents to which word pairs were learned were equivalent at the end of the acquisition phase in both repeated study and repeated testing conditions, indicating that repeated study did not produce faster and more efficient learning than repeated testing. While the absence of a difference between repeated study and repeated testing conditions in the 12th cycle could be regarded as a null "testing effect" in the immediate memory test, it should be noted that the "immediate" memory test reported in previous testing-effect studies was typically given about 5–10 minutes *after* the end of the acquisition phase, rather than *within* the acquisition phase.

To further examine the extent to which the lexical links between L2 and "L3" were built during the acquisition phase, we computed participants' mean intra-list intrusion errors, extra-list intrusion errors, and omissions in the acquisition phase (see Table 10.3). Intra-list intrusion errors refer to the cases in which participants responded with a wrong yet studied English translation equivalent to the Swahili word cue, extra-list intrusion errors refer to cases in which participants responded with a wrong and non-studied English translation equivalent to the Swahili word cue, and omission errors refer to cases in which participants skipped the trial without giving an answer. Similar to the proportion of cumulative recall, we conducted 2 (Condition) × 3 (Cycle: 4th, 8th, and 12th) repeated-measures ANOVAs, using a Greenhouse-Geisser correction for the potential violation of sphericity, for the three types of errors. The main effects of Cycle and Condition and their interaction were significant in omission errors [$F(1.05, 61.80) = 14.19$, $MSE = 0.02$, $\eta_p^2 = 0.19$; $F(1, 59) = 8.90$, $MSE = 0.01$, $\eta_p^2 = 0.13$; and $F(1.15, 67.95) = 7.99$, $MSE = 0.002$, $\eta_p^2 = 0.12$, respectively], intra-list intrusion errors [$F(1.27, 75.06) = 110.52$, $MSE = 0.02$, $\eta_p^2 = 0.65$; $F(1, 59) = 66.72$, $MSE = 0.01$, $\eta_p^2 = 0.53$; and $F(1.88, 110.97) = 34.10$, $MSE = 0.004$, $\eta_p^2 = 0.37$, respectively], and extra-list intrusion errors [$F(1.25, 73.65) = 31.51$, $MSE = 0.003$, $\eta_p^2 = 0.35$; $F(1, 59) = 13.25$, $MSE = 0.002$, $\eta_p^2 = 0.18$; and $F(1.43, 84.22) = 5.43$, $MSE = 0.002$, $\eta_p^2 = 0.08$, respectively]. Relative to repeated-study conditions, repeated-testing conditions showed fewer omission, intra-list intrusion, and extra-list intrusion errors across all cycles, all $p < 0.03$, except the difference in extra-list intrusion errors in the 8th cycle, $p = 0.33$, yet in the same direction. Relative to the 4th cycle, the repeated-study vs. repeated-testing difference was smaller in the 12th cycle for intra-list intrusion, extra-list intrusion, and omission errors, from 0.17 to 0.03, 0.04 to 0.01, and 0.04 to 0.01, respectively.

Final-recall phase The mean proportions of final recall of the Swahili–English word pairs acquired via repeated-study and repeated-testing procedures were 0.42 and 0.49, respectively. The 7 percent difference was small yet significant [$t(59) = 3.87$, $d = 0.71$], indicating an overall testing effect. As the cumulative proportions of recall were statistically equivlaent in repeated-study and repeated-testing conditions at the end of the 12th cycle, analyses on the proportion of word pairs forgotten in the final recall test mirrored the final-recall data; that is, 0.49 for repeated study and 0.43 for repeated testing [$t(59) = 2.68$,

Table 10.3 *Mean proportions of intra-list intrusion errors, extra-list intrusion errors, and omission as a function of condition in the acquisition phase and final cued-recall test*

Cycle	Intralist intrusion errors				Extralist intrusion errors				Omission errors			
	Repeated study		Repeated testing		Repeated study		Repeated testing		Repeated study		Repeated testing	
	M	SD	M	SD	M	SD	M	SD	M	SD	M	SD
2nd	–	–	0.26	0.11	–	–	0.10	0.08	–	–	0.07	0.13
4th	0.38	0.22	0.21	0.12	0.09	0.11	0.05	0.06	0.11	0.22	0.07	0.13
6th	–	–	0.16	0.11	–	–	0.02	0.03	–	–	0.04	0.08
8th	0.18	0.19	0.09	0.09	0.03	0.05	0.02	0.04	0.05	0.11	0.03	0.06
10th	–	–	0.06	0.08	–	–	0.01	0.03	–	–	0.02	0.04
12th	0.08	0.14	0.05	0.08	0.02	0.04	0.01	0.02	0.02	0.07	0.01	0.04
Final test	0.35	0.21	0.30	0.18	0.11	0.14	0.10	0.12	0.13	0.24	0.11	0.21

Note: In both repeated-study and repeated-testing conditions in the remaining cycles (i.e., 1st, 3rd, 5th, 7th, 9th, and 11th) participants received only study trials for the pairs. M = Mean; SD = Standard Deviation.

$d = 0.49$], respectively. Finally, as indicated in Table 10.3, relative to the repeated-study condition, repeated-testing condition showed fewer intra-list intrusion errors but equivalent extra-list intrusion errors and omission errors [$t(59) = 2.20$, $d = 0.41$, $t(59) = 0.67$, $d = 0.12$ and $t(59) = 0.92$, $d = 0.17$, respectively].

Correlational analyses   Table 10.4 shows the correlation matrix for the factor score for L1 proficiency, the factor score for L2 proficiency, proportion of final recall for pairs acquired through repeated study, proportion of final recall for pairs acquired through repeated testing, and the testing effect in the final recall phase. The testing effect was correlated with L2 proficiency but not with L1 proficiency, and this was probably due to the fact that L2 proficiency was, although only marginally, correlated with final-recall performance in the repeated testing condition, but not in the repeated study condition. The testing effect was still significantly correlated with L2 proficiency even after covarying out the influence of L1 proficiency, $r = +0.30$, $p < 0.05$, suggesting that L1 proficiency did not significantly affect "L3"–L2 acquisition, at least in the context of repeated-study and repeated-testing procedures (see Figure 10.3).

To investigate the relationship between the testing effect and L1/L2 proficiency in an alternative way, we performed partial correlation analyses. By controlling for the performance for pairs acquired through repeated study, the correlation between L2 proficiency and performance for pairs acquired through repeated testing was still significant, $r = +0.32$, $p < 0.05$, providing further evidence that the benefit of repeated testing increases as a function of L2 proficiency. In contrast to L2 proficiency, the correlation between L1 proficiency and the performance for pairs acquired through repeated testing was not significant, $r = +0.07$, *ns*. Finally, we divided the participants into two groups with equal N based on L1/L2 proficiency and performed a 2 (L1/L2 Proficiency Group: high vs. low) × 2 (Condition: repeated study vs. repeated testing) mixed-factor ANOVA, with L2/L1 proficiency factor score as a covariate. That is, when L1 Proficiency Group was entered, L2 proficiency factor score was covaried; when L2 Proficiency Group was entered, L1 proficiency factor score was covaried. The L2 proficiency significantly interacted with Condition (i.e., the testing effect) [$F(1, 57) = 4.46$, $MSE = 0.01$, $\eta_p^2 = 0.07$], indicating that the testing effect was larger for participants with high L2 proficiency [0.47 vs. 0.57, $t(29) = 4.85$, $d = 1.27$] than for those with low L2 proficiency [0.37 vs. 0.40, $t(29) = 1.18$, $d = 0.31$]. The overall recall performance was also higher for those with high L2 proficiency

Table 10.4 *Pearson correlation matrix*

	1	2	3	4	5
1 L1 (Chinese) proficiency (factor score)	1	.663*	.003	.041	.067
2 L2 (English) proficiency (factor score)		1	.098	.252^	.265*
3 Final recall in repeated study condition			1	.852*	-.362*
4 Final recall in repeated testing condition				1	.180
5 Testing effect in final recall					1

*$p < 0.05$; ^$p < 0.10$.

than for those with low L2 proficiency, as indicated by the main effect of L2 Proficiency Group [$F(1, 57) = 5.55$, $MSE = 0.10$, $\eta_p^2 = 0.09$]. In contrast, L1 proficiency did not interact with Condition [$F(1, 57) = 0.72$, $MSE = 0.01$, $\eta_p^2 = 0.01$], indicating that the testing effect was statistically equivalent for participants with high L1 proficiency [0.40 vs. 0.47, $t(29) = 2.98$, $d = 0.78$] and low L1 proficiency [0.44 vs. 50, $t(29) = 2.49$, $d = 0.65$]. The overall recall performance was also about the same for those with high and low L1 proficiency, as indicated by the nonsignificant main effect of L1 Proficiency Group [$F(1, 57) = 2.03$, $MSE = 0.10$, $\eta_p^2 = 0.03$].

Regarding intra-list intrusion errors, extra-list intrusion errors, and omission errors, none of the correlations between these error types (averaged across all cycles) in the acquisition phase and L1/L2 proficiency approached statistical significance, all $|r|s < 0.20$, $ps > 0.12$. There was only one marginally significant correlation between intra-list intrusion in the repeated-testing condition and L2 proficiency, $r = -0.22$, $p = 0.09$, suggesting that the more proficient a particpant's L2 was, the fewer intra-list intrusion errors they made during the acquisition phase because they were more likely to recollect the correct L2 translation equivalents to the "L3" cues. We split the participants into two groups: low vs. high L1/L2 proficiency (by median) and tested whether the effect of L1/L2 proficiency on various types of error was significant, with their L2/L1 proficiency factor scores being treated as covariates. We found only significant main effects of L2 proficiency on intra-list intrusion errors of repeated-testing [low: 0.17 vs. high: 0.11, $F(1, 57) = 10.33$, $MSE = 0.01$, $\eta_p^2 = 0.15$] and repeated-study conditions [low: 0.25 vs. high: 0.17, $F(1, 57) = 5.33$,

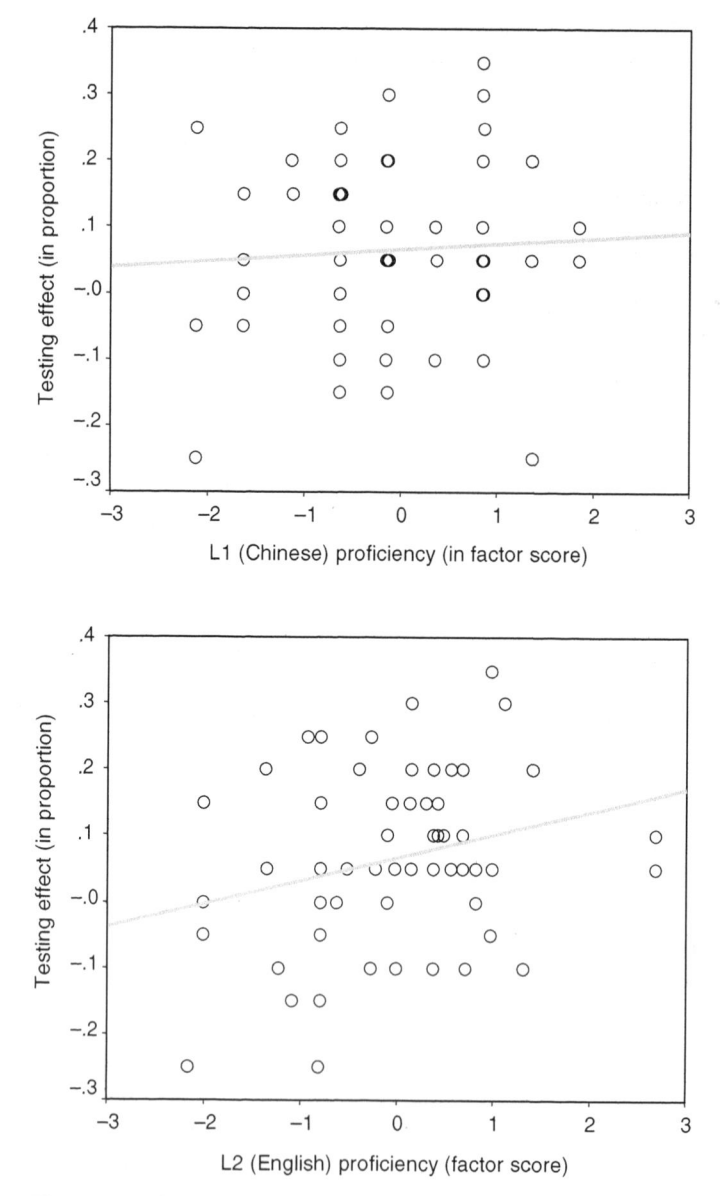

Figure 10.3 Scatterplot of testing effect and L1/L2 proficiency

$MSE = 0.02$, $\eta_p^2 = 0.09$] and of L1 proficiency on extra-list intrusion errors of repeated study [low: 0.04 vs. high: 0.03, $F(1, 57) = 4.97$, $MSE = 0.001$, $\eta_p^2 = 0.08$]. The last result was not interpretable. Finally, none of the correlations between the three error types in the final cued-recall test and L1/L2 proficiency was significant, all $|r|s < 0.19$, $ps > 0.14$, except that there was a marginally significant *positive* correlation between intra-list intrusion in the repeated-study condition and L1 proficiency, $r = +0.24$, $p = 0.07$, which was not easy to explain. Similar to the error data in the acquisition phase, we performed ANOVAs to test the effect of L1/L2 proficiency, with the participants being categorized into low vs. high L1/L2 proficency, and L2/L1 proficiency factor scores being treated as covariates. None of the effects of L1/L2 proficiency approached statistical significance, all $Fs < 1.95$, $ps > 0.17$, $\eta_p^2s < 0.03$.

Discussion

By manipulating repeated-study and repeated-testing conditions within participants in an "L3"–L2 paired-associate (i.e., Swahili–English word pairs) learning paradigm with the final recall test being given after a one-week retention interval, we found the typical testing effect (e.g., Karpicke & Roediger, 2008). Chinese–English bilingual participants showed better delayed recall performance for pairs acquired via the repeated-testing condition than those acquired via repeated study. Despite the differences in stimuli and design, the current findings replicated those reported in previous testing-effect studies in vocabulary learning (e.g., Barcroft, 2007; McNamara & Healy, 1995). By operationally defining participants' L1/L2 proficiency via their grades in standardized public examinations as well as Shipley's (1940) vocabulary subscales, we showed that participants' L2, but not L1, proficiency could modulate their testing effect on "L3"–L2 paired-associate acquisition: those who were more proficient in L2 benefited more by repeated testing (relative to repeated study) than those who were less proficient in L2. These results were confirmed in correlational analyses and in ANOVAs, with the participants being divided into two groups based on their L1/L2 proficiency. Finally, relative to repeated study, participants made fewer intra-list intrusion errors for pairs acquired via repeated testing, whether in the acquisition phase or in the final recall test given after a one-week retention interval. Those who were more proficient in L2 tended to make fewer intrusion errors, regardless of repeated-study or repeated-testing condition, than those who were not as proficient in L2, although this occurred only in the acquisition phase and not in the final cued-recall test. While one could argue that some of the intra-list intrusion errors could be attributed to participants' guessing, it is not clear why they were more likely to guess for the pairs acquired via repeated-study procedures than those acquired via repeated-testing procedures in the acquisition phase and why participants with lower L2 proficiency were more likely to use this guessing strategy than those with higher L2 proficiency. Hence, the findings of intra-list intrusion errors could not be explained by participants' use of guessing strategies, per se.

Before elaborating upon the theoretical and educational implications of the current findings, it is important to clarify the relationship between these findings and the literature regarding the acquisition of the third-language lexicon. Previous studies showed that relative to bilinguals' L1, their L2 is more likely to affect the process of L3 acquisition (Cenoz & Valencia, 1994; Hammarberg, 2001), even after taking into account the influences of other cognitive (e.g., general intelligence), psychosocial (attitudes and motivation), socioeconomic, and educational variables (e.g., number of years of studying English). In addition, L2 influence is favored if L3 is typologically close to L2 and even more so if L1 is more distant (e.g., Hammarberg, 2001). Given that Swahili (L3) is typologically closer to English (L2) than to Chinese (L1) for our Chinese–English bilinguals, this might account for the current findings that relative to L1, L2 proficiency plays a larger role in modulating the acquisition of L3 (i.e., Swahili)–L2 word pairs, thereby being consistent with the positive effect of bilingualism on L3 vocabulary acquisition reported in previous studies. This explanation seems to regard Swahili as the third language of our bilingual participants in the current study. However, it is noteworthy that the current study may not be comparable with the L3 acquisition studies because our participants did not know the Swahili language at all prior to their participation in the experiment. That is, Swahili words were just like nonwords to these participants, and this may be different from other studies where participants, who were labeled as late multilinguals, had already learned or even regularly used the L3 for some time (e.g., Bloch et al., 2009). To generalize the current findings to the area of third language acquisition, it is important to apply the repeated-study/repeated-testing paradigm to bilinguals who have at least a certain amount of knowledge in L3, for example, Chinese–English bilinguals who are currently taking intermediate or even an advanced Spanish course.

Theoretical implications of current findings on Kroll and Stewart's (1994) Revised Hierarchical Model of bilingual memory

In vocabulary learning, most of the bilingual memory models (e.g., Kroll & Stewart's, 1994, RHM) focus on (a) whether L2 learners encode the lexical forms of new L2 words, and (b) whether the new L2 word forms become connected to the concepts that they represent over time – the development of concept mediation (the L2 conceptual link). By pairing the "L3" Swahili words with their corresponding L2 English translation equivalents, the current study examined the extent to which L1/L2 proficiency, as reflected by L1/L2 conceptual links and the strength of the L1–L2 bidirectional link, could modulate the establishment of an "L3" → L2 link (see Figure 10.1) via repeated-study vs. repeated-testing procedures. Given the instructions of the "L3"–L2 cued-recall test, in the current study, participants should have been paying more attention to the build-up of the "L3" → L2 link in the acquisition phase. Relative to mere re-reading the pairs during repeated study, the demand that participants need to recall the L2 words in response to the corresponding "L3" word cues during repeated testing could further strengthen their "L3" → L2 link and thus produce the testing effect. Moreover, these findings were also consistent with previous survey studies that examine the relationship between strategy use and vocabulary learning performance (e.g., Gu & Johnson, 1996; Nation, 2008). For example, Gu and Johnson reported that the use of visual repetition of new words in vocabulary learning was the strongest negative predictor of vocabulary size.

If vocabulary learning merely involved the acquisition of the lexical link between the new, unfamiliar lexicon and the old, more familiar lexicon without necessarily involving the conceptual store, one would expect that learners' overall performance and the benefit of the testing effect, if any, would not depend on their L1 or L2 proficiency. On the other hand, if L1–L2 conceptual links were involved in the process of vocabulary learning (i.e., participants access the conceptual store when they establish the "L3" → L2 link), one would predict that learners' overall performance and the benefit of a testing effect would be modulated by their L1 or L2 proficiency. The current results showed that (a) overall final-recall performance was higher for those with high L2 proficiency than for those with low L2 proficiency, and (b) the testing effect was stronger for participants with high L2 proficiency than for those with low L2 proficiency. While the overall performance and testing effect were sensitive to participants' L2 proficiency, neither of these measures was affected by participants' L1 proficiency. Because our bilinguals were equally fluent in both L1 and L2, as supported by a strong correlation between L1 and L2 proficiency factor scores ($r = +0.66$), they were less likely to rely on the L2–L1 link as well as the L1 conceptual link to access the conceptual store. Hence, L1 proficiency did not modulate the testing effect. On the other hand, this finding could also be attributed to the demand of the Swahili-cued recall task that emphasizes the build-up of an "L3"–L2 link rather than the retreival of an L2–L1 link (not to mention the build-up of an "L3"–L1 link). Furthermore, the null effect of L1 proficiency should be interpreted with caution because the range was narrower for L1 proficiency factor scores (from −2.11 to 1.85) than for L2 proficiency factor scores (from −2.16 to 2.68), even though their means and standard deviations, in principle, were identical (i.e., $M = 0$ and $SD = 1$). Nevertheless, the current data clearly showed the involvement of a conceptual store (i.e., semantic information) when Chinese–English bilinguals learn the association between vocabulary of an entirely unfamiliar language (Swahili) and their L2 (English).

Before considering the educational implications of the current findings, it is important to highlight the intrusion-error findings that are relevant to previous testing-effect studies. Very few testing-effect studies using the paired-associate paradigm highlighted intrusion error data (but see Butler & Roediger, 2008; Fazio *et al.*, 2010; Marsh, Agarwal, & Roediger, 2009, for a discussion of intrusion errors in repeated testing procedures using multiple-choice question tests). Indeed, the interpretation of intrusion error data between repeated study and repeated testing conditions, which were manipulated between participants, could be clouded by a confound of sampling differences. Also, it is possible that the intrusion error rate was too low in previous studies, so the analyses would have been complicated by a floor effect. The current study demonstrated that relative to repeated study, repeated testing procedures could lower intralist intrusion errors during the acquisition phase, indicating the beneficial effect of repeated testing on strengthening the "L3" → L2 link and in turn minimizing the opportunities that participants might associate English translation equivalents with incorrect Swahili word cues.

Educational implications of the current findings on instructional method

As typically demonstrated in recent testing-effect studies (e.g., Karpicke & Roediger, 2007, 2008, see e.g., Roediger & Karpicke, 2006, for a review), the educational implication of the current findings is that language learners should be encouraged to recall (either in spoken or written form) newly learned words in a less familiar language in response to their translation equivalents in a more familiar language, rather than re-reading the word pairs over and over again. This has indeed been implemented in some computer-assisted language learning devices (e.g., Chen & Chung, 2008; Kwon *et al.*, 2010).

Despite the benefit of the repeated-testing procedure over the repeated-study procedure, repeated testing should not be regarded as the *only* way to enhance vocabulary-learning performance (see e.g., Nation, 2008, for other options). In fact, the effectiveness of repeated testing may be at odds with some recent findings. Barcroft (2009) explored how learner-selected strategies could affect their intentional picture-word L2 vocabulary learning and evaluated why some strategies might or might not be effective. He (see also Ahmed, 1989) found a positive correlation between the number of strategies participants reported having used and their vocabulary-learning performance, suggesting that students should be encouraged to use a variety of vocabulary-learning strategies, because the more varied their strategies are, the higher their scores are in vocabulary learning. Barcroft also found that the self-selected, most frequently used strategies during intentional L2 picture-word vocabulary learning were L2–picture association, L2–L1 association, L2–L1 translation, and repetition. The two association strategies, which are akin to strategies like imagery and the keyword technique (cf. Atkinson & Raugh, 1975), could yield higher recall performance than L2–L1 translation (i.e., retrieving L1 words in response to L2 cues) and repetition (i.e., simple word rehearsal), suggesting that repeated testing may not be the *best* strategy in vocabulary learning. Furthermore, Barcroft reported that L2–L1 translation was as efficient as repetition in terms of frequency of use (see also Schmitt, 1997) and in its influence on recall performance, which is quite surprising given the substantial evidence for the benefit of repeated testing on enhancing long-term retention. However, it is noteworthy that this study did not directly manipulate participants' use of strategies. In addition, in Barcroft's list of learning strategies, a much less frequently used strategy called *self-generate* target words may be more similar to the repeated-testing procedure than L2–L1 translation. This strategy was coded when participants reported attempting to produce a target word on their own. Indeed, recall performance was higher for those who used this self-generation method (14.5) than the L2–L1 translation method (11.6) in the cued-recall test with L2 cue words. Finally, Barcroft gave his participants only immediate cued-recall tests. As demonstrated in some testing-effect studies (e.g., Karpicke & Roediger, 2007, but see Royer, 1973), the benefit of repeated testing may be weak, if not non-existent, when only immediate memory tests are given. It is important that the acquired vocabulary should be maintained for a longer period without being forgotten, as tested in the current study. Indeed, Barcroft also mentioned that "whereas present findings speak to improved performance on vocabulary learning tested immediately after learning, future studies might examine the extent to which this relationship holds over extended periods of time" (2009, p. 86), highlighting the importance of using a delayed cued-recall test to compare the repeated-study and repeated-testing procedures.

Conclusions, limitations of the current study, and future directions

The current study clearly demonstrated (a) the positive effect of repeated testing, relative to repeated study, on bilinguals' vocabulary learning even when the new vocabulary items are from an entirely unfamiliar language, and (b) the importance of taking the relatively unfamiliar language (i.e., L2 in the current study) into account when introducing a novel, third language to bilingual learners.

However, it is important to point out some limitations in the current research, which may lead to a number of directions for future research.

1. Because the current study was conducted in one of the top universities in Hong Kong, most of the participants were advanced L2 users and this may restrict the range of L2 proficiency and in turn mask some effects that would have been revealed had participants with a wider range of L2 proficiency been recruited. As mentioned above, the difference in the range of L1 and L2 proficiencies might also have complicated the interpretation of the role of L1/L2 conceptual links in modulating the testing effect.

2. While the above discussion focused on the larger extent to which repeated testing could strengthen the "L3"–L2 link, relative to repeated study, it is not clear whether it was the strengthening of the "L3"– L2 link or the strengthening of "L3" conceptual links that might have contributed to the current findings. Future research should tease apart these two possibilities by using the pair of experiments described in Potter et al. (1984); that is, "L3"-L2 word translation and picture naming in "L3." It would be interesting to examine whether the L1/L2 conceptual links (i.e., L1/L2

proficiency) could differentially influence "L3"–L2 word translation and picture naming in "L3" tasks, as this should shed further light on the role of the conceptual store in learning vocabulary items in a new language.

3. The current study only involved one outcome of vocabulary learning, that is, "L3"–L2 translation in a cued-recall task. It is important to examine further whether the vocabulary learned via repeated testing can be successfully used in different contexts, such as text comprehension and language production. This notion is pertinent to the recent findings that the knowledge acquired via repeated testing can be transferred to other related domains (see Butler, 2010; Rohrer, Taylor, & Sholar, 2010). Elgort and Nation (2010) suggested that intentional vocabulary learning like paired-associate training has to be supplemented by other types of learning (e.g., exposing new vocabulary in various meaningful contexts), in order to create richer knowledge of the new L2 words and encourage learners to integrate their meanings with the existing conceptual store. Some researchers even pointed out that the quality of vocabulary knowledge gained through decontextualized paired-associate learning may not be directly correlated with the proficiency with which learners are able to *use* them in a real-world context (see e.g., Krashen, 1989, for a discussion). Future studies should test whether vocabulary knowledge can be transferred to other domains of language learning (e.g., text comprehension).

4. It is important to note that L1/L2 proficiency is not the only individual difference marker in modulating the effectiveness of repeated testing, relative to repeated study. In the literature on L2 vocabulary learning (e.g., Kroll & Linck, 2007; Tokowicz, Michael, & Kroll, 2004), individual differences in attentional and cognitive resources, which were reported to be more heavily tapped during L2 processing than during L1 processing, also influence the efficiency of vocabulary learning. Some studies have demonstrated a positive relationship between L2 proficiency and memory span (e.g., Atkins & Baddeley, 1998; Michael & Gollan, 2005). Learners' working memory capacity could modulate the extent to which they can suppress L1 in L2 processing, especially during the early stage of L2 acquisition (e.g., Kroll *et al.*, 2002). Hence, it is important to take more factors into account in future testing-effect studies in foreign vocabulary acquisition.

5. Although we focused on Kroll and Stewart's (1994) RHM in the current study, other more recent bilingual memory models, especially the computational ones like the Bilingual Interactive

Activation + (Dijkstra & van Heuven, 2002, see also Schoonbaert et al., 2009), should be tested to see if they can accommodate the current findings. Although the premises of the RHM have been criticized on various grounds (e.g., Altarriba & Mathis, 1997; Brysbaert & Duyck, 2010; see also Kroll et al., 2010, for rebuttals), most of the debates are related to lexical processing rather than memory processing. Hence, more research should be done to uncover the possibility of using this apparently "outdated" bilingual *memory* model to explain the data directly relevant to bilingual *memory* performance.

REFERENCES

Agarwal, P. K., Karpicke, J. D., Kang, S. H. K., Roediger, H. L., & McDermott, K. B. (2008). Examining the testing effect with open- and closed-book tests. *Applied Cognitive Psychology*, 22, 861–876.

Ahmed, M. O. (1989). Vocabulary learning strategies. In P. Meara (ed.), *Beyond words* (pp. 3–14). London: Centre for Information on Language Teaching and Learning.

Altarriba, J., & Basnight-Brown, D. M. (2007). Methodological considerations in performing semantic- and translation-priming experiments across languages. *Behavior Research Methods*, 39, 1–18.

Altarriba, J., & Knickerbocker, H. (2011). Acquiring second language vocabulary through the use of images and words. In P. Trofimovich & K. McDonough (eds.), *Insights from psycholinguistics: applying priming research to L2 learning and teaching* (pp. 21–48). Amsterdam: John Benjamins.

Altarriba, J., & Mathis, K. M. (1997). Conceptual and lexical development in second language acquisition. *Journal of Memory and Language*, 36, 550–568.

Atkins, P. W. B., & Baddeley, A. D. (1998). Working memory and distributed vocabulary learning. *Applied Psycholinguistics*, 19, 537–552.

Atkinson, R. C., & Raugh, M. R. (1975). An application of the mnemonic keyword method to the acquisition of a Russian vocabulary. *Journal of Experimental Psychology: Human Learning and Memory*, 104, 126–133.

Baddeley, A. D. (1990). *Human memory: theory and practice*. London: Lawrence Erlbaum.

Bahrick, H. P., Bahrick, L. E., Bahrick, A. S., & Bahrick, P. E. (1993). Maintenance of foreign language vocabulary and the spacing effect. *Psychological Science*, 4, 316–321.

Balota, D.A., Yap, M.J., Cortese, M.J., Hutchison, K.A., Kessler, B., Loftis, B., Neely, J.H., Nelson, D.L., Simpson, G.B., & Treiman, R. (2007). The English Lexicon Project. *Behavior Research Methods*, 39, 445–459.

Barcroft, J. (2007). Effects of opportunities for word retrieval during second language vocabulary learning. *Language Learning*, 57, 35–56.

(2009). Effects of synonym generation on incidental and intentional L2 vocabulary learning during reading. *TESOL Quarterly*, 43, 79–103.

Bloch, C., Kaiser, A., Kuenzli, E., Zappatore, D., Haller, S., Franceschini, R., et al. (2009). The age of second language acquisition determines the variability in activation elicited by narration in three languages in Broca's and Wernicke's area. *Neuropsychologia*, 47, 625–633.

Brisbois, J. I. (1995). Connections between first- and second-language reading. *Journal of Reading Behavior*, 27, 565–584.

Brysbaert, M., & Duyck, W. (2010). Is it time to leave behind the Revised Hierarchical Model of bilingual language processing after fifteen years of service? *Bilingualism: Language and Cognition*, 13, 359–371.

Butler, A. C. (2010). Repeated testing produces superior transfer of learning relative to repeated studying. *Journal of Experimental Psychology: Learning, Memory, and Cognition*, 36, 1118–1133.

Butler, A. C., & Roediger, H. L. (2008). Feedback enhances the positive effects and reduces the negative effects of multiple-choice testing. *Memory & Cognition*, 36, 604–616.

Carpenter, S. K., Pashler, H., & Vul, E. (2006). What types of learning are enhanced by a cued recall test? *Psychonomic Bulletin & Review*, 13, 826–830.

Carrier, M., & Pashler, H. (1992). The influence of retrieval on retention. *Memory & Cognition*, 20, 633–642.

Cenoz, J., & Valencia, J. F. (1994). Additive trilingualism: evidence from the Basque Country. *Applied Psycholinguistics*, 15, 195–207.

Chen, C. M., & Chung, C. J. (2008). Personalized mobile English vocabulary learning system based on item response theory and learning memory cycle. *Computers & Education*, 51, 624–645.

Chen, H. C., & Ng, M. L. (1989). Semantic facilitation and translation priming effects in Chinese–English bilinguals. *Memory & Cognition*, 17, 454–462.

Coady, J. (1997). L2 vocabulary acquisition through extensive reading. In J. Coady & T. Huckin (eds.), *Second language vocabulary acquisition* (pp. 225–237). Cambridge University Press.

Cobb, T., & Horst, M. (2004). Is there room for an AWL in French? In P. Bogaards & B. Laufer (eds.), *Vocabulary in a second language* (pp. 15–38). Amsterdam: John Benjamins.

Daller, H., Milton, J., & Treffers-Daller, J. (eds.) (2007). *Testing and modeling lexical knowledge*. Cambridge University Press.

de Groot, A. M. B., & Keijzer, R. (2000). What is hard to learn is easy to forget: the roles of word concreteness, cognate status, and word frequency in foreign-language vocabulary learning and forgetting. *Language Learning*, 50, 1–56.

DeKeyser, R. (1998). Beyond focus on form: cognitive perspectives on learning and practicing second language grammar. In C. Doughty & J. Williams (eds.), *Focus on form in classroom second language acquisition* (pp. 42–63). New York: Cambridge University Press.

Delaney, P. F., Verkoeijen, P. P., & Spirgel, A. (2010). Spacing and testing effects: a deeply critical, lengthy, and at times discursive review of the literature. *Psychology of Learning and Motivation*, 53, 64–111.

Dijkstra, T., & van Heuven, W. J. B. (2002). The architecture of the bilingual word recognition system: from identification to decision. *Bilingualism: Language and Cognition*, 5, 175–197.

Dupuy, B., & Krashen, S. (1993). Incidental vocabulary acquisition in French as a foreign language. *Applied Language Learning*, 4, 55–63.

Elgort, I. (2011). Deliberate learning and vocabulary acquisition in a second language. *Language Learning*, 61, 367–413.

Elgort, I., & Nation, I. S. P. (2010). Vocabulary learning in a second language: familiar answers to new questions. In P. Seedhouse, S. Walsh, & C. Jenks (eds.), *Conceptualising 'learning' in applied linguistics* (pp. 89–105). Houndmills: Macmillan.

Ellis, N. C. (2008). Usage-based and form-focused language acquisition. In P. Robinson & N. C. Ellis (eds.), *Handbook of cognitive linguistics and second language acquisition* (pp. 372–405). London: Routledge.

Fan, M. Y. (2003). Frequency of use, perceived usefulness, and actual usefulness of second language vocabulary strategies: a study of Hong Kong learners. *Modern Language Journal*, 87, 222–241.

Fazio, L. K., Agarwal, P. K., Marsh, E. M., & Roediger, H. L. (2010). Memorial consequences of multiple-choice testing on immediate and delayed tests. *Memory & Cognition*, 38, 407–418.

Francis, W. S. (1999). Cognitive integration of language and memory in bilinguals: semantic representation. *Psychological Bulletin*, 125, 193–222.

Gates, A. (1917). Recitation as a factor in memorizing. *Archives of Psychology*, 40, 1–104.

Glover, J. A. (1989). The "testing" phenomenon: not gone, but nearly forgotten. *Journal of Educational Psychology*, 81, 392–399.

Gu, Y., & Johnson, R. K. (1996). Vocabulary learning strategies and language learning outcomes. *Language Learning*, 46, 643–679.

Hammarberg, B. (2001). Roles of L1 and L2 in L3 production and acquisition. In J. Cenoz, B. Hufeisen, & U. Jessner (eds.), *Cross-linguistic influence in third language acquisition: psycholinguistic perspectives* (pp. 21–41). Clevedon: Multilingual Matters.

Heredia, R. R. (1997). Bilingual memory and hierarchical models: a case for language dominance. *Current Directions in Psychological Science*, 6, 34–39.

Hu, M., & Nation, I. S. P. (2000). Vocabulary density and reading comprehension. *Reading in a Foreign Language*, 13, 403–430.

Hulstijn, J. H. (2001). Intentional and incidental second language vocabulary learning: a reappraisal of elaboration, rehearsal and automaticity. In P. Robinson (ed.), *Cognition and second language instruction* (pp. 258–286). Cambridge University Press.

Jiang, N. (2004). Semantic transfer and its implications for vocabulary teaching in a second language. *Modern Language Journal*, 88, 416–432.

Kang, S. H. K., McDermott, K. B., & Roediger, H. L. (2007). Test format and corrective feedback modify the effect of testing on long-term retention. *European Journal of Cognitive Psychology*, 19, 528–558.

Karpicke, J. D., & Roediger, H. L. (2007). Repeated retrieval during learning is the key to long-term retention. *Journal of Memory and Language*, 57, 151–162.

(2008). The critical importance of retrieval for learning. *Science*, 319, 966–968.

Karpicke, J. D., Butler, A. C., & Roediger, H. L. (2009). Metacognitive strategies in student learning: do students practice retrieval when they study on their own? *Memory*, 17, 471–479.

Kornell, N., & Bjork, R. A. (2007). The promise and perils of self regulated study. *Psychonomic Bulletin & Review*, 14, 219–224.

Krashen, S. (1985). *The input hypothesis: issues and implications.* Torrance, CA: Laredo.

(1989). We acquire vocabulary and spelling by reading: additional evidence for the Input Hypothesis. *Modern Language Journal*, 73, 440–464.

Kroll, J. F., & Linck, J. A. (2007). Representation and skill in second language learners and proficient bilinguals. In I. Kecskes & L. Albertazzi (eds.), *Cognitive aspects of bilingualism* (pp. 237–269). New York: Springer.

Kroll, J. F., & Stewart, E. (1994). Category interference in translation and picture naming: evidence for asymmetric connections between bilingual memory representations. *Journal of Memory and Language*, 33, 149–174.

Kroll, J. F., Michael, E. B., Tokowicz, N., & Dufour, R. (2002). The development of lexical fluency in a second language. *Second Language Research*, 18, 137–171.

Kroll, J. F., Sumutka, B. M., & Schwartz, A. I. (2005). A cognitive view of the bilingual lexicon: reading and speaking words in two languages. *International Journal of Bilingualism*, 9, 27–48.

Kroll, J. F., van Hell, J. G., Tokowicz, N., & Green, D. W. (2010). The Revised Hierarchical Model: a critical review and assessment. *Bilingualism: Language and Cognition*, 13, 373–381.

Kwon, D.-Y., Lim, H.-K., Lee, W.-C., Kim, H.-C., Jung, S.-Y., Suh, T., et al. (2010). A personalized English vocabulary learning system based on cognitive abilities related to foreign language proficiency. *Transactions on Internet and Information Systems*, 4, 595–617.

Larsen, D. P., Butler, A. C., & Roediger, H. L. (2009). Repeated testing improves long-term retention relative to repeated study: a randomised controlled trial. *Medical Education*, 43, 1174–1181.

Laufer, B. (2005). Focus on form in second language vocabulary learning. In S. Foster-Cohen, M. P. Garcia Mayo, & J. Cenoz (eds.), *EUROSLA Yearbook 5* (pp. 223–250). Amsterdam: John Benjamins.

Lawson, M. J., & Hogben, D. (1996). The vocabulary-learning strategies of foreign-language students. *Language Learning*, 46, 101–135.

Marsh, E. J., Agarwal, P. K., & Roediger, H. L. (2009). Memorial consequences of answering SAT II questions. *Journal of Experimental Psychology: Applied*, 15, 1–11.

Marton, W. (1977). Foreign language vocabulary learning as problem number one of language teaching at the advanced level. *The Interlanguage Studies Bulletin*, 2, 33–57.

McDaniel, M. A., & Fisher, R. P. (1991). Tests and test feedback as learning sources. *Contemporary Educational Psychology*, 16, 192–201.

McDaniel, M. A., Roediger, H. L., & McDermott, K. B. (2007). Generalizing test-enhanced learning from the laboratory to the classroom. *Psychonomic Bulletin & Review*, 14, 200–206.

McNamara, D. S., & Healy, A. F. (1995). A generation advantage for multiplication skill training and nonword vocabulary acquisition. In A. F. Healy & L. E. Bourne, Jr. (eds.), *Learning and memory of knowledge and skills: durability and specificity* (pp. 132–169). Thousand Oaks, CA: Sage.

Melka, F. (1997). Receptive vs. productive aspects of vocabulary. In N. Schmitt & M. McCarthy (eds.), *Vocabulary: description, acquisition and pedagogy* (pp. 84–102). Cambridge University Press.

Michael, E., & Gollan, T. H. (2005). Being and becoming bilingual: individual differences and consequences for language production. In J. F. Kroll & A. M. B. de Groot (eds.), *Handbook of bilingualism: psycholinguistic approaches* (pp. 389–407). New York: Oxford University Press.

Nagy, W., Herman, P., & Anderson, R. (1985). Learning words from context. *Reading Research Quarterly*, 20, 233–253.

Nation, I. S. P. (2001). *Learning vocabulary in another language.* Cambridge University Press.

(2006). How large a vocabulary is needed for reading and listening? *Canadian Modern Language Review*, 63, 59–82.

(2007). The four stands. *Innovation in Language Learning and Teaching*, 1, 1–12.

(2008). *Teaching vocabulary: strategies and techniques.* Boston: Heinle.

Nelson, T. O., & Dunlosky, J. (1994). Norms of paired-associate recall during multitrial learning of Swahili–English translation equivalents. *Memory*, 2, 325–335.

O'Malley, J. M., Chamot, A. U., Stewner-Manzanares, G., Kupper, L., & Russo, R. P. (1985). Learning strategies used by beginning and intermediate ESL students. *Language Learning*, 35, 21–46.

Paribakht, T. S., & Wesche, M. (1999). 'Incidental' and instructed L2 vocabulary acquisition through reading: an introspective study. *Studies in Second Language Acquisition*, 21, 195–224.

Potter, M. C., So, K. F., von Eckardt, B., & Feldman, L. B. (1984). Lexical and conceptual representation in beginning and proficient bilinguals. *Journal of Verbal Learning and Verbal Behavior*, 23, 23–38.

Prince, P. (1996). Second language vocabulary learning: the role of context versus translations as a function of proficiency. *Modern Language Journal*, 80, 478–493.

Roediger, H. L., & Guynn, M. J. (1996). Retrieval processes. In E. L. Bjork & R. A. Bjork (eds.), *Memory: handbook of perception and cognition* (pp. 197–236). San Diego: Academic Press.

Roediger, H. L., & Karpicke, J. D. (2006). The power of testing memory: basic research and implications for educational practice. *Perspectives on Psychological Science*, 1, 181–210.

Rohrer, D., & Pashler, H. (2010). Recent research on human learning challenges conventional instructional strategies. *Educational Researcher*, 39, 406–412.

Rohrer, D., Taylor, K., & Sholar, B. (2010). Tests enhance the transfer of learning. *Journal of Experimental Psychology: Learning, Memory, and Cognition*, 36, 233–239

Royer, J. M. (1973). Memory effects for test-like events during acquisition of foreign language vocabulary. *Psychological Reports*, 32, 195–198.

Scarborough, D. L., Gerard, L., & Cortese, C. (1984). Independence of lexical access in bilingual word recognition. *Journal of Verbal Learning & Verbal Behavior*, 23, 84–99.

Schmitt, N. (1997). Vocabulary learning strategies. In N. Schmitt & M. McCarthy (eds.), *Vocabulary: description, acquisition and pedagogy* (pp. 199–228). Cambridge University Press.

Schneider, W., Eschman, A., & Zuccolotto, A. (2001). *E-Prime user's guide*. Philadelphia: Psychology Software Tools, Inc.

Schoonbaert, S., Duyck, W., Brysbaert, M., & Hartsuiker, R. J. (2009). Semantic and translation priming from a first language to a second and back: making sense of the findings. *Memory & Cognition*, 37, 569–586.

Shipley, W. C. (1940). A self-administering scale for measuring intellectual impairment and deterioration. *Journal of Psychology*, 9, 371–377.

Sumowski, J. F., Chiaravalloti, N., & DeLuca, J. (2010). Retrieval practice improves memory in multiple sclerosis: clinical application of the testing effect. *Neuropsychology*, 24, 267–272.

Swain, M. (2005). The output hypothesis: theory and research. In E. Hinkel (ed.), *Handbook of research in second language teaching and learning* (pp. 471–484). New Jersey: Lawrence Erlbaum.

Tokowicz, N., Michael, E., & Kroll, J. F. (2004). The roles of study abroad experience and working memory capacity in the types of errors made during translation. *Bilingualism: Language and Cognition*, 7, 255–272.

Tse, C.-S., Balota, D. A., & Roediger, H. L. (2010). The benefits and costs of repeated testing on the learning of face-name pairs in healthy older adults. *Psychology and Aging*, 25(4), 833–845.

Tseng, W., & Schmitt, N. (2008). Toward a model of motivated vocabulary learning: a structural equation modeling approach. *Language Learning*, 58, 357–400.

Tulving, E. (1967). The effects of presentation and recall of material in free-recall learning. *Journal of Verbal Learning and Verbal Behavior*, 6, 175–184.

Van Overschelde, J. P., Rawson, K. A., & Dunlosky, J. (2004). Category norms: an updated and expanded version of the Battig and Montague (1969) norms. *Journal of Memory and Language*, 50, 289–335.

Webb, S. (2008). Receptive and productive vocabulary sizes of L2 learners. *Studies in Second Language Acquisition*, 30, 79–95.

Weinstein, Y., McDermott, K. B., & Roediger, H. L. (2010). A comparison of study strategies for passages: rereading, answering questions, and generating questions. *Journal of Experimental Psychology*, 16, 308–316.

Wheeler, M. A., & Roediger, H. L. (1992). Disparate effects of repeated testing: reconciling Ballard's (1913) and Bartlett's (1932) results. *Psychological Science*, 3, 240–245.

Yap, M. J., Balota, D. A., Tse, C.-S., & Besner, D. (2008). On the additive effects of stimulus quality and word frequency in lexical decision: evidence for opposing interactive influences revealed by RT distributional analysis.

Journal of Experimental Psychology: Learning, Memory, and Cognition, 34, 495–513.

Yap, M. J., Tse, C.-S., & Balota, D. A. (2009). Individual differences in the joint effects of semantic priming and word frequency revealed by RT distributional analyses: the role of lexical integrity. *Journal of Memory and Language*, 61, 303–325.

Zachary, R. A. (1992). *Shipley Institute of Living Scale-Revised*. California: Western Psychological Services.

Zachary, R. A., Paulson, M. J., & Gorsuch, R. L. (1985). Estimating WAIS IQ from the Shipley Institute of Living Scale using continuously adjusted age norms. *Journal of Clinical Psychology*, 41, 820–831.

11 The lexicon in second language attrition: what happens when the cat's got your tongue?

Kathleen Bardovi-Harlig and David Stringer

Abstract

In this chapter, we expand the conceptual framework of research on second language attrition by invoking an expansive notion of the lexicon, which, in addition to vocabulary, contains items below the word level (i.e., affixes) and above the word level (i.e., phrasal structure stored in long-term memory). Although most syntactic structures are generated and then discarded, a vast number of phrases remain fixed in memory, such that procedural knowledge of grammar may be accessed through complex lexical items. In this light, all empirical research on second language attrition to date that offers evidence for ordering effects can be shown to involve issues of access to the mental lexicon. We examine how computational and psycholinguistic models of lexical activation and inhibition might be used to explain both catastrophic loss in cases of disuse, and apparently miraculous recovery in situations of re-immersion, as lexical retrieval breathes life into syntax.

In our earlier review of research on second language (L2) attrition, we developed a model that positions L2 attrition and retention as part of the life cycle of acquisition, identifying the crucial variables that interact with the presence and absence of continued L2 input, and plotting specific trajectories for different populations (Bardovi-Harlig & Stringer, 2010). In the current chapter, we expand the conceptual framework for research on L2 attrition by proposing a pivotal role for the lexicon in empirically established sequences of loss and retention, with a particular focus on multi-word lexical entries. In the following section, we briefly review the most prevalent hypothesis of L2 attrition, the Regression Hypothesis, and argue that the empirical evidence used for its support inevitably involves elements encompassed by our inclusive definition of the lexicon, which contains bound morphology, free morphemes (including content and function words), constructions, idioms, and conventional expressions. We note that such ordering effects hold even if these patterns of lexical attrition may be better explained by other hypotheses as yet untested in L2 attrition research, such the Activation Threshold Hypothesis (Paradis, 1993, 2004, 2007). We then consider more general L2 attrition findings that posit a difference in resilience between the lexicon and syntax, and suggest that a greater understanding of multi-word lexical entries might shed light on this distinction. In the sections that follow, we consider two avenues of thought, which together may help to explain two of the most mysterious attrition phenomena: dramatic loss in situations of disuse and dramatic retrieval in situations of re-immersion. The first line of reasoning puts together current work on phrasal syntax in the lexicon with recent investigations of the L2 acquisition of conventional expressions, in order to suggest that fragments of productive syntax are found in lexical memory. The second is that the lexicon is a network and should be explored as such. This perspective has long characterized computational and psycholinguistic models of lexical activation and inhibition, but has not significantly informed either formal theories of lexical semantics or linguistic accounts of L2 attrition. Finally, we consider attested examples of global loss and global reactivation, and consider how such phenomena might be demystified with interdisciplinary insight from linguistics, psychology and second language research.

Lexical aspects of second language attrition studies

On standard approaches to the lexicon in theoretical linguistics, elements stored in lexical memory include not only what are intuitively perceived as "words," but also bound morphology, all free morphemes (including content and function words), and multi-word units, such as idioms and expressions. In this light, the following subsection reveals a pattern visible in L2 attrition studies that have claimed empirical support for the Regression Hypothesis, in that the evidence is largely lexical in nature. It is then shown that previous findings generally indicate lexical loss without strong evidence for syntactic impairment. However, difficulties in interpreting the results of many studies suggest that a clearer understanding of the lexical interface with syntax must inform the design of future studies.

Revisiting the Regression Hypothesis

The Regression Hypothesis, which predicts that the path of attrition is the reverse of the path of acquisition (the first things learned remain longest in memory; the last things learned are the first things forgotten), has historically been the most influential hypothesis in L2 attrition research. We consider five studies that found support for this hypothesis (Cohen, 1975; Hansen, 1999; Hayashi, 1999; Kuhberg, 1992; Olshtain, 1989), all of which arguably involve attrition of the lexicon.

Cohen (1975) investigated attrition after summer vacation in three second-grade children whose development of L2 Spanish in an immersion program had been documented via six elicitation sessions over 20 months from kindergarten to first grade. Using the children's own acquisition record to compare changes in production on an oral elicitation task before and after summer vacation, Cohen found that two of the three children showed attrition of contrasts that had emerged before vacation, such as the distinction between the verbs *ser* and *estar* "to be," gender on masculine and feminine articles, and progressive vs. simple present morphology.

Olshtain (1989) found that irregular formation of plural nouns and past-tense verbs showed regression in the speech of 5–8 year olds, where irregular forms *gave, ate, slept, woke up, feet, men,* and *children* became *gived, sleeped, waked up, feets, mans,* and *childs* over time, although older children (8–14) retained the irregular forms.

The Regression Hypothesis was also tested for L2 Japanese negation investigating both adult missionaries (Hansen, 1999) and adults who as children had attended Japanese schools during the Japanese occupation of Micronesia (Hayashi, 1999). Japanese negation is expressed by bound morphemes that are suffixed to the element being negated. Note that use of fully productive morphology involves lexical access to separately stored representations. Given the established acquisition sequence for Japanese negation (V-Neg → N-Neg> NAdj-Neg → Adj-Neg), the Regression Hypothesis predicts that the order of attrition would be the reverse (Adj-Neg → NAdj-Neg → N-Neg → V-Neg).[1] The production data for both populations supported the Regression Hypothesis; the last acquired combination, negation with adjectives (Adj-Neg) showed the greatest loss.

Hansen and Chen (2001) studied the loss of numerical classifiers by L2 Japanese and Chinese learners, with reference to the universal Numeral Classifier Accessibility Hierarchy (NCAH), which is claimed to determine the order of acquisition of appropriate semantic categories. Their findings indeed showed that attrition was generally in the reverse order of acquisition, with two telling exceptions: the classifiers

---

[1] Abbreviations for syntactic categories are as follows: N (noun), V (verb), Adj (adjective), Adv (adverb), P (preposition/postposition), Neg (negation), Prt (particle); phrasal projections are abbreviated NP, VP, etc.

for *books* and *bicycles*. These were acquired at a rate not predicted by the hierarchy nor by general frequency counts for conversational Japanese (Downing, 1984), but, as noted by Hansen and Chen, were evidently high-frequency classifiers in this population of missionary learners. This suggests an account in terms of frequency analysis, rather than an order determined by the nature of semantic categories.

Kuhberg's (1992) comparison of the longitudinal attrition data of two Turkish L2 speakers of German with the acquisition of L2 German by a first language (L1) Turkish speaker showed "strong reverse" patterns in L2 attrition and L2 acquisition (p. 151) and that "L2 attrition, at least for the linguistic phenomena investigated, is to a large extent the mirror image of L2-acquisition" (p. 152). Using oral production data, Kuhberg compared acquisition and attrition on fourteen points considering patterns within the categories rather than across the categories: nonmodal verbs, modal verbs, modal particles, vocabulary (except verbs), verb morphology, tense, plural, prepositions, personal pronouns, articles, syntax, complex communicative skills, patterns of speech imitation, and basic communication patterns. These data are more difficult to evaluate than the negation data (cf. Hansen, 1999) because of the breadth of the inquiry.

It should be made clear that the pattern of loss found in studies such as these is open to other interpretations than reverse order of acquisition, as important variables often remained uncontrolled. Many early-learned, best-retained elements are high frequency, so studies of regression in L2 attrition ought to distinguish frequency and order of acquisition. Similarly, attention mechanisms may be more focused at the beginning rather than at the end of a school year or a semester abroad. It is quite plausible that frequency and attention are relevant to persistence in lexical memory, such that the ordering effects might be better explained by an account such as the Activation Threshold Hypothesis of Paradis (1993, 2004, 2007), discussed in more detail below. The intention here is not to evaluate the Regression Hypothesis as such, but to illustrate that the most convincing evidence for ordering effects involves elements that are stored in the mental lexicon.

The vulnerability of the lexicon

Beyond studies that have specifically targeted the Regression Hypothesis, other research on L2 attrition has highlighted the susceptibility of the lexicon to attrition. Such evidence comes from three main sources, which we consider in turn: studies of the lexicon as *words* or *vocabulary*, comparisons of lexicon and grammar, and studies of multi-word units.

The first source of evidence involves studies of the lexicon as words. In L2 attrition studies, word knowledge is generally defined as word meaning (often tested by translation or picture identification, and occasionally by knowledge of semantic category or antonyms). This is exemplified by the variety of measures of change which focus on the word level, including the number of different words or *lexical diversity* (Cohen, 1989; Tomiyama, 2008), lexical errors (de Bot & Lintsen, 1989), total words (Cohen, 1986; Russell, 1999), type–token ratios (Tomiyama, 2008), words per unit (Cohen, 1986, 1989; Olshtain, 1986; Tomiyama, 2008), and relative frequency of grammatical classes (i.e., N, V, Adj, Adv, Prep, and articles; Cohen, 1974, 1989; Kuhberg, 1992; Olshtain, 1989). Measures of knowledge in controlled tasks include number of correct lexical decisions when learners distinguish words from nonwords (Grendel, 1993; Verkaik & van der Wijst, 1986, cited in Weltens & Grendel, 1993; Weltens, 1989), translation from L2 to L1 (Bahrick, 1984; de Bot and Stoessel, 2000), and picture identification (Tomiyama, 1999b). De Bot and Stoessel (2000) point out that testing words in isolation prevents learners from using context to determine unknown lexical content. The controlled word-recognition/recall studies measure sound (as orthography)–meaning correspondences, not sound–syntax–meaning correspondences.

Studies of the lexicon have measured the decrease in active vocabulary not only in terms of size (e.g. Russell, 1999) but of access. Based on the fact that children in longitudinal studies can give the meanings of words that had been used in previous production samples, but that have since dropped out in subsequent elicitation sessions, Cohen (1989) and Olshtain (1989) concluded that there is reduction in lexical access during production, but not a loss of comprehension, hence no loss in vocabulary. Similarly, studies that compare recognition to recall often report that recognition scores are higher. Using a lexical decision task (word/nonword) which recorded reaction time and error rate, Verkaik and van der Wijst (1986) found that while error rates remained relatively steady across two learner groups, one that had just finished instruction and one that had two years of disuse, reaction times were considerably slower in the group with two years' disuse. As Weltens and Grendel (1993) concluded, this shows that the speed of the retrieval process is more affected than the success of the process.

Problems with lexical retrieval may also underlie several findings in studies investigating attributes of fluency, including speech rate, hesitations, filled and unfilled pauses, and repetition (Russell, 1999; Tomiyama, 1999b). These same attributes of fluency are linked to difficulties in word retrieval in oral production tasks (Cohen, 1986;

Olshtain, 1986, 1989). Reduction in speed of access can cause a breakdown in fluency which resembles attrition in tasks of free production.

The second source of evidence for the vulnerability of vocabulary comes from comparisons between words and grammar, in which the former is often claimed to show more attrition than the latter (Kuhberg, 1992; Tomiyama, 1999a, 2008). However, at least some of the comparisons consist of lexicon-as-words to grammar-as-morphology, although morphology has traditionally been considered to reside in the lexicon. For example, Tomiyama (1999a) concluded that morphological attrition was less evident than attrition of vocabulary, defined as lexical retrieval difficulty, in the oral production of an 8-year-old returnee to Japan during the first 19 months after return. In a broader comparison of lexicon and syntax in the production of two L2 child speakers of German (ages 7 and 9) who had returned to Turkey, Kuhberg found that German word order was retained until the very end of the study, surpassing the retention of morphology. In addition, he reported slower speech, more frequent deviations in the use of verb forms, articles and prepositions, increasing lexical difficulties with verbs and other word classes, lexical switching to Turkish, and mixing of Turkish verb stems with German morphology. Although Kuhberg concluded that his findings support the position that the lexicon shows greater attrition than grammar, he also noted that specific aspects of morphology are affected by attrition earlier than the open-class lexicon.

Some studies have reached the opposite conclusion, claiming that the lexicon is more resilient than grammar. However, the findings of these studies resist straightforward interpretation. In documenting later stages of attrition, Tomiyama (1999b) reported that the child's lexicon stabilized while syntax deteriorated over the course of multiple sessions involving narrative retells. The use of embedded sentences in these elicited production tasks decreased from session 9 to session 22 over four years, whereas word knowledge, defined as picture identification scores, was maintained over four years. It is not clear that this finding demonstrates syntactic attrition: the decrease in numbers of embedded clauses gives no precise information concerning knowledge of syntax, and could possibly be a result of processing difficulties caused by impaired lexical retrieval. In a more recent study, Tomiyama (2008) found that in the L2 English of a 7-year-old and a 10-year-old lexical productivity (measured as words/clause) was maintained, but we note that learners told the same story seven times during the attrition period. In line with the general understanding of the relative vulnerability of vocabulary, she also found that grammatical complexity was well maintained, in contrast to marked attrition in lexical diversity (which she termed "lexical complexity"). A further study to claim better lexical than grammatical retention was Moorcroft and Gardner (1987), which we discuss below.

The third kind of evidence sometimes used to point to the relative fragility of the lexicon derives from research on multi-word units in memory, although here the results are more mixed. Berko-Gleason (1982) suggested that researchers should undertake "a study to see if routinized or automatized language enjoys special status, e.g., are numbers especially retained" (p. 23), but the attrition or retention of routines and multi-word units has yet to be explored systematically. Nevertheless, longevity in memory has been observed in production data, not only for numbers, but sequences like days of the week and months, songs, emotionally laden phrases such as curses, idioms, and also social routines such as *How do you do?* or *Oh my goodness!* (e.g., Berman & Olshtain, 1983; Kuhberg, 1992; Moorcroft & Gardner, 1987; Olshtain, 1986, 1989). Berman and Olshtain (1983) reported that L1 Hebrew-speaking children who have returned from English-speaking countries generally retain the use of fixed expressions. The children used chunks such as *first of all*, *I'm crazy about*, and *that's a bore*, and social fillers such as *well I guess*, *you're welcome*, and *have a nice time*. In oral production data similar to that collected from children by Olshtain (1986, 1989), Kuhberg (1992) also reported that "basic communicative routine expressions" survived (p. 148).

Verb-particle combinations have proven easier to study than social expressions given their frequency of use and predictable occurrence. In contrast to the retention reported for social expressions, however, verb-particle combinations show some degradation following target-like attainment, including substitution of the target particle with another (*take off (shoes)* → *take out (shoes)*); omission of particle resulting in a bare verb (*put on* → *put*), and the replacement of the verb-particle combination with a single verb (*turn off* → *close*) (Olshtain, 1986, 1989).

Moorcroft and Gardner's (1987) claim of better lexical than grammatical retention is based partly on their study of multi-word units in tests which included oral and written open-ended questions administered to L2 French Grade 9 students before and after summer vacation. They included idioms as a category of analysis in the production data, although, as seen from their examples, many strings are not idioms based on a conventional understanding of the term. They included "weather" (no examples were given, although this was the largest subset in the idiom category), age (*il a sept ans*; literally "he has seven years"), use of articles (*il a les yeux bleus*; literally "he has the blue eyes"), and partitive constructions (*j'ai peur de*; literally "I have fear of"). Although Moorcroft and Gardner classified idioms as "grammatical structure" (Table 2, p. 333; pp. 331–332), they repositioned them as "vocabulary" in discussing the results. They observed, "idioms differ from the other grammatical elements tested in that they are fixed forms. As such, they can be compared to vocabulary, and, like vocabulary, they are not forgotten, at least not over a short period of time" (p. 336). The findings resist broad generalization due to (i) the short period of disuse (3 months), (ii) the open format of the test items which allowed participants to respond differently, and (iii) the categorization of materials (e.g., article use was categorized under "idioms," and then idioms were classified with vocabulary, so that article use was treated as vocabulary).

In contrast, Bahrick's (1984) controlled test of idioms yielded no long-term retention for either idiom recall or recognition by L2 learners of Spanish, instead showing noticeable decline. The idiom recall test asked for translation of L2 Spanish idioms into L1 English; the idiom recognition test was a multiple-choice translation from L2 to L1. Idioms included *hace mal tiempo* "it's bad weather," *hasta la vista* "see you later," *en vez de* "instead of," *sin embargo* "however," *tal vez* "perhaps," and *desde luego* "of course." (We note that these may not all be "idioms" by a strict definition, but they are all lexically stored.) The recall of English translations for Spanish idioms was similar to the recall for individual Spanish words; but the recognition for Spanish idioms showed more pronounced and continuous decline than the recognition for individual Spanish words. Bahrick attributed the low scores for recognition in part to task construction in which the multiple-choice options for some frequent Spanish idioms included a cognate "foil" that misdirected the respondent, e.g., the multiple choice item for *sin embargo* "nevertheless" offered the English word *embargo* as one of the distracters (Appendix A). In addition, we note that for this item at least, the first distracter contained a literal translation of *sin* "without," creating a second distraction. Both choices are arguably unnatural, as they would be unlikely to be an issue in natural contexts of recall and production. A comparison of retention of idioms in recognition and recall tasks (Bahrick, 1984) with production data (Moorcroft & Gardner, 1987) reveals conflicting findings with much stronger declines found by Bahrick (although these could be due in part to task effect) in contrast to the retention found by Moorcroft and Gardner.

Rethinking the lexicon–grammar divide in L2 attrition studies

The studies discussed above, whether specifically investigating the Regression Hypothesis, or more generally examining the relative vulnerability of the lexicon, collectively indicate that a simple distinction between a fragile lexicon and a robust syntax is rather too simple. First, even within single studies, it is clear that the lexicon is not undifferentiated with respect to attrition. Berman and Olshtain (1983) showed that some aspects of the lexicon were retained by English L2 speaking children returning to an L1 Hebrew-speaking environment, whereas other lexical features showed attrition. Child returnees were observed to appropriately use chunks such as *first of all* to structure discourse and expressions for social interaction. In addition, high function or emotional items were also retained. In contrast, lexical loss was most extreme in daily vocabulary for items or events that were typical in Israel (relating to school, sports and recreation, and household events) and invariably referred to in Hebrew. This was plausibly due to interference: access to these items may have been blocked by high activation of the Hebrew analogues, in line with the predictions of Paradis (2007, see below).

Second, a closer look at the comparisons of lexicon and grammar reveals that what many studies describe as "grammar" is in fact inflectional morphology, which is also stored in the lexicon. Kuhberg (1992) observed, "Not only is the attrition of vocabulary considerable, but also that of basic grammatical categories (plural; present tense endings of verb morphology; genitive, dative and accusative cases)" (p. 152), and "Comparing morphology, lexicon and syntax, it must be pointed out that, in the data, certain aspects of morphology are affected earlier by attrition than lexicon. Syntax, at least in its basic patterns, remains intact longest" (p. 150). Yoshitomi (1999) suggested that such comparisons are vacuous in L2 attrition as loss of an item in the lexicon (or access to an item) cannot be compared directly to the loss of a rule of grammar. We consider research into the attrition of grammar relevant to our inquiry in all cases where syntactic properties are encoded in lexical entries. In the studies discussed above, lexical elements that determine aspects of syntax included morphology such as classifiers (Hansen & Chen, 2001), negative suffixes (Hansen, 1999; Hayashi, 1999), irregular nouns and verbs (Olshtain, 1989), and multi-word units such as idioms (Bahrick, 1984; Berman & Olshtain, 1983; Moorcroft & Gardner, 1987).

It is striking that studies providing supportive evidence for sequences of attrition all implicate lexical knowledge in some way, which suggests that the nature of the lexicon itself must be re-examined if we are to interpret L2 attrition data. In the following section, we briefly examine recent work on lexical representation and L2 acquisition of multi-word units that suggests a more complex and intriguing relationship between lexical memory and syntax than has previously been assumed in the L2 attrition literature.

Creative syntax in lexical memory

At least since Bloomfield (1933), mainstream linguistic theory has traditionally regarded the lexicon as a list of morphemes that may be combined only following insertion into syntax. However, there are reasons to believe that relations between the lexicon and syntax are more complex. In this section, we consider the nature of multi-word lexical entries in light of recent research on representation and L2 acquisition, in order to deepen our understanding of lexicon–syntax relations in L2 attrition, and conclude that a considerable part of lexical memory is devoted to the storage of phrases, sentences, and texts, the recall of which involves active syntax. We draw on independent research by Jackendoff (1997b, 2002), who argues that the vast number of fixed expressions we commit to memory, subsuming compounds, collocations, idioms, clichés, and quotations "is of about the same order of magnitude as the single words of the vocabulary" (1997b, p. 156), and Bardovi-Harlig (2006, 2009), who provides empirical evidence for syntactic development in the pragmatic use of conventional expressions.

The lexicon in Parallel Architecture

In elaborating his theory of Parallel Architecture, Jackendoff (1997b, 2002) has taken issue with several assumptions in mainstream generative theory: (i) that fixed expressions are a marginal phenomenon, outside "core grammar" (Chomsky & Lasnik, 1993); (ii) that lexical items enter the syntactic derivation by means of insertion, substituting a syntactic node X^0 with phonological material; (iii) that semantic interpretation is necessarily post-syntactic and compositional; and (iv) that information in lexical entries is non-redundant. To this end, he cites a range of linguistic phenomena, from affixes through phrasal projections to whole sentences and even texts that must be stored in long-term memory even though they often involve productive syntax. The examples below show how by extending Emonds' (1972) original observations of the existence of discontinuous idioms with NP as an open variable (1), a broad class of constructional idioms can be identified, with other open variables. In (2), V is open, while NP and Prt are fixed; in (3), V and PP are open, while the NP is fixed (the *way*-construction); in (4), V is open, NP specifies a time period, and the Prt is fixed (the *time-away* construction); and in (5), the analysis is extended to resultatives.[2]

(1) a. take NP to task (*take to task NP). (Emonds, 1972, p. 549)
    b. bring NP to a head (*bring to a head NP).
(2) a. {talk/drink/read} one's head off. (Jackendoff, 2002, p. 173)
    b. {argue/cry/sing} one's heart out.
(3) a. Paddy {whistled/danced} his way to the station. (Stringer, 2005, p. 352)
    b. Paddy {*whistled a tune / *danced a jig} his way to the station.
(4) a. Bill slept the afternoon away. (Jackendoff, 1997a, p. 534)
    b. We're twistin' the night away.
(5) a. Wilma watered the tulips flat. (Jackendoff, 2002, p. 175)
    b. Clyde cooked the pot black.

Going beyond idioms, whether of the constructional type above or fixed idioms with no open slots (*bury the hatchet, kick the bucket, corner the market*), Jackendoff (1997b) discussed a striking variety of other types of fixed expressions, including eight different types of compound (e.g., N-N: *dream sequence*, [A-N]-N: *frequent-flyer program*); names of people, places and organizations (e.g., *Clint Eastwood, International Red Cross*), clichés (e.g., *look on the bright side, the face of an angel*), titles of songs, novels and television programs (e.g., *All You Need Is Love, Lady and the Tramp*), as well as quotations (e.g., *beam me up Scotty, you ain't seen nothin' yet*) most of which are taken from his *Wheel of Fortune* Corpus.[3] He estimated that over a ten-year-period, this television show presented about 10–15,000 such puzzles, with little or no repetition, and with no sense that it will ever run out of new material (p. 154). These items are

---

[2] It should be noted that while all the examples of idioms with fixed NP/PP/AP/Prt and V as a free variable must be encoded as constructions on any account, the case of resultatives is more complicated and more controversial. Jackendoff's flat structure representation offers the same linear account for both depictives (*The artist painted the model nude*) and resultatives (*The artist painted the statue red*). For a more complex account, expressing causality and result in the syntax, see Ramchand (2008).

[3] This is provided in the Appendix to Jackendoff (1997b). The *Wheel of Fortune* is an American television game show in which contestants are asked to guess well-known words and phrases, presumably almost all of which are stored in the lexicon of the average speaker of American English.

all instances of correspondences between phonological, syntactic, and semantic structure stored in long-term memory.

On the parallel-processing account, an operation *Unify* links outputs from the representational modules of phonology, syntax, and conceptual semantics. As such, fixed expressions can be accommodated in the lexicon in the same way as words, that is to say as stored links between phonological, syntactic and semantic structures. The simplified lexical entry for (1a) *take to task* involves the correspondences below (adapted from Jackendoff, 2002, p. 170).

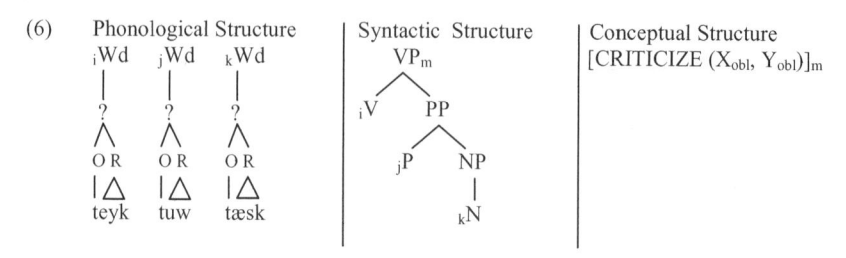

(6)   Phonological Structure | Syntactic Structure | Conceptual Structure
      $_i$Wd $_j$Wd $_k$Wd | VP$_m$ | [CRITICIZE (X$_{obl}$, Y$_{obl}$)]$_m$
                                | $_i$V   PP |
      O R   O R   O R | $_j$P   NP |
      teyk tuw   tæsk | $_k$N |

The pre-subscripts show the linking between phonological structure and syntactic structure (henceforth PS–SS correspondences), while the post-subscripts show the linking between syntactic structure and conceptual structure (henceforth SS–CS correspondences); this linking is necessary as idioms do not have word-by-word mapping. Thus it is at the level of the VP, in this case, that a lexical correspondence is made to CS. Jackendoff leaves open the mechanism by which the second obligatory semantic argument is mapped onto an NP in syntax (plausibly through classical subcategorization).

It is important to stress two observations with regard to such structural lexical entries. First, there may be varying degrees of redundancy in syntax–semantics correspondences. In the above example, the linking between SS and CS is strictly at the VP level (there is no *taking* or *task* involved). However, in semantically transparent phrases that are stored in long-term memory, the linking will remain tied to various levels of syntactic composition. In partially transparent idioms, there may be linking at more than one level. The fixed expression *The buck stops here* is linked at the level of the sentence by everyone who understands the meaning of the expression; the item *stop* is presumably also linked directly; however, even if the meaning of *buck* is not transparent to all speakers (i.e., equated with *blame* or *responsibility*), it may be processed without any particular meaning, or associated with a different meaning. This does not prevent entirely appropriate use of the phrase, due to the redundancy in linking the whole fixed expression at the higher level.

A second observation is that this approach does not reduce the whole of language to a set of constructions – most sentences, including the one you are reading, are not stored in long-term memory, but are creatively constructed online in working memory. A crucial question is what *must* be stored, and what *can* be stored (Jackendoff, 2002, p. 152). What must be stored is not controversial, and is generally understood as being any word or phrase whose meaning cannot be derived compositionally. It is the question of what can be stored that makes the implications of this line of inquiry so pregnant with possibility. Any utterance can be memorized, and many of our daily social interactions are rife with fixed expressions, both idiomatic and compositional. Estimates of how much first language natural discourse is formulaic range from 20 percent (Peters, 1983) to as high as 59 percent (Erman & Warren, 2000). Even adopting a more conservative estimate, this suggests that access to the lexicon in the course of normal speech necessarily involves the stimulation of unconscious syntactic processing routines, thus providing a bridge between sound–meaning correspondences in declarative memory and procedural knowledge of syntax. We now consider how this expanded notion of the lexicon can inform our understanding of second language acquisition and attrition, with specific reference to the role of conventional expressions. Contrary to standard assumptions in the L2 literature, such expressions are not always memorized "chunks," but are shown to be actively constructed syntactic representations subject to change over the course of development.

Conventional expressions in the acquisition of L2 pragmatics

Recent research in interlanguage pragmatics has investigated the issue of the grammar of formulaic sequences in second language development. Bardovi-Harlig (2009) adopted the term *conventional expression* to describe those social formulas that are routinely used in particular discourse contexts by native speakers, and that serve as both input and targets for second language learners. Adopting this term avoids the potential confusion of the more widespread term *formula*, which is used in a variety of different senses, and carries a (usually implicit) claim that such sequences are "stored and retrieved whole from memory at the time of use, rather than being subject to generation or analysis by the language grammar" (Wray, 2000, p. 465). It is desirable to avoid making this a priori psycholinguistic claim when the nature of such sequences is precisely the object of investigation. The findings of Bardovi-Harlig (2009) constituted the first major documentation of changes in the grammar of conventional expressions over the course of second language development, and thus allow us here to revisit the issue of representation in memory, retrieval, and online syntactic construction.

In given social contexts, native speakers predictably use conventional expressions such as *Nice to meet you, No problem, (I'm) sorry I'm late, I'm just looking* (while shopping), and *I gotta go* (on the telephone). Conventional expressions are by definition situationally dependent and community-wide in use (Myles, Mitchell, & Hooper, 1999). In order to investigate the relationship between L2 recognition and production of such phrases, Bardovi-Harlig (2009) conducted two tasks: (i) an aural recognition task testing knowledge of 60 expressions, and (ii) an oral production task eliciting responses to 32 scenarios. Participants included 122 learners of English from a variety of L1 backgrounds, placed in four levels of an intensive English program, and 49 native speakers of English, subdivided into peers and teachers. The oral production task yielded 5,504 responses (172 participants × 32 scenarios). That the selected conventional expressions tested were in fact what native speakers typically say in the circumstances described was experimentally confirmed. Of primary relevance to our concern in this chapter is the syntactic variation that emerged over the course of development. For example, consider the following scenario in the production task.

(7)   You made an appointment with your teacher. Unfortunately, you arrive five minutes late for the meeting. Your teacher says, "Hello. Come on in."
You say:

In such contexts, native speakers reliably use the conventional expression *(I'm) sorry I'm late*.[4] In attempting to construct this target expression, learners reveal that they are not simply retrieving a formulaic chunk, but are creatively combining elements in syntax, often resulting in forms of the type illustrated in (8), reflecting interlanguage syntax, or of the type exemplified in (9), which are grammatically acceptable

---

[4] This could be analyzed in one of two ways by native speakers. One possibility is that it could be two sentences idiomatically combined. While this is arguably not a legitimate derivation in syntax, several types of fixed expressions are syntactically deviant, as noted by Jackendoff (2002), for example *all of a sudden, by and large, up to your room with you, one more beer and I'm leaving*. Alternatively, this could simply be a standard matrix and embedded clause with a null complementizer, of the same form as *She was sorry (that) she was late*. It is also possible that different native speakers have different representations for the same surface form (McCawley, 1979, pp. 239–240).

in the target language but are not the preferred expression stored in memory by native speakers.

(8) a. I'm sorry for late.
    b. I'm sorry for I'm late.
    c. I'm sorry about late.
    d. I'm so sorry about my late.
    e. I'm so sorry to being so late.
    f. I'm sorry because I late.
(9) a. Sorry for being late.
    b. I'm sorry to be late.
    c. I'm sorry to come late.
    d. Sorry for coming late. (Bardovi-Harlig, 2009, p. 777)

The results also show development over the four levels of proficiency tested. In one "late" scenario, both lexical items *sorry* and *late* were used at a rate of 76 percent at the lowest level, and 96 percent at the most advanced level. The specific expression *(I'm) sorry I'm late* was used at 17 percent at the lowest level, 31–32 percent at the intermediate levels, and 48 percent at the most advanced level. Other conventional expressions such as *I'm just looking* (while shopping) showed similar patterns of development.

These data provide support for and allow for a refinement of Jackendoff's (1997b, 2002) lexical representations in Parallel Architecture, which were illustrated in example (6). It seems plausible to assume that despite the range of syntactic variation in learners' attempts to converge on the target formula *(I'm) sorry I'm late*, many share a target-like conceptual structure, stored in long-term memory. Thus, over the course of development, the linking between the highest structural levels of SS and CS representations essentially remains unchanged, despite the meaning not being idiomatic, while allowing for developmental changes within the syntax. The syntactic representation itself may be generated by either interlanguage or target-like principles of combination, and may exhibit variation even within individuals. Representational modularity also allows for the converse situation – there could be a change in the conceptual representation of a fixed expression that learners have mastered syntactically, as they realize that the precise semantic interpretation is not what was first assumed. In short, the kind of pragmalinguistic development described is insightfully captured in a model that distinguishes the independent generation of syntactic and conceptual structure, and in which well-formed utterances depend on correspondence rules between the outputs of representational modules.

What's in a word? A closer look at sound–meaning correspondences

Following our consideration of studies cited in support of the Regression Hypothesis, we speculated that a common denominator was the activation of the lexicon, as opposed to the implementation of the implicit knowledge involved in syntactic processing. However, this reconsideration of the nature of the lexicon allows us to refine our analysis. For many attrition studies, one-word retrieval paradigms were employed which test only sound–meaning relations (PS–CS correspondences). These correspondences are entirely arbitrary in a Saussurean sense, and of little relevance to linguistic computation. No L2 study of lexical attrition to date has specifically explored syntax–meaning relations (SS–CS correspondences) or full sound–syntax–meaning relations (PS–SS–CS correspondences), which are of primary concern to those interested in the language faculty. That an English learner of French can appropriately name or select a picture with grapes or pasta does not indicate "acquisition" of these lexical items. In order to use such words in sentences, learners must specify *raisin* "grapes" as a mass noun and *pâtes* "pasta" as a count noun, contrary to their English analogues. They must acquire the knowledge that *raisin* is masculine and singular, and that *pâtes* is feminine and plural. Otherwise, these nouns cannot be used appropriately in combination with either determiners, quantifiers, adjectives or verbs, and cannot be substituted by matching pronouns. As is well known, to acquire lexical entries for verbs is even more complex, and involves infinitely more than being able to say "yes" on a picture-matching task. The *Shorter Oxford English Dictionary* (1993) uses over three-and-a-half thousand words to define the verb *put*. Clearly, as argued by Bloom (2000, Ch. 2), acquisition of a word occurs incrementally with multiple exposures. Finally, we must note that lexical entries above the word level are still more complex. For example, stimulation of the conventional expression *I'm just looking* involves syntactic knowledge of pronouns, case assignment, contraction, adverbial modification, use of an irregular light verb, encoding of semantic verb class, and appropriate use of aspectual morphology.

Although this suggests a potential gold mine in essentially uncharted territory for attrition research, previous studies of the breakdown or retention of simple sound–meaning correspondences may nevertheless have interesting implications for more linguistically oriented studies of attrition. For example, the loss of a link between sound and meaning implies lack of access to syntactic information in the entry, such that a problem in declarative memory has a domino effect rendering inaccessible the relevant implicit syntactic processing routine. Conversely, the reactivation of a link between sound and meaning might automatically restimulate any linked syntactic information, without such procedural knowledge ever becoming conscious.

The consideration of the lexicon as a network allows us to take this idea to another level. Just as PS–SS–CS correspondences are linked within lexical items so that stimulation of any pairing can stimulate a third representation, lexical items themselves are linked in complex networks, ultimately forming the lexicon of a language in an individual mind. While most empirical research on the spreading of activation and inhibition in bilingual lexical networks has focused on temporary effects in particular situations, with states of linguistic knowledge being constant, the question arises of what happens over long stretches of time when one language is continually activated, and the other continually inhibited. A further question concerns reactivation of lexical items after long-term disuse. If each lexical item has multiple links in the system, might re-stimulation of many items have a cascade effect throughout previously suppressed representations? L2 attrition research has yet to address such questions, but may be informed by previous work in computational modeling and psycholinguistics. The following section considers examples of such work with potentially far-reaching implications of our understanding of both attrition, and recovery from attrition.

Losing one's inhibitions

Theories of lexicon-as-network have principally been developed in computational linguistics and in psycholinguistics. In this section, we consider both perspectives and briefly describe some models of activation and inhibition which might be profitably applied in research on L2 attrition.

The interconnectedness of the lexicon

In computational linguistics, Meara (2004) specifically addressed the relevance of lexical networks for attrition, although his insights have yet to be taken up in empirical L2 attrition research. To illustrate his point, he offered a highly simplified computational model of a 2,500-word lexicon in which all words have links to two other words, and all of which are either activated or non-activated. Some words are activated only following activation of both linked words, while others are activated by only one linked word. While the model is an abstraction rather than a representation of an actual mental lexicon, it succeeds in provoking thought about examining the "loss" of one word as an entity unrelated to any others. The deactivation (or attrition) of one word has effects on other words throughout the system. Meara maintains that successive deactivation of individual items weakens the structure of the lexicon as a whole. Thus, attrition events can build up silently within the system, with the result that it may look like one event can create an avalanche.

Another significant challenge from Meara (2004) is to consider how the number and types of words are chosen for inclusion in a task. The number of words should be considered in relation to the estimated vocabulary size. Meara (2005) reports that 250 words is the upper limit for a single session test for most respondents. Short tests are not likely to provide a good representation of the lexicon, as attrition in such cases could be under estimated. This may be illustrated by Weltens' (1989) finding in which the lowest score attained in a test of 40 words was 31/40 (77.5 percent) after four years of disuse, whereas the participants reported by means of self-assessment that they had experienced greater lexical attrition even by two years of disuse. It could very well be that the learners had a more representative sense of their vocabulary loss than the recognition test revealed.

One way to resolve the lexical sampling issue is to conduct longitudinal studies in which attriters are engaged in the same production tasks over time, as part of the general model of assessment proposed by Bardovi-Harlig and Stringer (2010). When participants complete a task in subsequent data collection periods and particular lexical items (morphemes, words, and fixed expressions) cease to appear, they are identified for further study. Such production tasks might involve conventional elicitation techniques, simulated role play, or, more ambitiously, audiovisual recordings of authentic social interactions.

Models of activation and inhibition

The question remains of the mechanisms by which attrition or reactivation can spread through the lexicon in situations of L2 disuse or re-immersion in an L2 environment. Possible answers to this question may be found in the literature on the role of inhibition in language choice in bilinguals. In Green's (1998) influential Inhibitory Control (IC) model, lexical nodes are marked with language tags, which identify the word as being, say, French or Hungarian. During language production by bilinguals, those words carrying the non-target language tag are subject to reactive inhibition. Thus, while lexical analogues in both languages are initially activated, activation of the non-selected items is subsequently suppressed. Due to this initial activation, the lexical nodes of the non-selected language interfere during processing, even though phonological activation appears to be restricted to the selected lexical item. The idea of inhibition linked to language tags lends itself straightforwardly to cases of global L2 attrition, on the assumption that continuous inhibition of all items with a particular tag eventually leads to more permanent suppression of the language.

In contrast to the IC model, which involves a simple access procedure but a complicated retrieval process involving degrees of inhibition, La Heij (2005, p. 290) characterizes his own proposed model as "complex access, simple selection." In this model, activation rather than inhibition is the key to lexical access – the preverbal message contains all necessary information, including affective and pragmatic features, to specify a single word uniquely. Language code is part of this information, so that choice of L1 or L2, and choice of register within these codes, directly affects activation level. The idea of complex preverbal messages in this model could be developed for application in L2 attrition research with or without language tags. On the assumption that lexical items lack precise translation equivalents (Stringer, 2010), a complex access process might suffice to pick out unique lexical entries using only phonological, syntactic, and semantic information.

Perhaps the psychological model of lexical access that melds best with the linguistic literature on attrition is the Activation Threshold Hypothesis (ATH) developed by Paradis (e.g. 1993, 2004, 2007). According to this hypothesis, an item is in an active state once it receives a sufficient number of neural impulses; this level of stimulus is termed its activation threshold. Subsequent activation of the item lowers the threshold, granting gains in speed of access. The selection of a particular lexical item in both monolingual and bilingual retrieval requires that it has a higher activation level than any competitors. Inhibition is a central construct in this model. In order to guarantee a sufficiently high level of activation, competitors must be inhibited, along the lines suggested by Green (1998). According to Paradis, "attrition is the result of long-term lack of stimulation" (2004, p. 28). Thus, while intensive exposure to a language leads to a lower activation threshold, lack of use leads to an inexorable rise in the activation threshold. The ATH claims that recency and frequency combine to determine the activation threshold: "The activation of a word or any other item (i.e., the amount of impulses needed to activate its neural substrate) will fluctuate as a consequence of it recency and frequency of use (and to some extent the recency and frequency of use of its immediate network and its entire subsystem)" (Paradis, 2004, p. 29). In applying this model to situations of attrition, one is not forced to choose between a language-wide tagging stem and local semantic networks; rather, it could be construed as the kind of psychological model that Meara's (2004) computational model set out to emulate, with activation spreading through increasing numbers of interrelated items producing the potential avalanche effects discussed earlier.

Combining the ATH with a strict distinction between declarative and procedural memory systems, Paradis (2007, pp. 121–122) makes the following predictions for L1 attrition, which, *mutatis mutandis*, also apply to L2 attrition: (i) language disuse leads to language loss; (ii) the most frequently used elements of L2 will replace their L1 counterparts; (iii) production is more vulnerable to attrition than comprehension, as the neurological mechanisms involved require a higher level of activation; (iv) elements dependent on declarative memory, such as "vocabulary" (e.g., the PS–CS correspondences discussed above), are more prone to attrition than those dependent on procedural memory, such as phonology, syntax, and "the lexicon" (i.e., SS–CS correspondences); (v) declarative items are more vulnerable to interference (attrition by substitution); and (vi) pragmatics and conceptual representations are also prone to attrition. Strong support for these predictions is found in the lexical studies of L2 attrition discussed earlier. Thus, differential attrition effects in production and comprehension were found by Cohen (1989) and Olshtain (1989), the predicted difference between vocabulary and syntax was found by Kuhberg (1992) and Tomiyama (1999a, 2008),[5] and high-frequency fixed expressions appear to persist more than general vocabulary (e.g., Berman & Olshtain, 1983; Kuhberg, 1992; Moorcroft & Gardner, 1987; Olshtain, 1986, 1989). The findings of Berman and Olshtain (1983) regarding the marked attrition of daily vocabulary relating to school, sports, and household events, in contrast to language-particular fixed expressions and emotionally charged items, provide further evidence for this model.

In her review of attrition in the context of heritage language learning, Montrul (2008) finds evidence for the ATH in the work on lexical attrition by Hulsen (2000) and Olshtain and Barzilay (1991), but notes that in studies that examined syntax, the only areas of syntax affected were those subject to transfer effects, such as pronominal binding in adult L1 attrition of Turkish with L2 English (Gürel, 2002), or impersonal passives in adult L1 attrition of Dutch with L2 English (Keijzer, 2007). Otherwise, knowledge of syntax remained relatively robust. Rather than being differentially affected, it may even be that certain aspects of

---

[5] As discussed earlier, Moorcroft and Gardner (1987) and Tomiyama (1999b) claim the opposite, but their results resist straightforward interpretation.

(L1) syntax and phonology are impervious to attrition (Montrul, 2008, p. 89).

The ATH also makes an interesting prediction regarding the difference between open- and closed-class items. Functional morphology (e.g., articles, plurality, agreement, tense) is often viewed as inherently problematic in L2 acquisition, leading some to suggest a stage with undefined syntactic feature values (Herschensohn, 2000) and others to posit an extended process of syntactic feature reassembly (Lardiere, 2009). On the Regression Hypothesis, one might expect late-acquired functional morphology to be susceptible to early attrition; however, on the ATH, these items are stored in procedural rather than declarative memory, making them *less* vulnerable to attrition. Interestingly, in Keijzer's (2007) Dutch–English study mentioned above, there was remarkably little L1 attrition of productive morphology. In L2 attrition, the open-class/closed-class distinction remains to be systematically investigated. In short, the predictions made by the ATH regarding the lexicon are largely supported by empirical studies of attrition, with further investigation required for functional morphology and syntax.

In this section, we have explored interconnectedness in the lexicon in terms of the potential for the spreading of either activation or inhibition through semantic networks, keeping in mind the question of long-term effects of frequent activation or continuous inhibition. Such spreading arguably takes effect throughout a specific language lexicon, either explicitly through a tagging system, or by specifying a language code in the preverbal message, or perhaps implicitly through multiple activation of items with myriad connections, leading to an avalanche effect. Research in this vein may further understanding of the mechanisms involved in the kinds of blanket loss and extensive recovery discussed in the following section.

Catastrophic loss, miraculous recovery: what happens on the ferry to Boulogne?

Research on attrition or reactivation of the lexicon *as a system* is thin on the ground, but we briefly summarize two empirical studies that attempted to document global loss and global recovery. Oller *et al.* (2007) provided tentative but suggestive evidence from L1 attrition research that for children, massive exposure to an L2 results in general inhibition of L1 vocabulary in production, though not (at first) in comprehension, in line with the ATH. They administered a battery of tests to children from Spanish-speaking and English-speaking families in Memphis at the beginning and at the end of their kindergarten year. Of the 30 Hispanic children, 13 had been exposed to English for one year prior to the baseline test, and the others were considered to be essentially monolingual. There were two comprehension tasks, one in English and one in Spanish, both involving 4-choice picture identification. There were also two production tasks, one in English and one in Spanish, both involving picture naming. At both times of testing, monolingual English-speaking children scored close to 100 percent, while the children from Spanish-speaking families revealed a stunning discrepancy between the comprehension and production tasks in Spanish (more than one-and-a-half standard deviations). It appears that very soon after entering the L2-dominant school system, a suppression mechanism impeded access to L1 vocabulary. Although this fits with anecdotal reports, a caveat must be sounded in interpreting the results. As argued in Bardovi-Harlig and Stringer (2010), the establishment of a peak of attainment is fundamental in the documentation of attrition. In this case, the baseline was late-established, at an unspecified time near "the beginning" (p. 476) of kindergarten. As the same comprehension–production discrepancy was found in pre- and post-test, and as the Hispanic children had spent an average of 4.4 (SD = 1.8) years in the USA *before* entering kindergarten, it is possible that the discrepancy was already in place before the period of investigation, and may even have been present from the outset of their heritage language learning.

The converse effect, where a language "comes flooding back" in situations of re-immersion, is also regularly confirmed in anecdotal reports but has yet to be comprehensively studied. To our knowledge, the only published attempt to document this in recent years was by Meara (2005), who coined it the Boulogne Ferry Effect, due to his own experience of the phenomenon. He noted that when visiting France from the UK, "the mere act of walking down the main street in Boulogne shortly after getting off the ferry can sometimes trigger the reactivation of a whole stream of dormant French vocabulary" (p. 271). Inspired equally by the many anecdotal reports of learners who report spontaneous reactivation of L2 vocabulary after short periods of re-immersion, and by similar processes of reactivation in his computational models (Meara, 2004), he set out to investigate the idea that the activation of small numbers of words can initiate "a ripple effect which works its way right through the entire lexicon" (p. 272).

Given the logistical and financial obstacles involved in sending groups of attriters on vacation to revisit old haunts, and the patience required of participants to test large numbers of words, Meara argues convincingly that there is merit in exploring single-case studies with cooperative volunteers, and presents the findings from one such investigation. The participant was an L1 English speaker who agreed to participate in a study while revisiting the Netherlands after 18 months without speaking Dutch. A list of 244 Dutch words was drawn up, taken from the participant's personal vocabulary notebooks created several years before. He was tested on his knowledge of these words once a day, for 12 consecutive days, six in the UK before taking his trip, three after his arrival in the Netherlands, and three after his return to the UK. When presented with an English translation equivalent, he was asked to consider if he could provide the target Dutch word, and then press one of four buttons corresponding to the responses: "I do not know this word"; "I think I don't know this word"; "I think I do know this word"; and "I'm certain I know this word." Some results were intriguing. He reported a significant increase in vocabulary awareness on the morning of the day he traveled, before any actual contact with Dutch speakers. In addition, his performance continued to improve after his return to the UK. The key finding, however, was the dramatic increase on days 7, 8, and 9 while he was in the L2 environment, during which time his active vocabulary more than tripled in size.

However, as Meara (2005) recognizes, findings from this initial exploration need to be treated with caution. The post-experiment interview made clear that the methodology was problematic in a number of ways. Some English words were ambiguous, allowing for unintended translations; the participant later said he could sometimes translate a word by adopting a paraphrasing strategy; he sometimes recorded a negative response only to have the word come to mind two or three seconds later; and, crucially, there was almost certainly an inescapable task effect – the participant reported that repeated testing of the same words facilitated his noticing of them in context in the Netherlands. If one steps outside of the theoretical framework of the study, other issues arise, such as how much we can rely on self-reports at all, how much recognition of simple sound–meaning correspondences tell us about knowledge of the lexicon, and what might happen in cases of recall of phrases, idioms, and conventional expressions. Nevertheless, this pioneering study provides a valuable platform for further research. It provides justification for more case studies in this area, and meets one of the most important criteria for the assessment of attrition and recovery laid out in Bardovi-Harlig and Stringer (2010) – the comparison of participants to themselves in longitudinal designs.

Moreover, although empirical evidence is lacking, anecdotal evidence abounds that when an L2 comes flooding back, speakers are not left with a mere list of Saussurean correspondences. Within a few days, phrases, sentences, and stretches of discourse also reveal a grammatical reawakening. It is a plausible hypothesis that the recall of common constructions, conversational idioms and conventional expressions in daily use all help to stimulate this recovery, as multi-word expressions are laden with syntactic information.

Conclusion

There appears to be a thread running through the maze of L2 attrition research. Empirical studies offering support for sequences of L2 attrition, whether in terms of the Regression Hypothesis or the various versions of the Threshold Hypothesis, may all be understood as centrally involving the retrieval of items from the mental lexicon. Generally speaking, reported findings are commensurate with the Activation Threshold Hypothesis of Paradis (2004, 2007), in which both recency and frequency of access determine the efficiency of lexical retrieval, comprehension is more resilient than production, and simple sound–meaning correspondences stored in declarative memory are prone to interference from lexical analogues in the dominant language. It is plausible to claim that vocabulary is more vulnerable than grammar in situations of disuse; however, such a claim requires clarification when sound–meaning correspondences are embedded in a more sophisticated account of the lexicon. Different types of lexical entries show different patterns of attrition. Moreover, the lexicon *contains* syntax, not only in the form of inherent and selectional features, but also due to its status as a reservoir of constructional idioms and fixed expressions. As revealed in the L2 acquisition of conventional expressions, complex lexical entries may differ between learners and may change over time, as varied syntactic structures are mapped onto a target conceptual structure. Moreover, computational modeling and psycholinguistic research reveal that lexical entries are interconnected in a system in which no lexical item is activated or inhibited in isolation. Successive attrition events may thus eventually result in global lack of access, and reactivation events may eventually result in global reactivation.

This fresh perspective on patterns of L2 attrition has yet to be comprehensively explored. One characteristic of previous work on multi-word units is that data were not targeted for elicitation but drawn from unplanned use in production. Using techniques from acquisition studies, such as the oral discourse completion task which simulates the time pressure of turn taking and explores specific mappings between conceptual and linguistic representations, future work may study attrition of the lexicon beyond the word more systematically. The proposal that continuous inhibition leads to eventual attrition remains a plausible if not proven account of language loss more generally. Without words, there is no syntactic expression, whether or not principles of syntax continue to abide in the bilingual mind. However, even if implicit syntactic knowledge is prone to attrition, our reconsideration of the lexicon as a vast repository of phrases, idioms, and conventional expressions provides a bridge between the recall of PS–CS correspondences sustained by declarative memory and SS–CS correspondences sustained by procedural memory. When the lexicon awakes, syntax is necessarily aroused from slumber.

REFERENCES

Bahrick, H. (1984). Semantic memory content in permastore: fifty years of memory for Spanish learned in school. *Journal of Experimental Psychology: General*, 113, 1–29.

Bardovi-Harlig, K. (2006). On the role of formulas in the acquisition of L2 pragmatics. In K. Bardovi-Harlig, C. Félix-Brasdefer, & A. S. Omar (eds.), *Pragmatics and language learning* (Vol. 11, pp. 1–28). Honolulu: University of Hawai'i, National Foreign Language Resource Center.

(2009). Conventional expressions as a pragmalinguistic resource: recognition and production of conventional expressions in L2 pragmatics. *Language Learning*, 59, 755–795.

Bardovi-Harlig, K., & Stringer, D. (2010). Variables in second language attrition: advancing the state of the art. *Studies in Second Language Acquisition*, 32, 1–45.

Berko-Gleason, J. (1982). Insights from child language acquisition for second language loss. In R. D. Lambert & B. F. Freed (eds.), *The loss of language skills* (pp. 13–23). Rowley, MA: Newbury House.

Berman, R. A., & Olshtain, E. (1983). Features of first language transfer in second language attrition. *Applied Linguistics*, 4, 222–234.

Bloom, P. (2000). *How children learn the meanings of words*. Cambridge, MA: MIT Press.

Bloomfield, L. (1933). *Language*. London: George Allen and Unwin.

Chomsky, N., & Lasnik, H. (1993). The theory of principles and parameters. In J. Jacobs, A. von Stechow, W. Sternefeld, & T. Vennemann (eds.), *Syntax: an international handbook of contemporary research, Vol. 1* (pp. 506–569). Berlin: de Gruyter.

Cohen, A. D. (1974). The Culver City Spanish Immersion Program: how does summer recess affect Spanish speaking ability? *Language Learning*, 24, 55–68.

(1975). Forgetting a second language. *Language Learning*, 25, 127–138.

(1986). Forgetting foreign language vocabulary. In B. Weltens, K. de Bot, & T. van Els (eds.), *Language attrition in progress* (pp. 143–158). Dordrecht: Foris.

(1989). Attrition in the productive lexicon of two Portuguese third language speakers. *Studies in Second Language Acquisition*, 11, 135–149.

de Bot, K., & Lintsen, T. (1989). Perception of own language proficiency by elderly adults. *I. T. L. Review of Applied Linguistics*, 83, 51–61.
de Bot, K., & Stoessel, S. (2000). In search of yesterday's words: reactivating a long forgotten language. *Applied Linguistics*, 21, 364–384.
Downing, P. (1984). *Japanese numeral classifiers: a syntactic, semantic, and functional profile*. Unpublished Ph.D. dissertation, University of California, Berkeley.
Emonds, J. E. (1972). Evidence that indirect object movement is a structure-preserving rule. *Foundations of Language*, 8, 546–561.
Erman, B., & Warren, B. (2000). The idiom principle and the open choice principle. *Text*, 20, 29–62.
Green, D. W. (1998). Mental control of the bilingual lexico-semantic system. *Bilingualism: Language and Cognition*, 1, 67–81.
Grendel, M. (1993). *Verlies en Herstel van Lexicale Kennis* [Attrition and recovery of lexical knowledge]. Unpublished Ph.D. dissertation, University of Nijmegen.
Gürel, A. (2002). *Linguistic characterizations of second language acquisition and first language attrition: Turkish overt vs. null pronouns*. Unpublished Ph.D. dissertation, McGill University.
Hansen, L. (1999). Not a total loss: the attrition of Japanese negation over three decades. In L. Hansen (ed.), *Second language attrition in Japanese contexts* (pp. 142–153). Oxford University Press.
Hansen, L., & Chen, Y.-L. (2001). What counts in the acquisition and attrition of numeral classifiers? *JALT*, 23, 90–110.
Hayashi, B. (1999). Testing the regression hypothesis: the remains of the Japanese negation system in Micronesia. In L. Hansen (ed.), *Second language attrition in Japanese contexts* (pp. 154–168). Oxford University Press.
Herschensohn, J. (2000). *The second time around: minimalism and L2 acquisition*. Philadelphia, PA: John Benjamins.
Hulsen, M. (2000). *Language loss and language processing: three generations of Dutch migrants in New Zealand*. Unpublished Ph.D. dissertation, University of Nijmegen.
Jackendoff, R. (1997a). Twistin' the night away. *Language*, 73, 534–559.
——— (1997b). *The architecture of the language faculty*. Cambridge, MA: MIT Press.
——— (2002). *Foundations of language: brain, meaning, grammar, evolution*. Oxford University Press.
Keijzer, M. (2007). *Last in first out? An investigation of the regression hypothesis in Dutch emigrants in anglophone Canada*. Vrije Universiteit Amsterdam, LOT: Netherlands Graduate School of Linguistics.
Kuhberg, H. (1992). Longitudinal L2-attrition versus L2-acquisition in three Turkish children: empirical findings. *Second Language Research*, 8, 138–154.
La Heij, W. (2005). Selection processes in monolingual and bilingual lexical access. In J. F. Kroll & A. M. B. de Groot (eds.), *Handbook of bilingualism* (pp. 289–307). Oxford University Press.

Lardiere, D. (2009). Some thoughts on the contrastive analysis of features in second language acquisition. *Second Language Research*, 25, 173–227.
McCawley, J. D. (1979). Some ideas not to live by. In J. D. McCawley, *Adverbs, vowels and other objects of wonder* (pp. 234–246). University of Chicago Press.
Meara, P. M. (2004). Modelling vocabulary loss. *Applied Linguistics*, 25, 137–155.
  (2005). Reactivating a dormant vocabulary. In S. H. Foster-Cohen, M. P. García Mayo, & J. Cenoz (eds.), *EUROSLA Yearbook* (Vol. 5, pp. 269–280). Amsterdam: John Benjamins.
Montrul, S. (2008). *Incomplete acquisition in bilingualism: re-examining the age factor*. Amsterdam: John Benjamins.
Moorcroft, R., & Gardner, R. C. (1987). Linguistic factors in second-language loss. *Language Learning*, 37, 327–340.
Myles, F., Mitchell, R., & Hooper, J. (1999). Interrogative chunks in French L2. *Studies in Second Language Acquisition*, 21, 49–80.
Oller, D. K., Jarmulowicz, L., Gibson, T., & Hoff, E. (2007). First language vocabulary loss in early bilinguals during language immersion: a possible role for suppression. In H. Caunt-Nolton, S. Kulatilake, & I.-H. Woo (eds.), *Proceedings of the Boston University Conference on Language Development* (pp. 474–484). Somerville, MA: Cascadilla Press.
Olshtain, E. (1986). The attrition of English as a second language with speakers of Hebrew. In B. Weltens, K. de Bot, & T. van Els (eds.), *Language attrition in progress* (pp. 187–204). Dordrecht: Foris.
  (1989). Is second language attrition the reversal of second language acquisition? *Studies in Second Language Acquisition*, 11, 151–165.
Olshtain, E., & Barzilay, M. (1991). Lexical retrieval difficulties in adult language attrition. In H. W. Seliger & R. M. Vago (eds.), *First language attrition* (pp. 139–150). Cambridge University Press.
Paradis, M. (1993). Linguistic, psycholinguistic, and neurolinguistic aspects of "interference" in bilingual speakers: the Activation Threshold Hypothesis. *International Journal of Psycholinguistics*, 9, 133–145.
  (2004). *A neurolinguistic theory of bilingualism*. Amsterdam: John Benjamins.
  (2007). L1 attrition features predicted by a neurolinguistic theory of bilingualism. In B. Kopke, M. S. Schmid, M. Keijzer, & S. Dostert (eds.), *Language attrition: theoretical perspectives* (pp. 121–133). Amsterdam: John Benjamins.
Peters, A. M. (1983). *The units of language acquisition*. Cambridge University Press.
Ramchand, G. (2008). *Verb meaning and the lexicon: a first-phase syntax*. Cambridge University Press.
Russell, R. A. (1999). Lexical maintenance and attrition in Japanese as a second language. In L. Hansen (ed.), *Second language attrition in Japanese contexts* (pp. 114–141). Oxford University Press.
Stringer, D. (2005). *Paths in first language acquisition: motion through space in English, French and Japanese*. Unpublished Ph.D. dissertation, University of Durham.

(2010). The gloss trap. In Z.-H. Han & T. Cadierno (eds.), *Linguistic relativity in SLA: thinking for speaking* (pp. 102–124). Clevedon: Multilingual Matters.

Tomiyama, M. (1999a). The first stage of second language attrition: a case study of a Japanese returnee. In L. Hansen (ed.), *Second language attrition in Japanese contexts* (pp. 59–79). Oxford University Press.

(1999b). The later stages of natural L2 attrition. In P. Robinson (ed.), *Representation and process: Proceedings of the 3rd Pacific Second Language Research Forum*, Vol. 1 (pp. 309–320). Tokyo: PacSLRF, Aoyama University.

(2008). Age and proficiency in L2 attrition: data from two siblings. *Applied Linguistics*, 29, 1–23.

Verkaik, O., & van der Wijst (1986). *Taalverlies en Woordherkenning in het Frans als Vreemde Taal* [Language attrition and word recognition in French as a foreign language]. Unpublished master's thesis, University of Nijmegen.

Weltens, B. (1989). *The attrition of French as a foreign language*. Dordrecht: Foris.

Weltens, B., & Grendel, M. (1993). Attrition of vocabulary knowledge. In R. Schreuder & B. Weltens (eds.), *The bilingual lexicon* (pp. 135–156). Amsterdam: John Benjamins.

Wray, A. (2000). Formulaic sequences in second language teaching: principle and practice. *Applied Linguistics*, 21, 463–489.

Yoshitomi, A. (1999). On the loss of English as a second language by Japanese returnee children. In L. Hansen (ed.), *Second language in Japanese contexts* (pp. 80–113). Oxford University Press.

12 Memory and first language forgetting

Ludmila Isurin

Abstract

Non-pathological first language forgetting is studied by socio- and psycholinguists. Psycholinguistic research relies on the same methodological approaches used in studies of bilingual memory. The present chapter gives a brief overview of theories, tasks, and findings pertaining to this domain of research. The reported empirical study contributes to the existing knowledge of first language (L1) attrition as well as shows a way in which the quantitative and qualitative methods of analysis can be used to provide deeper insight into bilingual memory. Three groups of Russian bilinguals with different second language backgrounds (English, Hebrew, and German) participated in a picture-naming study. Word frequency was found to be a decisive factor in L1 forgetting whereas the length of immigration proved only marginally reliable. Qualitative analysis of the data revealed retrieval failures at the semantic and word-form levels and showed how each of the second languages interfered with successful access of the L1 lexicon.

The role of memory in first language (L1) forgetting experienced by healthy individuals has been studied by psycholinguists over the last two to three decades. However, the obvious difficulty of conducting psycholinguistic research in a real – not experimentally simulated – setting, the diversity of the population groups studied, the lack of consistency in the use of methodologically robust approaches, and a relatively small group of researchers in the field leaves the topic largely unexplored. This chapter gives a brief overview of the psycholinguistic research on first language forgetting – commonly known as L1 attrition – and reports on the findings of an empirical study involving three groups of Russian bilinguals.

Theories of first language forgetting

The forgetting of the native language is a phenomenon that may sound puzzling to those individuals who take first language retention for granted and consider its gradual erosion inconceivable. However, psycholinguists and psychologists consider the forgetting of the native language in immigrants as natural as the forgetting of any other information stored in human long-term memory (LTM). The explanations for the diminished access to linguistic information lie in the realm of the existing theories of forgetting.

In his relatively recent overview of theories of forgetting, Ecke (2004) emphasized the relevance of existing theories to the language domain and summarized major studies and findings in the field of first and second language forgetting as they pertain to each theory. As the author pointed out, there are four major research issues raised by prior psycholinguistic studies on language forgetting: the definition of language forgetting, the causes of forgetting, the linguistic domains most vulnerable to forgetting, and the potential socio-psychological consequences of forgetting (Ecke, 2004). Among the causes of language forgetting are linguistic repression, linguistic distortion, language decay, linguistic interference, and retrieval failure. An example of linguistic repression would be the case of individuals (mostly children) who suppressed their native language due to a psychological trauma associated with it or due to social pressure toward a less prestigious language (Isurin, 2000; Kouritzin, 1999). Linguistic distortion may result in bilinguals having difficulty in identifying ungrammaticality in their native language due to a restructuring of their mental grammar under the influence of the second language (Major, 1993). Linguistic decay can occur in those cases where the individual experiences a gradual loss of linguistic knowledge as a result of non-use or aging. Also, linguistic interference and retrieval failure are the major identified causes of first language forgetting, manifested in the difficulty of accessing the target language. This has been identified as a major reason behind the failure of L1 lexical access.

The first three explanations, that is, linguistic repression, linguistic distortion, and language decay, are usually based on evidence obtained through qualitative research, whereas the last two, linguistic interference and retrieval failure, constitute the major focus of experimental psycholinguistic studies on memory in first language forgetting. The L1 lexicon has been found to be the most vulnerable by far in attrition studies (Ammerlaan, 1997; Hulsen, 2000; Isurin, 2000; Kaufman & Aronoff, 1991; Leyen, 1984; Olshtain & Barzilay, 1991). The high level of forgetting in the domain of the lexicon and the relative ease of probing into the mental lexicon using psycholinguistic experimental techniques make this area of L1 forgetting more likely to be investigated than others.

Picture-matching and picture-naming tasks have been used in studies probing into the forgetting of the L1 lexicon (Ammerlaan, 1996; Hulsen, 2000; Isurin, 2000). However, any psycholinguistic study on L1 forgetting becomes an inseparable part of a major field of bilingual memory. In order not to repeat general information on bilingual memory, the reader is referred to Bartolotti and Marian's overview of the major theories, theoretical frameworks and findings in this area (this volume). The next section will examine the existing literature on lexical access and retrieval failure in bilinguals as it is relevant to the findings reported in this chapter.

Findings from psycholinguistic studies on lexical access in bilinguals

Most scholars working on bilingual language processing have come to agree that during lexical access, both languages of the bilingual are activated simultaneously, and it is impossible to keep the non-target language completely deactivated (Costa & Caramazza, 1999; Costa, Ivanova, & Santesteban, 2006; Green, 1998; Hermans *et al.*, 1998). Conversely, when a Russian–English bilingual is presented with a picture of a dog and asked to name it in the L1 (Russian), it is possible that the individual may name it as English "dog" rather than Russian *sobaka* since both language systems are activated. There are a few psycholinguistic techniques routinely used in experimental studies on lexical access, one of which is picture naming. Most commonly, this involves showing pictures on a computer screen (standard black-and-white drawings) and asking participants to name them as quickly as they can. Reaction time, measured in milliseconds, serves as an indicator of lexical access and problems associated with lexical retrieval (routinely known as retrieval failure).

The task may look deceptively simple: all the participant needs to do is name an object that is shown. In reality, the process of naming the picture can be broken down into three processes that happen over the course of a few hundredths of a millisecond (ms). First, the participant needs to match the image of the object with a visual description associated with the object in LTM. Second, semantic information about the object is activated, leading to name retrieval. Only one candidate of the pool of activated lemmas in the semantic network should be retrieved as the correct one. The task becomes even more complex when we deal with bilinguals who need to deactivate their non-target language successfully when performing the naming task. Different outcomes are possible. The picture may not be recognized at all. Or the participant may accidentally retrieve an incorrect name from the same semantic category, which would suggest that the failure happened at the second level of the naming process. Yet another possibility is that the participant produces the word in the non-target language. Also, the word may be retrieved in a grammatically incorrect form, suggesting that the failure occurred at the word-form level that is believed to be the final stage of lexical access. It is not surprising that bilinguals are found to be slower than monolinguals in the picture-naming task due to the need to keep the non-target language deactivated (e.g., Gollan *et al.*, 2005).

Different psycholinguistic models account for the possible outcomes of this seemingly simple production task (for further information see de Bot, 1992, 2001; de Bot & Schreuder, 1993; Levelt, Roelofs, & Meyer, 1999). Here we will look only at those major findings that were reported in studies on bilingual speech production that are relevant to the present research. These came either from studies that employed a picture-naming paradigm or from other controlled psycholinguistic techniques. Moreover, the findings reported here pertain either to bilingual language processing in general or to first language attrition.

Word frequency

The effect of word frequency on naming latency has been explored both in the second language acquisition field (Barry *et al.*, 2001; Dent & Johnston, 2008) and in first language attrition studies (Ammerlaan, 1997; Hakuta & D'Andrea, 1992; Leyen, 1984; Olshtain & Barzilay, 1991; Soesman, 1997). Findings were consistent across studies: low-frequency words are retrieved at a slower rate and tend to be lost much faster in the attrition process. However, Isurin (2000) reported the opposite finding, that is, high frequency words become less accessible in the situation of rapid first language loss. The study was conducted on a Russian orphan removed abruptly from the native language environment and placed in an American English-speaking family. The process of first language forgetting was contrasted with that of second language acquisition. The same pictures were used alternately in the picture-naming task in both languages, Russian (L1) and English (L2). The possibility of semantic overlap as a cause of forgetting was suggested: the forgotten L1 words happened to be those for which the child had acquired translation equivalents in English. The latter finding was tested further and supported in a subsequent experimental study simulating the process of first language forgetting (Isurin & McDonald, 2001). Despite these findings, the majority of studies pinpoint low-frequency rather than high-frequency words as more problematic in lexical access.

Phonological and semantic interference effects

Another question that created much interest in the psycholinguistic research on lexical access concerned a possible interaction of phonological and semantic factors that interfere in the retrieval process of lexical information in bilinguals. This has been studied through the priming paradigm in picture-naming (e.g., Jared & Szucs, 2002) and lexical-decision tasks (e.g., Beauvillain & Grainger, 1987), through the use of a Stroop-like task (e.g., Sutton & Altarriba, 2008), or through the prism of the so-called tip-of-the-tongue phenomenon (TOT, e.g., Gollan *et al.*, 2005).

In contrast to picture-naming tasks, lexical-decision tasks do not target the direct naming of the picture after its presentation. Instead they explore the possible effect of a prime (a word phonologically or semantically related or unrelated to the target word) as well as the distance between the prime and the target word in the order of presentation. The participant is expected to say "yes" or "no" to the target word in regard to its lexicality, for example, whether it's a real word or a non-word. A variation of the Stroop test probing into lexical access phenomena is represented by a picture-word interference task where the participant is presented with a picture and a word that is semantically related or unrelated to the picture. The participant is instructed to ignore the word and just name the picture. TOT studies, on the other hand, manipulate the experimental procedure of induced lexical blocking by providing so-called interlopers that are related either semantically or phonologically to the target word or by using fillers, such as unrelated words.

By far the most consistent evidence was found for semantic interference in lexical access. Presumably, this effect causes a slower retrieval of the target word when accompanied by a semantically related word in a Stroop-like task or when it is primed with a semantically related word in a picture-naming task (Costa & Caramazza, 1999; Ehri & Ryan, 1980; Glaser & Dungelhoff, 1984; Goodman *et al.*, 1985; Hermans *et al.*, 1998; Schriefers, Meyer, & Levelt, 1990).

The evidence on phonological facilitation or inhibition effects has not been as consistent. Knupsky and Amrhein (2007) found robust activation of phonological representations by translation equivalents of word distracters which led to facilitation in naming, especially in the weaker L2. In Marian, Blumenfeld, and Boukrina's (2008) study, asymmetrical patterns of phonological effects were demonstrated for native (Russian) and non-native (English) languages. When performing in English, participants showed shorter response latencies and more accuracy in recognizing a picture that had a phonological overlap with their L1, Russian. The opposite was found for recognition in Russian, where a phonological overlap with English produced longer latencies and decreased accuracy rates in lexical decision.

Lack of strong evidence for any one effect characterizes the TOT studies. There is strong controversy in the literature regarding the possible effect of interloper words used in these studies. However, consistent support was found for phonological effects, both facilitation (Askari, 1991; Meyer & Bock, 1992) and inhibition (Jones, 1987, 1989; Maylor, 1990). Evidence of a strong semantic inhibition effect comes from Brown's (1979) study and the recent study by Gollan and her colleagues (2010).

Conversely, bilinguals' lexical access is likely to be influenced by within- and across-language activation of semantically related words. This may lead to longer latencies in naming the picture as well as general accuracy within the semantic category. The presence of phonological overlap between the two languages in naming an object may inadvertently affect participants' performance in L1.

Socio-linguistic factors in attrition research

Scholars studying L1 attrition use the psycholinguistic tasks described above. For the most comprehensive overview of the research in this field, see publications by Ecke (2004), Kopke and Schmid (2004), Schmid (2004, 2011). In addition to retrieval problems associated with word frequency and L2 interference, there are a number of socio-linguistic factors identified in the attrition literature. Several of these will be reviewed below.

Age Age of language acquisition mostly concerns second language acquisition (SLA) studies. As far as attrition is concerned, the studies break down into those that investigate L1 loss in adults (e.g., Schmid, 2002; Isurin, 2007) and those that specifically look at children (e.g., Isurin, 2000; Kaufman & Aronoff, 1991). Studies reporting on adult populations greatly outnumber those that deal with children (for more information, see Kopke & Schmid, 2004). The results indicate that L1 linguistic knowledge can indeed be significantly lost if attrition sets in well before puberty. In studies on adults, the age factor is usually studied with regard to the time when the person acquired the second language, which is often approximated as the age when the person migrated to the L2 country. The other reference point would be the age of onset of attrition, which is often hard to identify reliably. A different way to look at age and its possible effect on naming latency is through the age–word-frequency correlate. Dent and Johnston (2008) examined the possibility of combining the two factors in order to arrive at more comprehensive theories of picture naming. Their reasoning was that word frequency should not be treated as a more or less stable value that is equal for all speakers of the language. Rather, they suggest that the more years of exposure to the word a person had, the more stable its frequency effect should be.

Education Level of education is an important measure in attrition studies. Previous studies reported a difference in linguistic behavior depending on the person's educational background. In other words, there was a positive correlation between the level of education and the performance level among speakers, both monolinguals and bilinguals (Jaspaert & Kroon, 1989; Waas, 1996).

Amount of contact with L1 It may be reasonable to expect that lack of contact with L1 can lead to greater L1 loss. As Kopke and Schmid (2004) suggested, there is no direct way to measure that contact, such as the precise amount of daily exposure to and communication in the native language, or to find an ultimate socio-linguistic or psychological reason why a person has limited exposure to the native language, which may be due to the lack of a network in the area where the individual resides or to an attitude toward the community. Methodological issues involved in this parameter might also confound the data, since this information is usually based on self-reports on a questionnaire, and it is not clear to what extent this reflects reality rather than a self-image the person wants to create.

Length of residency in the L2 environment Number of years spent in the host country is a controversial factor and has not received any consensus in the literature. It may appear logical to expect that a person would lose L1 linguistic skills with a more prolonged stay in the L2 environment. However, as Kopke and Schmid (2004) point out, the majority of studies did not find a reliable effect of time on the attrition process, and some suggested that the time factor only plays a role when there is little or no contact with the native language. To summarize, compared with linguistic factors such as word frequency and semantic or phonological similarity, extra-linguistic factors are not as interpretable or reliable. Yet most researchers conducting their studies in the field of first language attrition do attempt to analyze the data against some of these socio-linguistic factors.

Point of reference: do we need a control group?

Finally, there has been debate about the validity of using a control group of monolinguals. Starting with Jaspaert, Kroon, and van Hout (1986) the question of studying monolinguals as a reference point in research on bilingualism has been raised on numerous occasions. The definition of a monolingual in a world where bilingualism becomes a persistent rule rather than an exception gets fuzzy. The psycholinguistic research does provide evidence for monolinguals being faster than bilinguals in lexical access (see Ivanova & Costa, 2008, for further references) but what does this tell us in terms of the attrition process? As Dewaele (2004) argues, the comparison should be made between bilingual attriters and bilingual non-attriters. We need to acknowledge the dynamics of the ever-changing linguistic environments where bilinguals and monolinguals reside. The comparison of attriters with monolingual controls may not contribute much to our understanding of L1 attrition. The native language of bilinguals, as well as the language of their monolingual counterparts, is changing constantly. The effect of borrowings and changes in the frequency of words in the language spoken today in the L1 country may not be the same as the language spoken by bilinguals prior to their immigration. Thus, controlled psycholinguistic studies on attrition do not necessarily benefit from having a control group as a reference point.

The present study

The current study looked at the process of L1 attrition in three groups of Russian bilinguals who resided in different countries and were exposed to three different second language environments, that is, English, German, and Hebrew. The picture-naming task with word frequency as the main variable was used in the study.

The research questions in this study partly were in line with the previous picture-naming studies probing first language attrition (Ammerlaan, 1997; Hakuta & D'Andrea, 1992; Isurin, 2000; Leyen, 1984; Olshtain & Barzilay, 1991; Soesman, 1997) and partly emerged from the specificity of the participating groups. First, it was hypothesized that low-frequency words would be retrieved at longer latencies than high-frequency words. Second, the length of residence in the host country was hypothesized to be a factor affecting lexical retrieval, that is, a longer time of immigration may result in longer latencies. However, a closer look should be taken at the amount of daily exposure to L1 when this factor is examined. As the review of prior studies showed (see e.g., Kopke & Schmid, 2004), these two factors are not necessarily reliable predictors of attrition when taken in isolation from other factors. Third, the specificity of the participating groups allowed us to look deeper into what would be viewed as "inaccurate" naming of the item. Since all participants shared the same native language in which they performed the task but had three different second language backgrounds, any trends within a group not observed in the other two might indicate a hidden effect of L2. This effect might be of a semantic or phonological nature. Thus, special attention was given to analyzing "inaccurate" recalls registered in the data.

In addition to the above research questions, this study aimed at combining quantitative and qualitative analyses in examining the data gathered through a picture-naming paradigm. Prior studies employing this technique were primarily quantitative ones where inaccurate responses were discarded and, mostly, reaction-time data were analyzed. This study attempted to show how the combination of the two approaches can allow us to look deeper into bilingual lexical access. Inaccurate or wrong responses can shed light on the architecture of a bilingual's mental lexicon. The participants in this study come from three different bilingual sets where the native language – the language in which they performed the task – remained the same. Analyzing inaccurate responses between the groups may reveal effects of the second languages affecting lexical access in the native language.

Method

Participants The participants in this study were Russian–English bilinguals (n = 50), Russian–Hebrew bilinguals (n = 52), and Russian–German bilinguals (n = 52), who will be referred to as American, Israeli, and German participants, respectively. All participants emigrated as adults and resided in their host countries at the time of the study. The study took place in three respective countries, the USA, Israel, and Germany. Table 12.1 summarizes the socio-linguistic data of the three groups.

The majority of the participants were college educated, with 4 percent, 2 percent, and 2 percent (for the USA, Israel, and Germany, respectively) having only high school diplomas.

Table 12.1 *Socio-linguistic background of the participants*

Group	Age	Residence	Daily contact with Russian (self-report, %)				
				Less than			More
	(mean)	(mean)	0%	10%	20–30%	50–80%	than 80%
American	53.1	15.0	0	58.0	36.0	0	6.0
Israeli	51.3	16.4	0	7.7	36.5	30.8	25.0
German	49.3	12.8	5.8	7.7	15.4	34.6	36.5

Materials and design The pictures were selected from a standardized set of 520 pictures used in the International Picture Naming Project (IPNP) and available for download at http://crl.ucsd.edu/~aszekely/ipnp/1stimuli.html (last accessed January 15, 2008). They included 175 pictures suggested for use by Snodgrass and Vanderwart (1980); the rest were complementary materials used in studies by Szekely *et al.* (2003, 2004, 2005). A pool of 130 standard black-and-white drawings representing concrete objects was used in the present study. The words were controlled for frequency and were split evenly between 65 low-frequency words (frequency below 10) and 65 high-frequency words (frequency above 50). The mean frequency for high-frequency (HF) words was 208; the mean frequency for low-frequency (LF) words was 4.4. The information on word frequency was obtained from a Russian dictionary on frequency (Zasorina, 1977). However, word frequency is not a stable phenomenon and it could be different if a more recent dictionary were used. We opted for this particular publication since the participants in this study lived in Russia in the late 1970s and immigrated in the late 1980s or early 1990s, so more recent publications would not reflect the linguistic environment to which they were exposed. The pictures were randomized into SuperLab stimuli lists, and the information on the actual name of the object and word frequency was hidden from the participants' view. The presentation was piloted on ten Russian–English bilinguals in order to test the clarity of the images and possible ambiguity of naming. A few pictures were replaced after the pilot test. The participants of the pilot study were excluded from the experiment.

The experiment followed a 2 (word frequency: HF vs. LF) × 3 (language group: English, German, Hebrew) factorial design, with word frequency as a within-group variable and the foreign language background of the participants as a between-group variable. The dependent variables were latency and accuracy of response.

Procedure The SuperLab software generated picture presentations on a standard laptop. The order of item presentation remained the same within and between groups. Each participant was tested individually by the researcher. First, the participant was asked to read the instructions on the screen. The language of instruction as well as the language of interaction with the researcher remained Russian. After the participant became familiar with the task, a practice trial was introduced. Then the experiment was run. The participant was encouraged to do one of three things: to name the picture, to say that the name cannot be recalled, or to indicate a problem with understanding the picture. After a picture was shown on the screen, the participant was supposed to name it in Russian and simultaneously press a computer key. Reaction time (RT) was measured as the time from the onset of picture presentation to the time when a key was pressed, derived from the experimental software's output. The participant was strongly discouraged from doing any self-correction. If they did self-correct, the data for that picture were discarded. If self-correction of the previous naming happened when the next picture was being presented, the data for that picture were discarded as well. The researcher observed the performance closely and took all necessary notes concerning any naming deviations, which included inaccurate or wrong answers, the participant's inability to recall the word, naming in the non-target language, or the picture's ambiguity. Such answers were later coded and the RT data on those were excluded from the quantitative analysis.

Coding and analysis All inaccurate responses were coded in the following way. If the participant admitted that the item could not be recalled, it was coded as unrecalled (UR). If the participant showed retrieval problems within the same category it was coded as a within-category confusion (WC) and notes were taken on the word(s) incorrectly retrieved. The latter also included cases where the participant eventually arrived at the correct response after a few failed attempts, for example, a picture of a grasshopper would be named by a sequence of names where only the last one was correct, such as, "insect, fly, grasshopper." The next category included those items that were retrieved in the non-target language (WR, standing for "wrong language"). Another category of inaccurate responses were the words that were retrieved as an alternative name for the picture, for example, "automobile" for "car." Since those words might have a different frequency that might confound the results they were coded as a separate category of alternative names (AN).

There was a group of wrong responses that did not fit into any of the above categories and they were simply coded as wrong answers (W). All these responses were excluded from the quantitative analysis. The next step in the analysis was to remove possible outliers. Latencies shorter than 350 ms and longer than two standard deviations (*SD*) from the mean were removed from the analysis. The exclusion of outliers, inaccurate responses, and the data discarded due to technical problems resulted in a total exclusion of 12.89 percent of the overall data set. A number of analysis of variance (ANOVA) measures, followed by a Tukey HSD test (where appropriate) and an additional set of *t*-tests were used to formally analyze the RT data. A Bonferroni correction was applied in cases of multiple comparisons. The coded inaccurate responses were also analyzed qualitatively and will be discussed in a separate section.

Results: findings from quantitative analyses

Frequency effect The RT results were submitted to an ANOVA with frequency (HF vs. LF) as a within-subjects variable and group (i.e. American, Israeli, and German) as a between-subjects variable. Although the overall interaction was not reliable ($p > 0.05$), this analysis revealed both a significant main effect of group [$F(1, 151) = 457.67$, $p < 0.001$] and a main effect of frequency [$F(2,151) = 457.67$, $p < 0.001$]. As expected, responses were significantly faster for HF than for LF words [$F(2, 256) = 148.56$, $p < 0.001$]. That is, within each participant group, there was a significant difference in mean reaction time for HF vs. LF words [$M = 1290$ vs. 1523; $M = 1281$ vs. 1475; and $M = 1437$ vs. 1655 for the American, Israeli, and German groups, respectively]. Additionally, there were longer RT latencies for the German group when compared with the Israeli group [*MD* (Mean Difference) $= 168.28$, $p < 0.001$], and with the American group [*MD* $= 143.56$, $p < 0.05$]. There was no significant difference between the American and Israeli groups [*MD* $= 24.72$, $p > 0.05$]. The results are illustrated in Figure 12.1.

Age effect The unexpected findings from the German group encouraged us to run an additional set of tests on an age factor. The mean age for this group was comparable with the other two groups, $M = 49$ (see Table 12.1) but there were more elderly participants in that group, which could have created a between-groups effect. The results of Bivariate Pearson Correlation analyses proved only marginally reliable for LF words [$M = 1649$, SD 392, $r = 0.25$, $p < .12$], suggesting that

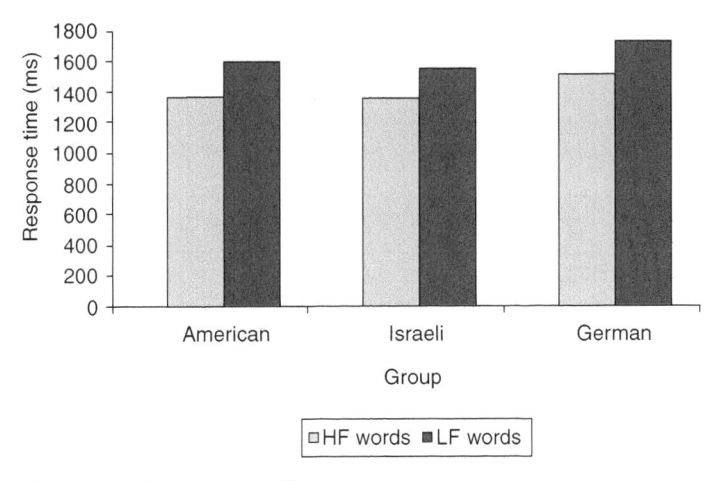

Figure 12.1 Frequency effect

the older German participants tended to recall LF words with longer latencies than younger participants. No significant effect was found for the other two groups. Two separate t-tests were run as a follow-up to the above analyses. There was a significant effect of frequency [$t(128) = 5.74, p < 0.001$].

Length of immigration effect   The results of Bivariate Pearson Correlation analyses indicated a positive relationship between RT and length of immigration for HF words in the American group [$M = 1284$, SD 201, $r = 0.36, p < 0.05$] but proved only marginally reliable for LF words [$M = 1512$, SD 261, $r = 0.29, p < 0.12$]. This indicates that the American participants with a shorter residency in the country named HF words faster than those who had spent a much longer time in the L2 country. No significant effects were found for the other two groups of participants. The results on LF words for the Israeli group proved only marginally reliable [$M = 1473$, SD 311, $r = 0.24, p < 0.12$].

Contact with L1   The amount of daily exposure to L1 (see Figure 12.2) was tested against naming latencies for each group. It should be acknowledged that there were certain limitations to these tests due to the grouping of participants according to their L1 contact level. The amount of daily contact with L1 was not equal across the groups. For example, if participants were grouped together in two groups, that is, those who had less than 30 percent of daily exposure to Russian and those who had more than 50 percent contact, then the

332   Isurin

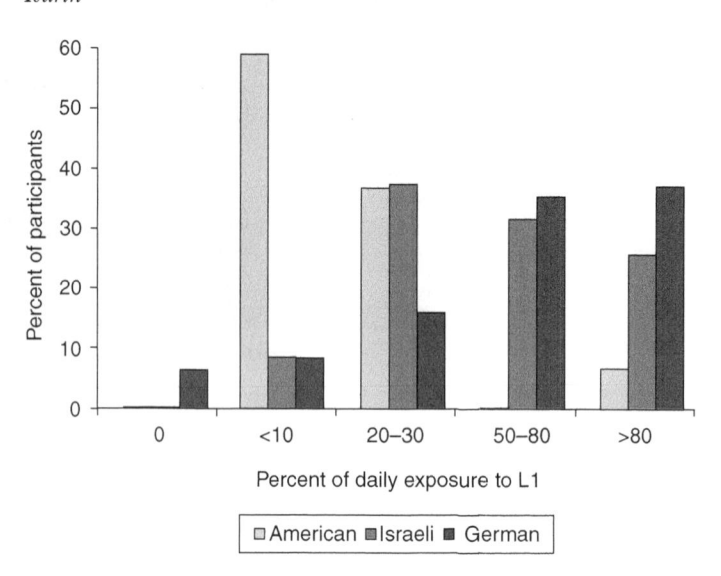

Figure 12.2 Contact with L1

two groups would show the following pattern: 94% vs. 6% (American), 44.2% vs. 55.8% (Israeli), and 28.9% vs. 71.1% (German). In order to create sizable groups for comparison in the above analysis, the participants were grouped slightly differently across the three groups and this might have confounded the results. For example, in the American group, the participants with 10% and below (n = 29) and 30% and above (n = 21) of L1 contact formed two groups. The Israeli participants were collapsed into the following two groups: those with 30% and below (n = 23) and 50% and above (n = 29); the analysis of the German group was based on those participants who were exposed to 30% and below (n = 15), 50–80% (n = 18), and 80% and above (n = 19).

Three separate ANOVA with the amount of contact as a between-subjects variable and word frequency as a within-subjects variable were run. The frequency effect proved reliable for the American group [$F(1, 48) = 0.228.72$, $p < 0.001$] and there was no effect of contact [$M = 221.95$ vs. $M = 235.83$]. The interaction between frequency and contact proved unreliable as well [$F(1, 48) = 0.21$, $p > 0.05$], showing no effect of the amount of daily exposure to Russian on word retrieval. A similar result was found for the Israeli group [$F(1, 50) = 157.14$, $p < 0.001$ for the frequency effect, $M = 191.9$ vs. $M = 206.38$ for L1 contact, and $F(1, 50) = 0.20$, $p > 0.05$ for the interaction]. However, the analysis of the German group found a significant effect for the

Table 12.2 *Semantic interference*

Group/responses	Total (% of all responses)	HF words (%)	LF words (%)
American	3.5	36	64
Israeli	4.8	45	55
German	5.5	34	66

interaction of the two variables [$F(2, 49) = 3.82$, $p < 0.05$] in addition to a main effect of frequency [$F(1, 49) = 121.71$, $p < 0.001$]. The interaction appears to be due to a smaller frequency effect in the group with 20–30% of daily exposure to L1 [$MD = 145.44$] compared with those participants who had less than 10% [$MD = 279.45$] or more than 50% [$MD = 232.31$] of daily contact with L1.

Results: findings from qualitative analyses

Retrieval failure that may not directly indicate L1 attrition The next step in the analysis was to look at the inaccurate responses that had been removed from the formal statistical analyses. These included unrecalled items, responses in the non-target language, responses that demonstrated semantic or word-form confusion, and responses that suggested a possible effect of corresponding second languages. First, we will look at those responses that may not necessarily indicate language attrition. Rather, they may be typical of lexical access in general and will shed light on retrieval problems in picture naming. Then we will examine those deviations that could suggest L1 attrition.

Semantic interference. One of the largest categories among inaccurate responses was words that were retrieved within the same semantic category. As in cases of unrecalled items and items retrieved in the non-target language, the majority of incorrect responses fell into the category of LF words. However, the percentage of HF words affected by semantic interference is much higher than for the other categories of inaccurate responses (Table 12.2).

Examples of such responses would be naming a bowl as "plate," "spoon," or "vase," or naming an ostrich as "duck," "penguin," or "turkey." Often, participants would offer a few incorrect names before arriving at the target one; for example, when naming an ant an Israeli participant would say "fly, bug, ant." This indicates a process of searching for the right label in the network of activated concepts. In some cases, the participant would name the picture by its general category, such as "dish" for "pan" or "insect" for "grasshopper." The most confused items were the names of animals, birds, and insects. For example, the LF word "grasshopper" was retrieved inaccurately as a name from the same semantic category by 25 percent of Israeli, 19 percent of German, and 14 percent of American participants. Another interesting observation concerns the inaccurate naming of drawer, which was named "shelf" by 17 percent of the Israeli and 5 percent of the German participants.

Retrieval failure at the word-form level. Russian belongs to the category of synthetic languages where word formation relies heavily on derivational and inflectional morphemes. Analyzing inaccurate responses across three sets of data revealed instances of morphological errors that led to wrong responses. For example, a picture of a swing (*kach-el*, feminine with an ending that is more dominant in masculine nouns) was retrieved as a word having the target root with the wrong suffix (*kach-alka*, feminine with a more standard feminine ending –*a*). Also, a few participants in each group incorrectly named a watering can (*lei-ka*, feminine, in Russian) as *po-liv-alka* (feminine) or *po-liv-alnik* (masculine). There was a problem with naming a paperclip and a clothespin in all three groups. The names (*s-crepka* and *pri-zhepka* in Russian) were retrieved with wrong prefixes such as *za-krepka* or *za-zhepka*. Another repeated error was with the word "light switch" (*vy-kluchatel* in Russian) which was retrieved as *pere-kluchatel* (a more technical term used in electrical engineering for a switch used for a different purpose).

Retrieval failure that indicates L1 forgetting The above examples show retrieval failures both at the semantic and morphological levels. This section will look at those specific instances of retrieval failure that could pertain to L1 attrition.

Unrecalled items. Failure to recall the word is a direct indicator of forgetting. However, the participants in this study showed much ambition in trying to name as many items as possible, even at the expense of accuracy in their responses. The percentage of unrecalled items was relatively low for each group and most of the retrieval failures came from the category of LF words (Table 12.3). Also, all three groups showed overlapping problems with remembering particular words, such as blimp, slingshot, lawnmower, Band-Aid, ghost, peacock, dustpan. However, there was no consistency between the groups in failing to recall the same HF words.

Memory and first language forgetting 335

Table 12.3 *Unrecalled items*

Group/responses	Total (% of all responses)	HF words (%)	LF words (%)
American	0.6	11	89
Israeli	0.8	8	91
German	1.0	14	86

Table 12.4 *Recall in non-target language*

Group/responses	Total (% of all responses)	HF words (%)	LF words (%)
American	0.6	19	81
Israeli	0.3	13	87
German	0.2	20	80

Recall in non-target language. Another indication of L1 attrition can be found in responses produced in the non-target language. This may suggest a higher level of activation of a particular lexical label in the second language. Surprisingly, the same category of LF words became more susceptible to L2 interference. As Table 12.4 demonstrates, the overwhelming majority of responses in L2 came from the category of LF words in all three groups.

Two words are of interest here. The picture of a sandwich was named as English "sandwich" by 21 percent of Israeli and 14 percent of American participants. The correct name in Russian would be *buterbrod*, which is a well-established borrowing from German. The English borrowing "sandwich" is used widely in contemporary Hebrew. No participant in the German group named it as "sandwich." Moreover, a few participants in the American group later argued that the presented picture showed a "sandwich" rather than a *buterbrod* since the Russian *buterbrod* has a single slice of bread.

Another word that was retrieved in English by 12 percent of the American group was Band-Aid. The word "ostrich" is *straus* in Russian and *shtraus* in German. Two German participants named the picture in German and another two failed to remember it in Russian. The other two groups did not register cases of naming this object in L2. These findings suggest that word frequency does not necessarily overlap in

L1 and L2, and the failure to suppress L2 during the naming task may be caused by different factors, such as a cognate effect (in the case of German *shtraus*) or conceptual non-equivalence (as in Russian *buterbrod*).

Lexical innovations. In some instances, the participant would struggle to recall the word and would offer a label that was either an incorrect name retaining the semantics of the target word or a made-up word. For example, the Russian word for the LF word "thimble" is *naperstok*, literally meaning an object that is put on a finger. The Russian word for finger is *paletz* but the word *naperstok* retains the Old Russian name for a finger, *perst*. Thus, the participant retrieves the word as *napalechnik*, which has the correct prefix but wrong root and makes the word still recognizable in Russian but renders it grammatically incorrect. Another odd name would be *letuchij zmei* ("flying snake") for "kite." The correct word would be *vozdushnyi zmei* ("air snake"). Note that in Russian, "snake" can be used in the feminine (*zmeja*) for a reptile or in the masculine as *zmei* for a kite as well as a name of a folk and biblical character. A participant in the German group used the wrong gender in naming a kite, which resulted in the odd name *zmeja*, which would be unacceptable in Russian.

Another example of a lexical innovation was the word *musorosbornik* ("trash collector") for a dustpan (*sovok*) that posed problems for some participants in all three groups. All the above concepts were very familiar to all participants from their time in Russia. However, there was a concept that may be less familiar to participants between the groups. There is no doubt that the concept of a lawnmower (*gazonokosilka* in Russian) is well known to the American participants, at least those who live in residential areas. It was therefore not surprising that among American participants, 4 percent named it in L2, 2 percent failed to recall it, and only 8 percent struggled with the right word. In the Israeli group, 2 percent could not recall it and 27 percent offered incorrect names. The corresponding numbers for the German group were 6 and 19 percent. The range of innovative terms for a lawnmower ranged from *senokosilka* ("haymower") to *pribor/machinka/apparat dlja podstrizhki travy* ("device/ machine/apparatus for cutting the grass"). As mentioned above, the word Band-Aid (*plastyr* or *leikoplastyr*) posed a recurring problem for participants. When retrieved, it often had the incorrect form of *nakleika*, *zakleika*, or *prilipuchka*, that is, made up words describing the function of the object (of being stuck to something). The above examples illustrate the way bilinguals deal with naming objects that are very familiar in their new reality but probably forgotten in their native language.

Evidence of a hidden L2 effect The linguistic background of the participants in this study allows us to take a closer look at those deviations in naming that may pertain to the effect of the second language. The task was performed in Russian while participants had knowledge of English, German, or Hebrew as their second language. In other words, if we look at deviant responses in Russian that are grammatically and semantically correct and find more in one group than in another or present only in one group, the answer may lie in the hidden effect of the second language of the participant.

When analyzing inaccurate responses, a category of so-called "alternative names" was created. As in any other language, Russian can have more than one name for the same concept. For example, horse can be named *loshad'* (a more general term) or *kon'* (male horse), and the latter would not point immediately to the gender difference. Since word frequency was an independent variable in the task, only one name, a more general one, was expected. Alternative names do not necessarily have the same frequency, and even if they were perfectly correct responses, they were discarded from the RT data. In this section, we will look at a few categories of responses that suggest an L2 interference effect.

Cognate effect: alternative names. The category of alternative names included those concepts that could be named correctly by more than one label but showed a consistent pattern of one name or another. The preferred alternative happened to be a cognate of the L2 translation equivalent. For example, like in English, a car can be named *machina* (car) or *avtomobil* (automobile) in Russian. Among the participants, 25 percent of German, 8 percent of Israeli, and 6 percent of the American responses were *avtomobil* (automobile). While English has a few possible names for a car, the more common and neutral term would be "car." In Hebrew, it would be *mehonit* and there is no cognate of "automobile" among other alternative names. However, the English borrowing "auto" is used in everyday Hebrew. German, on the other hand, has *auto* as the most common name for a car. If we see a much higher rate of naming a car as *avtomobile* by German participants we may suggest an obvious effect of L2.

Another interesting example would be the word "helmet." In Russian, it can be named as *shlem* and *kaska*. The latter normally would refer to a military helmet or a hard hat worn by a construction worker. The Hebrew name is *kasda* and does not differentiate lexically between the two types of helmets. The German translation equivalent of helmet is *kappe* or *helm*. In other words, only Hebrew has a name that is a cognate of one of the Russian labels. Thus, it is not surprising that 19 percent of Israeli participants opted to name helmet as *kaska* while only

4 percent of Americans and 6 percent of Germans chose this alternative name.

Another word in this category is "whip," which can be called *hlyst* or *plet'*. The latter was chosen by 24 percent of German participants but only 3 percent of Israeli participants, and there were no such responses in the American group. The German equivalent of "whip" is *peitsche*, which strictly cannot be called a cognate of Russian *plet'*, but we can argue that the onset consonant overlaps and all but one sound from the Russian name are present in its German equivalent. The concept of "church" (*tzerkov* in Russian) was retrieved as *kirha* (name of a Lutheran church) by 6 percent of German participants. No such responses were registered in the other two groups. The corresponding names in German and Hebrew would be *kirche* and *knisa*, respectively. Again, this indicates a possible effect of a German cognate on accessing the correct name in Russian. Clearly, the above examples show the hidden effect of L2 in the retrieval of the L1 word.

Lexically convergent and divergent pairs. The next category includes those concepts that are not lexically differentiated in one language, for example, "car" as a vehicle and "car" as a constituent of a train, but are differentiated in another (lexically convergent pairs), and the other way around, for example, "watch" and "clock" in English (lexically divergent pairs). There were a few instances of wrong naming that may be of interest here.

In Russian, a church bell and doorbell would have two different names, that is, *kolokol* and *zvonok*, respectively. A picture of a bell was named incorrectly as *zvonok* by 12 percent of Israeli and 2 percent of German participants. In Hebrew, both concepts have the same name, *tzeltul*. The American data did not register such a mistake regardless of a similar situation with lexically convergent pairs. However, while not being lexically distinguished, the English "bell" is more likely to be used with a modifier, "door" or "church," to specify the concept. Two percent of the American participants named a frying pan as a *kastrulja* (Russian for "pan") instead of the correct *skovorada*. These concepts are lexically differentiated in Russian. There were no similar mistakes in the other two groups.

If the above examples illustrate cases of lexically divergent pairs in Russian, the following findings concern the opposite phenomenon – a lexically convergent pair. The HF name for a drawer (*jazchik* in Russian) was not recalled by 6 percent of the German, 4 percent of the Israeli, and 2 percent of the American participants. Moreover, it was named *polka* (shelf) by 17 percent of the Israeli and 5 percent of the German participants. No such responses were registered in the

American data. Neither German nor Hebrew dictionaries helped shed light on this finding. However, the reason for the confusion may lie in the same phenomena as discussed above. The name for a drawer in Russian is *jazchik* ("box"), which also refers to a regular box. In order to differentiate the two, a modifier is usually used, for example, *jazchik shkafa* (a closet drawer). The same would apply to the word "table," which would refer to a dining table and a desk. Thus, in Russian, a desk would be specified by the use of a modifier (e.g., *pismennyi stol*, "table for writing"). Since in all three languages, English, German, and Hebrew, the concept of a drawer is lexicalized by a word that does not have an additional meaning of a box there is a possibility that participants had a problem retrieving it or recalled it incorrectly as "shelf" in their attempt to arrive at the correct name. However, there were no incorrect responses like "shelf" in the American group, which makes this suggestion rather speculative.

Semantic transfer. The category of semantic transfer includes those naming instances where the target word was incorrectly named in one language due to a possible extension of meaning in another. For example, a picture of a bow (*bant* in Russian) was named wrongly as *galstuk* (tie) in all three groups. The Russian equivalent of "bow-tie" would be *babochka* (homophone of "butterfly"). Another instance would be the incorrect naming of a tape (audiocassette) as *lenta* (tape in Russian, which never refers to an audiotape), or naming a syringe as *igla* (needle) instead of the Russian word *shpritz* by participants in the American group. The above examples do not show trends specific to any group; neither were there many instances of such incorrect responses. However, these observations are reported here to show how the data of inaccurate responses can be examined for evidence of first language change.

Qualitatively driven reanalysis of the RT data After the above qualitative analysis was complete, it was decided to exclude the above items that show evidence of an L2 effect from the RT data and see whether their removal would change the original findings. If these items indeed pose a difficulty for participants due to the hidden effect of their second languages, the RT on correct responses in their naming also could indicate retrieval problems. There were two ways to do this analysis. First, we could compare a group of those items with a random group of items of equal size. Second, we could exclude those items and run the analyses again. The first choice has its own limitations. It is extremely difficult to choose a random set of control items that would not have their own problems within or between groups. In addition, both sets should be controlled for frequency. Thus, we opted for the second alternative while being fully aware of its limitations.

An ANOVA with frequency (HF vs. LF) as the within-subjects variable and group as the between-subjects variable (i.e., American, Israeli, and German) was run. As in the original tests, word frequency produced a significant effect [$F(2, 226) = 142.73$, $p < 0.001$], showing that the removal of the above problematic items from the analysis did not change the general pattern of word retrieval; that is, HF words were recalled significantly faster than LF words across all three groups [$M = 1291$ vs. $M = 1528$ for the American group; $M = 1270$ vs. $M = 1484$ for the Israeli group, and $M = 1439$ vs. $M = 1651$ for Germans].

Discussion

The present study was aimed at providing additional evidence of first language attrition in bilinguals through the use of a picture-naming paradigm. The methodology of this study differed from others in which the same psycholinguistic technique was used. It combined two different sets of analyses, quantitative and qualitative. This approach allowed us to get a closer look at findings that might have escaped notice had only a statistical approach been used. Instead of discarding the incorrect and deviant responses – as is done in many of the psycholinguistic studies on lexical access – we examined them in order to gain insight into the effects of the second language on the forgetting of the first language.

In line with previous studies on lexical access in L1 attriters (see e.g., (Ammerlaan, 1997; Hakuta & D'Andrea, 1992; Soesman, 1997), word frequency proved to be a factor in picture naming. Low-frequency words showed a consistent effect, both within subjects and between groups. Conversely, low-frequency words were retrieved at a much slower rate than high-frequency words. Word frequency effects are not unique to bilinguals' performance. Prior studies reported such effects for monolinguals, as well (Huttenlocher & Kubicek, 1983; Schilling, Rayner, & Chumbley, 1998). What we attempted to see here was an indication of an interaction of frequency with other socio-linguistic factors, such as the length of residency in the foreign country or amount of contact that the participant retained with the native language. As mentioned earlier, these socio-linguistic factors are not always reliable measures in L1 attrition research and their validity has been questioned (Kopke & Schmid, 2004).

Thus, with those reservations in mind, we ran separate tests to examine the possible influence of socio-linguistic variables. The length of immigration showed a significant effect only for one group, Russian–English bilinguals. Furthermore, the effect was found only for HF words. This suggests that with prolonged stay in the L2 environment, access problems may affect HF words while LF words, which already pose more retrieval problems, remain unaffected. The amount of contact with L1 did not reach significance for any of the three groups but showed an interaction with frequency for the German group. Here we need to acknowledge certain limitations of this set of analyses. The American group had a much higher number of people with daily L1 contact of less than 10 percent (58% as compared with 7.7% for the other two groups). The obvious dominance of participants with limited exposure to L1 could suggest that contact might be a serious factor in their performance. However, since this information was gathered through a questionnaire and the amount of contact did not present a continuous variable, it was difficult to group participants along those lines. For example, nobody in the American group fell into the category of people having 50–80 percent of exposure and only 6 percent reported more than 80 percent (see Table 12.1). As a result, participants were grouped as follows: those with less than 10 percent and those who had 20–30 cent daily exposure to Russian. Clearly, there is no big difference between 10 percent and 20 percent when we are relying on self-reports. This may have confounded the results and did not show any significant effect of contact on overall performance.

A puzzling finding concerned the German group, which showed a significantly slower performance compared with the other two groups. Despite the relatively similar mean age for all three groups, there were more elderly people in the German group compared with the other two, for example, 11 percent of 70–75-year-olds compared with 4 percent and 6 percent for the American and Israeli groups. This led us to look at a possible effect of age. This variable did not reach significance, but a follow-up t-test revealed significant between-subject differences in the German group.

The quantitative analyses reported so far have given us a more general picture of lexical retrieval of HF vs. LF items in bilinguals' first language and the possible effect of a socio-linguistic factor of immigration on lexical access. However, the difference between this study and the majority of other psycholinguistic studies based on a picture-naming paradigm was in our attempt to utilize a qualitative analysis to investigate an area that may be restricted in any robust quantitative analysis. It concerned those items that were excluded from the quantitative analyses, namely, inaccurate responses. A closer look at those items, which granted were a relatively small percentage of the overall set of data, brings up a few points of interest.

The reported instances of semantic interference showed that the participants struggled to retrieve the right word from the pool of candidates in the activated semantic network. Keeping in mind the models of lexical access widely agreed upon by the majority of scholars (see the chapters by Bartolotti & Marian and Dijkstra, Haga, Bijsterveld, & Sprinkhuizen-Kuyper in this volume), we might suggest that a retrieval problem happened at the level of accessing lemmas. However, naming instances that produced a word in the incorrect grammatical form shows a retrieval problem at the word level. In this study, different examples of retrieval problems that happened at those two levels were discussed. They illustrated retrieval problems that are not necessarily specific to bilinguals.

The next step was to trace those responses that would allow us to shed light on the process of first language change under the influence of the second. The first category that we looked at was a group of items that were not recalled and can be viewed as forgotten. It was not surprising to find LF words were the majority of words in that category. Participants presumably had much less exposure to this lexicon before they immigrated and may have had even less exposure to those names in L1, in their host countries.

However, the results of the study also indicated that the majority of items recalled in the non-target language came from the same LF category. This may suggest two things. First, word frequency does not necessarily overlap across languages. For example, the word *dusha* (soul) is a HF word in Russian while it is a LF word in English (Wierzbicka, 1992). Thus the word could become more frequent in L2 and this may lead to the loss of its original label in L1. Second, the study did not test the participants' knowledge of the vocabulary items used in the task in their corresponding second languages. We can only hypothesize that the participants learned the L2 equivalent for the word that they were not exposed to very much in the native environment (e.g., a lawnmower). This calls for further studies where lexical access of translation equivalents would be tested within the framework of first language attrition.

Other evidence of attrition was revealed through the category of so-called "lexical innovations" where the participant produced words that carried the semantic information of the target word but failed to produce the correct form. The difference between this group and the group of deviations registered at the word level is that the retrieval failure not only affected derivational morphemes but also content morphemes and grammatical information, such as gender, presumably encoded in the lemma. The above examples of retrieval problems in bilinguals could provide evidence of L1 attrition.

However, we have mostly discussed inaccurate responses that were not characteristic of any group in particular and could be viewed as general problems experienced by bilinguals performing picture-naming or showing signs of attrition. The next step in the analysis was to look for any trends and indications that would pinpoint the effect of the second language. In other words, if one group showed a pattern of incorrect responses on a particular item and the other two did not, we may deduce that the effect comes from the bilingual's second language. All three groups of participants were bilingual in different languages, English, Hebrew, and German, while performing the task in their L1. Here, a few interesting trends were identified. First, a cognate effect revealed itself in the participants' preference for naming the item by its alternative name if that name happened to be a cognate of the translation equivalent in their L2. For example, German participants consistently retrieved the word "car" as "automobile" and Israeli participants named "helmet" by a less frequent alternative label.

Second, L2 interference was registered in cases of naming the object by a wrong label that would indicate lexical transfer from concepts that are lexically differentiated in L2 and not differentiated in L1 and vice versa. The prior finding from Isurin's (2000) study on L1 attrition indicated that lexically convergent concepts are vulnerable to forgetting. An example from the present study was the word "bell," which is not differentiated in English or Hebrew (church bell or doorbell) while it is lexically differentiated in Russian where a different word stands for each concept.

Finally, words suggesting semantic transfer from L2 were offered as additional evidence of the L2 effect; for example, naming an audiotape as "tape" is unacceptable in Russian and conveys a different meaning. All these examples lead us to suggest that during lexical access, both of a bilingual's languages stay activated and the non-target language may interfere with lexical retrieval in another language. From the perspective of attrition, the results of this study provide evidence of first language change under the influence of the second language.

Implications

Clearly, research on first language attrition within a psycholinguistic framework offers an additional perspective on memory in bilingual speakers. Often, the psycholinguistic studies on bilingual lexical access and bilingual memory in general are conducted in laboratory settings where robust methodological approaches and standard participant pools are used (e.g., undergraduate students who get psychology course credits for participation in the study). While this type of study is highly controlled and may be considered the most reliable in the field of experimental psychology, it is often removed from a real-life setting. Forgetting of the native language is a complex and very gradual process that does not happen overnight. Also, a group of individuals experiencing L1 attrition is usually not as uniform as the regular pool of participants in memory studies. In addition, collecting the attrition data during field work rather than in a laboratory setting brings in complications and may render it less reliable than the data gathered during lab testing. The differences between the two types of research practice call for integration of the accumulated knowledge in both parts of the field and the embracing of both types of analysis, that is, quantitative and qualitative. The strict adherence to the quantitative approach, as is evident in the majority of psycholinguistic studies on memory in bilinguals, and the entire removal of outliers and incorrect responses from the analysis may remind us of the proverbial baby being thrown out with the bathwater.

Conclusion

The present study looked into evidence of language attrition among Russian bilinguals coming from three different linguistic backgrounds. The psycholinguistic paradigm of picture naming aimed to look further into the process of lexical access in bilinguals as well as at retrieval problems due to attrition of the native language. The combination of quantitative and qualitative analyses revealed the following. LF words were retrieved at significantly longer latencies than HF words, and participants experienced more problems with recalling LF words and tended to name them in L2 more often than HF words. Partial support for the factor of immigration was found in this study, but this concerned only HF words. In addition to statistical evidence reported in the study, a few trends pertaining to L1 attrition were identified qualitatively. There was an obvious cognate-related effect registered in the data. In addition, evidence of lexical and semantic transfer was offered through the qualitative analysis of inaccurate responses. This study showed a way of combining a robust statistical approach with a more descriptive qualitative method. The combination of the two is believed to give a better insight into bilinguals' mental lexicons, as well as the process of first language attrition.

REFERENCES

Ammerlaan, T. (1996). "You get a bit wobbly...": *exploring bilingual lexical retrieval processes in the context of first language attrition*. Unpublished doctoral dissertation, Katholieke Universiteit Nijmegen.
   (1997). "Corrosion" or "loss" of immigrant Dutch in Australia: an experiment on first language attrition. In J. Klatter-Folmer & S. Kroon (eds.), *Dutch overseas* (pp. 69–97). The Netherlands: Tilburg University Press.
Askari, N. (1991). *Phonological and semantic priming effects on tip-of-the-tongue states in monolinguals and bilinguals*. Unpublished doctoral dissertation, Claremont Graduate School, CA.
Barry, C., Hirsh, K., Johnston, R., & Williams, C. (2001). Age of acquisition, word frequency, and the locus of repetition priming of picture naming. *Journal of Memory and Language*, 44, 350–375.
Beauvillain, C., & Grainger, J. (1987). Accessing interlexical homographs: some limitations of a language-selective access. *Journal of Memory and Language*, 26, 658–672.
Brown, A. (1979). Priming effects in semantic memory retrieval processes. *Journal of Experimental Psychology: Human Learning and Memory*, 5(2), 65–77.
Costa, A., & Caramazza, A. (1999). Is lexical selection in bilingual speech production language specific? Further evidence from Spanish–English and English–Spanish bilinguals. *Bilingualism: Language and Cognition*, 2(3), 231–244.
Costa, A., Ivanova, I., & Santesteban, M. (2006). How do highly proficient bilinguals control their lexicalization process? Inhibitory and language specific selection mechanisms are both functional. *Journal of Experimental Psychology: Learning, Memory, and Cognition*, 32(5), 1057–1074.
de Bot, K. (1992). A bilingual production model: Levelt's "speaking" model adapted. *Applied Linguistics*, 13, 1–24.
   (2001). A bilingual production model: Levelt's "speaking" model adapted. In Li Wei (ed.), *The bilingualism reader* (pp. 420–442). London: Routledge.
de Bot, K., & Schreuder, R. (1993). Word production in the bilingual lexicon: support for a mixed-representational system. In R. Schreuder & B. Weltens (eds.), *The bilingual lexicon* (pp. 191–215). Amsterdam: John Benjamins.
Dent, K., & Johnston, R. (2008). Age of acquisition and word frequency in picture-naming: a dual-task investigation. *Journal of Experimental Psychology: Learning, Memory and Cognition*, 34(2), 282–301.

Dewaele, J.-M. (2004). Perceived language dominance and language preference for emotional speech: the implications for attrition research. In M. Schmid, B. Kopke, M. Keijzer, & L. Weilemar (eds.), *First language attrition: interdisciplinary perspectives on methodological issues* (pp. 81–105). Amsterdam: John Benjamins.

Ecke, P. (2004). Language attrition and theories of forgetting: a cross-disciplinary review. *International Journal of Bilingualism*, 8(3), 321–354.

Ehri, L., & Ryan, E. (1980). Performance in bilinguals in picture-word interference task. *Journal of Psycholinguistic Research*, 9(3), 285–302.

Glaser, W., & Dungelhoff, F. (1984). The time course of picture-word interference. *Journal of Experimental Psychology: Human Perception and Performance*, 10, 640–654.

Gollan, T., Montona, R., Fennema-Notestine, C., & Morris, S. (2005). Bilingualism affects picture naming but not picture classification. *Memory and Cognition*, 33(7), 1220–1234.

Gollan, T., Ferreira, V., & Cera, C. (2010). Bilinguals reveal blocking mechanism underlying Tip-of-the-Tongue states. *Presented at the 51st annual meeting of the Psychonomic Society*, St. Louis, MO.

Goodman, G., Haith, M., Guttentag, R., & Rao, S. (1985). Automatic processing of word meaning: intralingual and interlingual interference. *Child Development*, 56, 103–118.

Green, D. (1998). Mental control of the bilingual lexico-semantic system. *Bilingualism: Language and Cognition*, 1(2), 67–81.

Hakuta, K., & d'Andrea, D. (1992). Some properties of bilingual maintenance and loss in Mexican background high-school students. *Applied Linguistics*, 13(1), 72–99.

Hermans, D., Bongaerts, T., de Bot, K., & Schreuder, R. (1998). Producing words in a foreign language: can speakers prevent interference from their first language? *Bilingualism: Language and Cognition*, 1(3), 213–230.

Hulsen, M. (2000). *Language loss and language processing. Three generations of Dutch migrants in New Zealand*. Unpublished dissertation, University of Nijmegen.

Huttenlocher, J., & Kubicek, L. F. (1983). The source of relatedness on naming latency. *Journal of Experimental Psychology: Learning, Memory, and Cognition*, 9, 484–496

Isurin, L. (2000). "Deserted island" or a child's first language forgetting. *Bilingualism: Language and Cognition*, 3(2), 151–166.

(2007). Teachers' language: the effects of L1 attrition. *The Modern Language Journal*, 91(3), 357–372.

Isurin, L., & McDonald, J. (2001). Retroactive interference from translation equivalents: implications for first language forgetting. *Memory and Cognition*, 29, 312–319.

Ivanova, I., & Costa, A. (2008). Does bilingualism hamper lexical access in speech production? *Acta Psychologica*, 127, 277–288.

Jared, D., & Szucs, C. (2002). Phonological activation in bilinguals: evidence from interlingual homograph naming. *Bilingualism: Language and Cognition*, 5, 225–239.

Jaspaert, K., & Kroon, S. (1989). Social determinants of language loss. *Review of Applied Linguistics*, 83–4, 75–98.

Jaspaert, K., Kroon, S., & van Hout, R. (1986). Points of reference in first language loss. In K. Weltens, K. de Bot, & T. van Els (eds.), *Language attrition in progress* (pp. 37–49). Dordrecht: Foris.

Jones, G. (1987). Phonological blocking in the tip-of-the-tongue state. *Cognition*, 26, 115–122.

(1989). Back to Woodworth: role of interlopers in the tip-of-the-tongue phenomenon. *Memory & Cognition*, 17(1), 69–76.

Kaufman, D., & Aronoff, M. (1991). Morphological disintegration and reconstruction in first language attrition. In H. Seliger & R. Vago (eds.), *First language attrition* (pp. 175–189). Cambridge University Press.

Knupsky, A., & Amrhein, P. (2007). Phonological facilitation through translation in a bilingual picture naming task. *Bilingualism: Language and Cognition*, 10(3), 211–223.

Kopke, B., & Schmid, M. (2004). Language attrition: the next phase. In M. Schmid, B. Kopke, M. Keijzer, & L. Weilemar (eds.), *First language attrition: interdisciplinary perspectives on methodological issues* (pp. 1–47). Amsterdam: John Benjamins.

Kouritzin, S. (1999). *Facets of first language loss*. Mahwah, NJ: Lawrence Erlbaum.

Levelt, W., Roelofs, A., & Meyer, A. (1999). A theory of lexical access in speech production. *Behavioral and Brain Sciences*, 22, 1–38.

Leyen, I. (1984). Native language attrition: a study of vocabulary decline. *Dissertation Abstracts International*, 46(9), 2602.

Major, R. (1993). Socio-linguistic factors in loss and acquisition of phonology. In K. Hyltenstam & A. Viberg (eds.), *Progression and regression in language* (pp. 463–478). Cambridge University Press.

Marian, V., Blumenfeld, H. K., & Boukrina, O. (2008). Sensitivity to phonological similarity within and across languages. *Journal of Psycholinguistic Research*, 37, 141–170.

Maylor, E. (1990). Age, blocking and the tip-of-the-tongue state. *British Journal of Psychology*, 81, 123–134.

Meyer, A., & Bock, K. (1992). The tip-of-the-tongue phenomenon: blocking or partial activation? *Memory & Cognition*, 20(6), 715–726.

Olshtain, E., & Barzilay, M. (1991). Lexical retrieval difficulties in adult language attrition. In H. Seliger & R. Vago (eds.), *First language attrition* (pp. 139–151). Cambridge University Press.

Schilling, H. E. H., Rayner, K., & Chumbley, J. I. (1998). Comparing naming, lexical decision, and eye fixation times: word frequency effects and individual differences. *Memory & Cognition*, 26(6), 1270–1281.

Schmid, M. (2002). *First language attrition, use and maintenance: the case of German Jews in Anglophone countries*. Amsterdam: John Benjamins.

(2004). Language attrition research: an annotated bibliography. In M. Schmid, B. Kopke, M. Keijzer, & L. Weilemar (eds.), *First language attrition: interdisciplinary perspectives on methodological issues* (pp. 317–349). Amsterdam: John Benjamins.

(2011). *Language attrition*. Cambridge University Press
Schriefers, H., Meyer, A., & Levelt, W. (1990). Exploring the time course access in language production interference studies. *Journal of Memory and Language*, 29(1), 86–102.
Snodgrass, J., & Vanderwart, M. (1980). A standardized set of 260 pictures: norms for name agreement, image agreement, familiarity and visual complexity. *Journal of Experimental Psychology: Human Learning and Memory*, 6(2), 174–215.
Soesman, A. (1997). An experimental study on native language attrition in Dutch adult immigrants in Israel. In J. Klatter-Folmer & S. Kroon (eds.), *Dutch overseas* (pp. 181–195). The Netherlands: Tilburg University Press.
Sutton, T. M., & Altarriba, J. (2008). Emotion words in the mental lexicon: a new look at the emotion Stroop effect. *The Mental Lexicon*, 3, 29–46.
Szekely, A., D'Amico, S., Devescovi, A., Federmeier, K., Herron, D., Iyer, G., et al. (2003). Timed picture naming: extended norms and validation against previous studies. *Behavior Research Methods Instruments and Computers*, 35(4), 621–633.
Szekely, A., Jacobsen, T., D'Amico, S., Devescovi, A., Andonova, E., Herron, D., et al. (2004). A new on-line resource for psycholinguistic studies. *Journal of Memory and Language*, 51(2), 247–250.
Szekely, A., D'Amico, S., Devescovi, A., Federmeier, K., Herron, D., Iyer, G., et al. (2005). Timed action and object naming. *Cortex*, 41(1), 7–26.
Waas, M. (1996). *Language attrition down under*. Frankfurt: Peter Lang.
Wierzbicka, A. (1992). *Semantics, culture, and cognition: universal human concepts in culture-specific configurations*. Oxford University Press.
Zasorina, L. (ed.) (1977). *Chastotnyi slovar' Russkogo jazyka* [Dictionary of frequency of the Russian language]. Moscow: Russkij Jazyk.

13 Future research directions: bilingualism, memory, and language

Jeanette Altarriba

Abstract

The current chapter is aimed at providing an overview of the main findings and research areas presented within this volume with an eye toward proposing various research questions and areas of inquiry that emerge from the previous pages. Additionally, several new and emerging areas of research interest, cutting across bilingualism, language, memory, and cognition, are identified that should aid in formulating future questions for novel and insightful investigation. These areas include the study of bilingualism and emotion, the area of bilingualism in infancy, the study of bilingualism and creativity, investigations into the representation of figurative language, and the exploration of the role of scripts in bilingual language processing and memory. These and many other areas of consideration are poised to serve as informed starting points from which new work should emerge within the more general field of bilingualism.

A volume of the current nature should clearly provide an up-to-date compendium of knowledge and findings that contribute new and novel insights to the areas of bilingualism, memory, and language. Additionally, it should also provide the reader and the researcher in the field with future directions for research, new and interesting questions to explore, and perhaps a set of "tools" with which to explore those new directions. The aim of the current chapter is to bring together some of the main findings and conclusions that have been reported in the current work and transform them into possible research questions that may help to direct the field for eager scholars, researchers, and scientists. The sections below reflect the overarching areas of scientific inquiry that have given rise to the organization and format of the current volume. A final section is devoted to those topics that it is also important to explore that were beyond the current scope but no less integral to the study of bilingualism, language, and memory.

The architecture of bilingual memory

Within this area of research inquiry, investigators seek to understand the fundamental structure and mechanisms that house the mental representations within and across languages and to model those structures in constructs that allow for further prediction and testing. Within the current volume, Bartolotti and Marian present the ways in which one might conceptualize bilingual memory using the traditional expressions of short-term and long-term memory, but add a newer twist in their focus on phonological memory processing and the processing of speech. They emphasize the real demands on a bilingual processing system – knowing when to operate individually, within a given language, and knowing when knowledge of a second language can impinge upon cognitive processing, for better or for worse. Yet they never lose sight of the fact that languages do not merely turn "on" or "off" at the flick of a switch, but rather, some cross-linguistic operations occur in parallel and it is the concepts that are represented by those languages that are shared, common, and, at times, alinguistic. What we gain further from this particular chapter is the notion that a certain amount of inhibitory control is also the crux of bilingual cognitive processing, and it is the very intricate interplay between automaticity and control that needs clarification, modeling, and further understanding. This work should incite the reader to explore the ways in which speech is processed within and between languages and how this changes across variables such as frequency, as compared to the written word. If it is the case that many more individuals are auditory/verbal bilinguals rather than both verbal and written bilinguals, then greater emphasis should be placed on studying the spoken word over print in bilingual research. That is, there is a large piece of the cognitive puzzle that still awaits exploration – that which involves the processing of phonological inputs across languages. From the current stepping stone, further work in this domain is called for.

Dijkstra and colleagues approach the issue of the mental structure of bilingual memory through the types of connectionist models that have previously been applied to monolingual language studies. However, the uniqueness of the current contribution lies in the utility of the model described there to capture the important processes occurring in second language learning and acquisition. What we learn from this work is the valuable insight that learning a second language is an act to be viewed in stages, and it is in the very components of those stages, how they relate to each other, and how essential each is to the learning process as a whole that is emphasized within the model unveiled in their chapter.

Future research directions 351

The notion that competition between languages also implies a degree of control or inhibition is also salient in the model. That is, an individual operating as a bilingual information processor has, simultaneously, to monitor inputs, attend to certain ones, filter out others, and then work toward interpreting and encoding the relevant inputs and distinguish which ones, and in which languages, are pertinent to the current situation. With the prevalence of cognates, homographic noncognates, "false friends," and other like stimuli across languages, the work of the bilingual speaker and thinker is truly quite challenging.

This work should goad others into exploring the ways in which cross-language processes can be modeled for languages that vary in script, tonal components, reading direction, and the like, in order to expand current knowledge of the acquisition of languages that might vary from each other in a number of ways. One might also apply these modeling techniques to a variety of age groups (e.g., does language control change with age?), in order to understand the developmental differences that might be predicted by models of a connectionist nature.

Explorations of working memory

Working memory is that repository in human memory wherein information is coded, rehearsed, interpreted, and otherwise processed in current consciousness for storage and future retrieval. But just what are the mechanisms that govern processing within this memory store when two (or more) different sets of languages, symbols, and possibly concepts are under consideration at any given moment in time? Working memory must encompass inputs of all types – words, objects, numbers, scenes, faces, and the like, and when multiple ways of coding these items based on language are at hand, it becomes increasingly challenging for bilinguals to process information. Yet they do so, quite elegantly. Works by Szmalec and Signorelli and their respective colleagues indicate that working memory plays an important role in acquiring new languages and in serving in an interpretive capacity between languages, respectively. Issues of nonselective language access and cognitive control are also very much part of the discussions on working memory.

Ultimately, we learn that the nature of second language learning should be understood as encompassing serial-order learning of features and components, as related to language (Szmalec), and that, in turn, componential analyses of words, phrases, and larger units of language are paramount to successful interpretation and translation (Signorelli). There is also a function that mentally "computes" an appropriate translation – a function that may help to explain why it is that, in certain instances, interpreters show superior working memory skills over non-interpreters. The careful review provided within the present volume would indicate that the degree to which working memory skills appear to be enhanced for interpreters over non-interpreters is moderated by such factors as mode (auditory, visual, etc.), years of experience, and knowledge of the topics and subject matter being interpreted. In short, this latter work underscores the value of generating a range of experiments on a given topic in order to triangulate or generalize findings across a number of variables and instances.

The topic of interpreting or translating is a fruitful one for future cognitive, empirical investigation as, through work in this area, researchers may uncover ways in which language training might lead to greater connections across languages between concepts that may have been thought to be "disconnected" or not "associated." What may also be interesting to pursue further is an investigation of the ways in which the often superior working memory abilities of interpreters transfer to other domains and other cognitive tasks (e.g., task switching with simulations of real-world tasks; Stroop color naming or other cognitive interference tasks; mental arithmetic and other related tasks). Additionally, are there age-related differences in the acquisition and use of these skills, such that one might want to engage in the training of interpreters at a younger age than perhaps is typical? Or could someone older with memory deficits gain greater mental agility by undergoing training as an interpreter later in life? These and other related questions might bring a broader context to the virtues of interpretive training and the benefits in terms of cognitive control and mental agility that such training may provide.

The bilingual brain

Advances in the techniques and tools used to further our knowledge of behavioral neuroscience set the stage for what promises to be the forefront of bilingual research – neurological investigations of the bilingual brain. Van Hell and Kroll provide a comprehensive overview of the procedures used when gathering event-related potentials (ERPs) in the study of language processing in monolingual and bilingual speakers. Emerging within the field of bilingualism research is the desire to bring both behavioral and neurological data to bear on important questions of processing, acquisition, retention, retrieval, and the like. Both types of research approaches complement one another, and the field is seeing the emergence of laboratories focusing more and more on training individuals in various methods to measure electrophysiological and neurological responses to stimuli. These approaches are revealing, yet again, that language access and processing is nonselective – that is, elements of both languages, consciously or subconsciously, appear to be operating in tandem while a bilingual is processing information. What is exciting about these new approaches to research is the ability to identify regions within the brain that may govern or control language and conceptual processing and that may, at the same time, be distinct for different languages and overlap in cases where languages might tap into the very same processes. How the brain processes multiple languages at the neural level was not known with the current level of precision until just recently; thus, this is an overarching area of research inquiry that stands to be quite prominent over the next few decades. More work on aspects of brain development will no doubt be executed in the coming years, as researchers will be able to model how the brain develops throughout the time course of acquisition, and how that time course may differ for young learners compared to older learners, for learners of distinct languages, and for those who learn a second language in a coordinate versus a compound manner. That is, it will continue to be important to understand how the brain comes to function in the way that it does in those research areas that have been studied in bilingual speakers. Understanding the mechanisms that are involved in cognitive processing by bilinguals could have applications to individuals who become aphasic or otherwise suffer brain injury and trauma.

Developmental issues in language learning

Thus far, a recurrent theme that seems to thread the earlier sections of the current volume is that developmental issues are important to understanding the overall structure of bilingual cognitive processing and function. How does one become bilingual and how does this occur over time? How might we model the development of the "successful bilingual" in such a way that we can devise and apply more efficient modes of language learning to new learners? One might conclude that one of the main reasons the area of bilingual language and memory development is important is that the most effective means of acquiring a language can be fruitfully developed, and few individuals would argue otherwise. Thus, all of the research provided within the current volume can, in multiple ways, contribute to this mission and do so validly and convincingly. Trofimovich and colleagues compared the learning of new foreign-language words in lists versus in isolation across varying age groups. Surprisingly, given the mode of acquisition that was used, they found no differences across groups, though the standard context effects emerged, indicating better memory when words are learned embedded in a meaningful context compared with when they are learned alone. As much as differences across groups or conditions are of importance in delimiting the range or applicability of a given theory or model, it can be just as informative to know when differences are not present and when a task or treatment of some kind can be utilized with equal success across varying samples or populations. Both kinds of data and evidence can speak to the generalizability of a given theory of learning or memory. Their effects were reported with *implicit* tests of memory – those that stem more from incidental exposures to information – versus intentional ones. Thus, other tests using explicit measures with different samples or populations or different language combinations may provide other findings and produce age-related differences. Yet those are avenues that still need further exploration and further study before definitive conclusions can be drawn.

The notion that the age-related cognitive deficits that are often reported in monolingual speakers may be attenuated in bilingual speakers was investigated by Goral. This is yet another topic that is emerging at the forefront of bilingual memory and language studies. Does being bilingual afford an individual some added "protection" against cognitive decline? In fact, Goral's chapter indicates that, particularly within the realm of tasks that involve cognitive control (e.g., switching tasks, interference tasks, and tasks that demand the inhibition or suppression of one language in favor of another), one finds particular performance benefits for bilingual speakers. Given the notion that bilingual speakers are often engaged in suppressing one language in favor of another, and then reversing the order of those operations, over what is sometimes a rapid time course, it is not too surprising that cognitive skills should develop accordingly in the bilingual brain and transfer to a variety of tasks. However, what is the extent of this apparent resilience? Is there a developmental stage at which it is "too late" to take advantage of such mental "training"? That is, the parameters that govern the applicability, broadly defined, of cognitive/attentional control in bilingual versus monolingual speakers have yet to be fully explored and developed. It is going to become increasingly important, as well, to understand the category of tasks and skills that ultimately do benefit from multiple language knowledge and to then understand what it is, exactly, that those tasks have in common. This would allow us to isolate the set of mechanisms that, in turn, could be encapsulated into a model of effective learning. In order to do so, the limits and boundaries of attentional control in bilinguals and the benefits that result need to be further explored so that comparisons can be drawn across tasks, as well as across languages.

It appears that both developmental and linguistic components may determine the frequency with which autobiographical memories are recounted during specific time periods within one's lifetime, as reported by Altman and colleagues. It has been known for quite some time that language features tend to be coded in memories such that participants tend to produce richer and more complete recall of personal events if recall takes place in the language that was most frequently used at the time of the original event. Less is known about how this effect interacts with immigration. The work described by Altman and co-authors indicates that "crossover memories" are more likely to occur post-immigration, in the sense that memories may be more often discussed or described in the language of the new environment than the language that was prevalent in the earlier environment. Thus, it is the case that when the dominant language "switches," as may occur when changing to a new cultural and linguistic environment, so too may the coding of new memories, in consonance. Of course, these effects are often moderated by the degree of acculturation and assimilation that is undergone by a given immigrant. This area of research inquiry is timely, particularly within the United States, as there is an ever-increasing population of immigrants who move from non-English-speaking countries and must then consider the ways in which they are to navigate in their new country and new language.

This area of work may be broadened with future questions revolving around the nature of language use and practice as governed by the motivation for immigration, and the political, socio-political, cultural, and historical influences surrounding both the country of origin and the new country, and the requirements that individuals may have in the new host country to speak and use its official language(s). Could memories also be altered as a result of these other influences apart from the dominance of a given language in a given location? Can this knowledge be used in psychotherapy where retrieval of autobiographical memories and manipulation of a bilingual's two languages may prove beneficial for their psychological health? These questions that may be part of sociological and socio-linguistic inquiry could also be amenable to cognitive investigations such that the definition of language-dependent memories could be broadened to include other variables or factors.

Questions related to the influence of culture on thought and the development of mental representations are a hallmark of work on linguistic relativity. To what extent does the learning of languages shape our views of the world and our awareness of our own thoughts and beliefs, in the metacognitive sense? These are the notions that are discussed in the chapter by Athanasopoulos and Aveledo. If it is indeed the case that acquiring a new language shapes our thoughts and beliefs, then one might argue that a bilingual or multilingual speaker enjoys the existence of many more concepts and ideas that are specifically afforded by each of their languages, as compared to a monolingual speaker. The implications of these conclusions are that bilinguals may have a certain "semantic richness" in being able to select concepts from one language over another based on the overall comprehensiveness or meaningfulness of a given concept.

More intriguing are the findings that language has been shown to moderate perceptual awareness, item discrimination (such as in the realm of color selection), and other tasks, based on the frequency with which a given language is being used for thinking and reasoning, on a daily basis. Could there be an adaptive advantage to learning to "think" like a member of one's new linguistic community, say, in the case of immigration? These kinds of questions are ones that future research will likely address, particularly in situations in which a given country is experiencing an increase in immigration. What these studies may consider is the degree to which this type of moderated thinking based on a second language and second culture becomes "automatized" and the extent to which these new ways of thinking are moderated by length of exposure and the nature of the exposure in the new environment. For example, would an immigrant's new language impinge upon their patterns of thinking differently if they were working in the medical profession versus in a blue-collar profession? That is, there are a whole host of variables that moderate the development of one's worldview, including those that are contextual and time-related, as well as those that are linguistically bound. Future research should work at systematically reviewing these variables and the ways in which they interact with notions of linguistic relativity across a diverse range of languages and cultures.

Finally, language learning issues were investigated with an eye toward a specific testing paradigm within the work of Tse and Pu. Newer research within the realm of cognitive psychology suggests that learning is enhanced in situations in which individuals are frequently tested on what they have learned compared to conditions that merely involve repetitive studying of the same material. So-called "testing effects" indicate that the act of retrieving information from memory serves to enhance our learning and make for more durable, longer-lasting memory traces. These kinds of effects are typically shown, as described by Tse, in experimental paradigms in which individuals exposed to new vocabulary either study that vocabulary various times, in multiple cycles, or alternate between study and test. Those who experience the latter conditions tend ultimately to recall a greater proportion of words than in the former case. What is significant about this research in the bilingual realm is that language acquisition is a fundamental area within this domain of research, and a primary question that is typically explored within the larger field revolves around the most effective methods for learning a new language. A direction for future extensions of this work lies in actually implementing these ideas in programs and methods of teaching a second language and investigating whether or not the effectiveness of these methods varies as a function of age of acquisition, the nature of the languages involved, and the setting in which the learning takes place. Are there limitations to the benefits that are accrued by using a study–test procedure in vocabulary learning? What are the boundaries under which this effect can be attenuated or increased? Can basic self-help methods that individuals use be enhanced by including more testing components within their guidelines and recommendations? These are all fruitful directions for the application of this relatively new perspective on enhancing the acquisition of a second language.

Language attrition

Language loss is an area of relatively little empirical study within the realm of bilingual research. Yet it is a provocative area of inquiry, given that many bilingual speakers often claim that once they have adopted a new language they have difficulty accessing words in their native language. Simply stated, usage and practice regarding a language is one way to maximize the ability to continue to access words and phrases in that language. When dominance undergoes a "switch" to a different language, then the frequency with which the former language is used and practiced decreases, leading to word-finding difficulties, interference in accessing information, and the like. An interesting exception to these general conclusions comes in the form of emotional stimuli, which are least likely to undergo attrition in the first language compared to other categories of stimuli. Interestingly, work in this area, as reported by Bardovi-Harlig and Stringer, has revealed that attrition may affect different levels of language representation and processing differentially. For example, the morphological components of a language might be more readily affected by attrition than its semantic components. Thus, a more fine-grained approach to the nature and characteristics of language attrition has been taken. However, this area of work in the empirical realm is in its infancy. Future research might focus on ways to minimize or reduce interference in memory that might block access to a given language, making it appear as though language has been lost. What are yet to be developed are more sensitive measures to detect whether apparently forgotten or lost elements of language are truly lost, or whether it is merely a case that their access has been inhibited. This is an area of inquiry that could benefit from greater understanding of the socio-linguistic, cultural, political, and developmental variables that lead to attrition. Could there be reasons why language access is blocked that are purely psychological in nature? Does attrition affect physiological or neural substrates in the brain? What might imaging techniques tell us about the biological correlates of language loss or apparent attrition? Can the lost childhood language be unblocked using hypnosis or related methods that examine the unconscious? These are questions for future work that bridge the ideas in the neural, behavioral, and developmental realms in what is a very intriguing area of research.

Isurin effectively argues, in fact, that studies of language attrition should encompass both quantitative and qualitative approaches, as it is indeed some of the very variables mentioned above that could contribute to language attrition. While tasks such as picture naming for objects, timed translation, or Stroop-interference paradigms are ways in which one could empirically measure the ease or difficulty of accessing a particular word or concept in a given language by means of reaction time, it is also important to consider the nature of the errors that are produced, the protocol and ordering of the output for these tasks, the frequency with which certain words are used over other valid alternatives, and an overall qualitative approach to the data that are reported. There are occasions, however, when words that are difficult to access in a given language nonetheless produce a sense of "knowing" and ultimately simply result in a tip-of-the-tongue (TOT) state. An interesting avenue of exploration that has received little attention to date involves investigating the nature of TOTs across languages as a function of category of word, length of language usage, immigration status, education, work status, family life, and the like. How is access to words in a given language moderated by variables that influence the mental representation of those words as a function of the settings or context in which they are used? This kind of multi-level investigation has not yet been accomplished with regard to lexical access, TOT research, and bilingualism, but it could certainly address extant issues in the attrition arena within the larger domain of bilingualism. A comprehensive examination of the various classes of words both grammatically (e.g., verbs, nouns, adjectives) and by type (e.g., abstract, concrete, emotion, cognate, noncognate) is needed in the area of attrition and the production of TOTs, both within and across languages. Perhaps this work could lead to more general conclusions regarding the types of linguistic devices that need to be reinforced while learning due to a high likelihood of attrition versus those aspects of language that seem to be impervious to loss.

Additional avenues of inquiry and investigation

While not expressly covered within the chapters in the current volume, the role of *emotion* in the processing of language and in the development of memory represents an entire realm of investigation that is in its infancy in the empirical, cognitive domain. The work of Altarriba and colleagues (Altarriba & Basnight-Brown, 2011; Altarriba & Canary, 2004) represents some of the earliest research in this area that has included cognitive tasks and experimental, laboratory-based paradigms in the investigation of emotion-word representation in bilingual memory. While it is known that emotion seems to code memory such that highly emotional events, particularly negative events, appear to be better recalled than positive or neutral events, interactions with language or language use have rarely been investigated within the bilingual realm. Noteworthy examinations that are socio-linguistic in nature have been published by Pavlenko (2008), Dewaele (2008), and others, but investigations into the automatic processing of emotion stimuli in two languages from an empirical perspective are almost nonexistent. Future research directions in this topic area could focus on such questions as are emotional events truly more deeply coded in an individual's first language rather than their second language, and what factors moderate this finding? Are results such as these moderated by language type, topic of the emotional event, gender, age, or other demographic variables? The relationship between emotion, memory, and bilingualism appears to be a highly important area of investigation that should lead to many useful and interesting results.

Interest has grown in recent years in investigating cognitive processing and *bilingualism in infants* (e.g., Byers-Heinlein, Burns, & Werker, 2010; Werker & Byers-Heinlein, 2008). Evidence of the emergence of bilingualism can be found as early as the first few months of development within newborns. What are the factors that determine the rate at which newborns acquire a new language? How do the features of language representation (e.g., morphology, phonology, semantics) begin to develop and what factors mediate their development over the first few years of an infant's life? Do infants show a preference for a given language early in their bilingual development? This fascinating field of inquiry stands to attract a great many individuals who will expand upon these and many other questions, rounding out what is known about the complete life cycle of the bilingual speaker. Future research are likely to be directed toward these questions and will also merge these questions with those examining the neurological substrates of early acquisition.

Another emerging area of research that is novel in the bilingual domain is the study of *creativity* (see e.g., Kharkhurin, 2010a, 2010b; Simonton, 2008). How is creativity associated with language use and linguistic knowledge in bilingual speakers as compared to monolingual speakers? Does bilingualism afford the kind of creative thinking that stems from having multiple ways of representing concepts and meaning across languages? Would learning a new language or languages enhance an individual's overall creative capacity? There is currently little work related to these questions, while clearly this is an area of investigation that could lead to important insights and findings related to problem solving, reasoning, intelligence, mental awareness, and similar topics.

Another avenue of novel research investigation in the realm of bilingualism includes the focus on *figurative language* and the ways in which bilingual speakers appear to access idiomatic expressions, metaphors, and the like, that may appear linguistically specific but might generalize to situations that occur in a different language (see e.g., Harris *et al.*, 1999; Vaid & Martinez, 2001). Figurative language is language that appears ambiguous in that the literal meaning of the words or phrase does not directly convey its meaning. Examples include metaphors, idiomatic expressions, and slang or taboo words. The apparent transfer of knowledge between associated information across languages that might help to disambiguate a phrase or sentence that appears to have a nuance specific to a certain language should prove to be yet another way in which bilingual speakers demonstrate creativity and mental flexibility due to the nonselectivity of language usage. Very few works have been reported uncovering the exact mechanisms by which bilingual speakers process idiomatic expressions and metaphors in either language, how information transfers across languages for those expressions that seem to have an analogy across languages, and how one learns those "cognate" metaphors in a new language versus those that are completely new semantically and syntactically. This area of investigation appears equally novel and ripe for new exploration and study.

Finally, not much attention has been paid to the role of *orthography or scripts* in the multitude of ways in which language is processed and remembered in bilingual speakers. Very few articles have been published on the effects of different scripts on bilingual language processing (see e.g., Hoshino & Kroll, 2008). While it has been thought that orthography plays a part in the processing of spoken languages, few researchers have focused on the exact role that the physical attributes of a language play in all facets of bilingual language use and memory. From effects in terms of acquisition, to the study of word memory and word recall, to the exploration of how different writing systems affect the perceptual processes involved in their reading, the influence of orthography has been largely ignored and has received little to no attention. Future directions in the study of language encoding, storage, and retrieval within bilingual populations could focus on the nature of the orthography of the languages involved in order to address concerns as to how this level of language representation influences the development of the overall mental architecture of the bilingual mind.

Summary and conclusions

The current volume explores the ways in which bilingual speakers' knowledge of language and its representation in memory is moderated by a host of variables and factors determining everything from the degree to which speakers can switch between languages, to the mechanisms involved in language acquisition and attrition. A wealth of other related topics remain to be explored using methods that have been developed with ever-increasing precision and with new technologies that allow for a more comprehensive overview of the bilingual mind and its processes and functions. Future research directions are those that can focus on characteristics such as emotional content or orthography, and those that involve the pragmatic or social uses of language, such as in the processing of figurative language. It is hoped that the current volume will serve as a springboard for all of these ideas and more, as exploration continues in the area of bilingualism, language, and memory.

REFERENCES

Altarriba, J., & Basnight-Brown, D. M. (2011). The representation of emotion vs. emotion-laden words in English and in Spanish in the Affective Simon Task. *International Journal of Bilingualism*, 15, 310–328.

Altarriba, J., & Canary, T. M. (2004). Affective priming: the automatic activation of arousal. *Journal of Multilingual and Multicultural Development*, 25, 248–265.

Byers-Heinlein, K., Burns, T. C., & Werker, J. F. (2010). The roots of bilingualism in newborns. *Psychological Science*, 21, 343–348.

Dewaele, J.-M. (2008). The emotional weight of 'I love you' in multilinguals' languages. *Journal of Pragmatics*, 40, 1753–1780.

Harris, R. J., Tebbe, M. R., Leka, G. E., Garcia, R. C., & Erramouspe, R. (1999). Monolingual and bilingual memory for English and Spanish metaphors and similes. *Metaphor and Symbol*, 14, 1–16.

Hoshino, N., & Kroll, J. F. (2008). Cognate effects in picture naming: does cross-language activation survive a change of script? *Cognition*, 106, 501–511.

Kharkhurin, A. V. (2010a). Bilingual verbal and nonverbal creative behavior. *International Journal of Bilingualism*, 14, 211–226.

(2010b). Sociocultural differences in the relationship between bilingualism and creative potential. *Journal of Cross-Cultural Psychology*, 41, 776–783.

Pavlenko, A. (2008). Emotion and emotion-laden words in the bilingual lexicon. *Bilingualism: Language and Cognition*, 11, 147–164.

Simonton, D. K. (2008). Bilingualism and creativity. In J. Altarriba & R. R. Heredia (eds.), *An introduction to bilingualism: principles and processes* (pp. 147–166). New York: Lawrence Erlbaum Associates.

Vaid, J., & Martinez, F. (April, 2001). *Figurative language and thought across languages: what transfer?* Poster presented at the Third International Symposium on Bilingualism, University of the West of England, Bristol, UK.

Werker, J. F., & Byers-Heinlein, K. (2008). Bilingualism in infancy: first steps in perception and comprehension. *Trends in Cognitive Science*, 12, 144–151.

Index

Note: Page numbers in italics are figures; with 't' are tables; and 'n' are notes.

Abutalebi, J. 87
access
  bilingual memory 7–8, 14–23
  cross-linguistic lexical 18–19, 35–36, 120–121
  and episodic memory 14–17
  semantic memory 18
Acenas, L. A. R. 85
acquisition (SLA) 2, 7, 306
  and age 154, 324–325, 352
  in the Chinese–English vocabulary study 270–272, 273
  and Repeated Study/Testing 270–272
  and Working Memory (WM) 76–84
activation
  Activation Threshold Hypothesis 292, 294, 309–311, 314
  parallel language 22, 36–37
  see also Bilingual Interactive Activation model (BIA)
advantage, bilingual 201–202
age 3–4
  and acquisition 154, 324–325, 352
  age-related change 188–203
  and conceptualization 247–248
  and episodic memory access 14–17
  and immigration 223–226
  L2
    at earlier 34, 58, 151–154
    at later 32, 33–34, 58, 60
  and short-term memory 12–13
  see also age effects
age of acquisition 154, 248, 357
age effects
  L1 attrition, psycholinguistic study 330–331
  in L2 learning 161–167, 353–354
    study 167–183, 170t, 176t
age-related change 188–203, 354–355
Agnoli, F. 238, 239
Allport, A. 85

Altarriba, Jeanette 5, 263, 359
Altman, Carmit 4, 355
Alvarado, N. 240
Alvarez, R. P. 139–140, 141, 142, 146
Alzheimer's disease *see* dementia
American Sign Language 134–135, 164
amnesia, infantile 212–213
Amrhein, P. 323
analytical ability 164–165
aphasia 196, 353
Arabic 88
  and French, and age-related decline 201
artecey (RTC) task 79
articulation repression 106–107, 112, 116–117
aspect/non-aspect languages 244
Astaneh, H. 33
asymmetry/symmetry, and translation priming 133–134
Athanasopoulos, Panos 4, 240–242, 243–244, 247–249, 250, 356
Atkinson, R. C. 9
attention, control of 201–202
attrition 5, 199, 357–359
  L1 319–321
    study 326–345
  L2 291–300, 314–315
auditory stimuli *98–125*
  and written stimuli 115–119, 123
autobiographical memory 4, 355
  and English–Hebrew immigrant study 211–233, 228t, *236–224*
  and episodic memory 14, 15–17, 23, 36
Aveledo, Fraibet 4

Baddeley, A. D. *11–25*, 75, 76, 77–78, 84, 96–98, 122, 260
Bahrick, H. 298–299
Bajo, M. T. 104–105, 106–107

363

balanced/unbalanced bilingualism 144–145
Balota, D. A. 268
Barberá Mata, A. 79–80
Barcroft, J. 260, 261, 281–282
Bardovi-Harlig, Kathleen 5, 300, 303–305, 308, 312, 313, 357
Bartolotti, James 2, 35–36, 321, 350
Barzilay, M. 310
basal ganglia 87
Basnight-Brown, D. M. 359
Basque
　and Spanish 145, 152, 154
　and translation priming studies 145, 147–148
　and Spanish to English 35
Bassetti, B. 243
Bates, E. 191
behavioral neuroscience 352–353
Berko-Gleason, J. 297
Berman, R. A. 297, 299, 310
Bialystok, E. 84, 86–87, 200, 201–202
biculturalism 16–17
bilingual advantage 201–202
bilingual cognition 237–238, 246–249
　and colour perception 239–242
　and grammatical number 242–244
Bilingual Interactive Activation model (BIA) 24, 26, 27–28
　BIA+ 26, 28–29, 52–54, 57, 59–63, 68, 283–284
Bilingual Language Interaction Network for Comprehension of Speech model (BLINCS) 24, 26, 29
bilingual lexical processing 261–262
bilingual memory 36–37, 350–351
　access 7–8, 14–23
　models 261–262
　　Concept Mediation model 262–263
　　Word Association model 262–263
　　see also Revised Hierarchical Model (RHM)
　processing 7–8, 13–14, 23–36
　　models 23, 49–51
　structure 7–9
Bilingual Single Network (BSN) model 54–59
　Revised 56, 62, 63–65, 68
Binet, A. 74
Bloom, P. 306
Bloomfield, L. 300
Blumenfeld, H. K. 323–324
Boroditsky, L. 248
Boston Naming Test (BNT) 189–190, 192–194
Boukrina, O. 323–324

Boulogne Ferry Effect 312–313
brain damage/disease 97, 122, 353
　aphasia 196
　dementia 84, 194–196, 239
　multiple sclerosis 260
Bransford, J. D. 166
Brenders, P. 151, 152
Brown, A. 249, 324
Bugelsky, B. R. 214
Burgess, N. 81
Buschkuehl, M. 88
Bylund, E. 244–246, 247, 248, 250

Cañas, J. J. 104–105, 106–107
Caplan, D. 83
Carpenter, P. A. 75–76, 108, 113
Carreiras, M. 145
Carroll, P. J. 110–111
Casasanto, D. 241–242
Caskey-Sirmons, L. 239–240
Catalan
　and Spanish
　　age-related decline 195, 200–201
　　and executive control 85–86
　　and translation recognition 148–149
Catalan–Spanish, and English study 33
catastrophic forgetting 55
CELT English Proficiency Test 33
Cenoz, J. 35
central executive 96
Chamot, A. U. 259
Chen, C. 87
Chen, Y.-L. 293–294
Cheung, H. 82
children
　and attrition 311–312
　infantile amnesia 212–213
　infants 359–360
　and new word learning 78, 79
　and verbal memory 82
　see also age effects
Chincotta, D. 98–125
Chinese
　and English
　　and age effects 248
　　cross-linguistic lexical access study 18–19
　　digit span tasks 105
　　and executive control 87
　　L3 vocabulary learning 256, 257, 265–284, 268t, 269t, 275t
　　listening span study 113
　　and SOMBIP 56
　　Thierry and Wu study 134
　　and translation recognition 150–151

and Japanese, regression study
    293–294
Christoffels, I. *98–125*
Cochran, B. P. 164
codeswitching (CS) 212, 216–217, 219,
    220, 231
  in crossover memories 227–228, 228t
cognate/noncognate homographs 26, 31,
    54–55, 61, 68–69, 351
cognates 351
  effect 337–338, 344–345
  and executive control 85
  and L2 learning 35
  and late bilinguals 65
  metaphors 360
  and semantic memory access 17–18, 20
  and TOT experiences 22
cognitive decline, age-related 196–203
cognitive neuroscience *see* behavioral
    neuroscience
cognitive processing
  and age effects 163–167
    study 167–183
  see also working memory (WM)
cognitive reserve 188, 202
Cohen, A. D. 293, 295, 310
Cohen-Mansfield, J. 202
Collentine, J. 83–84
colour perception 237, 239–242, 247,
    249–250
Comesaña, M. 152
competition *see* lexical competition
complex span tasks *see* reading span tasks
Comprehensive Test of Phonological
    Processing (CTOPP) 108
computational linguistics 307–308
computational modeling 51
Concept Mediation model 127, 130,
    262–263
conceptual processing 166–167
Conceptual Span Task 98
Conceptual Transfer Hypothesis (CTC)
    244–246
conceptualization 251
  and bilingual cognition 246–249
  motion events 244–246
conflict processing 87
connectionist models 51, 350
  see also distributed connectionist
      models; localist connectionist
      models
contact time with L1, and attrition 325,
    331
control of attention 201–202
control group in L1 attrition study 326

Controlled Productive Ability Test 33
conventional expressions 303–305
convergent/divergent pairs,
    psycholinguistic study 338–339
Cook, V. 243
correlational analyses, in
    Chinese–English study 274–277,
    275t
Costa, A. 20, 85–86, 87
Cowan, N. 76
Craik, F. I. M. 84, 86, 202
creativity 360
Crinion, J. 87
cross-language facilitation 20
cross-linguistic lexical access
  English–Chinese study 18–19
  interference 35–36
  and simultaneous interpreters 120–121
crossover memories (COs) 4, 212,
    214–216, 217, 220, 226–228, 355
  codeswitching (CS) 227–228, 228t
cue word technique, and immigrant
    autobiographical memory study
    218–219
cued recall tasks 112–113
  and bilingual memory access 15
  and simultaneous interpreters 98, 117,
    123
culture, and linguistic relativity 4,
    236–251, 355–356

Damjanovic, L. 240–241, 250
Daneman, M. 75–76, 108, 113
Danish
  and Polish 16–17
  crossover memories 215–216
Darò, V. *98–125*
de Bot, K. 295
De Boysson, C. 140–141
de Groot, A. M. B. 105–106, 131, 147, 251
decay, linguistic 320
declarative memory 164–165
DeKeyser, R. M. 165
dementia 84, 239
  and age-related decline 194–196, 199,
      202
Dent, K. 325
Dering, B. 241–242
DevLex-SOMBIP models 54
Dewaele, J.-M. 326, 359
digit names, English/Spanish memory
    test 13
digit span tests 74–75
  and simultaneous interpreters *98–125*
  and non-interpreters 111–112

Dijkstra, Ton 2, *27–29*, 56, 61, 69, 151, 350–351
Dimitropoulou, M. 145
distortion, linguistic 320
distributed connectionist models 53–56, 62
  and lexical competition 48–49, *63–67*, 68–48
Dong, Q. 87
Dufour, R. 131
Duñabeitia, J. A. 145, 146, 147, 154
Dunlosky, J. 267
Durazo-Arvizu, R. 232
Dutch
  and English *59*
    and ATH 310, 311
    and the Boulogne Ferry Effect 313
    and connectionist models 56, *59–60*, 62, *65–67*
    and the RHM 128
    sentence stimuli 109
    and translation priming 147
    and translation recognition 151–152
    word-list stimuli 105–106
  and German, grammatical aspects 246
  and Stroop performance 197
Duyck, Wouter 79–80
dyslexia 80

early bilinguals, learning L1 and L2 words *59–60*, 64–65
Ecke, P. 320, 324
education, and attrition 325
educational effect, of Chinese–English vocabulary study 280–282
electroencephalogram (EEG) 136
electrophysiological measures 3
  English–Chinese cross-linguistic lexical access study 19
  see also translation
Elgort, I. 283
Ellis, N. C. 121
Emergent 63
Emmorey, K. 86–87
Emonds, J. E. 300–301
emotion 359
encoding specificity 15
English
  and American Sign Language 134–135
  and Chinese
    and age effects 248
    cross-linguistic lexical access study 18–19
    digit span tasks 105
    and executive control 87
    L3 vocabulary learning 256, 257, 265–284, 268t, 269t, 275t
    listening span study 113
    and SOMBIP 56
    Thierry and Wu study 134
    and translation recognition 150–151
  and Dutch *59*
    and ATH 310, 311
    and the Boulogne Ferry Effect 313
    and connectionist models 56, *65–66*, 67
    and the RHM 128
    sentence stimuli 109
    and translation priming 147
    and translation recognition 151–152
    and word-list stimuli 105–106
  and Finnish, and verbal memory 82
  and French 88
    codeswitching 217
    translation priming studies 146
  and German
    and executive control 87
    motion events 250
  and Greek, colour perception 240, 247
  and Hebrew
    and codeswitching 217
    immigrant autobiographical memory study 212, 217–233
    and lexicon-grammar divide 299
  and Indonesian 248
  and Italian, and cross-linguistic differences 121
  and Japanese
    colour perception 240–241
    and crossover memories 215
    and executive control 87
    grammatical number 242–244
    and length of stay 249
  and non-words, vocabulary learning 261
  and Russian
    autobiographical memory 229
    and crossover memories 214
    L1 attrition 322–323
    and lexical access 321
    phonological effects 324
    psycholinguistic study 327–345
    and semantic memory access 18
    translation priming studies 140, 146, 154
  and Spanish
    and age-related decline 191–194
    attrition in children study 311–312
    autobiographical memory 229
    bilingual memory access test 15
    crossover memory study 214

Index

digital names test 13
and executive control 87
idiom retention 298
motion events 249
translation priming 139–140, 146, 154–155
translation recognition 149–150
verbal working memory 84
and Tamil, and Simon-effect 86
and Turkish
and ATH 310
repeated testing 260–261
and Welsh, and cross-linguistic differences 120
and Yucatec, grammatical number 242
episodic buffer 76, 97, 123
episodic memory 9–10, 14–17, 36
and N400 *137*
Ervin, S. 239–240
event-related potentials (ERP) 19n, 136–155, 241–242, 352
executive control 84–87
Executive Function (EF) 197
experience, and expertise in simultaneous interpreters 120
explicit memory 3, 9–10, 14, 164–165
and age effects study 167–183
explicit recall 175–176, *177–179*
in L1 processing and learning 165–167
explicit recall, and age effects 175–179, 176t
Eyal, N. 202

Fabbro, F. *98–125*
false friends *see* cognate/noncognate homographs
Farkas, I. *31*
figurative language 360
final recall *98–125*
phase in Chinese–English study 272, 273, *276*
Finnish, and English, and verbal memory 82
Fischler, J. 60
flanker tasks 86–87
Flecken, M. 246
fluid intelligence tasks 88
fonts
in age effects study 173, 174
in Chinese–English vocabulary learning study 268
forgetting *see* attrition
Francis, W. S. 231
Franks, J. J. 166

free recall, and simultaneous interpreters *98–125*
Freed, B. 83–84
Freedman, J. 84, 202
French, L. 82, 88, 89
French
and Arabic, and age-related decline 201
and English 88
codeswitching 217
translation priming studies 146
frequency effect, L1 attrition psycholinguistic study 330, *331–332*
Fromholt, P. 215–216

García-Albea, J. E. 148–149
garden-path sentences 83
Gardner, R. C. 297–299
Gaskins, S. 243
Gathercole, S. E. 77–78
Gedanken experiments 61–62
Genesee, F. 216
Gennari, S. 249
Gentner, D. 243
German
and Dutch, grammatical aspects 246
and English
and executive control 87
motion events 250
and Japanese, colour perception 240
and Russian, L1 attrition psycholinguistic study 327–345
and Turkish
lexical retrieval 296
regression study 294
Geyer, A. 140, 141, 142, 145
Gibson, T. 311–312
global loss/recovery 311–314
Gollan, T. H. 85, 87, 192, 193, 195, 324
Goral, Mira 3–4, 193–194, 354–355
Grainger, J. *27–28*, 52, 57, 139–140, 141–144
grammar 296–297, 299–300
grammatical aspect 237, 244, 245–246
grammatical number 237, 242–244, 247
grammatical sensitivity 165
Greek, and English, colour perception 240, 247
Green, D. W. *30–31*, 239, 308–309
Grendel, M. 295
Grosjean, F. 192
Gu, Y. 279
Guasch, M. 147–148
Gullberg, M. 249
Guo, T. 150–151

Gupta, P. 80–81

Haarmann, H. J. 98, 108
Hansen, L. 293–294
Harley, B. 164–165
Hart, D. 164–165
Hartsuiker, R. J. 142–143
Havelka, J. 149–150
Healy, A. F. 260
Hebb repetition effect 79–80
Hebbian learning processes 52, 57
Hebrew
  and English
    codeswitching 217
    immigrant autobiographical memory study 212, 217–233
    and lexicon-grammar divide 299
  and Russian, L1 attrition psycholinguistic study 327–345
Hennelly, R. A. 121
Hernandez, A. E. 87, 191, 192, 200–201
Hickerson, N. 239–240
Hitch, G. J. 75, 76, 77, 81
Hoff, E. 311–312
Hogben, D. 259
Holcomb, P. J. 52, 57, 139–140, 141–144
homographs, cognate/noncognate 54–55, 61, 351
Hoshino, N. 143–144, 146
Hulsen, M. 310
Hummel, K. 82, 89
Hunt, E. 238, 239

Iluz-Cohen, P. 216–217, 228
Imai, M. D. 243
immersion/re-immersion 154–155, 293, 308, 312
immigration
  and autobiographical memory 230, 355
  Polish-Danish study 16–17
  psycholinguistic study of L1 attrition 344
  see also autobiographical memory
Immigration Effect 219–220, *221–222*
  and Reminiscence Bump (RB) 219–226, 226–229
implicit memory 3, 9, 164–165
  and age effects study 167–183
    word stem completion tests 176, 178–176, 171–179
  in L1 processing and learning 165–167
incidental vocabulary learning 258–259
Indonesian, and English 248
infantile amnesia 212–213
infants, and bilingualism 359–360
inhibition 36

  and activation 308–311, 315
  and age-related decline 199–200
Inhibitory Control model 24, 29–31, 308–309
intelligence testing 74–76
intentional vocabulary learning 258–259
Interactive Activation (IA) models
  see localist connectionist models
interlingual homographs *see* cognate/noncognate homographs
International Picture Naming Project (IPNP) 328
interpreters, simultaneous
  see simultaneous interpreters
Isurin, Ludmila 5, 322, 358
Italian, and English, and cross-linguistic differences 121
Ivanova, I. 85, 86

Jackendoff, R. 300–303, 305–306
Jacobs, J. 74
Jaeggi, S. M. 88
James, W. 8
Jameson, K. A. 240
Japanese
  and English
    colour perception 240–241
    and crossover memories 215
    and ERP translation priming studies 144, 146
    and executive control 87
    grammatical number 242–244
    and length of stay 249
  and German 240
  and Portuguese, and dementia 195
  and regression 293–294
Jarmulowicz, L. 311–312
Jarrold, C. 76, 79
Jarvis, S. 244–247, 248
Jaspaert, K. 326
Johnson, R. K. 279
Johnston, R. 325
Jonides, J. 88

Kasai, C. 243, 247, 247–249
Kaushanskaya, M. 34
Kavé, G. 202
Keijzer, M. 311
Keshavarz, M. H. 33
Klein, D. 140–141
Klein, E. 34
Klein, R. 86
Knupsky, A. 323
Kohnert, K. J. 191, 192
Köpke, B. *98–125*, 324, 325
Kousaie, S. 201

Krajciova, A. 240–241
Kroll, Judith F. 3, *25*, 105–106, 127, 128–129, 130, 131, 134–135, 150–151, 154–155, 251, 256, 257, 261, 263, 352
Kroon, S. 326
Kuhberg, H. 294, 296, 297, 299, 310
Kuipers, J. 241–242
Kupper, L. 259

L1
 and age-related decline 195–196
 attrition 319–321
  psycholinguistic study 326–345, 333t, 335t
 and explicit/implicit memory 165–167
 and L2 language performance 121–122
L2
 acquisition, lexical competition in localist and distributed connectionist models 48–49
 attrition 291–300
 effect and L1 attrition 336–337
 and L1 language performance 121–122
 word-to-concept mappings 146, 152–153
L3
 "L3"
  vocabulary learning 257, 264–265
  Chinese–English study 256, 265–284
 vocabulary learning 4, 33
La Heij, W. 309
Laka, I. 145
language acquisition, and working memory (WM) 76–84
language attrition 5, 199, 357–359
 L1 319–321
  study 326–345
 L2 291–300, 314–315
language learning 23, 353–357
 and processing 32–36
Language Proficiency 119–120, 256–257, 259
 in Chinese–English study 274–278, 279–280, 282
language-as-strategy hypothesis 249
language-dependent memory 2, 15, 355
language-focused learning 258
languages *see* American Sign Language; Arabic; Basque; Catalan; Chinese; Danish; Dutch; English; Finnish; French; German; Greek; Hebrew; Indonesian; Italian; Japanese; Polish; Portuguese; Russian; Spanish; Swedish; Tamil; Turkish; Welsh; Yucatec

Larsen, S. 215–216
late bilinguals
 and L2 words of different frequencies *60–63*, 65, *66–67*
 processing L1 and L2 words *59*, 64
 and special types of L2 words 65, *67*, 68
Late Positivity Complex (LPC) 138
lateral inhibition 51, 56, 62, 66, 69
Lawson, M. J. 259
LEABRA 56, 63
length of stay 241–242, 248–249
 and L1 attrition 325–327, 331
Lenneberg, E. H. 161–162
Leoné, Frank 56
"less is more" hypothesis 163–164
Levinson, S. C. 237
Levy, B. A. 170–171
lexical access, psycholinguistic studies 321–326
lexical activation 21, 50, 227
 Activation Threshold Hypothesis 292, 294, 309–311, 314
lexical competition 66, 351
 and bilingual memory models 2
lexical cueing, and crossover memories study 215–216
lexical decision tasks 323
lexical innovations, in non-target language, psycholinguistic study 336, 342–343
lexical memory, and creative syntax 300–307
lexical retrieval 251
 and aging 188, 189–190, 191, 193–194, 314
 and attrition 295–297, 326–327
 failure 320, 321
lexical/semantic system 127
Li, P. *31*, 54, 56
Linck, J. A. 154–155
linguistic decay 320
linguistic distortion 320
linguistic relativity 4, 236–251, 355–356
linguistic repression 320
linguistic transfer 36
linguistically mediated thinking, and working memory (WM) 249–250
listening span studies *98–125*
Liu, M. 110–111, 113–114, 117, 119, 121
localist connectionist models 51, 52–53, 56
 and lexical competition 48–49, *59–63*, 68–48
 Multilink 61
Loncke, M. 80

long-term memory (LTM) 9–10, 14, 76
    and short-term memory 10–13
    and word stimuli 118
LPC (Late Positivity Complex) 138
Lucy, J. A. 237, 242, 243
Luk, G. 86–87

McClelland, J. L. 53–54, 68
McDonald, J. L. 164
MacLeod, C. M. 180
McNamara, D. S. 260
MacSwan, J. 216
Mahn, A. C. 33–34
Majerus, S. 81, 82
Mandarin *see* Chinese
Marian, Viorica 2, 29, 34, 35–36, 214,
    215, 229, 321, 323–324, 350
Martin-Chang, Sandra 170–171
Masson, M. E. J. 180
Mathis, K. M. 263
Matsumoto, A. 214–215
Mazuka, R. 243
meaning-focused learning 258
Meara, P. M. 307–308, 310, 312–313
Meguro, K. 195
memory *see* autobiographical; bilingual;
    declarative; episodic; explicit;
    implicit; language-dependent;
    lexical; long-term; phonological
    working; procedural; semantic;
    Serial Order Memory;
    short-term; verbal; working
    memory (WM)
memory consolidation theory 9–10
memory span 98–103, 120–121
Mendez, M. F. 195
mental lexicon, and attrition 291–300,
    314
Mercier, J. 140–141
metalinguistic knowledge 35, 36
Meuter, R. F. I. 85
Midgley, K. 52, 57, 140, 142, 143–144,
    146
Milin, P. 88, 89
Miller, G. A. 12, 75, 232
Misra, M. 150–151
models *see also* Bilingual Interactive
    Activation (BIA); Bilingual
    Interactive Activation + (BIA+);
    Bilingual Language Interaction
    Network for Comprehension
    of Speech; Inhibitory Control;
    Revised Hierarchical Model
    (RHM); Self-Organizing Model of
    Bilingual Processing (SOMBIP)

monolinguals
    age-related decline 189–192, 196–198,
        200–201
    control group in L1 attrition
        study 326
    and dementia 84
    language processing 32–33, 60, 62
    and working memory capacity 87–89
Montrul, S. 310
Moorcroft, R. 297–299
Morford, J. P. 134–135
morphology 293–294, 296, 306, 311
    bound 291, 292
Morris, C. D. 166
Moser-Mercer, B. 120
Mosse, E. K. 79
motion events 244–246, 249, 250
multi-word lexical entries 291–292,
    297–299, 300–307, 314–315
multilinguals 353
    and age-related decline 192–193,
        195
Multilink 61
Multiple Memory Trace theory 10
multiple sclerosis 260

n-back task 88
N250 137, 141–142
N400 19n, 136–138
    and Thierry and Wu study 134
    see also translation priming
names, proper 21–22
naming latency, and word frequency
    322–323
Nation, I. S. P. 257, 258, 259, 260, 283
Neisser, U. 214, 215, 229
Nelson, T. O. 267
Nespoulous, J-L. *98–125*
neurocognition *see* behavioral
    neuroscience
neurophysiological techniques, event
    related brain potentials (ERPs)
    241–242
Nicoladis, E. 217, 228
non-digit word stimuli 105–106
non-word repetition task 107–108
    and L2 processing 88
    and simultaneous interpreters 108,
        109–110, 118–119
non-words, and English, vocabulary
    learning 261
noncognate/cognate homographs 26, 31,
    54–55, 61, 68–69, 351
noncognates, and late bilinguals 65
Norris, D. 79

numbers reversed test, Woodcock Johnson III Tests of Cognitive Abilities 170
Numeral Classifier Accessibility Hierarchy (NCAH) 293
Nusbaum, H. C. 232

Oberauer, K. 76
Obler, Loraine 2–3, 108
O'Brien, I. 83–84, 88
Oller, D. K. 311–312
Olshtain, E. 293, 295, 297, 299, 310
O'Malley, J. M. 259
opportunity to use language 248, 251
orthographical neighbors 17–18
orthography 360–361
Otoya, M. T. 214

P200 136–137
Padilla, F. 104–105, 106–107
Padilla, P. *98–125*
Page, M. P. A. 79–80
paired-associate vocabulary learning, and testing effect 260–261, 277–278, 280
Palmer, S. D. 149–150
Papagno, C. 77, 88
Paradis, J. 217, 228, 294, 299, 309–310, 314
Parallel Architecture 300–303, 305–306
Parallel Distributed Processing (PDP) models *see* distributed connectionist models
parallel language activation 22, 36–37
Parault, S. J. 164
Pashler, H. 260
Pavlenko, A. 246–247, 359
Penfield, W. 161
perceptual processing 166, 181–182
Pérez-Ollé, J. 148–149
Perrig, W. J. 88
Phillips, N. A. 140–141, 201
phonological interference 323–324
phonological loop 96, 98–103, 118, 122–123
phonological mismatch negativity (PMN) 140–141
phonological working memory 13–14, 35, 36
phrase-span task 113–114
picture naming 87, 129–130
 and age-related decline 189, 191
 and attrition in children 312
 and L1 attrition
  lexical retrieval 321–322

psycholinguistic study 321, 326–327, 328–330, 340, 344–345
Piñar, P. 134–135
Plaut, D. C. 53–54
Polish
 and Danish
  autobiographical memory 16–17
 crossover memories 215–216
Poncelet, M. 82
Poplack, S. 216
Portuguese, and Japanese, and dementia 195
Positron Emission Tomography studies 87
Potter, M. M. C. 24, 127, 129–130, 262–263, 282
pragmatics 303–305
primacy effect 80, 98
Prince, P. 259
Principles of Psychology (James) 8
print stimuli *see* written stimuli
Prior, A. 87
procedural memory 164–165
processing
 bilingual memory 7–8, 13–14, 23–36, 350
 and language learning 32–36, 57
 models 23
 second language, and working memory (WM) 74–89
 timecourse of 127, 133–134
 and working memory (WM) 74, 82–84, 89
productive vocabulary 257–258
proficiency (language) 119–120, 256–257, 259
 in Chinese-English study 274–278, 279–280, 282
proper names 21–22
psycholinguistic studies
 and lexical access in bilinguals 321–326
 present study on L1 attrition 326–345, 328t, 333t
psychology, cognitive 9
Pu, Xiaoping 4–5
Pulvermüller, F. 162
Pyers, J. E. 86–87

Ransdell, S. E. 60
Rawson, K. A. 267
re-immersion/immersion 154–155, 293, 308, 312
reading comprehension 83, 84
reading-span studies 75–76, 89, *98–125*

recall, in non-target language, psycholinguistic study 334–336, 335t
recency effect 80–81, 98, 213
receptive vocabulary 257–258
regression 199–200
Regression Hypothesis 195–196, 291
Regression Hypothesis 291, 292–294, 311
Rekké, S. 61
related word stimulus tasks *98–125*
Reminiscence Bump (RB) 211–221, 223–226, 229–230
  and Immigration Effect 219–226, *236–224*
repeated study 256–257, 259–260, 273, 280–282
  acquisition phase 270–272
  final-recall, phase in Chinese–English study 272
repeated testing 256–257, 259–261, 273, 282–283
  acquisition phase 270–272
  final-recall, phase in Chinese–English study 272
  and language learning 280–282
repression, linguistic 320
retrieval failure 320, 321
  and L1 attrition 333–339, 343
Revised Bilingual Single Network (RBSN) model 56, 62, *63–64*, 68
Revised Hierarchical Model (RHM) 24, 25, 49–51, 263–265, 283–284
  and novel word learning in Chinese–English bilinguals study 256, *264–271*, 279–280
  and the testing effect 261
  and translation 127–137, 152, 153–155
Roberts, L. 161
Roediger, H. L. 260
Rosselli, M. 193
Royer, J. M. 260–261
Rubin, D. C. 211, 213–214, 215–216, 218, 220–221, 226, 229, 230–231
Russian
  and English
    autobiographical memory 229
    and crossover memories 214
    L1 attrition 322–323, 327–345
    L1 attrition psycholinguistic study 327–345
    and lexical access 321
    phonological effects 324
    and semantic memory access 18
    translation priming studies 140, 146, 154
  and German, L1 attrition psycholinguistic study 327–345
  and Hebrew, L1 attrition psycholinguistic study 327–345
Russo, R. P. 259
Ryan, J. 86

same language memories 226–228, 228t
Sandoval, T. C. 191–192
Sankoff, D. 216
Santesteban, M. 85–86
Sanz, C. 33
Sapir, Edward 236–237
Sapir-Whorf hypothesis *see* linguistic relativity
Sasaki, M. 240–241, 243
Schacter, D. L. 165
Schallert, D. L. 110–111
Schmid, M. 324, 325
Schmitt, N. 258, 259
Scholastic Aptitude Test 75
Schoonbaert, S. 142–143
Schrauf, Robert 211, 213–214, 215–216, 218, 220–221, 226, 229, 230–231, 232
Schumann, J. H. 162
scripts 143–144, 360–361
second language *see* L2
Segalowitz, N. 83–84
Seidenberg, M. S. 53–54, 68
Self-Organizing Model of Bilingual Processing (SOMBIP) 24, 30, *31*, 56
  DevLex- 54
semantic interference 323–324, 333–335, 342
semantic memory 9–10, 14, 36
  and language comprehension 17–19
  and language production 19–23
semantic transfer 343
  psycholinguistic study 339
semantic word generation tasks 193–194
"sensitive periods controversy" 161–163, 247–248
sentence parsing 83–84
sentence stimuli, and interpreters/non-interpreters 108–110, 113–114, 117, 123
sentence-span tasks 98–103
separate sentence interpretation resource 83
sequence, learning 34–35
Serial Order Memory 78–82, 89
Service, E. 82
Shallice, T. 53–54

Index

Shanks, D. R. 183
Shiffrin, R. M. 9
Shipley Institute of Living Scale 256, 266, 277
Shook, A. 29
Shorek, A. 202
short-term memory 9, 10–13, 75, 76
　and digit span tests 75
　new word learning 78, 81–82
Shorter Oxford English Dictionary (1993) 306
Signorelli, Teresa M. 2–3, *98–125*, 351–352
Simon task/effect 86–87, 200
Simon, Th. 74
simultaneous interpreters 2–3, 95, 99, *103–116*, 122–95, 351–352
　comparison of the studies 114–122
　and non-interpreters 103–114
Slobin, D. I. 237, 244
Small, S. L. 232
Snodgrass, J. 328
socio-linguistic factors
　and L1 attrition 324–326, 328–333, 340–342
　and L2 5
sound–meaning correspondences 306–307, 313
Spanish
　and Basque 145, 152, 154
　and Catalan 85, 145
　　age-related decline 200–201
　　and executive control 85–86
　　and translation priming 147–148
　and English 33
　　and age-related decline 191–194
　　attrition in children study 311–312
　　autobiographical memory 229
　　bilingual memory access test 15
　　crossover memory study 214
　　digital names test 13
　　and executive control 87
　　idiom retention 298
　　and L3 learning study 35
　　motion events 249
　　translation priming 139–140, 146, 154–155
　　translation recognition 148–150
　　and verbal working memory 84
　and regression study 293
　and Swedish 247
　　grammatical aspect 245–246
special words 57, 351
　and late bilinguals 65
　see also cognates

Stanny, C. J. 214–215
Stephens, D. A. 216
Stewart, E. 25, 127, 128–129, 130, 256, 257, 261, 263
Stewner-Manzanares, G. 259
Stoessel, S. 295
Stringer, David 5, 308, 312, 313, 357
Stroop Task 197, 200–201, 323
Sunderman, G. 154–155
Swahili *see* vocabulary, learning, Chinese–English study
Swedish
　and Spanish 247
　　grammatical aspect 245–246
switching 355, 357
　and age-related decline 199
　end executive control 85–86
symmetry/asymmetry, and translation priming 133–134
syntax, and the lexicon 300–307
Szekely, A. 328
Szmalec, Arnaud 2, 79–80, 351–352

Takahashi, J. 243
Talamas, A. 131, 151
Tam, J. W. 150–151
Tamil, and English, Simon-effect 86
testing effect 257, 260–261
　vocabulary learning in Chinese–English bilinguals 256, 274–277, 278, 356–357
Thierry, G. 18–19, 134–135, 150, 241–242
"thinking out loud" 16
thinking for speaking hypothesis 244–246
third-languages, learning 33, 34–35
Thomas, M. S. C. 54, 55, 62
timecourse
　of processing 127, 133–134
tip-of-the-tongue (TOT) 21–22, 85, 323, 324, 358–359
　and age-related decline 190, 191
Tomiyama, M. 296, 310
top-down feedback 51
Towse, J. N. 76
transfer, linguistic 36
transfer-appropriate processing (TAP) framework 166, 167–168, 179
translation 126–128, 351–352
　and the RHM 127–137
translation priming 132–134
　and ERP 138–148
translation production 128–131
translation recognition 131–132
　and ERP 148–153

Trofimovich, Pavel 3, 353–354
Tse, Chi-Shing 4–5, 356–357
Turkish
  and English
    and ATH 310
    repeated testing 260–261
  and German, and regression study 294
Tzou, Y. *98–125*

Ullman, M. T. 164
unbalanced/balanced bilingualism 144–145
Underwood, G. *98–125*
Uribe-Etxebarria, O. 145

Vallar, G. 88
Van der Elst, W. 197
Van der Linden, M. 82
van der Wijst, P. 295
van Hell, Janet 3, 33–34, 147, 151, 352
van Heuven, W. J. B., *27–29*, 55, 62
van Hooff, J. C. 149–150
van Hout, R. 326
Van Overschelde, J. P. 267
Vanderwart, M. 328
Vandierendonck, A. 79–80
Vejnovic, D. 88, 89
verb particles 297
verbal memory 2, *97–103*
  and second language learning 76–89
  and working memory (WM) 76–78
verbal models of bilingual processing 49–51
Verkaik, O. 295
Vigil-Colet, A. 148–149, 150
Villwock, A. 134–135
visual Mismatch Negativity (vMMN) 241–242
visuospatial information 76–77, 84
visuospatial sketchpad 96
vocabulary
  learning 256–265
    Chinese–English study 256, 265–284, 269t
  and the lexicon 294–298

Walters, Joel 216–217, 228
Wang, Y. 87
Waters, G. S. 83

Weekes, B. 82
Welsh, and English, and cross-linguistic differences 120
Weltens, B. 295, 308
Whorf, Benjamin Lee 236–237
Wide Range Achievement Test (WRAT-3) 169, 170–176
Wiggett, A. 241–242
Wilkinson, E. 134–135
Woodcock Johnson III Tests of Cognitive Abilities (WJ-III) 170–176
Word Association model 127, 130
  of bilingual memory 262–263
word frequency, naming latency 322–323
word lexicon *see* mental lexicon
word stem completion tests, and age effects study 171–179
word-length effect 98
word-list recall *98–125*
word-span tasks *98–125*
word-to-concept mappings 146, 152–153
working memory (WM) 2–3, 96–98, 351–352
  Baddeley's model *11–25*
  capacity and bilingualism 87–89
  and linguistically mediated thinking 249–250
  phonological 13–14, 35, 36
  and second language acquisition 2
  and second language processing 74–89
  and short-term memory 10
  and simultaneous interpreters 2–3
  and the Woodcock Johnson III Tests of Cognitive Abilities 170–176
  see also simultaneous interpreters
written stimuli *98–125*
  and auditory stimuli 115–119, 123
Wu, Y. J. 18–19, 134–135, 150

Xue, F. 87
Xue, G. 87

Yoshitomi, A. 299
Yucatec, and English, grammatical number 242

Zdravkovic, S. 88, 89
Zentella, A. C. 216
Zied, K. M. 201
Zollinger, H. 240